James Macaulay

Speeches and Addresses of H. R. H. the Prince of Wales

1863-1888

James Macaulay

Speeches and Addresses of H. R. H. the Prince of Wales
1863-1888

ISBN/EAN: 9783337164744

Printed in Europe, USA, Canada, Australia, Japan

Cover: Foto ©ninafisch / pixelio.de

More available books at **www.hansebooks.com**

Albert Edward P

SPEECHES AND ADDRESSES

OF

H.R.H. THE PRINCE OF WALES:

1863—1888.

EDITED BY

JAMES MACAULAY, A.M., M.D. Edin.,

AUTHOR OF "VICTORIA R.I., HER LIFE AND REIGN."

WITH A PORTRAIT.

LONDON:

JOHN MURRAY, ALBEMARLE STREET.

1889.

LONDON:

PRINTED BY WILLIAM CLOWES AND SONS, LIMITED,
STAMFORD STREET AND CHARING CROSS.

To the Memory of

HIS ROYAL HIGHNESS

THE PRINCE CONSORT,

THE "NOBLE FATHER OF OUR KINGS TO BE,"

ALBERT THE WISE AND GOOD.

PREFACE.

THE year 1888, that of the Silver Wedding of the Prince and Princess of Wales, is also the 25th anniversary of the year when the Prince first began to appear in public life. It is, therefore, a fit time to present some record of events in which His Royal Highness has taken part, and of services rendered by him to the nation, during the past quarter of a century. The best and the least formal way of doing this seemed to be the reproduction of his Speeches and Addresses, along with some account of the occasions when they were delivered.

Some of these speeches, in more recent years, are known to all, and their importance is universally recognised; such as those relating to the various International Exhibitions, the foundation of the Royal College of Music, and the establishment of the Imperial Institute. But throughout the whole of the twenty-five years, there has been a succession of speeches, on all manner of occasions, of many of which there is no adequate record or remembrance. It is only due to the Prince to recall the various services thus rendered by him, especially during those earlier years when the loss of the Prince Consort was most deeply felt, and when the Queen, whose Jubilee has been so splendidly celebrated, was living in retirement. A new generation has come on the stage since those days, and there are comparatively few who remember the number and variety of occasions upon which Royalty was worthily represented by the Prince of Wales, and the important and arduous duties voluntarily and cheerfully undertaken by him.

Before carrying out this design, it was advisable to ascertain if there might be any objection on the part of the Prince of Wales. There might, for instance, be a purpose of official publication of these speeches. On the matter being referred to the Prince, he not only made no objection, but, in most kind and gracious terms, gave his sanction to the work, and hoped it might be " useful to the various objects which he had publicly advocated and supported."

The number and diversity of occasions on which the Prince has made these public appearances will surprise those who have not personal recollection of them. The speeches themselves will surprise no one. The Prince has had education and culture such as few of any station obtain ; directed at first by such a father as the Prince Consort, and by tutors who carried out the design of both his parents. Accomplished in Art, and interested in Science, in Antiquities, and most branches of learning; with some University training at Oxford, Cambridge, and Edinburgh, and with his mind enlarged by foreign travel, we might expect the fruits of such training to appear in his public addresses. Add to this the kindliness which comes from a good natural disposition, the sympathetic influence of a genial manner, and the grace which is given by a training from childhood in the highest station, and we can understand how the speeches even of the earliest years were heard with pleasure and approval. Some of the speeches are very brief, but are always to the point, and present the gist of the subject in hand. It was Earl Granville who once said, in proposing his health, that, " if the speeches of His Royal Highness were usually short, they were always, to use a homely expression, as full of meat as an egg." Even where there has been no formal speech, we are interested in knowing what the Prince has done as well as what he has said; and therefore some important occasions are included when no speech was made.

It is the variety of subjects that will strike most readers, Let it be noted, moreover, that the speeches now reproduced are only those addressed to meetings where reporters for the press were present. There have been innumerable meetings besides,— meetings of Commissions, of Boards, of Councils, of Committees, at none of which has the Prince ever been an inactive or silent member, but rather the guiding and moving spirit. If the voluntary offices of His Royal Highness were printed at length, they would far outnumber those mere honorary titles with which the College of Arms concerns itself; and are such as imply thought and work, in many useful and beneficent ways.

Long may His Royal Highness have the health and the will for such offices and duties. If his future career is equal to the hopes and promise of his early life, and the performances of the last twenty-five years, he will leave a name illustrious and memorable in the history of the British Empire.

** *The frontispiece portrait, under which the Prince of Wales has been pleased to put his autograph, is etched by W. Strang, from a recent photograph by Van der Weyde.*

TABLE OF CONTENTS.

THE EARLY YEARS OF THE PRINCE OF WALES.

As the record of Public Speeches in the following pages does not begin till 1863, it may bo well to give a few dates and incidents of previous years in the life of the Prince of Wales.

He was born on the 9th of November, 1841, at Buckingham Palace. From Windsor, to which the Court removed on the 6th of December, the Queen wrote next day to King Leopold, "We arrived here safe and sound, with our awfully large nursery establishment, yesterday morning. . . . I wonder very much whom our little boy will be like. You will understand how fervent are my prayers, and I am sure everybody's must be, to see him resemble his father in *every* respect, both in body and mind."

The Prince, named Albert Edward, was baptized in St. George's Chapel, Windsor, on the 25th of January, 1842. King Frederick William of Prussia was invited to be the boy's Godfather, and he came over personally to undertake the office. The other Sponsors, six in number, were members of the Houses of Saxe-Coburg and Saxe-Gotha, and of the English Royal family. There was a full choral service at the christening. A special anthem had been composed by Sir George Elvey. On the Prince Consort being told of this, and asked when it should be sung, he answered, "Not at all; no anthem. If the service ends by an anthem we shall all go out criticising the music. We will have something we all know —something in which we can all join—something devotional. The Hallelujah Chorus; we shall all join in that, with our hearts." The Hallelujah Chorus ended the service accordingly. The incident is noteworthy, as showing how the infant Prince was committed, at his baptism, not in outward form only, but in devout spirit, to the care of the Heavenly Father.

When the Queen told King Leopold of the removal of the Court to Windsor, she had made special mention of "the nursery establishment." No mother in any rank of life ever paid greater attention to this part of the home, wherever the Court might be. In Memoirs and Recollections of the Queen, by those who have belonged to her household, many anecdotes are found which show

s s B

the watchful care and the personal superintendence of the Royal Mother.

It is only this year, in the autumn of 1888, that Mrs. Hull, who entered Her Majesty's service as nurse to the Prince of Wales, died, in her seventy-ninth year. She was a kind and conscientious attendant to every one of the Royal children, and the Queen ever retained great regard for the faithful nurse—" Dear old May," as she used to call her. When she retired from the Royal service, and lived in recent years in Windsor, she was always welcome at the Castle. The Queen herself and the Princesses often saw her, and the Prince of Wales frequently brought her handsome presents. In reading the account of her funeral, it is pleasant to see that on the card attached to one of the many wreaths laid on her coffin were the words: " A mark of affection and gratitude from Victoria R. I." A beautiful wreath sent by the Prince and Princess of Wales bore the inscription: " In remembrance of dear old May."

When the Royal children came to be under governesses and teachers, they were taught well the usual branches of early education, and were also trained in practical ways, the boys in the use of tools, and the girls in household work, especially when the Swiss Cottage at Osborne was occupied by the young folk.

In the story of the ' Early Years of the Prince Consort' there is an amusing reference to the interruptions of the schoolroom studies by the old Duke of Saxe-Coburg, who loved to carry off the two boys, and take them on excursions. The Prince himself did this sometimes, as when the two elder children, in the autumn of 1846, were taken with their parents in the *Victoria and Albert* to Portland, Weymouth, Guernsey, Dartmouth, and Plymouth, between August 8th and 25th; and to Jersey, Falmouth, St. Michael's Mount, and the Duchy of Cornwall, between September 2nd and 9th. Of these excursions details are given in the Queen's ' Leaves from a Journal.' The Queen tells how, at several places off the Cornish coast, " boats crowded round us in all directions, and when Bertie showed himself the people shouted, ' Three cheers for the Duke of Cornwall! ' " . . . In the Journal, under date September 7th, Prince Albert having that day landed to visit some mines, the Queen has this entry, " The Corporation of Penryn were on board, and very anxious to see the Duke of Cornwall, so I stepped out of the pavilion with Bertie, and Lord Palmerston told them that that was the Duke of Cornwall; and the old Mayor of Penryn said that ' he hoped he would grow up to be a blessing to his parents, and to his country.' "

On September the 2nd, on the evening of the day when the Royal yacht left Osborne for the Channel Islands, " Bertie put on his sailor's dress, which was beautifully made by the man on board who makes for our sailors. When he appeared, the officers and sailors, who were all assembled on deck to see him, cheered, and seemed delighted with him.

In 1847 there was another holiday journey, this time to Scotland, the Queen and the Prince taking with them, as before, the two eldest children, with Miss Hildyard, their governess. They embarked at Osborne, in the Royal yacht, on the 11th of August. On the 14th they were at Pembroke, when the dockyard and the castle were inspected: thence along the coast of Wales, landing at Bangor, from whence there was an expedition to Penryn Castle, and thence past the Isle of Man to the Scottish coast. Of this journey a detailed account is given in a letter to Baron Stockmar. At Rothesay in the Isle of Bute, the Prince Consort says, "The people were as much rejoiced to see the Duke of Rothesay as the Welsh were to salute the Prince of Wales on their native ground." It was this enthusiasm about local associations that led the Queen, after the first visit to Ireland, to desire for the Prince the title of Earl of Dublin.

During 1848 and the following year there was much in the state of public affairs, at home and abroad, to occupy the attention of the Queen and the Prince Consort, but they were anxiously considering the plans for the future education of the Prince of Wales. In May 1848 negociations had been opened with Mr. Birch, who had been highly recommended as tutor. In the spring of 1849 the appointment was made, and Prince Albert, in a letter to the Dowager Duchess of Gotha, dated Windsor Castle, 10th April, thus wrote, " The children grow more than well. Bertie will be given over in a few weeks into the hands of a tutor, whom we have found in Mr. Birch, a young, good-looking, amiable man, who was a tutor at Eton, and who not only himself took the highest honours at Cambridge, but whose pupils have won especial distinction. It is an important step, and God's blessing be upon it, for upon the good education of Princes, and especially of those who are destined to govern, the welfare of the world in these days very greatly depends."

Of the course and conduct of the studies of the Prince, under Mr. Birch, from 1849–1851, and under his successor, Mr. Gibbs, from 1851–1858, it is not necessary to speak. His other teachers were efficient in their departments, such as Mr. Corbould, who taught drawing to all the Royal children; and M. Brasseur, the French teacher, to whom the Prince paid a visit when in Paris in 1888. As in the earlier years, so when he was under tutors, the real education for public life was less in study than in the companionship and the example of his parents. A man of wide knowledge and of varied accomplishments like the Prince Consort had higher views of education than mere scholastic routine. He took his son to all places where a love of arts and sciences might be encouraged and fostered, and hence the Prince obtained knowledge and acquired tastes not universal among young Englishmen, in times before the subjects of academic training and honours had been enlarged, mainly through the influence of the Prince Consort, as Chancellor of the University of Cambridge. From his father also he inherited the taste for music which has been since turned to national benefit. But above all, he was often taken to meetings and festivals connected with charitable institutions, a Princely duty in which the son has been proud to follow the example of his lamented father.

The extra-scholastic education of the Prince was continued throughout the time that Mr. Gibbs, his classical tutor, remained with him. He was also gradually introduced to public life, and initiated in affairs of modern as well as ancient history,—events reported in the newspapers of the day, as well as those recorded by the historians of antiquity. As early as the 3rd of April, 1854, when the Addresses from both Houses of Parliament were presented to the Queen, in answer to Her Majesty's message announcing the opening of war with Russia, we are told that "the Prince of Wales took his place, for the first time, beside the Queen and Prince Albert upon the throne." In the succeeding years these appearances in public were frequent, and in 1857 he accompanied the Queen and the Prince on their memorable visit to the Art Treasures Exhibition at Manchester. The Princess Royal, the Princess Alice, Prince George, and Prince Frederick William of Prussia, were also guests at Worsley Hall during this visit. In Manchester, as recorded by the Queen in her Diary, "The crowd was enormous, greater than ever witnessed before, and enthusiastic beyond belief—nothing but kind and friendly faces." Upwards of a million people were computed to have been in the streets that day. Not only were the treasures of the Exhibition carefully inspected, but visits were paid to some of the great manufacturing works of the town. On the day that the Queen drove to see the statue of herself recently erected in the Peel Park, the Prince Consort, with his two eldest sons, and Prince Frederick William, went to the Manchester Town Hall, to receive the address which the Corporation presented to the Prussian Prince on his approaching marriage with the Princess Royal.

In July of that year, 1857, the Prince of Wales went to Königswinter, for the purposes of study. He was accompanied by General Grey, Sir Henry Ponsonby, and several companions, among whom were Mr. C. Wood, son of Lord Halifax, Lord Cadogan, and Mr. F. Stanley, son of Lord Derby. With Mr. Gibbs was now associated the Rev. Canon Tarver, who, on the retirement of Mr. Gibbs in 1858, was appointed Director of Studies and Chaplain. In this capacity he accompanied the Prince to Rome, Spain, and Portugal, and afterwards went with him to Edinburgh, remaining with the Prince till the autumn of 1859, when his education ceased to be conducted at home.

Of the principal events of the year 1858 as regards the Prince, a most interesting statement is given in a letter of his father to his old friend Stockmar. It is dated Windsor Castle, April 2nd. "Yesterday the Confirmation of the Prince of Wales went off with great solemnity, and I hope with lasting impression on his mind.

The previous day his examination took place before the Archbishop and ourselves. Wellesley (Dean of Windsor) prolonged it a full hour, and Bertie acquitted himself *extremely well.* To-day we take the sacrament with him." In a Memorandum by Her Majesty, it is said that the Prince Consort "had a very strong feeling about the solemnity of this act, and did not like to appear in company either the evening before or on the day on which he took the sacrament ; and he and the Queen almost always dined alone on these occasions." With such habitual feelings about the solemnity of the service, the "First Communion" of his eldest son must have deeply touched his heart.

In the letter to Stockmar the Prince continues his statement about the educational plans for his son. "Next week he is to make a run for fourteen days to the South of Ireland, with Mr. Gibbs, Captain de Ros, and Dr. Minter, for recreation. When he returns to London he is to take up his residence at the White Lodge, in Richmond Park, so as to be away from the world, and devote himself exclusively to study, and prepare for a military examination. As companions for him we have appointed three very distinguished young men, of from 23 to 26 years of age, who are to occupy in monthly rotation a kind of equerry's place about him, and from whose more intimate intercourse I anticipate no small benefit to Bertie." These companions were Lord Valletort, eldest son of Lord Mount-Edgecombe, Major Teesdale, R.A., of Kars celebrity, and Major Loyd-Lindsay, V.C., of all of whom the Prince expresses to Stockmar his high opinion. "Besides these three, only Mr. Gibbs and Mr. Tarver will go with him to Richmond. As future Governor I have as yet been able to think of no one as likely to suit, except Colonel Bruce, Lord Elgin's brother, and his military secretary in Canada, who now commands one of the battalions of Grenadier Guards. He has all the amiability of his sister (Lady Augusta Bruce, afterwards Lady Augusta Stanley), with great mildness of expression, and is full of ability."

Fortunately for the Prince, the wish to obtain the services of Colonel Bruce was successful. On the 9th of November, 1858, writing from Windsor Castle to the King of Prussia on political affairs, which in Prussia were then in troubled condition, the Prince adds : " I ought not to tease you just now with family trifles, still I will let you know that Bertie, who to-day solemnizes his eighteenth birthday, proposes to pay a fortnight's visit to his sister, and asks leave to present himself to you. It will not be a State, but purely a family visit ; and we, therefore, beg you only to show him such slender courtesies as are suitable to a member, and a very young one, of the family. To-day he becomes a Colonel in the Army, unattached, and will receive the Garter. Colonel Bruce, Lord Elgin's brother, has become his Governor."

The Prince speaks of family events as trifles, compared with great political affairs, but he felt deeply every change in the home life. A few weeks earlier, he had taken his son, Alfred, to his ship at Spithead, from which he went to sea at once. On the day before, the father wrote, "His departure will be another great trial to us: the second child lost to our family circle in one year."

On the 10th of January, 1859, the Prince of Wales started on his Italian tour. He had previously been hard at study. He had opportunities of seeing much that was interesting in his continental journey, but the stay at Rome, which was greatly enjoyed, had to be abruptly ended. The restless ambition of the Emperor of the French had brought about war with Austria, and a French descent on Sardinia. Orders were sent to the Prince of Wales to leave Rome and repair to Gibraltar, which he reached on the 7th of May. The plan now arranged was that he was to visit the south of Spain and Lisbon, to return to England in the middle of June, and in July and August to take up his head-quarters in Edinburgh for study.

All this was well carried out, and on the 11th of September the Prince joined his parents at Balmoral. The Court had left Osborne on the 29th of August for the Highlands, and reached Balmoral on the 31st, after spending a day and a night in Edinburgh. Writing to Stockmar a few days after, the Prince Consort says they had "travelled for the first time by night, straight through from London to Edinburgh, in order to gain a day for that place. The experiment proved a complete success, and the Queen was not at all tired. When in Edinburgh I had an educational conference with all the persons who are taking part in the education of the Prince of Wales. They all speak highly of him, and he seems to have shown zeal and good will. Dr. Lyon Playfair is giving him lectures on Chemistry in relation to Manufactures, and at the close of each special course he visits the appropriate manufactory with him, so as to explain its practical application. Dr. Schmitz, the Rector of the High School of Edinburgh, a German, gives him lectures on Roman History. Italian, German, and French are advanced at the same time; and three times a week the Prince exercises with the 16th Hussars, who are stationed near the city. Mr. Fisher, who is to be tutor at Oxford, was also in Holyrood. Law and History are to be the subjects on which he is to prepare the Prince."

All this shows the care taken in regard to the education of the Prince. The Royal pupil had rather a stiff course of study in these days, but he stuck manfully to all his work, which had been carefully planned by his good father, who held that little relaxation should be allowed even during holiday time. In a letter of 17th September, 1859, to Mr. Tarver, who was still Director of Studies, he wrote, "I should be very sorry that he" (the Prince of Wales) "should look upon the reading of a novel, even by Sir Walter Scott, *as a day's work*." Fond as he was himself of high-class works of fiction, the Prince held they should be sparingly laid open to young people during years which should be devoted to study.

In December 1859 the Prince Consort wrote to the old Duchess of Coburg, who ever retained lively interest in all the family affairs, "The visit of Prince Frederick William of Prussia and his Princess came to a close on the 3rd. He has delighted us much. Vicky has developed greatly of late, and yet remained quite a child,—of such is the Kingdom of Heaven." With sad interest we recall this, after recent events. Also it is written about the same time, "The Prince of Wales is working hard at Oxford."

The year closed, and the new year dawned very peaceably and happily, the Queen saying in her Diary, "I never remember spending a pleasanter New Year's Day, surrounded by our children and dear Mama. It is really extraordinary how much our good children did for the day, in reading, reciting, and music."

In the early spring arrangements were being made for the proposed visit of the Prince of Wales to America. A promise o this visit had been given to the Canadians during the Crimean War for which Her Majesty's loyal subjects in the Dominion had levied and equipped a regiment. A request was then made that Her Majesty would visit her American possessions. On this being pronounced inexpedient, the Canadians asked that one of the Queen's sons might be Governor-General. Their youth made this impossible, and then the promise was made that the Prince of Wales, as soon as he was old enough, should visit Canada. It was now announced that this visit should be early in the autumn of 1860, and that it should be signalised by laying the foundation stone of the new Canadian Parliament House at Ottawa. It was also arranged that the Prince should be accompanied by the Duke of Newcastle, Secretary of State for the Colonies.

This no sooner became known on the other side of the water than the President of the United States, James Buchanan, addressed a letter to the Queen, dated on June 4th (Independence Day), offering a cordial welcome to the States, and assuring Her Majesty that the Prince would be everywhere greeted in a manner that could not fail to be gratifying to the Queen. A reply was sent, in the same friendly spirit, informing the President that the Prince would return from Canada through the United States, and that it would give him pleasure to have an opportunity of testifying in person to the President that the feelings which prompted his invitation were fully reciprocated on this side of the Atlantic.

After a short visit to Coburg in the early summer, the Prince started for the New World on the 10th of July, and on the 25th landed at St. John's, Newfoundland. His arrival caused a fever of excitement. "If all the Colonies feel towards the Prince as Newfoundland does," wrote one who witnessed the scenes, "it was a most politic step to have sent him on this tour." The rough fishermen and their wives were delighted, and were full of admiration. "God bless his pretty face, and send him a good wife!" was their most frequent exclamation. The manner of the Prince to the venerable Bishop of Newfoundland was "very beautiful, so gentle, and quite reverential," that all were touched, and the old man said, "God bless my dear young Prince! I hope he will carry away a favourable impression of this almost unknown rugged island."

The same enthusiasm was shown everywhere in Canada, and the Duke of Newcastle writing to the Queen on the 23rd of September, from Dwight in Illinois, after he had crossed into the United States, thus summed up the results of the visit: "Now that the Canadian visit is concluded, the Duke of Newcastle may pronounce it eminently successful, and may venture to offer Her Majesty his humble but very hearty congratulations. He does not doubt that future years will clearly demonstrate the good that has been done. The attachment to the Crown has been greatly cemented. . . . The Duke of Newcastle is rejoiced to think that this is not the only good that has sprung out of this visit. It has done much good to the Prince of Wales himself, and the development of his mind and habit of thought is very perceptible. The Duke of Newcastle will be much disappointed if your Majesty and the Prince Consort are not pleased with the change that has been brought about by this practical school, in which so many of the future duties of life have been forced upon the Prince's daily attention. He has certainly left a very favourable impression behind him."

Besides laying the foundation stone of the buildings for the Parliament House at Ottawa, the Prince performed another memorable action in driving home the last rivet of the magnificent Victoria Bridge at Montreal.

The enthusiasm caused by the visit to the States was immense. Chicago was the first great town reached after leaving Niagara, and here the reception was remarkable. It was the same at Cincinnati, and at St. Louis. In fact everywhere the friendly spirit of the people was the same, and the courtesy of the civic authorities, and of the educated classes, most marked. A pleasant record of the prevailing feeling is given in a letter from a well-known American author. "The Prince is decidedly a popular character with us, and he may consider himself a lucky lad if he escapes nomination for President before he reaches his home-bound fleet. The funny part of the whole affair is to note the unwillingness of people to be *shabbed* off with a sham title (Baron Renfrew, under which name he travelled in the States), instead of His Royal Highness the Prince of Wales, a real up and down and out and out Prince, and of the right stuff too; coupled with a hope he may long remain so; for there is not a living being more sincerely beloved by our people than his Royal mother."

Washington was reached on the 3rd of October. The most memorable incident of his stay at the capital was an excursion, on the 5th, in company with the President to Mount Vernon, the home and the burial-place of George Washington. The reporter of the *Times* thus speaks of the event, "Before this humble tomb the

Prince, the President, and all the party stood uncovered. It is easy moralizing on this visit, for there is something grandly suggestive of historical retribution in the reverential awe of the Prince of Wales, the great-grandson of George III., standing bareheaded at the foot of the coffin of Washington. For a few moments the party stood mute and motionless, and the Prince then proceeded to plant a chestnut by the side of the tomb. It seemed when the Royal youth closed in the earth around the little germ, that he was burying the last faint trace of discord between us and our great brethren in the West."

The Prince left Washington for Richmond on the following day, and closed his American tour at Boston, after having had a magnificent welcome at New York from the vast population of that city. In an American paper of the day it was said, " All our reminiscences, the history, the poetry, the romance of England for ten centuries, are concentrated in the huzzahs with which we greet the Prince of Wales."

The Prince landed at Plymouth on the 13th of November and the same evening arrived at Windsor. On the 15th of January he went to Cambridge for his first term, and resumed his studies, under his preceptors, at Madingley Hall. At the end of his second term he went to the camp of the Curragh of Kildare during the summer vacation.

In the autumn of 1861 he went to Germany, with the intention of meeting the Princess Alexandra of Denmark, with the view to marriage, if the meeting should result in mutual attachment. The meeting, which took place at Speier and at Heidelberg, led to their engagement. The Prince returned to Madingley Hall, from whence he was summoned to Windsor on the day before his beloved father's death, on the 14th of December, 1861.

It is not our purpose to encroach further on the office of the future biographer of the Prince of Wales. In the 'Life of the Prince Consort' the sad incidents of that December are described with touching pathos. Neither do we propose to narrate the events that occurred between the death of the Prince Consort and the marriage of the Prince of Wales, to the Princess Alexandra, on the 10th of March, 1863. These events are fresh in the recollection of many to whom the incidents of the earlier life of the Prince are less known. It is enough to say as to these years, that he continued to be diligent in the acquirement of varied knowledge; that he carefully attended to his military duties; that he took active part in the volunteer movement; and in town and country was alike popular, from his love of manly sport as well as of the pursuits of art.

The coming of age of the Prince was not celebrated with great ceremony, for he was abroad at the time, and the shadow of sorrow was still over the Royal household. But when the Prince brought his bride to England the joy of the nation was unbounded. The passage of the Prince and Princess through the streets of London was a scene of popular enthusiasm such as has seldom been witnessed, so tumultuous was the outburst of joy. The magnificent splendour of the marriage itself was as nothing compared with that national demonstration. In the following pages it will be seen how the Prince and Princess were one in public life, as they were in heart and home.

When the Prince and Princess were returning from Osborne, where they spent the honeymoon, on arriving at Portsmouth, *en route* to Windsor, the Mayor and Corporation presented an address, upon the deck of the Royal yacht *Fairy*. This was the first of a succession of "addresses," which were merely marriage congratulations, couched in complimentary strains, and responded to in a few grateful and gracious words. These addresses were so numerous that they came to be merely mentioned in list, and in that early time might have been troublesome, but for the courtesy and good nature of the Prince. These demonstrations continued throughout the summer, the last being at Edinburgh, where their Royal Highnesses remained for a night on the way to Abergeldie, their Highland home near Balmoral. They did not go to Holyrood Palace, but to Douglas' private hotel, in St. Andrew's Square. Here a vast crowd assembled, and the Prince and Princess had to appear and bow their acknowledgments from the open window, till the multitude dispersed. But before going to the North, the Prince had already made public appearances, and his voice had been heard, in the City of London. The words were few, but the occasions were so important that with them may be commenced the record of the Speeches of His Royal Highness. The earliest appearance in a public assembly was at the banquet of the Royal Academy of Arts, on the 2nd of May, 1863.

SPEECHES OF H.R.H. THE PRINCE OF WALES.

AT THE ROYAL ACADEMY BANQUET.

May 2nd, 1863.

THE annual banquet given by the President and Council of the Royal Academy of Arts, at Burlington House, is one of the chief events of the London season, or rather, it marks the opening of the season. It always takes place on the Saturday preceding the first Monday in May, when the Exhibition of Pictures is opened to the public. Seldom can a more distinguished company of men, eminent in art, science, and literature, as well as in social position and public life, be seen together than on these occasions. The Prince of Wales has been a very frequent guest, and his speeches have been so numerous, that it seems best to group them together, at a later part of this volume. But the first speech at the Academy banquet was so interesting an occasion that it is given under the date of its delivery.

The presence of the young Prince, and so soon after his marriage, gave unusual *éclat* to the banquet of 1863. At that time Sir Charles Eastlake was President, and the rooms of the Academy were at Trafalgar Square. After the toast of "The Queen," the President made touching reference to the loss which the nation as well as the Royal Family had recently sustained. He gave "The memory of the great and good Prince Consort," which was drunk in deep silence. Then followed the toast of "The Prince of Wales, and the rest of the Royal Family." "The Council of the Royal Academy," said the President, "had that day the honour of offering their respectful and heartfelt congratulations to His Royal Highness on his marriage to a Princess, whose personal attractions and gracious manners enhance the impression of Her Royal Highness's amiable character."

The Prince, in replying, spoke (as was said at the time) "evidently under deep emotion, but in a peculiarly clear and pleasing tone of voice, and with great impressiveness of manner" :—

"Sir Charles Eastlake, your Royal Highnesses, my Lords, and Gentlemen,—It is with the most contending feelings of pleasure, pride, and sorrow that I rise to return you thanks in the name of myself and the Royal family for the kind terms in which you, Sir Charles, have proposed our health, and for the very cordial way in which this distinguished assembly has received it. I cannot on this occasion divest my mind of the associations connected with my beloved and lamented father. His bright example cannot fail to stimulate my efforts to tread in his footsteps : and, whatever my shortcomings may be, I may at least presume to participate in the interest which he took in every institution which tended to encourage art and science in this country, but more especially in the prosperity of the Royal Academy. Adverting to my marriage, I beg you to believe how grateful I feel for, and I may be permitted to add how sincerely I appreciate, the sentiments you have expressed with reference to the Princess. I know that I am only speaking her mind in joining her thoughts to mine on this occasion. We neither of us can ever forget the manner in which our union has been celebrated throughout the nation ; and I should be more than ungrateful if I did not retain the most lasting as well as most pleasing recollection of the kind expressions and reception which my attendance at your anniversary meeting has evoked this evening."

Among the speakers at this banquet of 1863 were Lord Palmerston, Mr. Thackeray, and Sir Roderick Murchison.

FREEDOM OF THE CITY OF LONDON.

June 8th, 1863.

THE first event of importance in the public life of the Prince of Wales, after his marriage, was the taking up the freedom of the City of London, on the 8th of June, 1863. As far back as the 12th of March the following resolution had been passed by the Court of Common Council :—

"That His Royal Highness Albert Edward, Prince of Wales, be very respectfully requested to take upon himself the freedom of the City, to which he is entitled by patrimony ; and that upon his acceding to this request His Royal Highness be presented with the copy of the freedom, enclosed in a casket, in testimony of the affection and profound respect entertained by the Court for his person and character."

Having signified his assent to the request, the 8th of June was fixed as the day when the Prince would come to Guildhall to take up the freedom. The Lord Mayor and the civic authorities thought that this would be the fittest time for the official reception of the Prince and Princess, and for an entertainment, worthy of the occasion of the marriage, and of the ancient hospitality of the City of London. Invitations were accordingly issued to about two thousand guests to meet the Royal visitors, and the list included all the most eminent persons in public life or in society, and the ambassadors and representatives of foreign countries. Immense and costly preparations were made, both in the decoration of the Hall, and for the reception of the guests. Shortly after 9 P.M. the sound of trumpets announced that the Royal party had arrived. The Prince wore his military uniform, and the Riband and Star of the Garter. The Princess wore a rich but simple white dress, with coronet and brooch of diamonds, the wedding present of her husband, and the splendid necklace of brilliants which the City of London had presented. With them came Prince Alfred, the Duchess of Cambridge, the Duke and Princess Mary of Cambridge, and other Royal personages, followed by a numerous retinue. The Royal party were conducted to the daïs, in front of which was a table at which the Lord Mayor (Alderman Rose, M.P.), and the City officials took their places, and there resolved themselves into a Court of Common Council. All wore their robes and insignia of office, the sword and mace laid on the table before the Lord Mayor. The resolution passed on the 12th of March having been read, and also the official record of His Royal Highness's title to the freedom, the Prince then read aloud and afterwards subscribed the following declaration :—

"I, Albert Edward, Prince of Wales, do solemnly declare that I will be good and true to our Sovereign Lady Queen Victoria; that I will be obedient to the Mayor of this City; that I will maintain the franchises and customs thereof, and will keep this City harmless, in that which in me is; that I will also keep the Queen's peace in my own person; that I will know no gatherings nor conspiracies made against the Queen's peace, but I will warn the Mayor thereof, or hinder it to my power; and that all these points and articles I will well and truly keep, according to the laws and customs of this City, to my power.

"ALBERT EDWARD."

Mr. Benjamin Scott, the Chamberlain, then read an address, at the close of which he offered the right hand of fellowship as a citizen of London, and presented the gold casket containing the record of the freedom. The Prince, in reply, said :—

" My Lord Mayor, Mr. Chamberlain, and Gentlemen,—It is, I assure you, a source of sincere gratification to me to attend here for the purpose of being invested with a privilege which for the reasons you have stated you are unable to confer upon me, and which descends to me by inheritance. It is a patrimony that I am proud to claim—this freedom of the greatest city of the commercial world, which holds its charter from such an ancient date. My pride is increased when I call to memory the long list of illustrious men who have been enrolled among the citizens of London, more especially when I connect with that list the beloved father to whom you have adverted in such warm terms of eulogy and respect, and through whom I am here to claim my freedom of the City of London. My Lord Mayor and Gentlemen, the Princess and myself heartily thank you for the past—for your loyalty and expressions of attachment towards the Queen, for the manifestations of this evening towards ourselves, and for all your prayers for our future happiness."

When the ceremony was ended, the Prince and the Royal visitors withdrew from the Hall, but soon returned to join in the festivities, which began with a ball. "The Lord Mayor led off in a spirited quadrille with Her Royal Highness the Princess, and the Prince with the Lady Mayoress." So runs the record, with details of the dances, and the names of the dancers in the area kept clear, in front of the daïs, for the special guests. Attempts were occasionally made to keep up dancing in the body of the Hall, but the crowd was so great that, till after supper, and the retirement of the Royal party, the fête was more of a grand assembly than a ball. Under whatever name, it was a magnificent entertainment, and aged citizens tell us that Guildhall had never witnessed a scene so splendid and joyous.

BRITISH ORPHAN ASYLUM.

June 24th, 1863.

ONE of the earliest appearances of the Prince and Princess of Wales in support of a charitable institution was when they opened the new buildings erected at Slough for the British Orphan Asylum, on the 24th of June, 1863. The scholars belonging to the Asylum had so largely increased in number that the Board of Directors resolved in 1862 to move the whole establishment from Clapham Rise, its former locality, to more spacious premises at Slough. They bought the freehold of the well-known and large Royal Hotel, which had been closed since the old coaches had been driven off the road by the railway. The situation was admirable, and the grounds spacious, and by adding an additional story the building was readily adapted to its new purpose.

The fine weather and the presence of the Prince and Princess attracted a large assemblage. On the arrival of their Royal Highnesses the pupils sang the Old Hundredth Psalm, the National Anthem having been previously played by military bands as the procession moved towards a daïs, beneath a marquee on the lawn. An Address was read, concluding with the expression of a hope that the Prince and Princess would allow their names to be enrolled as Vice-Patron and Vice-Patroness of the Asylum, of which the Queen is Patron. The Prince made the following reply :—

"It has given the Princess and myself great pleasure to be present at the opening of your most excellent Asylum, and to have been invited to take part in so good a work. The benevolent purposes of this widely-extended institution speak for themselves. It is one in which the Queen and my lamented father, the promoter of every scheme for the relief of the miserable, evinced a warm interest, and the details which you have given of its formation and progress furnish another appeal for aid from those whose highest enjoyment it is to give a home and education to the fatherless and destitute. It is a privilege, I assure you, that the Princess and myself value greatly to have our names associated with the British Orphan Asylum."

The Prince then formally declared the building to be for ever dedicated to the purposes of the British Orphan Asylum, and also announced the munificent gift of £12,000 from Mr. Edward Mackenzie to the building fund. The Bishop of Bath and Wells offered prayer; a choral was sung, and many purses were presented in the offertory. Trees were also planted in commemoration of the day.

Eleven years later, the Prince presided at the anniversary festival of the Asylum. He then said that he felt a special interest in the institution, which he had visited along with the Princess of Wales so many years before. In his speech at that festival he spoke more fully of the objects and merits of the Asylum, as will be seen in the report under the date of the festival in May 1874.

AT MERCERS' HALL.

July 8th, 1863.

AFTER the visit to Guildhall, the common hall of all the City Guilds or Companies, the civic event of most importance was when, on the 8th of July, 1863, the Prince went to the City to take up his freedom in the Mercers' Company, and to enroll his name on their records.

It was a fitting thing thus early to show his attachment to ancient Guilds and Corporate Constitutions. The Mercers' Company is the first in rank, and the most ancient of all the great City Guilds, and its roll of members is one of the most illustrious. Its existence as a Metropolitan Guild can be traced as far back as the year 1172, and the Company received its incorporation in 1392 from Richard II., who conferred upon it the honour of becoming one of its brethren. Besides the Royal names of King Henry VIII. and Queen Elizabeth, the Company can boast those of Sir Richard Whittington, William Caxton the Printer, Sir Thomas Gresham, and Dean Colet, the founder of St. Paul's School. The address to the Prince was read by the Master Warden, the Rev. Markland Barnard, who had the distinction of representing the fourteenth generation of his family, who had been freemen or wardens of the Company ever since the third year of Henry IV.

To this address the Prince listened with marked attention, and then replied, in a clear and pleasing tone, which those who heard it said he inherited from his Royal mother :—

" Master and Court of Assistants,—I am glad to avail myself of the last opportunity which my stay in London affords me of attending here this day to receive the freedom of your ancient and honourable company. The oldest of the city companies, the Mercers', is hardly exceeded by any in the amount of its charities, or in its capabilities of doing good. How these powers have been exercised, the list of the foundations of the company and of the distinguished persons whom you have enumerated as benefactors and freemen tells us. Among the latter, the great Sovereign, who was herself a sister of the company, stands conspicuous ; and commerce and science appear equally to have lent their representatives to ennoble the Mercers' Company. To be associated with such names in the freedom and history of your company is an honour and privilege I am proud to have conferred upon me. I thank you sincerely for the terms in which you have mentioned the names of my beloved mother and the Princess, and for the happiness you desire for us both."

The Prince then subscribed the Oath of the Company, with its quaint old phraseology, affixing his usual signature, ALBERT EDWARD, P.

The Clerk then presented His Royal Highness with the formal document which enrolled him as a Freeman, enclosed in a massive gold casket of exquisite design and workmanship. The numerous visitors who had witnessed the ceremony afterwards had a *déjeuner* in the Banqueting Hall, the Prince with a small number of select guests being at the same time entertained in the Council Room.

THE ROYAL LITERARY FUND.

May 18th, 1864.

IN the last annual Report of the Royal Literary Fund, for 1888, it is said: "The anniversary of 1864 was memorable as the first public dinner presided over by the Prince of Wales, to whose presence in the chair the Institution is indebted for a success altogether unprecedented in the history of its anniversaries."

The annual Report for 1864 contains a detailed account of the proceedings at that meeting, the seventy-fifth anniversary of the Institution. It was natural that a large number of eminent men should assemble to support the youthful Chairman, whose illustrious father had presided at the fifty-third anniversary, in 1842. In the long list of Stewards, in 1864, appear the names of almost all those most distinguished at that time, not only in Literature, but in Art and Science, and in every department of the public service. Upwards of four hundred attended, and the special donations to the fund at the dinner amounted to £2328 17s., a sum then far in advance of any profit of former anniversaries. This amount has only once since been exceeded, when the King of the Belgians presided, in 1872.

In commemoration of Prince Albert's presidency, Her Majesty was graciously pleased to grant to this Institution the privilege of bearing the Crown as an addition to its Armorial bearings, and the style of the Institution was thenceforth that of "The Royal Literary Fund." Her Majesty confers upon it the sanction of her name as its Patron, and has shown her interest by an annual benefaction of One Hundred Guineas, ever since the year of her Accession.

By the donations and subscriptions of members of the Corporation, with the addition of legacies, and the profits obtained at the anniversary festivals, the Royal Literary Fund has been enabled,

C

since its foundation in the latter part of the eighteenth century, to dispense upwards of £105,000 to needy persons of the literary class.

The importance and the benefits of the Institution will more clearly appear from a brief statement of the proceedings at the Festival over which H.R.H. the Prince of Wales presided. The dinner was served in St. James's Hall on Wednesday, May 18th. Grace was said by the Lord Primate of Ireland. After the removal of the cloth, and the singing of the " Deum Laudate," the Prince rose to propose the first toast :—

" The first toast I have the honour to propose is ' The health of Her Majesty the Queen, our munificent Patron ; ' a toast which I feel sure will be drunk with the enthusiasm which it elicits on all public occasions. Although the Queen is now compelled, to a certain extent, to withdraw from public life, still her interest in every institution of this country, and particularly in charitable institutions, remains undiminished. Gentlemen, I give you ' The Queen.' "

The next toast was proposed by the Marquis of Salisbury, " The health of Her Royal Highness the Princess of Wales, and the rest of the Royal Family." The toast was drunk with all the honours and responded to by His Royal Highness the Chairman. " The Church " having been proposed by the Rt. Hon. Edward Cardwell, and responded to by the Archbishop of Armagh, H.R.H. the Chairman proposed the toast of " The Army, Navy, and Volunteers," saying :—

" This is a toast which it gives me especial pleasure to propose from the circumstance of my having served for a time with both infantry and cavalry. Short as my service was, it has been long enough to impress me with the conviction of the efficiency of all ranks composing the British army. I have also had an opportunity during my voyage to America in 1860, and on many other occasions, of witnessing the able manner in which the duties of the navy are performed. The volunteers demand our warmest thanks and approbation for the zeal with which they came forward when they thought their services were required, a zeal which they still evince on every occasion afforded to them. I beg to couple with ' the Army and Volunteers,' the name of my illustrious relative the Duke of Cambridge, who so ably fills the arduous post of Commander-in-Chief entrusted to him by the Queen, and to whose practical and liberal administration the army owes its present high state of efficiency. With 'the Navy,' I will couple the name of Rear-Admiral Sir Alexander Milne, who has only lately returned from the successful discharge of the difficult duties attaching to the command of the North American Station. Gentlemen, let us drink to the 'Army, Navy, and Volunteers.' "

The Duke of Cambridge and Admiral Sir Alexander Milne having responded, His Royal Highness the Chairman then gave the toast of " The Royal Literary Fund," saying :—

" Your Royal Highness, my Lords, and Gentlemen, I have now the honour to propose the most important toast of the evening, it is 'Prosperity to the Royal Literary Fund.' Although the most important, it is nevertheless the toast upon which, perhaps, I can say least, certainly I can give you no new information, as every one here present knows better than I do the character of this institution. Still it is right that I should offer a few remarks on the working of this Society. You are all aware, gentlemen, of the immense advantages which have been derived from it in support of literature and science. One of its principal features is that it is not limited to our own country-men, but is often extended to literary men of all nations ; so that we may feel proud to think that by our timely assistance, we not only advance the literature of our own country, but that of other nations. In this way, many eminent men who would otherwise be incapacitated from carrying on their labours, and from making their talents known to the world, are enabled to do so. The second important feature is the secrecy with which this timely aid is given,—a secrecy so sacredly observed that in the whole number of cases, which amount to 1,645 since the foundation of this Corporation in the year 1790, there is not a single case of any indiscretion having been committed ; and if cases have been brought to light at all, it has only been through the acknowledgment of the literary men thus assisted, who have been anxious to express their gratitude. I ought here to mention the name of an eminent man of letters, whose loss must be deeply deplored in all literary circles. I allude to Mr. Thackeray. I allude to him, not so much on account of his works, for they are standard works, but because he was an active member of your committee, and always ready to open his purse for the relief of literary men struggling with difficulties.

"Gentlemen, some of those here present do not perhaps know that in France, since 1857, an Institution similar to ours, and founded by M. Thenard, has been in existence for the benefit of scientific men only, and that a few days ago M. Champfleury, a distinguished writer, proposed to form a Literary Society adopting some of our principles. It is to be hoped that some day these two societies may form sister Literary Funds; and if administered on our model, I think we may augur for the new institution a large measure of success. We shall at all times be most happy to enter into communication with it, and show it the result of our long experience and of the unwearied zeal and exertion of the Officers of this Corporation.

"I will not detain you much longer, gentlemen, but I cannot sit down without bringing back to your recollection the deep interest which my dear and lamented father took in everything connected with literature and science, and particularly in the labours of this Society. Nobody has forgotten that the second time he spoke in public in this country, was as chairman of the Literary Fund dinner. And we all, I am convinced, deeply regret that the speeches made on that occasion were not reported at full length, as every word falling from those lips could not fail to command universal admiration. Gentlemen, let us drink ' Prosperity to the Royal Literary Fund.' "

The list of subscriptions and donations having been read, including a donation of £110 from the Prince of Wales, Earl Stanhope, as President of the Institution, responded. Speeches being delivered by Earl Russell, Mr. Anthony Trollope, Lord Houghton, and H. E. M. Van de Weyer, Earl Stanhope proposed the health of the Chairman, which was received with much enthusiasm, and the Prince thus replied:—

"Your Royal Highness, my Lords and Gentlemen, I thank you most sincerely for the kind and cordial manner in which you have drunk my health, and I feel proud to have occupied the chair for the first time, on so interesting and important an occasion. I must now take the opportunity to congratulate this Corporation on the great advantage which it enjoys, in the services of the distinguished nobleman who now fills the high office of your President, and who has contributed so much to historical literature.   I can give him no higher praise, than by saying that he is a worthy successor of a nobleman who was for more than twenty years your president; who throughout a long political career never made an enemy, and who always found time to assist in the advancement of literature and art.   I allude to the late Marquess of Lansdowne.   Gentlemen, allow me to propose one more toast.   In the presence of a Society, accustomed to cultivate with such signal success the flowers of literature, it would be unpardonable to forget the flowers of society.   I propose the health of ' The Ladies,' who, by their numerous attendance here this evening, evince the interest they take in the Literary Fund."

The toast was received with the usual honours.   It should have been mentioned that nearly 400 ladies were present, but in the galleries, not at the tables as guests, as is the better custom at some anniversaries.

IRISH INTERNATIONAL EXHIBITION OF 1865.

May 9th, 1865.

THE city of Dublin has seldom presented a scene of more general joy than when the Prince of Wales opened the International Exhibition, on the 9th of May, 1865.   The weather was superb, the loyal demonstrations in the streets were enthusiastic, and the great Hall where the opening ceremony took place, decorated with the flag of all nations, was densely crowded with the most distinguished assembly that Ireland could bring to welcome the heir of the throne, and the representative of the Queen.   There were no disloyal feelings nor discordant sounds in the Palace that day.   The Duke of Leinster, the Earl of Rosse, and the highest and most distinguished of the nobles of Ireland were there.   The Lord Mayor and Corporation of the City appeared in their civic robes.   The Mayors of Cork and Waterford and Londonderry walked together; and the Lord Mayors of London and York, and the Lord Provost of Edinburgh, with many official personages, joined in the procession.   When His Royal Highness took his place in the chair of State, the orchestra, 1000 strong, performed the National Anthem, and 10,000 voices sent up their loyal cheers at its conclusion.

The Duke of Leinster read the address of the Committee, to which the Prince replied:—

"My Lords and Gentlemen,—I thank you for your address. It is a source of sincere pleasure to me to discharge the duties confided to me by Her Majesty the Queen in thus inaugurating your Exhibition. It is not less in accordance with my own feelings than with those of Her Majesty to assist in every measure calculated for the happiness and welfare of the Irish people. The example of my lamented and beloved parent will, I trust, ever be present to my mind as a stimulus in the encouragement of every work tending to advance international prosperity, and to develope the powers and resources of our own country. The cultivation of the fine arts, in itself so powerful an auxiliary in the civilization and refinement of the human race, has been an important object in these Exhibitions, and seems already to have produced most satisfactory results. Believe me very sensible of your kind wishes on behalf of the Princess of Wales. Her regret at being unable to accompany me equals my own, and you may rely upon her anxiety to come among you, assured of the welcome she will receive."

Then from the grand organ and choir rose the ever impressive music of the Hundredth Psalm, the most Catholic of all strains of praise and thanksgiving. At its close there was another address, giving an account of the origin and history of the Exhibition. A copy of the Catalogue, and the key of the building, having been presented to the Prince, the organ and orchestra pealed forth Handel's Coronation Anthem. Then came another address, presented by the Lord Mayor and the Corporation of Dublin, in their civic robes. This was read and handed to His Royal Highness, who thus replied:—

"My Lord Mayor, Aldermen, and Burgesses of the City of Dublin,—I return you my hearty thanks for the kind welcome you have given me, and for your loyal expressions towards Her Majesty the Queen. I regret that circumstances should prevent the extension of my visit to a longer period. It would have been very gratifying to the Princess had she been able to accompany me, and I request that you be assured that we look forward to another occasion when she will have the opportunity of appreciating the hearty welcome which my own experience leads me to anticipate for her. You justly ascribe to me a peculiar interest in this day's ceremony. As the son of that revered and lamented parent to whose wisdom, energy, and influence you truly state exhibitions such as these owe their origin, I may well feel proud in being able to assist in the inauguration of the one we are about to open. May your prayers be granted that it will be the means of producing the usual result attending well-directed labour, and conduce to the prosperity of Ireland and to the happiness of her people."

Then followed more music, from Haydn's Creation, and the State procession moved from the centre of the nave, and made a tour of the Exhibition. The Committee had arranged that music should form a notable feature of the ceremonies, for when the Prince returned to the daïs, the orchestra gave with grand effect Mendelssohn's 'Hymn of Praise.' At its conclusion the Prince rose and commanded Sir Bernard Burke, Ulster King-at-Arms, to declare the Exhibition open. This was done amidst a flourish of trumpets, and on a rocket being sent up as a signal, salvos of artillery were fired from the forts and batteries, and from the ships of war off Kingstown.

Such was the opening ceremony. In the evening the Lord Mayor gave a ball at the Mansion House. The city was brilliantly illuminated. Next day there was a review in the Phœnix Park, the number of spectators on the ground being greater than on any occasion since the visit of the Queen in 1849. The Prince of Wales, who wore the uniform of the 10th Hussars, of which regiment he is Colonel, was received with the utmost enthusiasm.

This was the first State visit of the Prince of Wales to Ireland. His second visit, along with the Princess of Wales, was a time of even greater brilliancy, and evoked equal enthusiasm of loyalty. If later visits were marked with less unanimity of rejoicing, the causes of the apparent disloyalty are well understood, and the disaffection is known to be partial and temporary. Nothing has ever occurred to lessen the personal popularity of the Prince of Wales, nor to give reasonable cause for the reception of any of the Royal Family being less cordial and enthusiastic than that of the Prince in 1865. The Exhibition of that year was held under the patronage of the Queen, who wished every success to the "patriotic undertaking," as she called it. They can be no true patriots who seek to lessen the Queen's interest in the welfare of Ireland.

INTERNATIONAL REFORMATORY EXHIBITION, HELD IN THE AGRICULTURAL HALL, ISLINGTON.

May 19*th*, 1865.

AFTER the great national and international Exhibitions, in which were seen the most advanced displays of art, fostered by wealth, skill, and training, it is pleasant to look back upon other exhibitions, of a humbler but not less useful kind, which were encouraged and patronized by the Prince of Wales. One of the most memorable of these, the pattern and parent of many local exhibitions of similar kind, was the Reformatory Exhibition held in the Agricultural Hall, Islington, in 1865. It was to exhibit the productions of various schools connected with the Reformatory and Refuge Union. The articles were the veritable manufacture of poor boys and girls of the lowest classes, many of them utterly destitute and hopeless as to any usefulness in life, until rescued and taught various industries, by the efforts of Christian and philanthropic men.

The good and venerated Lord Shaftesbury was the President of the Union, of which the Prince of Wales had gladly allowed himself to be named Patron. In an address read by Lord Shaftesbury, it was stated that the objects exhibited were contributed by workers in above two hundred separate institutions in London and other great towns. An invitation had been sent out for contributions from foreign schools of the same class, and this was responded to by articles being sent from almost every part of Europe, and some from Africa and America. Hence the title of international could be fairly given to the show. The representatives of several foreign governments were present on the occasion. The opening of the meeting by the Archbishop of Canterbury, and the sacred choral music performed by about one thousand children from the Reformatory and Refuge Schools, showed that moral and religious training was associated with the industrial work of the Union.

To the address of Lord Shaftesbury, the Prince replied as follows :—

" Your Grace, your Excellencies, my Lords, Ladies and Gentlemen,—I have gladly taken a part in the proceedings of this day, and complied with your request that I should attend, as patron of this society, with the greatest satisfaction. The benevolent purpose of this Exhibition cannot fail to be followed by deserved success, and claims the co-operation of every one who has the interests of the industrious poor at heart, and who desires to forward the object which the Reformatory and Refuge

Union has in view—namely, industrial and moral training. The Committee do me justice in believing that I cordially sympathize in the welcome this society offers to those representatives of foreign countries who have responded to the invitation they have received by their presence and contributions. In doing so they have borne testimony, in common with ourselves, to the value of these international exhibitions in promoting the growth of those Christian and kind feelings towards each other which we ought to pray should animate the whole of the nations of the world."

This reply, read in a clear, sonorous voice, was heard in every part of the building, and at its conclusion the cheers were loud and prolonged. Prayers were then offered up by the Archbishop of Canterbury, after which, and the singing of a hymn composed by the late Prince Consort, His Royal Highness declared the Exhibition opened.

The Prince then spent considerable time in examining various parts of the Exhibition, and delighted many youthful manufacturers by the very numerous purchases of every description, from the girls' as well as the boys' stalls, such as lace and crochet work to take to the Princess of Wales. The heartiness with which the Prince entered into the spirit of the occasion charmed all who were present.

On an earlier day of the same year, on the 1st of March, the Prince had visited an Exhibition got up by the South London Working Classes. No formal address or speech marked this visit, but the interest taken by the Prince, and his liberal purchases, of which all the neighbourhood soon heard and spoke, secured the success of the Exhibition. One exhibitor wished the Prince to accept a toy cart, which had attracted his notice, but the Prince good-humouredly declined such irregularity, however kindly intended, and insisted on paying for this as for all the purchases during the visit.

THE SAILORS' HOME, LONDON DOCKS.

May 22nd, 1865.

THE objects and the advantages of Sailors' Homes are now so universally known, that few words are needed for introducing a brief report of the visit of the Prince of Wales to the Home at the London Docks, on May 22nd, 1865. This institution has now for above fifty years afforded protection, comfort, and instruction to

all classes of the mercantile marine service. With increase of the
trade and shipping of London, new accommodation was required ;
and in 1863 the foundation stone of a new wing to the Sailors'
Home was laid by Lord Palmerston.

It was to open this completed building that the Prince of Wales
made his visit to the east of London. The event was regarded as
a great honour by the crowded and busy population of that quarter,
and a general holiday was held on the occasion. Many distinguished persons, including some of the Foreign Ministers, were
present. Foreign seamen in the British mercantile service are
admitted to benefits of the Home. An address having been read
by Admiral Sir William Bowles, President of the Institution, the
Prince replied :—

"Sir William Bowles, your Excellencies, my Lords, and
Gentlemen,—It is very gratifying to me to comply with the
invitation I have received to take a part in this day's proceedings
and to preside at the opening of the new wing of this institution.
The beneficial results attending the establishment of a Sailors'
Home for our immense mercantile navy are shown by the statements and figures which you have now given, and which
establish in the most satisfactory manner the necessity of adding
to the original building. The interest taken by my lamented
father in the religious welfare of this institution, evinced by his
laying the foundation stone of the Seamen's Church adjoining,
will not, I trust, be less in his son, who is well aware of the
sentiments of loyalty and devotion to the Throne which distinguish the mercantile navy of Great Britain."

ROYAL DRAMATIC COLLEGE.

June 5th, 1865.

How much the Prince of Wales has, from early life, favoured
dramatic art, and encouraged its professors, is universally known.
While enjoying the drama for his own recreation, amidst more
arduous labours, he has been always ready to support any well-
devised and well-directed scheme for the benefit of the dramatic
profession. It was with this feeling that he accepted the invitation
to inaugurate and formally open the Royal Dramatic College at
Woking.

There was a great gathering on the occasion, and the hall was
well filled, principally by ladies, before the proceedings commenced.

Mr. Webster, the Master of the College, having presented the Prince with a massive gold key, symbolical of the ceremony, and having read an address describing the objects of the Institution, His Royal Highness replied as follows :—

"Gentlemen,—It is truly gratifying to my feelings to find myself this day called on to take a part in the final completion of a building the foundation of which was the work of my lamented father, as it was also an object which he had much at heart. My satisfaction is increased by finding his beneficent plan carried out in a manner worthy of the cause and of the profession for the benefit of which the Dramatic College has been instituted, and that, as the inevitable hour approaches, he who has so often administered to your amusement, blended with instruction, will here find a retreat open for age and its infirmities, in grateful recognition of a debt due by the world at large. I am happy to learn that the funds are progressively increasing towards conferring the inestimable boon of education on the children of men who, whether by their performances or by their writings, have themselves laboured so well in the cause of literature, and so justly earned this provision for their offspring. The inauguration of the building we are now in completes the three purposes which you have enumerated as forming the original design of this institution. After having provided for the material wants and comforts of those who are entitled to seek a shelter in this asylum, the last object is to cheer their evening of life, and to embellish its closing scenes with the books, memorials, and records of their art, that they may again live in the past, and make their final exit in a spirit of thankfulness to God and their fellow-creatures."

FISHMONGERS' HALL DINNER.

June 11th, 1865.

ON the 11th of June, 1865, a banquet was given to the Prince of Wales by the Fishmongers' Company in their hall at London Bridge. Two years before, in 1863, the name of the Prince was added to the roll of the Company, so that on this occasion he appeared as a member as well as a guest. Allusion was made to this by the Prime Warden, James Spicer, who, as Chairman, proposed the health of the Prince and Princess of Wales, and the rest of the Royal Family. Reference was also made to the recent birth of another infant Prince, so that there was prospect of two Royal members, who would in due time have the right of inscribing their names on their freemen's roll. Some of the Prime Warden's words are worth reproducing, as showing at how early an age the Prince had exhibited the traits of character, and the line of action, by which he has now so long been distinguished. The Prime Warden said that "he was not using the language of flattery, but simply recording a fact with which the people of these realms, from one end of the kingdom to the other, were conversant, when he said that the esteem and the affection with which His Royal Highness was regarded by Her Majesty's subjects were owing no less to his amiable manners, his kindly disposition, and the condescension which he invariably displayed in his intercourse with all the classes of the community, than to the exalted position which he occupied, and the relation in which he stood as heir apparent to the British Throne. There was another circumstance which had endeared him to the people of England, and that was that he had followed so closely in the footsteps of his ever-to-be-lamented and illustrious father, by lending his high sanction to the promotion of those industrial exhibitions that tended so much to elevate and improve the tastes and habits of the people."

The Prince of Wales, in acknowledging the toast, said :—

" Mr. Prime Warden, your Royal Highness, my Lords, Ladies, and Gentlemen,—I thank you very much for the kind manner in which my name and that of the Princess of Wales, and the other members of the Royal family, have been proposed and received. I need hardly tell you that it is a source of sincere gratification to me to be present here this evening ; not only as a guest, but as a member—a freeman of this corporation. I have not forgotten that soon after I came of age the first freedom of any of the ancient guilds of this city with which I was presented was that of the Fishmongers' Company in 1863. I am proud also to think that I have been thus enrolled as a member of a company into which so many of my relations have been admitted, whose portraits adorn these walls. Although this is a joyous occasion, I cannot forbear alluding to the loss of one whose name is intimately connected with the city of London, Mr. Cubitt, who was twice elected Lord Mayor of London, and who was your Prime Warden three years ago when I took up my freedom in this company. I need not recall to your memory how anxious he was to promote every kind of charity, and I feel sure you will not think it unbecoming in me or inopportune to mention his name on this occasion. In conclusion, I beg again to thank you for the kind manner in which you have alluded to a recent event, and the cordial wishes you have expressed for the speedy recovery of the Princess. I can assure you my heartfelt wish is that my two sons may learn to emulate and follow the bright example of their revered grandfather."

SPEECH DAY AT WELLINGTON COLLEGE.

July 3rd, 1865.

On the 3rd of July 1865, the ceremony of distributing prizes at Wellington College was performed by the Prince of Wales, in presence of a distinguished company. The Governors of the College were in attendance, the Bishop of Oxford, the Earl of Derby, Earl Stanhope, Lord Eversley, Lord Chelmsford, Mr. Walter, M.P., and Mr. Cox. At the luncheon, which followed the proceedings in the large hall of the College, the head master, Mr. Benson (now Archbishop of Canterbury), having proposed the toast of the Prince of Wales, thanking him for his presence that day, and for the kind favour and interest with which he had uniformly regarded the institution, the Prince replied :—

"My Lords and Gentlemen,—I am deeply sensible of the manner in which Mr. Benson has proposed my health, and in which it has been received by the company assembled here to-day. I need hardly assure you that it is a source of sincere gratification to me to find myself once more within the walls of Wellington College, taking part in the proceedings of 'Speech Day,' and distributing prizes to the successful competitors. Allow me, Mr. Benson, to congratulate you, and through you the whole college, on the highly efficient state in which I find it. I feel convinced that my young friends have not forgotten that it bears the name of one of the greatest soldiers England ever knew. In the success of this institution Mr. Benson has already mentioned, and I need hardly remind you, that the Queen takes a strong interest; a still greater interest was taken by my father, to whose exertions the college really owes its origin. I have now, my lords and gentlemen, a very pleasing task to perform, and that is to make an announcement which I hope will not be considered indiscreet on my part. At the last meeting of the Governors of Wellington College, Lord Derby intimated that it was his intention to devote the profits of his justly celebrated translation of 'Homer' to the production of a prize to be given annually as a reward to the foundationer who within the year of his leaving the college should conduct himself to the entire approbation of the Head Master—be considered, in fact, the most industrious and well-conducted boy or young man in the school. I feel certain that this announcement will be received with great pleasure. It will show you the interest which the noble lord takes in this institution, and will be a stimulus to increased exertion on the part of those within its walls. I thank you, Mr. Benson, for proposing, and you, my lords and gentlemen, for drinking, my health so cordially; and I assure you it affords me great gratification whenever I can do anything to promote the welfare of Wellington College."

The report of the proceedings states that this speech was "delivered with a heartiness which elicited corresponding enthusiasm in the audience." The other speakers were Sir John Pakington, who said he had the most gratifying proof of the efficiency of the College in the progress made by his son as one of the pupils; and Lord Derby, who said that no worthier and suitable memorial of "the Great Duke" could have been erected in his honour than this institution, which was not merely a military school, but a college for training young Englishmen for the Universities, and for every department of public life, although all the foundationers are sons of deceased officers. Lord Derby also referred to the prize instituted by him, such rewards being usually given only to ability and successful study, while his object was to hold forth a stimulus to general study, and persevering good conduct. He would not have referred to the gift which it was his happiness to make, had not the matter been mentioned by His Royal Highness the Prince of Wales.

The Prince was again at Wellington College on the 17th of June, 1867, and he has ever since taken personal interest in the institution, as one of its Governors.

INSTITUTION OF CIVIL ENGINEERS.

May 9th, 1866.

THE President and Council of the Institution of Civil Engineers had the honour of entertaining the Prince of Wales, Prince Alfred, as he was then styled, and a very distinguished company, at dinner, in Willis's Rooms, on the 9th of May, 1866. Among the guests were the veteran Sir John Burgoyne, the Dukes of Sutherland and Buccleuch, Earl Grey, Lord Salisbury, Sir John Pakington, Sir Edwin Landseer, Professor (Sir Richard) Owen, Baron Marochetti, the Presidents of the Royal Society and of the Royal Institute of British Architects, and representatives of various departments in the public service. The members and associates of the Institution, numbering nearly two hundred, included all the civil engineers most eminent at that time, or who have since risen to distinction. Some of the names recall notable events and achievements in our time, sometimes called "the age of the engineers." Rennie, Armstrong, Bidder, Hawkshaw, Scott Russell, Hawksley, Cubitt, Penn, Fairbairn, Brunlees, Brassey, Samuda, Bramwell, Bessemer, Maudsley, Rawlinson, Vignoles, are on the list of those present on this memorable occasion. Mr. Fowler, President of the Institution, presided at the dinner, and in proposing the loyal toasts which are given at all such meetings, said of the Prince of Wales, that, "notwithstanding the numerous duties of his exalted station, His Royal Highness has always taken the greatest interest in those works which occupy the thoughts and lives of engineers, and therefore it is a source of peculiar gratification to the profession that His Royal Highness has been pleased to join the Institution of Civil Engineers, which had the honour to rank as its most distinguished honorary member His Royal Highness the Prince Consort."

The Prince of Wales in returning thanks, said :—

"Mr. President, your Royal Highness, my Lords and Gentlemen, I have indeed every reason to feel deeply flattered and gratified at the very kind manner in which you, Mr. President, have proposed this toast, and for the way in which it has been received by the company present. Under any circumstances, it would have afforded me sincere pleasure to have been present this evening—present at a meeting of so distinguished a body as the Civil Engineers of Great Britain ; but it is still more agreeable to me to find myself here in the position of one of your honorary members. I thank you for the manner in which you have mentioned my name regarding me as one of yourselves. I feel proud to think that my lamented father was also an honorary member of this distinguished Institution. Mr. President and Gentlemen, perhaps it is a difficult task for me to address so eminently scientific a body, more especially to eulogize them; but I cannot forbear adverting to the names of two most distinguished members of it—I allude to Mr. Brunel and Mr. Stephenson, whose names will never be obliterated from our memory. The important services they have rendered to this country can never be forgotten. Let us look round at the vast works which have been completed, or which are in the course of completion in this country. Though it may, perhaps, seem unnecessary, I think it is right I should on this occasion ask you to look for a moment at the vast extension of our docks all over this country—at the great improvements in the electric telegraph, and also in our steamships, and, in fact, in the general steam navigation on our waters. Let us look at what has been done at home—and when I say at home, I mean in this Metropolis. No one can walk over Westminster-bridge without being struck by those magnificent quays which are being built on either side of the river, and are commonly called the Thames Embankment. These constitute the most important works of the day. I must also refer to the Metropolitan Underground Railway, which is owing to the continued exertions of your distinguished President, and which, although not entirely completed, has been in use for nearly three years, and has, I believe, to a considerable extent diminished the traffic in our streets. Let us look also at our colonies, and see the many important works which our engineers have contrived there. I would allude more especially to one—the celebrated bridge built over the St. Lawrence, called the Victoria-bridge, which is close to Montreal, and which was constructed by one of your most renowned engineers, Mr. Stephenson. I had the honour of inaugurating that bridge in the name of Her Majesty the Queen. I have to be thankful to you all in many ways; but I have to be particularly thankful to Mr. Stephenson for having built such a bridge, because, perhaps, I should never have had an opportunity of visiting our North American colonies and a portion of the United States if I had not received an invitation to inaugurate that great work. Let me thank you once more, Mr. President, for the honour done me, and for the kind way in which the name of the Princess of Wales has been received. And let me assure you that it affords me the deepest gratification to have the honour of being present this evening as one of your members."

The Chairman then gave the toast of "the Army, Navy, and Volunteers," coupling with it the names of Prince Alfred, Sir John Burgoyne, and Colonel Erskine. The speech of Prince Alfred, in reply, is worth recalling, as one of the earliest occasions on which he represented the profession in which he now holds so high a position :—

" Mr. President, your Royal Highness, my Lords, and Gentlemen,—I need scarcely tell you with what pleasure I rise to respond to this toast, nor how proud I feel to hear my name associated with the Royal navy. Within the last few years the navy has become more connected with the civil engineers than ever it was before. Many improvements we owe—in fact, I may say all the later improvements we owe—to the civil engineers. There is only one thing they have not succeeded in doing, and that is making us look more beautiful than we did before. Indeed, I am afraid they have rather caused us to deteriorate in appearance. I need not add that I take, and shall continue to take, the greatest interest in this body ; the more so from the fact of my father having been an honorary member of the institution, and from my brother having now for the first time taken his place in the same character."

THE BRITISH AND FOREIGN BIBLE SOCIETY.

June 11th, 1866.

THE foundation-stone of the stately edifice in Queen Victoria Street, the head-quarters of the British and Foreign Bible Society, was laid by the Prince of Wales, on the 11th of June, 1866. On the ground near St. Andrew's Hill, Doctors' Commons, a spacious awning stretched over an area with ranges of seats for above 2000 persons. On the platform were many good and eminent men, most of whom—Lord Shaftesbury, Lord Teignmouth, the Archbishop of York, the Bishops of Winchester and Carlisle, the Dean of Westminster, Dr. Binney—are with us no more.

The proceedings commenced with prayer, praise, and reading some portions of Scripture appropriate to the occasion. An address was then read by the Rev. S. B. Bergne, one of the

D

Secretaries, giving a summary of the history of the Society, and stating its objects and operations.

The Earl of Shaftesbury then formally requested His Royal Highness "to undertake the solemn duty of laying the foundation stone of an edifice which shall be raised for the glory of God, and for the promotion of the best interests of the human race." The Prince duly and formally laid the stone, and then replied to the address that had been read :—

" My Lord Archbishop, my Lords and Gentlemen,—I have to thank you for the very interesting address in which you so ably set forth the objects of this noble Institution.

"It is now sixty-three years ago since Mr. Wilberforce, the father of the eminent prelate who now occupies so prominent a place in the Church of England, met, with a few friends, by candlelight, in a small room in a dingy counting-house, and resolved upon the establishment of the Bible Society.

"Contrast with this obscure beginning the scene of this day, which, not only in England and in our colonies, but in the United States of America, and in every nation in Europe, will awaken the keenest interest.

"Such a reward of perseverance is always a gratifying spectacle ; much more so when the work which it commemorates is one in which all Christians can take part, and when the object is that of enabling every man in his own tongue to read the wonderful works of God.

"I have an hereditary claim to be here upon this occasion. My grandfather, the Duke of Kent, as you have reminded me, warmly advocated the claims of this Society ; and it is gratifying to me to reflect that the two modern versions of the Scriptures most widely circulated—the German and English—were both, in their origin, connected with my family. The translation of Martin Luther was executed under the protection of the Elector of Saxony, the collateral ancestor of my lamented father ; whilst that of William Tyndale, the foundation of the present authorized English version, was introduced with the sanction of the Royal predecessor of my mother the Queen, who first desired that the Bible 'should have free course through all Christendom, but especially in his own realm.'

"It is my hope and trust, that, under the Divine guidance, the wider diffusion and the deeper study of the Scriptures

will, in this as in every age, be at once the surest guarantee
of the progress and liberty of mankind, and the means of
multiplying in the purest form the consolations of our holy
religion."

The Archbishop of York then invoked the Divine Blessing on
the work. The Bishop of Winchester, as one of the oldest living
members of the Society, expressed the grateful acknowledgments
of the Committee to the Prince, for his presence among them, and
for the act performed at their request. Two verses of the National
Anthem having been sung, and the benediction pronounced, the
meeting dispersed.

The Lord Mayor, with true civic hospitality, invited the Prince
of Wales, the officers of the Society, and all who had taken any
part in the ceremony to luncheon at the Mansion House. On
the health of the Prince and the Princess of Wales being proposed, the Prince acknowledged the compliment in the following
words:—

"I am, indeed, deeply touched and gratified by the toast
which has just been proposed by the Lord Mayor, and by the
very kind and feeling manner in which you have drunk to the
health of the Princess and myself. It is to me a source of
sincere gratification to receive again the hospitality of the Chief
Magistrate of the City. I can never forget, nor can the Princess
ever forget, the manner in which she was received on her first
entry into London; and although she is not here to-day—a fact
which I most deeply regret—I can bear testimony that she has
never forgotten, and never will forget, the reception given to her
three years ago. The occasion which has brought me here to-day
has given me sincere gratification. I shall be happy on all
occasions to do any thing that may tend, as the Lord Bishop of
Winchester said this morning, 'to alleviate the sufferings of
man.' But I feel sure that the work I have been enabled to
perform, small as it may be, will bear testimony to the great
good done to the poorer classes by a Society which has existed
for so many years. Sincerely I thank you for the opportunity
you have given me in coming forward on this interesting occasion,
and I shall always be happy to render every assistance in my
power to an institution which is calculated to render such
important benefits to the world. I return my best thanks for
the greeting I received this morning at the ceremony, and also

for the kind manner in which I have been received on this occasion."

Her Majesty the Queen signified her interest in the proceedings of the day by sending £100 to the Building Fund, and £100 was also contributed by the Prince of Wales.

The Bible Society has, since its establishment in 1804, issued about 113 millions of Bibles, Testaments, or portions thereof. Its issues yearly are now about four million copies. The full income in 1887 amounted to £116,761; and the sum received for Scriptures sold was £104,880. The Society has aided the translation of the Bible into 280 languages or dialects.

FRIEND OF THE CLERGY CORPORATION.

June 13th, 1866.

THE sixteenth anniversary festival of this institution was celebrated at Willis's Rooms on the 13th of June, 1866. Among the guests were the Archbishops of Canterbury, York, and Armagh, and numerous dignitaries in Church and State, the Marquis of Salisbury presiding. The Prince of Wales honoured the company with his presence, and on his health being proposed by the chairman, he said :—

" My Lord Chairman, my Lords and Gentlemen,—I feel, indeed, deeply flattered and gratified by the kind terms in which you have spoken of me, and by the kind manner in which my health has been received by the company, and I have earnestly to thank you in my own name and in the name of the Princess of Wales and of the other members of the Royal family. Among the many charities in this country, I believe there are few which demand our sympathy and support more than the Friend of the Clergy Corporation. Its object is to assist the orphans and unmarried daughters of clergymen of the Church of England, and to afford temporary aid to their necessitous parents. We have met here this evening to advocate the cause of the institution, and I believe that at the present moment the pensions which it distributes amount to the large sum of £4000 per annum, and that it helps to maintain 106 pensioners, while there are 60 more persons applying for its bounty. One remarkable characteristic of the institution is that its pensions, which never exceed £40 a year, are granted for life, and another is that these pensions are bestowed on members of the Church not only in England, but also in Ireland and the colonies. Young though I am, I think I may state that I am aware from my own personal knowledge how low are the stipends received by many of our clergymen, and I can, therefore, support most cordially this institution. I feel, however, some diffidence in alluding to that subject, because I know I shall thereby be trenching on the special province of our noble chairman. But I believe he will forgive me for saying that I think we ought upon this occasion to show the greatest possible liberality, and, if I may use the expression, that we ought freely to open our purses. I can again assure you that the Princess of Wales and the other members of the Royal family are most ready to participate with me in the feeling of sincere gratitude with which I now acknowledge the compliment you have just paid us. I now thank you, too, for the kind manner in which you have just listened to me, however imperfectly I have expressed myself."

In giving the toast of "Prosperity to the Institution," the noble chairman said, that after the speech which they had just heard in its favour from His Royal Highness it was scarcely necessary for him to say another word. He could fully confirm everything which had been said by His Royal Highness as to its value, and the urgent need of such an institution was proved by the fact that there were in this kingdom no less than 10,000 clergymen who occupied benefices of less value than £150 a year. How was it possible for men with such incomes, who had to move in a respectable sphere of life, to lay by anything for a period of distress or to make a provision for their widows and orphans? He therefore cordially concurred in the eloquent appeal made to them by His Royal Highness.

The result of the appeal was a subscription list amounting to £1200, including 100 guineas from the Prince of Wales.

It may be added that now (1888) there are about 100 pensioners, besides special grants for urgent cases. Last year's receipts were £6,000, and the invested funds are about £18,500.

WAREHOUSEMEN AND CLERKS' SCHOOL.

June 18th, 1866.

ONE of the earliest public functions undertaken by the Prince (July, 1863) was laying the foundation stone of the School, near Croydon, for children of warehousemen, clerks, and agents of wholesale houses and manufactories, so employed in any part of the United Kingdom. The building was not completed till the spring of 1866, and on the 18th of June of that year, the Prince, on being applied to, at once and cordially agreed to preside at the inauguration or formal opening of the Asylum.

The Prince was received by Earl Russell, President of the Charity, the Bishop of Winchester, the Lord Mayor of London, the High Sheriff of Surrey, and other official and distinguished persons interested in the Institution. Having thoroughly inspected the building, the arrangements of which are admirable, and having heard an address explaining the origin and purposes of the Institution, briefly replied as follows :—

"My Lords and Gentlemen,—It is a sincere pleasure to me to see the work which we commenced in July, 1863, brought to a happy conclusion. Such a consummation, when we reflect on the numerous classes of the great commercial community of our country whose interests it promotes, cannot but be gratifying to every one present, and will induce us all gratefully to invoke the Divine blessing on the ultimate success of this undertaking. The attention that has been paid to the details of the building and to the comforts and wellbeing of the children it is destined to shelter, I may say, without presumption, merits this success. And if, as you have stated, 'that which is worth doing at all is worth doing well,' be a truth requiring any corroboration, I have only to point to this structure for the most unanswerable argument in its support. It only remains for me to thank you, my lords and gentlemen, for the kind expressions you have used with reference to the part I have taken in this day's proceedings."

Prayer was then offered by the Bishop of Winchester, and a thanksgiving hymn sung. The ladies present then came forward with their collection purses, and amusement was caused by the hugeness of the heap of offerings that rose before the Prince, exceeding even the large sum presented when the foundation stone was laid. On this occasion upwards of one thousand ladies presented the charitable gifts, and above £5000 in money or subscriptions proved to be the gratifying result. Prayer and thanksgiving were again offered, and the Prince, amid much enthusiasm, declared the Asylum open.

The schools, first established in 1853, had been formerly conducted in three separate houses at New Cross, under many disadvantages. The building inaugurated by the Prince of Wales is one of the most commodious and beautiful structures possessed by any charity. Its imposing appearance and picturesque site must have been admired by many travellers on the Brighton and South Coast Railway, near Caterham Junction. The prosperity of the Institution has been in keeping with its auspicious beginning.

MERCHANT SEAMEN'S ORPHAN ASYLUM.

June 28th, 1866.

THE object of the Merchant Seamen's Orphan Asylum is sufficiently indicated by its name. Founded in 1817, the institution had for nearly fifty years been carried on with success. Upwards of 800 children had found shelter and training, but this number represents a very small proportion of the orphans left destitute through the calamities of which merchant seamen are constantly in peril. This asylum was at first located in the parish of St. George's-in-the-East, and subsequently removed to the Borough Road, where the first stone of a new building was, in 1861, laid by the Prince Consort. The building was opened by Earl Russell in 1862. The support given to the charity encouraged the building of the present asylum, near Snaresbrook, in a healthy and beautiful part of the country.

It was for the opening ceremony of the erection of a new dining-hall that the Prince and Princess of Wales visited the Asylum, on the 28th of June, 1866. Received by a guard of honour of the Hon. Artillery Company, their Royal Highnesses were conducted to a tent where luncheon was served. In proposing the health of the Royal visitors, Lord Alfred Paget, who presided, said that "he had known His Royal Highness almost, he might say, before he knew himself, and that he could bear testimony to the interest he took, not only in every manly English sport, but in everything which tended to contribute to the advancement of such institutions as that whose success he testified by his presence on that occasion his desire to promote."

In returning thanks the Prince of Wales said :—

" I am, indeed, deeply sensible of and deeply grateful for the excessively kind manner in which the noble lord has proposed my health and that of the Princess of Wales, as well as for the very kind manner in which you all have been good enough to receive the toast. My presence here to-day affords me the greatest satisfaction, because we have come to honour a work which to me is particularly interesting, inasmuch as the foundation stone of this asylum was laid by my lamented father in 1861. But, under any circumstances, it would be a pleasing and a proud moment for me to be here on such an occasion as this. We must all know how important a part our mercantile navy plays at the present moment, and how important it is that we should provide for the orphans of those brave men who are exposed to so many dangers. As you are well aware, this institution has furnished an asylum since its opening in 1862 for upwards of 180 boys and girls at a time, and it must, I am sure, be greatly gratifying to us that I should to-day be called upon to lay the foundation stone of an additional room, which I understand will embrace part of the plan of the original building. I beg again to thank you, on my own behalf and on that of the Princess, than whom, I assure you, nobody takes greater interest in the work which we are assembled to promote."

Lord A. Paget next proposed the toast of " Prosperity to the Merchant Seamen's Orphan Asylum," which was responded to by Mr. Green, one of the directors.

The Prince of Wales then rose and said :—

" I have to give you the health of our noble chairman, to whom, I think, we ought all to be very grateful for the kind manner in which he has undertaken to perform the duties of his position on this occasion, as well as for the interest which he manifests, not only in this great and important charity, but in the welfare of the sailor all over the world. I felt almost inclined to blush at the terms in which he alluded to his friendship for myself, and I can never forget the kindness which he has shown towards me since my early boyhood."

The toast was very cordially drunk, and shortly after Lord A. Paget had briefly responded to it their Royal Highnesses paid a brief visit to the beautiful chapel, which has been endowed for the use of the asylum at the sole cost of Lady Morrison. An address was afterwards read, expressing the gratification which the friends of the institution derived from the presence of their Royal Highnesses, and their thankfulness for the interest thus manifested in its prosperity. In reply the Prince said :—

"My part in the proceedings of the day is attended with peculiar pleasure from the circumstance of its being the anniversary of the inauguration of this building by my lamented father. The call for its extension by the increased numbers applying for admission tells its own story. The steady support which the institution has continued to receive from its commencement encourages us to persevere in the good work so auspiciously begun. The interest of the Queen in its welfare is, I can assure you, fully participated in by me, and it only remains for me now to invoke the Divine blessing on the benevolent objects which have led to this undertaking."

The foundation stone was then laid with the usual formalities, and after a religious service, conducted by the Archbishop of Armagh, the Royal visitors left, amidst the cheers of the assemblage.

ROYAL VISIT TO NORWICH IN 1866.

August, 1866.

FROM the time of making his home at Sandringham, the Prince of Wales, like all English country gentlemen, has felt that his county had special claims on his public spirit and personal exertions. Norfolk has not been slow to understand these claims, and the Prince has more than met the expectations formed of him in regard to his county life. In the record of future years it will be seen how heartily he has associated himself, not with the agriculture only, but with the various occupations and industries, the works and the sports, the schools and the charities of Norfolk.

One of the earliest public appearances of the Prince and Princess of Wales in the county chosen as their home, was at Norwich in the autumn of 1866. The time chosen by the Mayor and Corporation for the invitation to visit their city was that of the Norwich musical festival of that year. Her Majesty the Queen of Denmark, and the Duke of Edinburgh, accompanied the Prince and Princess on this visit, which was in every way a most enjoyable and successful one. Among the attractions of the musical festival was the performance for the first time of Sir Michael Costa's oratorio

Naaman. The Norwich concerts of 1866 were remarkable both in the richness of the programmes, and the rare excellence of the performances. Seldom has opportunity been afforded of hearing such variety of classic music, performed by the greatest vocal and instrumental artists of the time.

The musical festival was not, however, the sole attraction. The capital of the Eastern Counties was in high festival, and other entertainments were provided. Advantage was also taken of the Prince's presence for the ceremony of opening the Drill-shed recently erected for the Norwich Volunteers. Colonel Black, the commander, in addressing the Prince, referred to the great interest always taken by him in the organization and efficiency of the volunteer force of the country, and they had therefore sought the honour of his inaugurating the building erected for military purposes, by the volunteers of the ancient and loyal city of Norwich. The Prince replied that he had the greatest pleasure in complying with the request; and, having complimented the commander on the efficiency of his corps, and the suitability of the building for its purposes, he declared the hall open. The chaplain of the battalion then offered a brief prayer. The planting of memorial trees, and other incidents associated with the Royal visit, will long be remembered by the people of Norwich.

ROYAL NATIONAL LIFE-BOAT INSTITUTION.

March 1st, 1867.

In a maritime country like this, with seas crowded with shipping, and with coasts dangerous from rocks or shoals, a lifeboat service for preservation of life from shipwreck is a necessity. The Royal National Life-boat Institution meets the want. It has now, in 1888, nearly 300 stations, all round the coast. The wreck chart, which is published annually with the Society's Report, shows at a glance where wrecks are most numerous, and there the boats of rescue are most required. It is not only British coasting vessels that are thus provided for, but the ships coming from foreign seas, and of all nations, as they crowd towards our estuaries and ports, benefit by the lifeboat service.

On the 1st of March, 1867, the Prince of Wales took the chair at the annual meeting of the Institution held, through the courtesy of the Lord Mayor, in the Egyptian Hall of the Mansion House. Received in the State Drawing-Room, by the chief magistrate of London, attended by the sword and mace bearers of the Corporation, the Prince was thence conducted to the Hall, where a numerous and distinguished company had assembled. On taking the chair, the Prince said:—

"My Lord Mayor, my Lords, Ladies, and Gentlemen,—It affords me very great pleasure to occupy the chair to-day, upon so interesting an occasion as the present. Among the many benevolent and charitable institutions of this country there are, I think, few which demand our sympathy and support more, and in which we can feel more interest, than the National Life-boat Institution. An institution of this kind is an absolute necessity in a great maritime country like ours. It is wholly different in one respect from other institutions, because although lives are to be saved, they can in those cases in which this society operates only be saved at the risk of the loss of other lives. I am happy to be able to congratulate the Institution upon its high state of efficiency at the present moment, and upon the fact that by its means very nearly one thousand lives have been saved in the course of the past year.

"Lifeboats have been given by many benevolent individuals —some as thank-offerings from the friends of those whose lives have been saved, and others in memory of those who are unhappily no more. I am happy also to be able to say that lifeboats do not only exist upon our coast, but that our great example in this matter has been imitated by many foreign maritime countries, and they have chosen our institution as the model for their own. I beg upon this occasion to tender, in the name of the Institution, our warmest thanks for the kindness and courtesy of the Lord Mayor in allowing us to hold our meeting in this hall. It is indeed a peculiarly fitting place in which to hold such a meeting, closely connected as the Institution is with the City of London. Very nearly half a century ago the Institution originated in this city. In 1850 the late Duke of Northumberland became its president. My lamented father was also a vice-patron, and took the warmest interest in its prosperity. I am happy to say the respected secretary, Mr. Lewis, occupied that position at that time, as, indeed, he had long before that time. He has held it ever since, and much of the success of the Institution is owing to his long experience, and the energetic manner in which he has directed its working has raised the Institution to its present high state of efficiency.

"I may say that there are 174 lifeboats afloat, and that in

the course of the past year 33 have been called into existence, at a cost of no less than £17,000, the whole of which has been defrayed by benevolent individuals.   Before concluding the brief remarks which I have addressed to you, however imperfectly, upon this occasion, I call upon you once more to offer your support to so excellent an Institution.   I am certain you must be convinced that it is one which is really a necessity for a great maritime nation like this.   I congratulate you that it has arrived at so efficient a state, and I feel quite sure that you would be the last to wish it to decay from want of funds."

The Secretary having read the Report, and various speeches having been delivered, donations were announced to the amount of £1200.   At the luncheon, which was afterwards given in the Long Parlour, the Prince hoped that the proceedings of that day would advance the prosperity of the Institution, the benefits of which had only to be more widely known, to be more largely supported.

We may add that the receipts, as stated in last year's report (1887), were £56,970, and the expenditure £74,162.   During the year 368 lives had been saved by the Society's boats, and ten vessels saved from destruction.   Besides medals and other testimonials, £3345 had been granted in rewards.   Since the formation of the Society it has voted as rewards 97 gold and 996 silver medals or clasps, 139 binocular glasses, 15 telescopes, and money to the amount of £96,700.   These statistics are furnished by the present secretary, Mr. Charles Dibdin, a descendant of the Dibdin whose naval songs are known to all sailors.   British seamen are always ready to risk their lives to save their fellow men, and there is never any difficulty found in manning the lifeboats, but it is necessary to have a permanent staff, and to keep up the stations, while those who volunteer to imperil their own lives ought to have reward, in order to help to provide for others dependent on them.   The Prince again presided at the Annual Meeting in 1884.

SOCIETY OF ANCIENT BRITONS.

March 1st, 1867.

A WELSH charitable institution might claim the patronage of the Prince of Wales, from his title, apart from the sympathy shown by him towards benevolent works amidst all classes of the people. On St. David's Day, March 1st, 1867, the Prince presided at the 152nd anniversary festival of this ancient and useful charity, the origin of which dates back from the year 1715, shortly after the accession of George I.

Caroline, the Princess of Wales, was born on the 1st of March of that year; and as there were divisions and intrigues at the period, many influential Welshmen combined to show their loyal attachment to the House of Hanover.

At first the combination was probably prompted by political motives, but the Society soon took up practical work, and founded a school for the education of poor children of Welsh parents in London. The Scotch had already formed similar patriotic institutions, and at a later period the Irish followed the example. On the present anniversary the Prince was supported by a distinguished company, including several of the most eminent and influential natives of the Principality.

The Health of the Queen having been drunk with enthusiasm, that of the Prince and Princess of Wales was proposed by the Duke of Cambridge, who said that every one would agree with him in expressing the high sense which every body entertained of the admirable way in which His Royal Highness had supported not only the general interests of the country, but also those of individual societies. The Prince responded in a few hearty words, saying he would always be found ready to assist charitable objects, whether as an onlooker, or as a participator in the proceedings, as he was that night. Having returned warm thanks for the reception given to the toast, and the good wishes expressed towards himself and the Princess of Wales, he then proposed the toast of the evening: "Prosperity to the Welsh Charity School, and Perpetuity to the Honourable and Loyal Society of Ancient Britons."

"I feel sure, Gentlemen, I shall not have to call upon you twice to respond most heartily to this toast. You all of you must know, perhaps far better than I can tell you, the history of this society; but at the same time it may be well that I should go back and give you a brief sketch of the society from its commencement. In 1715 it was founded on St. David's Day, which was the birthday of Caroline, Princess of Wales. My ancestor, George II., then Prince of Wales, became the first patron of the society. The Princess took great interest in the well-being of the society, independent of the fact of its having been founded in commemoration of her natal day. The school in those times was nothing more than a day school. It was found to be too small, and was removed to Clerkenwell, and there it flourished for some time. In 1771 it was removed to Gray's-inn Lane, and in 1818, at the death of the much lamented Princess Charlotte of Wales, whose loss the whole country most

deeply felt, 50 additional children were, by means of a public
subscription, sent to the school in remembrance of her name.
The school continued to flourish, but it was thought advisable,
if it could be effected, that the institution should be removed
into the country, in order, among other advantages, that the
children might derive the benefit of the fresh air.   Accordingly
in 1854 the school was removed to Ashford, and on the 13th of
July, 1857, my lamented father inaugurated and opened the
school on its present site.   I am happy to say that I accompanied him on that occasion, and from that time to this you will
believe me when I assure you that I have felt the deepest
interest in the prosperity of the school.   It has frequently
occurred on my journey from Windsor to London by the South-
Western line for me to notice the school as I have passed by it,
but that circumstance alone would not be required to remind
me of its claims.   When the school was removed from London
to the country considerable expense was incurred; so much so
that it was rendered necessary to reduce the number of children
from 200 to 150, but I am happy to be able to inform you that
in the course of the last century and a half as many as 3000
Welsh children have been by means of this institution clothed,
fed, and educated, and afterwards sent forth into the world provided, to a certain extent, for their future career.   This must be
a gratifying announcement, and brief and imperfect as the
sketch may have been which I have now given you, still I trust
I have said enough to call upon you most heartily to continue
that support which in past years you have given on the occasion
of these annual festivals.   Gentlemen, I thank you for the kind
manner in which you have been pleased to receive these
remarks, and I beg to propose to you, in a bumper, the toast of
the evening."

Other toasts and speeches followed, and a most liberal collection
was made for the Charity, which is now generally known under
the name of "High School for Welsh Girls."

LONDON INTERNATIONAL COLLEGE.

July 10th, 1867.

ON the 10th of July, 1867, His Royal Highness the Prince of Wales inaugurated this institution, established under the auspices of the International Education Society. Some years previously a Committee, of which Mr. Cobden and M. Michael Chevalier were members, proposed the formation of an International College, having four principal establishments, in England, France, Germany, and Italy. The pupils were to pursue their studies at each branch in succession. It was to inaugurate the English branch of this institution, at Spring Grove, under the direction of Dr. Leonard Schmitz, formerly Rector of the High School of Edinburgh, that they assembled this day.

After inspecting the building and grounds, the visitors assembled at luncheon, the chair being occupied by Mr. Paulton, the treasurer of the College, having on his right the Prince of Wales, and on his left the Duc d'Aumale. The Prince de Joinville and the Comte de Paris were also among the guests. On the health of the Prince of Wales being proposed, he replied as follows :—

"Mr. Chairman, Ladies, and Gentlemen,—I beg to thank you for the kind manner in which you have drunk my health, and for the feeling and touching sympathy you have evinced for the Princess of Wales. I can assure you it gives me the greatest gratification to be present to-day to inaugurate this College under the auspices of the International Education Society. I sincerely trust that this propitious weather and the goodly company I see around me may be omens of the future of this institution. The site of this College is all that can be desired, and I know that its management will be so administered as to fulfil to the utmost the anticipations of its promoters. There is now room for 80 pupils within its walls, and when the new wings are completed it will be capable of accommodating twice, probably treble, that number. There are, I understand, two sister institutions abroad—one in Germany, and the other in France ; and after the pupils have completed their studies here they can avail themselves of the advantages of these institutions to perfect themselves in modern Continental languages.

"I am not going to discuss the relative claims on our attention of the living and dead languages ; but I believe it to be most important that modern languages should form one of the principal subjects of study on grounds of practical utility. No persons were ever more deeply impressed with this fact than my late lamented father, and another man whose name is now celebrated through England, Richard Cobden. I have travelled a great deal on the Continent, and I am confident that I should have found my sojourn in these countries far less pleasant than it was if I had not possessed a considerable knowledge of the vernacular of the people.

"I thank you again sincerely for the manner in which you have drunk my health, and I shall convey to the Princess the deep sympathy you have evinced for her in her illness, the enthusiastic affection with which you have received her name, and your warm good wishes for her speedy restoration to health. Before sitting down I beg to propose a toast, which I am sure you will receive with every demonstration of approbation. It is "Success to the London College of the International Education Society." With that toast I beg to couple the name of Dr. Schmitz, whose pupil, I am proud to say, I once was while studying in the city of Edinburgh."

The toast having been received with great enthusiasm, Dr. Schmitz, in reply, said he had to thank His Royal Highness for the kindness of heart with which he had spoken of his humble name, and hoped that the College so happily inaugurated would have a prosperous issue. The distinctive feature of the institution was that in it the study of modern languages and natural sciences were to be largely pursued. The dead languages, however, were not to be ignored. They protested only against the exclusive study of classical literature. He had himself devoted his life to letters, but at the same time he fully recognized the claims of the modern continental tongues and the natural sciences, by which the civilization and progress of the world were unquestionably advanced. Professor Huxley then proposed the "Health of the Committee of Management," coupling with it the name of the chairman. The Chairman having briefly replied, the meeting broke up, and the visitors dispersed throughout the grounds for promenade.

THE VICEROY OF EGYPT, ISMAIL PASHA, AT THE MANSION HOUSE.

July 11th, 1867.

AMONG the many illustrious rulers of foreign nations who have been entertained by the Lord Mayor of London, have been three Viceroys of Egypt. On the 11th of July, 1867, at a banquet at the Mansion House, a distinguished company assembled to meet his Highness the Viceroy, Ismail Pasha. Twenty-one years previously, the father, and on a subsequent occasion the brother of the Viceroy had been similarly honoured in the capital of the British Empire. The Prince of Wales, the Duke of Cambridge, Prince Teck, Prince Edward of Saxe Weimar, many of the ambassadors of foreign powers, and the most eminent men of all shades of political opinion were among the company.

The reply of the Viceroy, to the toast, given by the Lord Mayor, was responded to in his native tongue, and interpreted by Nubar Pasha in French: "If Egypt had rendered services to England, chiefly in facilitating communication with India, his country was only acknowledging the debt due to this country for the benefits received in promoting the material and the moral progress of his people."

The next toast was the health of the Prince and Princess of Wales, and the other members of the Royal Family, to which the Prince thus responded:—

"My Lord Mayor, your Royal Highnesses, my Lords, Ladies, and Gentlemen, I beg to thank you most warmly and sincerely for the kind manner in which you, my Lord Mayor, have proposed my health and that of the Princess of Wales, and the other members of the Royal Family ; and to thank the company here present for the way in which it has been received. I need not assure you, my Lord Mayor, that to have been invited here this evening has been a source of great pleasure to me. Under any circumstances I always feel it a great compliment to be invited to the hospitable board of the Lord Mayor and the Corporation of the city of London.

"But this evening we have been invited here to do honour to a guest, and that guest the Viceroy of Egypt. As the Lord Mayor has very truly remarked, England and Egypt, though far distant from one another, though very different from one another in religion and in habits, are countries

E

which have been, and will continue to be, closely allied to one another.   We have every reason to be grateful to the Viceroy and to his Government for the means he has afforded us of visiting that country, and for the great hospitality that he has shown to us on all occasions.   I myself received distinguished marks of kindness under the rule of his brother, the late Viceroy, in 1862.   Nothing could exceed the kindness and courtesy with which I was treated, and the facilities with which I was enabled to visit that most interesting country.   We are also indebted to the Viceroy and the Egyptian Government for the great facilities he has afforded our troops in their transit to India.

"Egypt, as has been remarked, is a country that is fast improving in every way.   Manufactures are rising on all sides— especially the manufacture of cotton.   I myself visited a very important sugar manufactory, and it was interesting to find that there were English, French, and German workmen employed in that manufactory.

"I do not wish, my Lord Mayor, to take up more of your time this evening, knowing that there are other toasts to be proposed.   I will, therefore, conclude by again thanking you once more for the honour you have done me in drinking my health, and for the very kind expressions you have used towards the Princess of Wales.   I know I only express her feelings when I say that she has been deeply touched by that universal good feeling and sympathy which has been shown to her during her long and painful illness.   Thank God she has now nearly recovered, and I trust that in a month's time she will be able to leave London and enjoy the benefits of fresh air."

FESTIVAL OF ST. PATRICK.

March 17th, 1868.

ON various occasions, the Prince of Wales has shown on Irish soil, his sympathy with the people of the Sister Isle, and has been always welcomed with warm and loyal feeling by the mass of the population.   He has given practical proof of his good feeling for the Irish nation by being a patron and supporter of the Benevolent Society of St. Patrick, in the schools of which the children of poor Irish parents residing in the Metropolis receive education and other benefits.

The annual festival has long been well attended and supported, but never before was there so great and brilliant a gathering as when the Prince of Wales, on the 17th of March, 1868, presided at the dinner, at Willis's Rooms. Among the company were the Archbishop of Armagh, the Bishop of Derry, and many members of the House of Lords, and of the House of Commons, connected with Ireland, with other distinguished persons of all classes interested in the charity. The London Irish Volunteers formed a guard of honour in front of the building, and the Prince on entering, and taking his place as president, was greeted with enthusiastic cheers.

The usual loyal toasts having been given, and responded to by the Prince, with warm appreciation of the good-will, especially directed towards the Princess of Wales, on her health being proposed by the Archbishop of Armagh, the Prince proposed " The Army and Navy, the Militia and the Volunteers," saying some suitable words as to each branch of the united services.

The Earl of Longford briefly replied for the Army. Mr. Corry, in responding for the Navy, said he believed that St. Patrick had never been so far south as that fine harbour which was "*statio bene fida carinis.*" Complaints had been made from time to time that the Government had not availed themselves of the facilities which Cork harbour afforded for dockyard accommodation, but after the works at Haulbowline were completed, he hoped that the people of Cork would see that the Admiralty had no desire to do any injustice to Ireland in respect of the navy. He was glad to announce to the company that on the occasion of the forthcoming visit of the Prince of Wales to Dublin a division of the armour-clad vessels of the Channel fleet would be sent to the Bay of Dublin, where, weather permitting, the ships of the division would anchor and remain during the time His Royal Highness was to stay in Ireland.

Captain M. J. O'Connell, in returning thanks for the Volunteers, remarked that in the London Irish there never had been any political or polemical disputes.

At this stage of the proceedings there occurred a scene thoroughly " racy of the soil " of which most of the noblemen and gentlemen present were natives. The children of the schools were brought into the room, and "St. Patrick's Day" having been struck up by the band, the boys and girls proceeded to make the circuit of the tables. The national air of Ireland told alike on the benefactors and the recipients of the charity. The children looked with glistening eyes on the company, and the latter, as the young ones passed by, loaded them with fruit and cakes to such an extent that before the juvenile procession had made its exit from the apartment the tables had been cleared of the entire dessert, which was a very liberal one. The boys and girls raised a loud cheer as they left the room, and the entire company, including the illustrious President, appeared all the happier for having made the festival the means of so unusual a treat for the little sons and daughters of poor Irish parents struggling for their living in London.

After the performance of a selection of Irish airs, the Prince of Wales again rose and said :—

"My Lords and Gentlemen,—The next toast which I shall have the honour of proposing to you is the toast of the evening. We are here to-night for a very excellent and charitable purpose. The objects of the Benevolent Society of St. Patrick have been so often stated—so many able speeches have been made at so many successive anniversaries of this festival, that there is very little left for me to say; but having accepted, which I did with pleasure, the post of chairman this evening, I feel it is due to the institution and to this company that I should make a few observations. I may as well at once say that I am about to call upon you to drink prosperity to the Benevolent Society of St. Patrick. This Society was instituted in 1784, with the object of relieving the necessitous children of Irish parents resident in London. One of its first patrons was my grand-father, the Duke of Kent. I have always understood that he took a very great interest in the Society, and I may further observe that several of my grand-uncles acted as presidents at your annual dinners. At the present moment I believe the schools are in what may be called a flourishing condition. They afford education to as many as 400 children. That the boys and girls are in good health and thriving is, I think, pretty evident, from the appearance they presented as they passed through the room just now. A special feature in the conduct of the schools is that no doctrinal teaching is permitted. They are entirely national and non-sectarian schools. At the same time the children are strongly advised to attend the instructions given by the ministers of the religion in which their parents wish them to be brought up, and they are afforded an opportunity of doing so every week. If it is thought desirable, the children are apprenticed on leaving school. This system has been found to work remarkably well. Inducements are held out for proficiency and good conduct by rewards given after examination. A comparatively new feature in the management of the institution is this—that at times when the parents are enduring hardships and perhaps privations owing to the want of work—when they may not have a sufficiency of daily bread for the maintenance of their families, as, for instance, during severe winter weather, when many poor people find it difficult to obtain employment—a daily meal is given to children who are in want of it. This has been found to afford much assistance to the parents as well as the children, and may therefore be regarded as a satisfactory addition to the arrangements of the managers. I am informed that of late years the institution has lost many valuable patrons and supporters, but I should hope that any void in this way may speedily be filled up. My Lords and Gentlemen,—though this may be called an annual festival in aid of a charity, and in this respect it is exceedingly useful, it has also another advantage. It has long been regarded as an occasion when Irishmen living in London may meet together without sectarian feelings or political allusions. Such meetings are beneficial, and they must be all the more so when their main object is the furtherance of a most excellent institution like the Benevolent Society of St. Patrick, prosperity to which I now ask you to drink."

The illustrious President next gave " The Lord-Lieutenant of Ireland," and in doing so said, " he was sure every one would agree with him in thinking that Lord Abercorn had filled his high office with credit to himself and benefit to the country. His Excellency had had a very arduous task to perform. During Lord Abercorn's administration there had been great troubles in Ireland, but it was to be hoped that these were almost at an end."

The Earl of Mayo, in returning thanks for the Lord-Lieutenant, expressed his opinion that the Prince of Wales on his forthcoming visit to Ireland would experience such a reception as would induce His Royal Highness to go there again.

The Earl of Kimberley, in proposing the health of the illustrious President, said he thought the friends of Ireland ought to feel much obliged to His Royal Highness for his presence there that evening. He was convinced that good would result from it. Having on one occasion, while filling the office of Lord-Lieutenant, had the honour to receive the Prince of Wales at Dublin, he could state from his own knowledge that His Royal Highness took the deepest interest in all that concerned the welfare of Ireland, and showed the greatest anxiety to make himself acquainted with her affairs. The Prince had made himself acquainted with her affairs, and was in a position to give an intelligent and a just opinion on the matter. This was of great importance for Ireland. He thought he might venture to say that the Prince of Wales felt an affection for Ireland.

The toast was drunk with all the honours, and with unusual enthusiasm. The Prince of Wales said :—

"I am exceedingly gratified by the very kind terms in which my noble friend has proposed my health, and the more than cordial manner in which you, my lords and gentlemen, have received it. I hope I need not assure you that it has been a source of great pleasure to me to take the chair at a dinner in aid of a society which does so much for the benefit of so many children of the poorer Irish in London. My noble friend has alluded to my approaching visit to Ireland. I shall only say that I am glad to visit a portion of the United Kingdom in which I have experienced such extensive kindness from all parties. I agree with the noble Lord the Chief Secretary for Ireland. If this visit should tend to give pleasure to the people of Ireland I hope there may be a longer visit hereafter. During the course of the last two years there has been much that has been disagreeable to loyal Irishmen ; but I am convinced that the people of Ireland generally are thoroughly true and loyal, and that the disaffection which has existed will only be of short duration. It has not been engrafted on the minds of any portion of the Irish people by the Irish people themselves. But as we are assembled here for a purely charitable object this is not the place for political allusions. I shall, therefore, conclude by once more thanking you for the kind way in which you have drunk my health, and for the manner in which you have supported me this evening."

The amount contributed to the funds of the charity was about £1200, which included 100 guineas from the Queen, and a similar sum from the Prince of Wales.

DUBLIN AND CARNARVON.

April 15–25th, 1868.

THE projected visit to Ireland, referred to in a previous article on St. Patrick's festival, took place in April, 1868. It was a successful and memorable visit in every way. On the 15th of April the Prince and Princess of Wales, who had started from Holyhead at 4 A.M., arrived in Kingstown Harbour at 9.30, and landed amidst salutes from the fleet attending the Royal yacht. On the way to Dublin Castle they were received with enthusiasm by the crowds. The streets and houses were profusely decorated with banners and evergreens. " Welcome to Erin " was the burden of the mottoes. No troops lined the way, but reliance was put on the loyal and hospitable spirit of the people, who kept the track clear for the cortège, and when the escort had passed the crowd closed in behind, like the waters in the wake of a ship which has passed through. At night the city was brilliantly illuminated. Next day the royal party went to Punchestown races in open carriages, and were greeted with enthusiasm as great as on the first entrance to Dublin. On Saturday the Prince was installed, with great ceremony, a Knight of St. Patrick, in St. Patrick's Cathedral.

The Prince was belted with the same sword worn by George IV. In the evening his Excellency the Lord-Lieutenant entertained the Knight, the Royal visitors, and a distinguished company, at dinner in St. Patrick's Hall. In proposing the health of the Prince and the Princess of Wales, the Lord Lieutenant said that "the shouts of acclamation that for four successive days have rung in our ears, will have shown to the illustrious Heir of these Kingdoms, better than any words of mine, the kindly nature of the Irish people, and the attachment that may be awakened in their generous and warm hearts."

His Royal Highness, in returning thanks, said:—

" Your Excellency, your Royal Highnesses, my Lords, Ladies, and Gentlemen,—In the name of the Princess of Wales and myself, I beg to tender you my warmest thanks for the very kind and flattering manner in which this toast has been proposed, and for the cordial way in which it has been received by the company present here this evening. Under any circumstances I should feel it a great honour to have my health proposed by his Excellency the Lord-Lieutenant, but to-night the circumstances under which it has been proposed are peculiar, for I appear here as a Knight of the Illustrious Order of

St. Patrick. I can assure you that I feel very proud to wear this evening for the first time the star and riband of this illustrious Order; and I am very grateful to Her Majesty the Queen for having given it to me. On former occasions I have received the Orders of Great Britain from Her Majesty's own hands; and, although I cannot but regret that on this occasion she has not been able to give this Order to me herself, still it was the Queen's wish that I should receive it on Irish soil, from the hands of her representative, the Lord-Lieutenant.

"This Order was first founded, now more than 80 years ago, by my great-grandfather, King George III., and was instituted by him as a mark of his goodwill and friendship towards this country, and it is my hope that, as his great-grandson, having to-day received it on Irish soil, I may also be instrumental in evincing in this country, in the name of my Sovereign and my mother, her goodwill and friendship towards Ireland. I feel also proud that I have been not only invested with the insignia of this Order, but installed in the magnificent Cathedral of St. Patrick, for the restoration of which we are indebted to the great munificence of a private gentleman of Ireland, whose name is so well known that I need not mention it to you, more particularly as I have the pleasure of seeing him at this table.

"My Lords and Gentlemen, I am very glad to have this opportunity of stating to you, on behalf of the Princess and myself, how deeply gratified we are by the reception which has been accorded to us in this country, not only, as the Lord-Lieutenant has observed, by the higher classes, but by the sons of the soil as well. After the sad times of the past year it might, perhaps, have been thought by some that our reception would not have been all that could have been wished. I myself felt confident that it would, and my hopes have been indeed realised. I beg, therefore, to offer, not only to those present who participated more immediately in our reception, but to the whole Irish people, our thanks for the cordial, hearty, and friendly welcome which we have received. I will not weary you with more words, but thank you once more for the honour you have done us in so heartily drinking our healths."

The Prince, we are told, spoke with an unaffected earnestness which deepened the impression left by his words. The reference to "the sad times of the past year" included the wretched Clerkenwell explosion affair, the perpetrators of which outrage were on their trial in London, at the very time when the people of Dublin were showing their loyal attachment to the throne, and observing the most remarkable order and decorum, even in the most crowded and poverty-stricken districts.

Besides an incessant round of banquets, receptions, concerts, balls, and what are humorously called "entertainments," the Royal visitors devoted much time to inspecting museums, libraries, hospitals, colleges, schools, including some sights not usually attractive to strangers, such as the collections of preparations and curiosities in the College of Surgeons, and the College of Physicians. The antiquities in the Royal Hibernian Academy's rooms were duly inspected; a conversazione at the Royal Dublin Society attended; a flower-show at the Rotunda; The Catholic University in Stephen's Green visited; and above all there were splendid doings at Trinity College, where the Prince (and at the same time, the Duke of Cambridge, and Lord Abercorn) received the investiture of honorary Doctor of Laws. After this the Royal LL.D. went out, unrobed, to unveil the statue of Edmund Burke.

Then there was the Cattle Show, for it happened that the usual spring meeting of the Royal Dublin Society fell at the very time of the Prince's visit. Of course there was also a review in Phœnix Park, and on this occasion the military spectacle was of unusual brilliancy.

On Sunday, the 19th, His Royal Highness attended the service in Christ Church, a cathedral exceeded by few in historic interest.

In addition to the many engagements in Dublin, visits were paid to Lord Powerscourt's beautiful domain, with the romantic and classical scenes of county Wicklow; and to the Duke of Leinster at Carton, and to Maynooth College, fifteen miles off. The President, Dr. Russell, with the officials, formally received the Prince, while the hundreds of students gave him a cheerful welcome in the great quadrangle.

It would occupy too much space to mention all the incidents crowded into the days of the Irish sojourn. They are all recorded in full detail, in the newspapers of the period, and especially in the columns of the *Times*, who sent a special correspondent to chronicle the events, day by day. In a leading article of the *Times*, the writer gives a summary of the proceedings, and makes comments on what might be the result of the Royal visit. Some sentences of this article we quote as showing what was the impression made at the time by the Prince himself :—

"Any reader of our daily correspondence could easily make out a hundred distinct occasions during these ten days on which the Prince, most frequently with the Princess, had to be face to face with some portion of the people, in some ceremony or other, and had to perform a part requiring all the graces and gifts of Royalty. There were presentations and receptions; receiving and answering addresses; processions, walking, riding, and driving, in morning, evening, military, academic, and mediæval attire. The Prince was invested as a Knight, robed as an LL.D., and made a Lord of the Irish Privy Council; he had to breakfast, lunch, dine, and sup with more or less publicity every twenty-four hours. He had to go twice to races with fifty or a hundred thousand people about him; to review a small army and make a tour in the Wicklow mountains, of course everywhere receiving addresses under canopies, and dining in state under galleries full of spectators. He visited and inspected institutions, colleges, universities, academies, libraries, and cattle shows. He had to take a very active part in assemblies of from several hundred to several thousand dancers, and always to select for his partners the most important personages. He had to introduce the statue of Burke to the wind and rain of his country. He had to listen to many speeches sufficiently to know when and what to answer. He had to examine with respectful interest pictures, books, antiquities, relics, manuscripts, specimens, bones, fossils, prize beasts, and works of Irish art. He had never to be unequal to the occasion, however different from the last or however like the last, and whatever his disadvantage as to the novelty or the dullness of the matter and the scene. He was always before persons who were there at home, on their own ground, and amid persons and objects familiar to them, and sometimes in a manner made by them. Be it Cardinal, Chancellor, Rector, Mayor, Commanding Officer, President, Chairman, or local deputation, he had to hold his own, without even seeming to do so— that is, without effort or self assertion. All this he had to do continually for ten days. Now, men of common mould know what an anxious thing it is to have to do this even once, and how utterly they may be upset by the concurrence of two or three such occasions."

All this and more the Prince had to do and to suffer during his visit. The speeches if not long, were numerous and appropriate. Altogether the Irish campaign of 1868 was not an easy one. Let it be remembered with the more honour.

On the 25th of April, the Royal visitors returned to Holyhead, and stopping at Carnarvon, the birthplace of the first Prince of Wales, received a public greeting, and an address. At a banquet subsequently given, the Prince thus responded to the toast given by the High Sheriff of the County:—

" On behalf of the Princess and myself I return our warmest thanks for the kind way in which our health has been proposed, and for the manner in which it has been received. It has afforded the Princess and myself the very greatest pleasure to come to North Wales and visit the ancient castle of Carnarvon.

It is particularly interesting to us to come upon this day, the anniversary of the birthday of the first Prince of Wales. For a long time it had been our intention to pay a visit to Wales, and I regret that that intention has been so long in the fulfilment ; but the cordial reception which we have received to-day will, I am sure, lead us to look forward with great pleasure to another visit on some future day. We deeply regret that our stay should be so short, and that, it being necessary for us to go homewards, we cannot remain longer with you. I thank you once more for the kind way in which you have received the few words I have addressed to you, and for the welcome we have received from the people of Carnarvon."

His Royal Highness concluded by proposing the health of the Lords-Lieutenant, the High Sheriffs, and the Mayors of the towns and counties of North Wales.

SOCIETY OF FRIENDS OF FOREIGNERS IN DISTRESS.

May 5th, 1868.

THERE is no form of charity more obviously suitable and good, than helping distressed strangers in a strange land, and especially foreigners in London. The sixty-second anniversary of the " Society of Friends of Foreigners in Distress " was celebrated on May 5th, 1868, at Willis's Rooms, under the presidency of H.R.H. the Prince of Wales. The guests included many representatives of various nations, the charity itself being cosmopolitan, and helping the distressed of all races and regions.

In proposing the health of " The Queen, the Protectress of the Society," the Prince observed that " Her Majesty had shown a deep interest in the charity, ever since 1837, the year of her accession to the throne, when she became an annual subscriber ; and his lamented father became its protector at his marriage, and continued to subscribe to its funds."

In proposing the health of the Prince and Princess of Wales, Sir Travers Twiss, her Majesty's Advocate-General, said that he was not merely following the high example of his august mother and lamented father, but was moved by his own kind disposition. As it was not generally known, he took the liberty of mentioning, even in his presence, that the Prince, in the course of his Eastern travels, passed through no great city without having visited its institutions in aid of suffering humanity; and it was still fresh in the memory of those who were around him how much his heart was touched at the sight of the shelter afforded by British and American philanthropy to the unfortunate Syrian Christians, who had been driven from their homes at Damascus, and found a temporary asylum among the European residents at Beyrout.

His Royal Highness, in returning thanks, expressed the high pleasure it was to be present in support of the institution, and proposed the health of the " Foreign Sovereigns and Governments— protectors and patrons of the Institution," coupling with the toast the name of his Excellency the Prussian Ambassador; to which Count Bernstorff responded.

In proposing the principal toast of the evening, His Royal Highness said that he was sure it would be received with enthusiasm :—

" The 'Society of Friends of Foreigners in Distress' was the first of the kind established in London, and its object was to afford assistance to deserving and necessitous foreigners in this country, without distinction of nationality, religion, age, or sex. This institution, which had now existed for more than sixty years, was even at the time of its initiation thought to be a work of necessity; how much more so had it become such since the means of communication between country and country had been so vastly increased, and trade, manufactures, and commerce had so largely attracted the people of other nations to our shores !

" The charitable objects of the society were first to grant allowances to deserving foreigners in their old age. Pensioners were elected by the governors, and the Board of Directors paid the pensions annually. The second object was to grant temporary relief in time of sickness. These cases were inquired into with the greatest care, and sums from a few shillings up to £5 or £10 were sometimes given where the cases required it. A third object was to afford temporary assistance to the younger members of families when the heads of the families were by infirmity or ill health unable to support them; but when such relief had been once afforded to any extent a period of eight weeks was required to elapse before any further help was rendered, unless in cases of great emergency. The fourth and last object of the society was to afford means by which foreigners might be able to return to their native country. As many as 243 families had been enabled to return to their native country by the assistance rendered to them by this society. Several of the families so assisted had been induced to quit their native land in that unfortunate expedition to Mexico. They had engaged in what they thought was a good cause, but when that fell to the ground, owing to events that occurred last year, those poor creatures were totally unprovided for, and then it was that the society granted them the means of returning to their native country.

"There were some almshouses at Lower Norwood belonging to the society, in which several families were comfortably lodged and maintained. Since the origin of the society as many as 116,000 cases had received its attention and aid. Last year 3000 persons were assisted, not including the 243 families that were enabled to return to their native home. Similar societies had recently sprung up, but they all differed from the one they were then celebrating in this respect, that they confined their assistance to the natives of certain countries, while this society had for its object the giving relief to foreigners of all nations. He had one more statement to make which had only been mentioned to him a few minutes ago. There was a gentleman present who was well known to them, but did not wish his name to be announced, who had already given £1000 to the society, and who had expressed himself ready to give an additional £100 if he could find nine other gentlemen who would each give a like sum. He hoped the society would be able to find those nine gentlemen to assist them. Having made this brief statement, he begged to propose that the toast be drunk up-standing with three times three."

The call was heartily responded to, and, after some further complimentary and formal toasts, His Royal Highness and the principal guests retired.

———

ST. BARTHOLOMEW'S HOSPITAL.

May 13th, 1868.

As President of the Governors of St. Bartholomew's Hospital, the Prince of Wales has always taken a warm and active interest in the affairs of that great charitable institution. On the 13th of May, 1868, he took the chair at what is called the annual "View" dinner. It is the custom on that day for some of the Governors to make a visitation of the wards and other departments of the Hospital. On this occasion the Royal President visited six of the wards. At the dinner he was supported by Prince Christian, the Bishop of Oxford, and other distinguished guests, as well as the officials of the Hospital. After dinner the Royal President rose and said :—

"My Lords and Gentlemen,—The first toast which I have the honour to submit to you I propose in the form in which it has always been given at this anniversary festival; it is 'The Church and the Queen.' I need hardly remind you that the Queen takes the liveliest interest in the hospitals of the country, and she has to-day evinced that interest by laying the foundation-stone of the sister hospital of St. Thomas. Although the Queen, as I understand, has never visited this hospital, I trust that before long I may induce her to do so, and that I may have the honour of showing her over it."

The Bishop of Oxford responded, and in proposing the health of "The Prince and Princess of Wales, and the rest of the Royal Family," said that the presence of the Royal President that day was not only a tribute to humanity, most graceful in the heir of a hundred kings, but it was also a tribute to the highest of human science, a tribute as much to the noble profession of medicine, to those who ministered to the relief of human sufferings, as to the sufferers themselves.

The Royal President said :—

"My Lords and Gentlemen,—I thank you for the toast that has just been given by the right rev. prelate, and has been so kindly received. In responding to the very kind words in which my health has been proposed, I can assure you it has given me more than ordinary pleasure to be President of this hospital and to take the chair, for the first time, at its anniversary festival. My only regret has been and is, that the many duties devolving upon me do not allow me to come here oftener than I have done; but you may be sure I take the greatest interest in the hospital, and the more the Treasurer tells me of what is going on in the hospital the better I shall be pleased. Whenever I have availed myself of an opportunity of visiting the hospital I have found it in a condition which left nothing to be desired. The Princess of Wales has also taken as great an interest in it as I have done, and as soon as she could move about after her return from abroad she accompanied me on a visit to this hospital. In the name of the Princess of Wales and the other members of the Royal Family I return thanks for the manner in which this toast has been drunk."

In proposing the next toast, "The Army, Navy, Militia, and Volunteers," the Royal President said :—

"I always think that this is a puzzling toast for a chairman to give, although at the same time it is an easy one, because so many have given it, and will continue to give it, that there is, unfortunately, little scope for originality and variety in proposing it. On such an occasion as this, however, and in a hospital, too, it is a most appropriate toast, because medical departments are essential in our army and navy, and medical science is specially invoked by their active services. Alas that it should be so! But, fortunately, in our last campaign, in Abyssinia, there was less call than ever for medical science on our own side, as only one person was wounded in action."

Other customary toasts having been given, the Royal President again rose, and said :—

"The toast I have now the honour to propose you will receive with enthusiasm: it is, 'Prosperity to St. Bartholomew's Hospital, and Health and Ease to the Patients.' It gives me the greatest pleasure to propose this toast. This hospital, the largest and most ancient of the metropolitan hospitals, was founded in 1123 by Rahere, and was then attached to the Priory; and on the suppression of the monasteries, in 1544, it had a charter granted to it by Henry VIII., whose portrait occupies the wall on my right. At that time the hospital had only 100 beds, one physician, and three surgeons; it has now 650 beds, 12 physicians, and 12 surgeons, besides an array of lecturers, dispensers, and other officers. We may regard this as a grand day, and those who have gone through the wards of the hospital will have found everything in good order; but I once took the officers by surprise, and I came here in the winter, practically without giving notice.. I can assure you I found everything on that occasion in the same condition as to-day—nurses and attendants in their places, and surgeons and physicians punctiliously discharging their duties.

"I may here advert to the terrible event which occurred in the winter—the Clerkenwell explosion. That showed how well organized the hospital is, and how admirable its arrangements are adapted to such an emergency. Almost immediately after the explosion as many as 40 patients were safely housed in the hospital, while many had their wounds dressed and were sent away. I came here, and found that the sufferers were receiving every possible attention. Much is, no doubt, due to the unremitting care and supervision of the Treasurer; and if one of the surgeons — Mr. Holden — were not present, I would express my appreciation of his valuable services in terms which, I am sure, many in this room would be ready to endorse. Every one is satisfied of the thorough efficiency of the hospital; but there is still wanting a convalescent hospital. True, there is the Samaritan Fund, out of which you aid patients when they are dismissed; but still, when they are nearly well, you wish to send them into the country to recruit their health, so that they may return to their homes thoroughly convalescent. When this question is mooted I shall take the greatest interest, and do all I can to promote the establishment of the additional hospital. I have the greatest pleasure in coupling with this toast the name of the Treasurer, and no one will more heartily drink his health than I shall. He has been called upon to act as Treasurer to Christ's Hospital too, and, although he will conscientiously serve it, he will not forget his first love—St. Bartholomew's."

Mr. Foster White, the Treasurer, in responding, said that such had been the demand upon the resources of the hospital during the past year that its income had been exceeded by £4,000, which was owing, however, chiefly to the high price of provisions. At the time of the Clerkenwell explosion he was prepared, if it had been necessary, to make a ward of the dining-room, feeling sure the Governors would have supported him. The Governors of this hospital and the Merchant Taylors' Company were in communication, with the object of erecting conjointly a convalescent hospital, at an expenditure of £45,000 each corporation. In conclusion, the Treasurer denounced with some warmth the taxation of charities.

The Royal President proposed "The Medical Staff," coupling the toast with the names of Dr. Frederic Farre and Mr. Paget. To the latter he tendered his heartfelt recognition of the services he had rendered during the severe illness of the Princess of Wales.

Dr. Farre and Mr. Paget having responded, the "Corporation of London" was proposed from the Chair, and responded to by Mr. Alderman Finnis, and this terminated the proceedings.

This 13th of May was a day of special interest in connection with Metropolitan Hospitals, the Queen having in the morning, with great state ceremony, laid the foundation stone of the new St. Thomas's Hospital, when the Prince and Princess of Wales were also present.

The informal visit paid to St. Bartholomew's Hospital, referred to by the Prince in his speech, was on the 17th of February of that year, when he was accompanied by the Princess of Wales. The Princess had long wished to see the Hospital, and attention was then recalled to it by the announcement of the reception there of the sufferers from the Fenian outrage at Clerkenwell. They were conducted over the whole establishment by the Treasurer and principal surgeons. The Royal visitors had the opportunity of seeing all the Clerkenwell sufferers and of expressing their sympathy with them. Before leaving, they inspected the beautiful little church of St. Bartholomew the Less, which stands within the walls of the Hospital, and is, in fact, the Hospital chapel. The informal visit of their Royal Highnesses, which afforded great gratification to the authorities of the institution, lasted about an hour and a half.

The visits of the Prince to St. Bartholomew's have been frequent in subsequent years, one interesting occasion being on the presentation of a testimonial to Sir James Paget in 1871, on retiring from the post he had long held.

LAYING FOUNDATION STONE OF NEW BUILDINGS, GLASGOW UNIVERSITY.

October 8th, 1868.

WHATEVER else Scotland may have to boast of, she may point with pride to her parish schools and her universities. These have contributed largely to raise her among the nations, and laid the foundation of much of the enterprise, energy, and success in life, which have long characterized the Scots at home and abroad, and given them an honourable place in letters, science, and commerce.

Next to St. Andrews, and later only by a few years, Glasgow is the oldest of the Scottish Universities. It owes its origin to the Church in pre-Reformation times, being founded A.D. 1450, and was at first connected with the Cathedral. The buildings did not assume their collegiate form till after the Reformation. The front and gateway facing the High Street were not erected till 1660. Many still remember the dingy-looking old building, with its quaint barred windows, and projecting balconies over the gateway, surmounted by the Royal Scottish Arms, in the style and period of the last of the Stuarts. The visitor passed through the four open courts, on to the handsome modern building, the Hunterian Museum, containing the valuable collection of Dr. William Hunter, bequeathed by him in grateful remembrance of his connection with this University.

The venerable old College, having served its purpose through successive generations, for more than three centuries, the Senate of the University and the citizens of Glasgow determined to provide new buildings, upon a site and on a scale more suited to the requirements of the time. Subscriptions, in response to the appeal of the Senate, were obtained, to the amount of over £160,000 ; and this being supplemented by the money for the sale of the old building and the old site, with a parliamentary vote of £120,000, gave a total of £440,000.

The site chosen for the new buildings was the rising ground called Gilmore Hill, on the west of Kelvin Grove. The plans were prepared by Gilbert Scott, and all the world knows how the magnificent structure in due time rose, to be the pride and ornament of the western capital of Scotland—in wealth and population the second city in the United Kingdom.

It was an imposing spectacle when the Prince of Wales, accompanied by the Princess of Wales, laid the foundation stone of the new building, on the 8th of October, 1868. A vast concourse of people witnessed the ceremony. An address was presented by the Lord Provost and Corporation, the Prince having previously received the freedom of the city.

Another address was then presented by the Principal and Senate of the University, in replying to which the Prince said:—

" It affords me the highest satisfaction to become a member and graduate of your University, and at the same time to visit a city the close connection of which with you has been so beneficial to both, as well as to the interests of learning and knowledge. The presence of so many of all classes of the citizens of Glasgow around me, and their liberal subscriptions for the prosecution of the work, the value they attach to its completion, and their sense of the advantages they and the people of Scotland derive from our institutions, the interest which my lamented father took in the advancement of every branch of science and education, would stimulate me to follow his example, and promote by every means in my power the success of your University and the objects for which it has been founded. We may confidently expect that the eminent men educated here in times past are only the precursors of a long train equally to be distinguished by every scientific acquirement. The Princess of Wales rejoices in the opportunity afforded her of taking part in this day's ceremony and cordially thanks you for your kind wishes."

FOREIGN TOUR, 1868–1869.

November 17th, 1868—May 13th, 1869.

THERE is a long break in the record of proceedings or speeches on account of the Foreign Tour on which the Prince started in November 1868, returning in May 1869. Of this time of travel it is not necessary to say much here, as the chief events and incidents are before the public in various works. Full reports appeared in the *Times,* and other journals, during the movements of the Royal party on the Continent, in Egypt, and Palestine. Reference is made to this interesting and memorable tour in several of the speeches made by the Prince after his return ; and at a later time, as when he spoke at the meeting about the neglect of the Crimean graves, and at that for the memorial to Dean Stanley.

Only one incident of the tour, and the one of greatest historical interest, may be mentioned, the visit to the Cave of Machpelah and the Sepulchres of the Patriarchs. In this event, not only the personal interest, but the national importance of the Prince's Eastern Tour, may be said to culminate. Never before had Christian pilgrims, since the days of the Mohammedan conquest, or of the Crusades, been allowed to see so much of the holy tombs of the Patriarchs. The sanctity with which the Mussulmans have invested the place is a living witness of the unbroken veneration with which men of Jewish, Christian, and Mohammedan creeds have honoured the memory of Abraham, the father of all the faithful. Hebron is known among the native population by no other name than El-Khalil, the Friend of God.

It was the high position of the Prince of Wales, as son of Queen Victoria, that obtained for him the rare privilege of access to this sacred spot. Nor was it obtained for him without some difficulty. Mr. Finn, the English Consul at Jerusalem, prepared the way by requesting an order from the Porte; and the reply of the Grand Vizier left the matter very much to the discretion of the Governor, the Pasha of Jerusalem. He gave his consent on the condition that only a small number should accompany the Prince; and precautions were taken that the experiment should be made with as little risk as possible. The approach to Hebron was lined with troops, and guards were posted on the house-tops, in case of any outbreak of fanatical opposition to entering the holy places. A guard attended the Prince up to the entrance of the sacred enclosure. Even then two of the Arab Sheiks were inclined to give annoyance, but these the Governor of Hebron ordered out, or rather escorted them out himself, and the remainder were very courteous and complimentary to the Prince, saying that they were glad to have the opportunity of showing any civility in their power to one of the Princes of England, to whom their Government and people were so much indebted for kind offices.

Dr. Rosen, well known to travellers in Palestine for his knowledge of sacred geography, was fortunately one of the party admitted, and he was able to make a ground plan of the platform. This, with the observations recorded by another of the Prince's party, has given clearer knowledge of this world-renowned spot. The existence and exact situation of the cave, the views of the enclosure within and without, the relation of the different tombs to each other, and the general conformity of the traditions of the mosque to the accounts of the Bible, and of the early travellers, were now, for the first time, clearly ascertained.

The Prince's visit was on the 7th of April, 1869. The story of the visit spread throughout the lands of Islam; and therefore this one incident of the Prince's Eastern Tour is here referred to as showing its national importance, and that the prestige of England is still great in these lands. But we must resume the record of speeches in England, where it so happens that the first of consequence was made at a meeting of the Royal Geographical Society.

THE ROYAL GEOGRAPHICAL SOCIETY.

May 24th, 1869.

OF all the "learned societies" in London, the Royal Geographical is the most popular. Perhaps it is because there is less "book learning" required for its membership, than that love of travel, enterprise, and adventure, which characterizes all true Englishmen. Professor Owen once said that in the new Hall of the Geographical Society a statue of 'Robinson Crusoe' should be the central figure. It was a wise and suggestive, though humorous proposal, for few geographers have not received early impressions from Defoe's immortal book. The whole globe is embraced in the objects of the Society, whether in the Old World or the New, whether the explorations are in the frozen regions of the Pole, or in the deserts and forests of tropical Africa.

The anniversary meeting of the Society was held on the 24th of May, 1869, in the Royal Institution, under the Presidency of Sir Roderick Murchison, to whose energy and enthusiasm geographical discoveries, and the prosperity of the Society, have been so largely due.

When the health of the Prince of Wales, as their Royal vice-patron was given, the President referred to the appointment of Sir Samuel Baker, the Society's medallist of the year, to the government of Equatorial Africa. The good-will and patronage of the Viceroy in this instance was essentially obtained through the personal influence of the Prince of Wales. Among the guests at their table was the young Egyptian Prince Hassan.

His Royal Highness the Prince of Wales said:—

"Sir Roderick Murchison, your Highness, my Lords, and Gentlemen,—Under any ordinary circumstances it would have given me great pleasure to be present at this interesting meeting—the anniversary dinner of the Royal Geographical Society; but I feel doubly proud to be here this evening as a vice-patron of so useful and celebrated an institution. Sir Roderick Murchison has had the kindness to allude to me as a traveller; I can only say that I feel ashamed almost to stand here with the name of a traveller, when I see around me so many distinguished persons who have travelled, I may almost say from one end of the world to the other. But I cannot be too grateful that my lamented father at an early period gave me an opportunity of travelling and seeing foreign countries; and the same permission being granted to my brother, I feel certain that we have both derived great benefit from seeing those interesting countries which it has been our happiness to visit. No doubt much knowledge and learning may be obtained by reading books of foreign travel, but I feel convinced that all those gentlemen who are members of this society will coincide with me when I say that you cannot form so full or favourable an idea of the countries described by reading of them in books as you can by visiting them yourselves.

" I am greatly flattered and deeply sensible of the kind manner in which Sir Roderick Murchison has mentioned me in connexion with the name of one whose presence we must all very much miss this evening—I mean my late travelling companion, Sir Samuel Baker. I cannot but regret that he was forced to leave this country rather suddenly in order to make arrangements for his great and important undertaking, and could not, indeed, take farewell of all his friends. Sir Roderick has stated that I was in some way instrumental in helping Sir Samuel Baker to carry out the enterprise in which he is engaged. His Highness the Viceroy of Egypt, I know, has deeply at heart the great importance of that noble enterprise—to put down slavery on the White Nile, and I need hardly tell you that anything I could do in the matter was done with the utmost pleasure and satisfaction. Such an enterprise must meet the approval not only of every Englishman, but of every philanthropist. There are great difficulties connected with it. These difficulties must be great to any one, and they must still be more trying to a European; but I know Sir Samuel Baker to be a man of energy and perseverance, and whatever the difficulties he may have to encounter he is certain, if it lies in his power, to attain the end of his mission."

We may here say that when Sir Samuel Baker gave a detailed account of his experiences, in the Hall of the London University, the Prince moved the vote of thanks, in a speech equally eulogistic.

The Prince again rose after the toast of " The Army and Navy, and Auxiliary Forces," had been given. He apologized for responding for the Army, in presence of so many distinguished officers; but he spoke by command of the President, and a soldier's first duty is obedience.

Admiral Sir George Back, the veteran Arctic explorer, and a leading officer in the Society, returned thanks for " The Navy."

The President next proposed the health of Professor Norden-skiold, of Stockholm, and of Mrs. Mary Somerville. The former received " the Founder's " Medal, for his Arctic discoveries; and to Mrs. Somerville, then in her eighty-ninth year, had been awarded the Patron or Victoria Medal, for her scientific and astronomical researches, and her works on physical geography.

Sir Roderick then proposed the health of Professor Owen, and the Duke of Sutherland, and Dr. Russell, who had been companions of the Prince in his Egyptian journey. Dr. Russell had, through the *Times*, been the reporter and historian of the expedition. The speech of Professor Owen was in happiest vein. Indeed, the whole of the speeches of the meeting, including those of Sir Francis Grant, the Duke of Sutherland, Dr. Russell, and Sir Henry Rawlinson, who proposed the health of the President, made this a memorable anniversary of the Society.

EARLSWOOD ASYLUM.

June 28th, 1869.

ALL travellers on the London, Brighton and South Coast Railway, have admired the palatial and splendidly situated building near Red Hill, Surrey, known as the Earlswood Asylum. It is an institution for the care and education of the idiot and imbecile. Everything that can be done by kindness and skill to ameliorate the lot of these classes, is here in exercise. By far the larger number show some capability of improvement, and not a few have learned some trade or industry, sufficient for their own support. There are now nearly 600 inmates, from all parts of the kingdom. At each half yearly election, there are about 150 applicants of whom the Board usually can elect 30 to 35. The receipts of last year were nearly £25,000, and the charity has £20,000 invested funds.

The first stone of the Asylum was laid by the Prince Consort in 1853, and the building was opened by him in 1855. To lay the first stone of additional buildings, on part of the 80 acres belonging to the Asylum, the presence of the Prince of Wales was asked, and was very cordially given. Accompanied by the Princess of Wales, he went to Earlswood for this purpose on the 28th of June, 1869. The Mayor and the magistrates of Reigate came to the Earlswood railway station with an address of welcome, to which the Prince made reply.

Sir Charles Reed, son of the Rev. Dr. Andrew Reed, founder of the Institution (as he was of other important charities), conducted the Royal visitors to the gate of the Asylum, to which they had driven from the station. From the Board Room a procession was formed, to the place of laying the stone. Here another address was read, in reply to which the Prince said :—

" My Lords and Gentlemen,—I thank you for the kind expressions contained in your address. I cannot but rejoice that my presence should be considered an encouragement, and conducive to the prosperity of an institution that lays claim to our warmest support. Apart from all other considerations, the fact of my lamented father having taken so active a part in the early formation of the society would, in itself, be sufficient to enlist my sympathy and interest in its welfare. The necessity for affording more extended accommodation, in consequence of the increased number of applicants, is the best proof of the success which has followed your first efforts. We must all appreciate the comprehensive principle which regulates, without regard to social or religious distinction, the admission of all classes of our fellow-creatures suffering under an affliction which reduces them to one common level. Finally, I have to assure you, gentlemen, how sincerely I feel your expressions of devotion and attachment towards the Queen, the Princess of Wales, and the Royal family. I am persuaded they, equally with myself, will watch with increasing interest the success of an institution this day enlarged under such hopeful circumstances."

The Treasurer then handed to the Prince a silver trowel, and Sir Charles Reed, M.P., presented the mallet, which had been used by the Prince Consort on laying the first stone of the " Infant Orphan Asylum" at Wanstead, and which His Royal Highness had afterwards given to Dr. Andrew Reed. A good supply of mortar having been brought to the Prince of Wales in a mahogany hod, His Royal Highness spread a sufficient quantity to make a setting for the stone. Then, amid cheering, the stone was slowly lowered, and the Prince tapped it with the mallet, tested it by rule and plumb, and amid a flourish of trumpets, followed by the National Anthem, pronounced it to be well and truly fixed. The Archbishop of Canterbury then offered an appropriate prayer, which was followed by a hymn, of which there was an instrumental performance by the band of the Grenadier Guards, while the words were sung by the entire company.

The Prince and Princess then took their seats, and, to the March of King Christian IX., of Denmark, there was an interesting and, for the charity, a most gratifying procession. It was one of ladies, who to the number of 380 in single file ascended the dais where the Prince sat, and deposited in all 400 purses. The Prince had previously, immediately after fixing the stone, handed to the Treasurer, a check for a hundred guineas. A *déjeuner* followed, and planting of memorial trees and other festivities.

THE ALEXANDRA DOCK AT LYNN.

July 7th, 1869.

SIX centuries ago Lynn was, next to London, the chief port on the east coast. It is nearer than any other port to Holland and North Germany. In course of time the foreign trade of the place had fallen into decay, and the town itself was outstripped in business by Hull, Grimsby, Yarmouth, and other eastern seaports. A time of revival having come, it was considered that the prosperity of the ancient borough would be secured by the formation of docks and accommodation for foreign trade, as the manufacturing districts of the Midland Counties might be brought into connection with Lynn as the shortest route to Amsterdam, Rotterdam, the Texel, and Hamburg. In hope of benefiting the trade and industry of the town, the Lynn Dock Company was formed, and obtained from Mr. Brunlees, C.E., the plans for a great dock, which in due time was completed, and was inaugurated by the Prince and Princess of Wales, on the 7th of July, 1869.

Arriving from London, by special train of the Great Eastern Railway, the Royal visitors were received, with great ceremony, in the Council Room of the Town Hall of Lynn. An address was presented by the Recorder, in which gratification was expressed at their Royal Highnesses having selected an abode in the neighbourhood of the borough, and in showing their interest in its welfare by having graciously undertaken to inaugurate their new dock.

His Royal Highness made the following reply:—

"Mr. Mayor and Gentlemen,—I thank you for this address, for the loyalty and attachment you express towards the Queen, and for the kind welcome you offer the Princess and myself. It is peculiarly gratifying to us to visit you on an occasion like the present. The revolutions of time and science would have had the same effects upon King's Lynn as upon other commercial ports but for the energies of the inhabitants. Without them its ancient name would have become interesting only for its antiquity. But in the century in which we live it is permitted neither to town nor to community to rest quiet or to stand still. The energies I have referred to, I have learned to appreciate from living in your neighbourhood, and, indeed, I have been called on to participate in them as regards the navigation of your waters. I fervently pray that the Dock we are about to open this day, may, under the fostering auspices of a beneficent Providence, open out new sources of wealth and commerce, shedding the blessings which are derived from them on your town, and contributing to the prosperity of our beloved country."

The Royal party then visited the Grammar School, where the Prince received and responded to an address from the Masters and Scholars, and presented to the successful competitor the gold medal, given annually, through the munificence of the Prince, as a prize for classical and modern languages in alternate years. The Prince presented the prize, saying :—

"I have great pleasure in presenting you with this medal. On a former occasion I presented it at Sandringham, but it is more pleasure to you to receive it among your schoolfellows. I hope this medal will contribute to your success in future life, and that it may be a stimulus to you for further exertion."

On arriving at the Dock, the circumference of which was densely crowded, the Royal visitors were greeted with cheering, bell-ringing, and every demonstration of welcome. When it came to the ceremony of declaring the dock open, an agreeable surprise was added by the terms in which the announcement was made :—

I DECLARE THIS DOCK NOW OPEN, AND THAT HENCEFORTH IT IS TO BE CALLED THE ALEXANDRA DOCK.

The announcement was received with vociferous acclamation. The Prince's intention had been signified to the Chairman of the Dock Company only a few minutes before, and was quite unknown to the mass of the spectators, who expressed their delight by repeated salvos of cheering.

At a banquet afterwards given, when the toast of the Royal visitors was given, by Mr. Jarvis the President, the Prince said that he regarded King's Lynn as his country town, and should always feel the deepest interest in its welfare.

———

VISIT TO MANCHESTER.

July, 1869.

THE annual show of the Royal Agricultural Society was held in 1869 at Manchester, which the Prince of Wales visited on the 29th of July, accompanied by the Princess of Wales.

There are some who remember the first visit of the Queen and Prince Consort to Manchester in 1851. The Royal party then proceeded along the canal to Worsley from Patricroft, where the wonderful engineering works of James Nasmyth were inspected. In 1869, the Prince and Princess of Wales were conducted along the same canal, but in reverse direction, the barge going from Worsley, through Patricroft, to Old Trafford. The Prince and Princess, with their host and hostess, the Earl and Countess of Ellesmere, drove from the Hall to the stage where the royal barge was waiting. A large flotilla of boats followed as a guard of honour, including some of the Manchester Rowing Clubs. It was a strange and picturesque canal scene, the barges being towed by horses ridden by postillions, and the towing path all along the route, for five or six miles, being kept clear by mounted patrols in livery. It was a great gala day in those densely peopled regions.

In passing through Salford an address was presented by the Mayor, Aldermen, and burgesses of that borough, in the Reading Room of the Royal Museum. The address expressed the great pleasure experienced by this, the second visit of the Prince to their town, enhanced by the presence there, for the first time, of the Princess of Wales: " We cherish a lively and affectionate remembrance of the visit of Her Most Gracious Majesty the Queen to Peel-park in the year 1851, when she witnessed the assemblage of 80,000 Sunday-school scholars, and listened, not unmoved, while they sang the National Anthem. This event was commemorated by the erection of a marble statue to Her Majesty in the park, which was publicly inaugurated by the late and much revered Prince Consort, who on that occasion inspected and manifested a deep interest in the free museum and library in the park. We deeply deplored the loss of the late Prince Consort, and erected a marble statue to his memory, in close proximity to that of the Queen, and near the spot where he stood when inaugurating the statue of Her Majesty."

The Prince made the following reply :—

" Mr. Mayor and Gentlemen,—The Princess of Wales and myself thank you very cordially for your address, and for the sentiments you are good enough to express towards us. It is very gratifying to us to have the opportunity of paying you a visit, and to observe the evidences of the growing wealth and population which have raised Salford to the position she now occupies in the Empire. It will be highly satisfactory to the Queen to learn how deeply engraven on your hearts is the recollection of the visit she paid you in 1851, and how cherished and beloved is the memory of my lamented father. On my own part, I can but acknowledge the kindness of the terms in which you have alluded to my past years. For those which are to come I can only say that it will be the one effort of my life to merit the good opinion of the people I am so proud to call my fellow-countrymen."

In driving through the park the Royal visitors had been conducted past the white marble statues of the Queen and the Prince Consort, and those of Richard Cobden and Joseph Brotherton. Leaving the park, the streets and ways being everywhere densely thronged, they reached the Manchester Town Hall, where another address was delivered, expressing joyous welcome from the loyal citizens, and especially the feelings of satisfaction at the presence of the Prince, as President of the Royal Agricultural Society, ": believing the same to be an evidence of the deep interest manifested by your Royal Highness in the success of all movements which have for their object the advancement of art and science and the progress and welfare of the people of this great empire. It has been the special privilege of your Royal Highness to an unusual extent to visit and personally to become acquainted with other Courts and countries, and with distant portions of Her Majesty's dominions, and we rejoice to believe that the valuable experience thereby acquired gives to all classes of Her Majesty's subjects an assurance that your Royal Highness will ever be foremost in all efforts to extend true liberty and civilization, and to develope those free institutions which are the pride and glory of our country."

To which address the Prince replied:—

"Mr. Mayor and Gentlemen,—I thank you for the kind expressions of loyalty and devotion towards the Queen, the Princess of Wales, and myself contained in your address. I have gladly availed myself of the opportunity afforded me, in the fulfilment of my duties as President of the Royal Agricultural Society, to visit a city second to none in the Empire in commercial importance, to become better acquainted with its history, its locality, and the sources of its prosperity. The wise provision of my lamented father and of the Queen, my dear mother, has secured for me at an early age the advantages of visiting the centres of the world, the most remarkable and the most deserving of study for their interest and for their development of the elements of wealth. In admiring, and, I trust, appreciating, the successful result that has distinguished foreign exertions, I have also learnt to look with increased admiration on those wonderful works of human ingenuity, perseverance, and industry, the products of the heads and hands of my own countrymen, and especially of those who now surround me. May we all be grateful, gentlemen, to a superintending Providence, which has blessed the efforts of our commercial enterprise and the free institutions of our country,—themselves a pledge of our future prosperity."

The Prince presided at a general meeting of the Council of the Society, and opened the proceedings by a brief speech which was loudly applauded. He also received in his own marquee a numerous deputation from the Agricultural Society of France. At the close of the meeting the Royal visitors drove to a station on the Manchester South Junction line, where a train was waiting to take them to Brough, near Hull, viâ Normanton ; the Prince having engaged to be at Hull in the afternoon in order to inaugurate the new Western Dock at that town.

The principal object of the Prince's visit was to see the Royal Agricultural Show, the members mustering in great force for the occasion from all parts of England. At the midday luncheon the Chairman, the Earl of Sefton, gave the toast of " The Queen," who was deeply interested in the agricultural affairs of the Kingdom, and set the practical example of being an exhibitor at the present Show. The Chairman next proposed " The Health of their Royal Highnesses the Prince and Princess of Wales." He said the present toast should be the last. He had to ask them to drink to the health of the President of the Royal Agricultural Society of England, His Royal Highness the Prince of Wales, coupled with the toast of Her Royal Highness the Princess of Wales. He had looked forward to this meeting for a long time, and it was with the greatest pride they learnt that it was to be held under the presidency of His Royal Highness. The reception their Royal Highnesses met with the day previous and that day sufficiently testified to the loyalty and attachment of the people of this country to the Crown. It was difficult to allude to the good qualities of His Royal Highness, but he was ever foremost in the furtherance of works of charity and usefulness. They also experienced the warmest attachment and the truest loyalty towards the Princess.

His Royal Highness the Prince of Wales, in replying, said :—

" I thank you from the bottom of my heart for the kind way in which you have received this toast. My health has been proposed twofold—first for myself, and also in my position as President of the Royal Agricultural Society of England. I can assure you it was great honour that was conferred upon me when I was asked to assume this presidency, and my only regret is that this office has been a mere nominal one, and that I have not been able to be of so much use as I should have liked. At the same time I feel a pride in being President of a Society which has existed for so long, and which is one of the greatest agricultural societies anywhere, always helping forward improvements in agriculture. It was a great satisfaction to this Society to hold one of its annual meetings at Manchester, one of the greatest manufacturing towns of England. It is my duty as President of the Society to return, in the name of the Society, our most cordial and our warmest thanks for the extensive and liberal way in which the local committee have made their arrangements. It is to them we owe this magnificent entertainment in this fine tent, and also the excellent arrangements which we see before us. Lord Sefton told us not to make many speeches or long ones. I will, therefore, not make any further remarks, but, before sitting down, allow me to thank you in the name of the Princess for the kind way in which you have received her. I can assure you it has given her great pleasure to be present at this second visit to the Royal Agricultural Society, and this her first visit to Manchester. We both feel deeply grateful for the kind and hearty welcome which we have received, not only from Manchester, but from the inhabitants of Lancashire."

THE PEABODY MEMORIAL. UNVEILING OF THE STATUE IN THE CITY OF LONDON.

July 23rd, 1869.

THE best memorials of George Peabody, American citizen and philanthropist, are the piles of buildings which stand as monuments of his generous liberality, and of his desire to advance the physical and moral welfare of the poor of London. He received from the Queen of England, and from many public and official bodies, warm recognition of his beneficence. But it was also fitting and right that in some public place a Statue should be erected, to perpetuate his name and his likeness, as well as to commemorate his good deeds. The citizens of London, headed by all the leading men of the Metropolis, subscribed for the Statue, which now adorns the site on the east of the Royal Exchange. The Prince of Wales, having consented to perform the ceremony of unveiling the Statue, was received at the Mansion House by the Lord Mayor, where a distinguished company had assembled. In response to the toast of his health, the Prince said :—

"I thank you for the compliment you have paid me in drinking my health. I assure you it is always a pleasure to me to be present here at the Mansion-house. It is not, indeed, the first time I have received the hospitality of the Lord Mayor and of the City of London. We are assembled to take part in a great ceremony, and I accepted with much pleasure the invitation and the privilege of unveiling the statue of Mr. George Peabody. After the appropriate remarks the Lord Mayor has made concerning him I have little to say except to indorse what has been so well expressed by his Lordship. He is a man whose name will go down to posterity as a great philanthropist, and you, my Lord Mayor, and the citizens of London in particular, can never be sufficiently grateful to him for what he has done."

After the luncheon His Royal Highness was escorted to the site of the memorial. Here Sir Benjamin Phillips, Chairman of the Committee, addressed the Prince, concluding with these words :— " Let us hope that this statue, erected by the sons of free England to the honour of one of Columbia's truest and noblest citizens, may be symbolical of the peace and goodwill that exist between the two countries, and that a people springing from the same stock, speaking the same language, and inspired and animated by the same love of freedom and progress may live in uninterrupted friendship and happiness. Your Royal Highness may remember the language so beautifully expressed by George Peabody, in the letter that accompanied his last noble gift, when, speaking of America he said, ' I will pray that Almighty God will give to it a future as happy and noble in the intelligence and virtue of its citizens as it will be glorious in unexampled power and prosperity.' Your Royal Highness, these are the sentiments uttered by a man of ripe age, and alike applicable to the land of his birth and to the country of his adoption. May they inspire us, may they animate us, and may they find an echo throughout the length and breadth of our own free and happy homes."

His Royal Highness the Prince of Wales than presented himself to speak, and was hailed with enthusiastic cheers. He said :—

"Sir Benjamin Phillips, my Lord Mayor, Ladies, and Gentlemen,—I feel sure that all those who have heard the words which have just been uttered cannot but be gratified with what has been said. Allow me to say to you that among the many duties which I have to perform, and which I have the privilege of performing, none could have given me greater pleasure than to assist and take part in the unveiling of this statue on this occasion. The name of George Peabody is so well known to all of you that really I feel some difficulty in saying anything new of that remarkable man; but, at the same time, it affords me the deepest gratification to join in paying a mark of tribute and respect to the name of that great American citizen and philanthropist—I may say, that citizen of the world. England can never adequately pay the debt of gratitude which she owes to him—London especially, where his wonderful charity has been so liberally distributed. For a man not born in this country to give a sum, I believe, more than a quarter of a million of pounds sterling for purposes of benevolence is a fact unexampled. His name will go down to posterity as one who, as Sir Benjamin Phillips so justly remarked, has tried to ameliorate the condition of his poorer fellow-citizens, and especially to benefit their moral and social character. I have not yet had the opportunity of seeing the statue which is about to be unveiled, but having had the privilege of knowing the sculptor, Mr. Story, for a space of now about ten years, I feel sure it will be one worthy of his reputation, and worthy also of the man to whom it is dedicated. Before concluding the few imperfect remarks which I have ventured to address to you, let me thank Mr. Motley, the American Minister, for his presence on this occasion, and assure him what pleasure it gives me to take part in this great and I might almost say, national ceremonial of paying a tribute to the name of his great and distinguished countryman. Be assured that the feelings which I personally entertain towards America are the same as they ever were. I can never forget the reception which I had there nine years ago, and my earnest wish and hope is that England and America may go hand in hand in peace and prosperity."

At the conclusion of His Royal Highness's address the Statue was uncovered, and at a signal from the Lord Mayor a loud and prolonged cheer was raised on its being exposed to view.

His Excellency, the American Minister, then addressed the vast audience. He said, towards the close of his speech, "It is a delightful thought that the tens of thousands who daily throng this crowded mart will see him almost as accurately as if in the flesh, and that generations after generations—that long, yet unborn, but I fear, never ending procession of London's poor—will be almost as familiar in the future with the form and features of their great benefactor as are those of us who have enjoyed his acquaintance and friendship in life."

Mr. Story, the sculptor, having been called on, said he had no speech to make. He added, significantly pointing to the Statue, "That is my speech,"—a remark which occasioned much merriment and cheering.

The ceremony was then brought to a close, and the Prince took his leave. His Royal Highness, as he did so, was repeatedly cheered.

THE SCOTTISH HOSPITAL.

November 30th, 1869.

THE Scottish Corporation is commonly called the Scottish Hospital, but this is rather misleading as to the uses of the charity. Its objects are to assist, by pensions, poor aged natives of Scotland living in London, to afford temporary relief to Scotchmen in distress, or to aid them to return to their own country; and also to educate poor Scottish children. The last-named object is also carried out by a kindred institution, the Royal Caledonian Asylum, which receives some children of indigent Scotchmen in London, although its main purpose is the maintenance and education of children of soldiers, sailors, and marines, natives of Caledonia. The Scottish Hospital possesses funded property to the amount of £40,000, and the annual receipts are about £5000. In trust to the Scottish Hospital there is also attached the "Kinloch Bequest," for granting pensions to Scottish soldiers and sailors, resident in the United Kingdom, who have been wounded or have lost their sight in the service of the country, and whose incomes do not exceed £20 from other sources.

The anniversary festival of the Scottish Corporation is always held on the 30th of November, St. Andrew's day. In 1869 His Royal Highness the Prince of Wales presided at the dinner. The guests at this festival are mostly Scottish, and a large muster of Highland Chiefs and Lowland Lairds, as well as prosperous Scotchmen of London, supported the Royal chairman upon this occasion. Prince Christian and other distinguished visitors were also present. Many of the stewards wore the garb of old Gaul, and the tartans, scarves, flags, and decorations made the Hall of the Freemasons' Tavern assume a national appearance. The "bagpipes" were also in honourable use, the Prince being conducted to the chair to the tune of the Highland laddie, played by the Queen's piper, the Prince's first piper, and the piper of the Royal Caledonian Asylum. The Prince had previously been received by a guard of honour of the London Artillery, whose band played the National Anthem, while the band of the London Scottish Volunteers performed a selection of Scotch music during the dinner.

G

The three pipers also, at intervals, paraded the hall, and regaled the guests with their stirring strains.

The health of the Queen was drunk with enthusiasm, specially as the patroness of the Scottish Hospital. To the toast of "the Princess of Wales and the rest of the Royal Family," proposed by the Duke of Roxburghe, the Prince responded, and then gave: "The Army, Navy, Militia, and Volunteers," referring in his speech to the Kinloch Bequest, which provides pensions for about 400 disabled soldiers and sailors. A Scotch vocalist, Mr. Maclagan, sang "Scots wha hae wi' Wallace bled." Then the Prince rose to give the toast of "Prosperity to the Scottish Hospital" :—

"Your Royal Highness, my Lords, and Gentlemen,—I have now to give you the toast of the evening: 'Prosperity to the Scottish Hospital.' I feel assured that it is a toast which the numerous assembly I see before me will drink in bumpers. As you know, the Queen is patroness of this hospital; she has been so for thirty-seven years, and she has contributed to its funds between £3000 and £4000. At twenty different anniversaries the late King William, as Duke of Clarence, presided. The Duke of Kent, the Duke of Sussex, and the Duke of Cambridge also presided at various anniversaries, and contributed largely to the funds of the hospital.

"The hospital, as no doubt most of you know, was originally founded in the reign of James I. Its first charter was given to it by Charles II., in 1665, and a second charter of incorporation was granted by the same Monarch, in 1676, containing more extended privileges. It became necessary, however, to enable the corporation to extend its relief, to obtain a new charter, which was granted by King George I., in 1715.

"By the paper which has been placed in my hands I observe the pensions which are contributed by this ancient corporation are very numerous. I see that a sum is set apart for the support of five persons exceeding 65 years of age who have occupied a respectable social position, and who have a permanent income of not less than £15, but not more than £30 per annum; for 20 poor and infirm persons exceeding 72 years of age, to whom a pension of £15 each per annum is allowed; for 110 above 68, to whom a pension of £12 each is allowed. Pensions of £6 are granted to 50 persons selected from the casual list. Monthly casual relief to upwards of 200 is awarded by the committee, and free passages to Scotland are given to such as require them.

"The charity of the Scottish Hospital is applicable to the poor natives of Scotland and their children resident in the Metropolis and its immediate neighbourhood, who, not being in receipt of parochial relief in this country, would in age and poverty, in sickness or distress, or when in want of employment, be exposed to the utmost wretchedness, or to discreditable beggary, but for the fostering relief afforded them by this institution. Those natives of Scotland resident in London who may desire to spend the remainder of their days in Scotland have free passages granted to them by the corporation. From the accumulation of a subscription which was raised in India thirty years ago the corporation is also enabled to allot £120 a year to the ministers and Kirk Sessions of the several congregations of the Scottish churches in London and Westminster, for the purpose of affording education to the children of Scottish parents at the schools attached to these churches.

"I am happy to say that the Scottish Hospital is in a more prosperous state this year than at any former period. But at the same time further demands have been made upon its funds. The claims during the past year have been in excess of any previous year, and several of the cases relieved have been of a very pressing and urgent nature. Pensions of £6, £12, £15, and £25 per annum have been granted to nearly 200 respectable men and women, whose means of support have been greatly increased by the timely aid afforded. Nearly 300 monthly applicants have had sums given to them by the directors, in several instances amounting to £5 at one time. In addition to these, more than 1300 persons have had casual assistance at the office of the corporation. Passages to Scotland have been granted to about 200 deserving persons. But for the intervention of this corporation many would have been compelled to apply to an English parish for relief, and by doing so would have lost that feeling of independence which every Scotsman cherishes and desires to maintain. Upwards of 208 children of Scottish parents resident in the Metropolis have during the year been educated at the expense of the corporation. Soldiers and sailors, natives of Scotland, to the number of nearly 400, have been in receipt of pensions from the Kinloch Bequest.

"Although the facts must be known to most of you, I have

nevertheless thought it necessary to mention a few of them in order to stimulate your generosity this evening, and induce you to contribute as largely as you can for the benefit of this excellent charity. I hope you will drink the toast of 'Prosperity to the Scottish Hospital' in full bumpers. I have great pleasure in coupling with the toast the name of the noble Duke on my left, who has been president for four successive years."

The Duke of Roxburghe, in responding to the toast, announced that His Royal Highness had kindly consented to allow his name to appear as that of President of the Corporation for the ensuing year. As Duke of Rothesay he had a warm welcome that evening, and in the name of his brother Scotchmen he gave his heartfelt thanks for appearing among them. "Nay more, I thank him in the name of the aged recipients of this great charity, many of whom have seen better days, but who now, bowed down by poverty, look to you for assistance in the hour of need. I also thank His Royal Highness in the name of all whose sorrows have been lessened, and whose homes have been brightened, by the ministrations of this Society." He proposed the health of the Prince of Wales.

The toast was drunk with "Highland honours." His Royal Highness, who was loudly cheered, said:—

"Your Royal Highness, my Lords, and Gentlemen,—Allow me to return you my most hearty thanks for the excessively kind way in which my health has been proposed and received by you. On any ordinary occasion I should have been deeply gratified by the kind feeling displayed towards me, but I am deeply touched by the enthusiasm you have manifested just now in drinking my health with Highland honours. I can only say it has afforded me great pleasure to preside here this evening. Although for some years past the Duke of Roxburghe asked me to take the chair, different circumstances unfortunately prevented me—being absent from the country two years ago—and again last year being on the Continent. I feel, therefore, exceedingly happy that I have been enabled to be present this evening, and to discharge what I have found to be the very easy duties of chairman. My lords and gentlemen, let me thank you once more for the honour you have done me in drinking my health, and for the support you have given me this evening."

His Royal Highness then announced that telegrams had been received during the evening from meetings with similar objects held in New York, Glasgow, Belfast, Ipswich, and Aberdeen, and answers had been returned expressive of kindly feeling to the different associations. The secretary then read a list of contributions received, among which were 100 guineas from Her Majesty the Queen, 100 guineas from His Royal Highness the Prince of Wales, 100 guineas from the Highland Society of London, 300 guineas from the Caledonian Society of London—in all about £2500, being by far the largest subscription received at any anniversary of the Scottish Hospital.

ROYAL MASONIC INSTITUTION FOR BOYS.

March 30th, 1870.

THE seventy-second anniversary festival of this institution was held at Freemason's Hall on the 30th of March, 1870. The Prince of Wales presided, and was supported by Earl de Grey and Ripon, G. M. elect, the Duke of Manchester, the Earl of Jersey, Earl Percy, the Marquis of Hartington, and a numerous company of above six hundred brethren, all of whom wore dress of the craft. The galleries were crowded with ladies.

After dinner His Royal Highness, in giving the toast of " The Queen," said that Her Majesty had been patroness of the institution since 1852, and on this occasion sent a donation of a hundred guineas, in addition to the annual subscription.

The next toast was "The health of the Earl of Zetland," the retiring Grand Master, who had held the honourable and useful post for more than a quarter of a century. The Grand Master elect, the Earl of Ripon, in giving the toast of the Prince and the Princess of Wales, said that the Prince had entered the craft determined to discharge his duties to the fullest extent, and he had taken the earliest opportunity of presiding at one of the festivals of the craft. The Prince of Wales, in responding, said :—

" Brethren, I feel deeply touched by the excessively kind manner in which this toast has been received by you. I wish to take this opportunity of thanking you for the kind reception you have given me this evening, and I desire especially to express to you the pride I feel at being so heartily received among you as a brother Mason. I feel deeply grateful for the kind words which have fallen from the Deputy Grand Master, and I can assure him and you of my desire to follow the footsteps of my grand uncles, who were so long connected with the craft. Brethren, much has been said against Freemasonry by those who do not know what it is. People naturally say they do not approve secret societies; but I maintain that the craft is free from the reproach of being either disloyal or irreligious; and I am sure you will all support me in that assertion, for I am convinced that Her Majesty has no more loyal subjects than are the Freemasons of England. Brethren, I desire to remind you that when, about 70 years ago, it became necessary for the Government of that day to put down secret societies, my rela- tive the late Duke of Sussex urged in his place in Parliament that Freemasons' lodges ought to be exempt from such a law, and the force of his appeal was acknowledged. From that time Freemasonry has been devoid of politics, its only object being the pure and Christian one of charity. Brethren, I once more thank you heartily for the welcome you have given me this evening, and let me assure you that the interests of Freemasonry shall be always upheld and respected by me."

Other toasts, usual at Masonic festivals, having been given, the Prince of Wales proposed success to the institution, and made a statement respecting its position and progress :—

" Freemasons had fully recognized the importance of educa- tion—a subject which had of late so much occupied the public mind—and had founded many schools. The Royal Masonic Institution for Boys was founded in 1798, when six boys were admitted. In 1810, when the jubilee of the reign of George III. was celebrated, the number was increased to 50, and now there were 110 in the school. The total cost of the new building had been £47,000 of which £5000 was still owing, while there were other matters which raised the total liability to £10,200. There were now 155 candidates for admission, but there were only nine vacancies, although 20 more boys could be admitted if the institution was free from debt. He was sure he had only to mention these facts to so distinguished an assemblage of Masons to insure a response which would greatly forward the prosperity of the institution."

INTERNATIONAL EDUCATIONAL EXHIBITION.

April 4th, 1870.

In everything pertaining to Exhibitions, national or international, the Prince of Wales has never grown weary, even when the public interest has seemed to flag. On the 4th of April, 1870, His Royal Highness presided at the rooms of the Society of Arts, in connection with the "Educational Section" of a series of proposed International Exhibitions. On rising to open the proceedings, the Prince said :—

"We are assembled here for the purpose of organizing the educational section of the Exhibition to be held in 1871. I appear before you on this occasion in a double capacity, for I hold the position of President of your Society, and I am President of the Royal Commission of 1851, having succeeded in this post the late lamented Lord Derby, whose name will always be remembered among the names of our great statesmen, and who will be greatly missed from that Commission, the interest of which he had so much at heart.

"The long-standing connection of the Society of Arts with Exhibitions is well known, and in these very rooms the Exhibitions of 1851 and 1862 were first planned. This Society is, I consider, well qualified to deal with the subject before it, and I assure you that it is a great gratification to me to preside here and show that I am entirely alive to the great question of the day—that of education.

"I have now to state that the meeting to-day is of members of a large Committee, of persons eminent in their various stations for the interest they have displayed in education, and that it has been appointed without reference to politics, party, denomination, or social position, for the purpose of obtaining the best possible representation in 1871 of the various materials and apparatus used in teaching, and exhibiting, as far as practicable, the results of the many systems of instruction which are in operation in this country and in other nations of the world. Under the first class we find such objects as affect the sanitary condition of schools—the desks and stools used, maps and globes, books, pictures, scientific diagrams, objects of natural history, and the like. Under the second class will be shown illustrations of modes of teaching, drawing, reading, writing, music, and gymnastics, and the interesting work of educating those whom nature has deprived of sight, speech, and hearing, with examples of the successful results.

"In this Exhibition of Education, foreigners as well as British subjects will take their share, and I am happy to say that Sweden has already applied for permission to exhibit a full-sized model of one of its parish schools. The duty of this Committee is to see that such work as I have sketched out shall be completely accomplished, that exhibitors shall come forward and offer their productions, that the best only shall be selected for exhibition, and that discussions on systems of instruction shall be organized. I indulge a sanguine hope that the labours of this Committee may teach lessons which will lead to the improvement of the quality of primary education, and to the extension of that secondary instruction in science and art so much needed for the industrial progress of this country, a necessity proved at the Exhibition of 1851, originated and conducted by my illustrious father, and confirmed again in 1862, and at Paris in 1867, where our own artisans showed by their remarkable reports how strong were their convictions on this point. Difficulties there are, as there must ever be, in the completion of a great work, and here I am reminded how fully the difficulties connected with this work of education were appreciated by my father as long ago as 1851. But my visit with the Princess of Wales to the Middle Class Schools in the City of London on Wednesday last, and the reports on Faversham School and the District Union Schools of the Metropolis, which have been published by our Society, lead me on to hope that even these difficulties may admit of solution.

"By improved organization of schools and teaching power, I think that it is shown that instruction may be so given as to enable earning and learning to go hand-in-hand together. I close these few remarks by bidding 'God speed' to this Committee in the great work that is before them. Two resolutions will be offered for your acceptance, and any explanation which may seem necessary will be afforded."

The resolutions, moved by Sir John Pakington, and by the Hon. W. Cowper Temple, were to the effect that the meeting warmly approved of the proposed International Educational Exhibition, which would not only receive His Royal Highness's sanction, but his personal assistance and co-operation. It was explained that the feature of these Exhibitions would be the arrangement of objects illustrating the progress of art and industry, not according to countries, but according to classes. On the proposal of a vote of thanks to the chairman of the meeting, the Prince said :—

"I require and desire no thanks at all. It has given me great pleasure to be here to open the proceedings, and I cordially thank all the gentlemen who have so kindly supported me on this occasion. I beg again to assure you that I take a very deep interest in this question—that of education, and that I shall be always ready to give my hearty co-operation on a subject of this important bearing."

ROYAL GENERAL THEATRICAL FUND.

May 16th, 1870.

THIS Fund grants relief in annuities to members of the dramatic profession, to singers and dancers, and also to the widows and orphans of members. At present, upwards of £2000 annually is paid to fifty annuitants. The invested capital is about £12,000. The institution has the merit of not being a mere charity, but is largely supported by the actors themselves. In this respect it holds a more honourable position than even the Royal Literary Fund; no attempt to establish a guild for mutual help among men of letters having, as yet, been successful.

The Theatrical Fund was established as long ago as 1839 by a few actors, and was incorporated by Royal charter in 1853. Part of the income comes from subscribers to the fund; but it is necessary also to appeal to the public, in the method common to all charities; the resources of the profession not being sufficient to maintain a mutual insurance society on financial unaided by benevolent principles.

His Royal Highness the Prince of Wales presided at the 25th anniversary festival of the Fund at St. James's Hall on the 16th of May, 1870. There was a large attendance, including the leading members of the profession, and some zealous supporters of the drama, among whom were the Nawab Nazim of Bengal, with his two sons, the Princes Ali and Suleiman. Grace having been sung after dinner the Prince gave "The Health of Her Majesty the Queen," the patroness of this institution, and an annual subscriber to its funds. The Duke of Sutherland, in proposing the health of

" The Prince and Princess of Wales, and other members of the Royal Family," adverted to the constant support given by their Royal Highnesses to the drama.

The Prince of Wales, in returning thanks, said "he rejoiced that ever since his childhood he had had opportunities of going to the theatre and witnessing some of the most excellent plays, and appreciating the performances of some of the best actors of the present day, many of whom he saw on either side and before him on this occasion. The few remarks he had to make regarding this most excellent fund must be reserved till a later period of the evening, and therefore he would not then detain the company ; but he must observe that not only had the Princess and himself derived considerable amusement from what they had witnessed at the theatres, but they had given their patronage to the drama because it was their wish to encourage a noble profession."

The usual toast of the Army, Navy, and Volunteers having been given and responded to, the Prince rose, and said :—

" The toast which he had now to propose was the so-called toast of the evening, which was ' Prosperity to the Royal General Theatrical Fund.' It afforded him great pleasure to propose this toast, and when he saw the numerous assembly before him he felt no doubt of the great interest taken by all present in this excellent charity. What charity, he asked, could be more deserving of support ? When they considered how much amusement and pleasure they all derived by going to the theatre, did it ever occur to them that it was to the actors and actresses a life of drudgery and hardship ? Those same actors and actresses who appeared in some comic character might have near and dear relations lying sick at home. Then, also, when a time of life arrived in the course of nature in which they were unable longer to appear upon the stage ought they to be left to starve ? Certainly not, and it was to prevent aged actors who were incapable of work from starving, that this fund had been instituted.

" This charity was still more meritorious, because it was supported by the actors themselves. The charity was established in 1839 by a few London actors, and in 1853 it was incorporated by Royal charter. The fund was raised to provide annuities for aged and decayed members of the charity, and in special cases for granting temporary assistance to the families of deceased members. Any member of the profession, on the payment of a small annual subscription, ranging from 21s. 4d. to £28 9s. a year, according to a special scale, provided he had been performing three years in a theatre licensed by the Lord Chamberlain or by the local magistrates, was eligible to receive the benefits of the fund, but no member had a claim unless he had been a subscriber for seven years. Should he then be incapacitated from further work, he had the option of either receiving a life annuity or one-half the payments made by him while a subscriber. On his death an allowance of £10 was granted towards defraying funeral expenses. At 60 years of age any member was at liberty to claim an annuity if he had subscribed to the fund for 12 years, and female members were allowed to cease their subscriptions when 55 years old. Since the opening of the charity 322 members of the profession had been admitted associates. To 61 of these life pensions had been granted, varying from £30 to £90 a year. In 1846, the first year in which pensions were granted, the receipts amounted to £565, and the annuities to £98. Last year the total income was £1370, and the amount expended in pensions was £1614. The receipts of 1869 therefore exceeded those of 1846 by £805, and the pensions, &c., by £1516. Again, while in 1846 only seven members received annuities, the number of annuitants had increased to 33 in 1869. The total disbursements, however, of last year exceeded the income by £368, and it had been found necessary therefore to draw that sum from the reserve fund.

"These few remarks would perhaps induce those who heard him to come forward liberally to the assistance of the charity, and to make up the £300 which it had been necessary to draw from the reserve fund. His Royal Highness concluded by calling upon the company to drink 'Prosperity to the General Theatrical Fund,' coupled with the name of one who, he was sure, they would receive with the greatest enthusiasm, as he was one of their oldest and ablest actors. He had known Mr. Buckstone personally ever since his childhood, and had repeatedly laughed and roared at his drollery and humour."

Mr. Buckstone made a very amusing and characteristic speech, but with good sense underlying the drollery. With regard to the presence of the Prince in the chair, he said: "That His Royal Highness is a constant and warm supporter of the drama is evident from his frequent visits with the Princess to all the London theatres, and his ready appreciation of every worthy novelty. This taste for the drama may in some measure be attributed to his early introduction to dramatic art at Windsor Castle, where, on having the honour of appearing there by invitation of Her Majesty and the lamented Prince Consort, I have frequently seen His Royal Highness with his brothers and sisters, seated at the feet of their father and mother, witnessing with delight the various representations.

"The members of our fund cannot be too grateful for the kindness and goodness of heart which have induced His Royal Highness to come here to-night, as the calls upon his time have now become so many, and the duties he has to perform so numerous and fatiguing, that we can only wonder how he gets through them all. Even within these few days he has held a levée; on Saturday last he patronized a performance at Drury-lane in aid of the Dramatic College; then had to run away to Freemasons'-hall to be present at the installation of the Grand Master; and now we find him in the chair this evening; so what with *conversaziones*, laying foundation stones, opening schools, and other calls upon his little leisure, I think he may be looked upon as one of the hardest working men in Her Majesty's dominions. Still, it is this ready kindness that endears him to the nation, as the Princess, by her charming qualities, is so firmly fixed in the heart of every Englishman and Englishwoman.

"And now, my Lords, Ladies, and Gentlemen, I must inform you that Her Gracious Majesty has again sent us her handsome donation of £100; and although, unfortunately, she does not now visit our theatres, yet she does not forget us; and so, my Lords, Ladies, and Gentlemen, with such a truly Royal example before you, I can only conclude by hoping that, according to your generous feelings and your worldly means, you will come and do likewise."

Lord W. Lennox proposed "The Visitors," coupling with it the health of the Nawab Nazim of Bengal, who during his residence in England had identified himself with the charities of this country. The Nawab had been a liberal patron of theatrical performances, and had, he understood, only one subject of regret in connection with our London theatres—that the plays of Shakespeare were not more frequently performed in them. The subscriptions of the evening amounted to £700, including £100 from the Prince of Wales, and £50 from the Nawab Nazim of Bengal.

ST. GEORGE'S HOSPITAL.

May 26th, 1870.

On the 26th of May, 1870, a public meeting was held at the Queen's Concert Rooms, Hanover Square, in aid of the funds of St. George's Hospital, especially with the view of enabling the Governors to open the wards of the new wing. The meeting was one of unusual interest, not only from the wide publicity given to the claims of the institution, but also from the announcement that His Royal Highness the Prince of Wales would preside, and from the high distinction of the speakers who were to take part in the proceedings. The Princess of Wales manifested her interest in the charity by accompanying the Prince to the meeting. The room was densely crowded, and a number of distinguished persons were in the company.

His Royal Highness, on taking the chair, said :—

"My Lords, Ladies, and Gentlemen,—Before opening the proceedings of this meeting, allow me to express to you the satisfaction I have in being able to accept the invitation to preside at a meeting to-day which has for its aim such excellent and important objects. We are met here to-day to discuss whether it is expedient to open the new wing that has been added to St. George's Hospital. Last year a meeting was held for the same purpose for which we are met to-day, and it was then thought that the subscriptions, although they were to a great extent liberal subscriptions, were not sufficient in amount to authorize the Governors of the Hospital to open the new wing. It has also been much discussed whether it was not an extravagance on the part of the authorities to build this new wing. I must say—and I think I speak for those on my right and left—that the authorities did perfectly right in building that wing, as a piece of ground had been presented to them at a nominal rent by the late lamented Marquis of Westminster, who always came forward voluntarily to assist any great and important work. Besides that, a further sum of £5000 was given by Miss Williams to the building fund.

" As regards this wing, we all know that St. George's Hospital lies near the South-Western and Great Western districts. We also know that it lies within the precincts of Kensington, Mayfair, and Belgravia. One would have thought that there would have been no difficulty, and that the large number of inhabitants in those parts, who are increasing monthly, and even weekly, would have been able to come forward and contribute sufficiently to this excellent institution.

"It has been said that the Hospital of St. George is a rich one, but that is a great mistake. One would indeed think that it would be rich from its important position, and when one remembers how full its wards invariably are. To go back to the new wing. After all, it is not a very large sum that is required to maintain these wards. The sum only amounts to £2500 a year. Is it not, therefore, a scandal, ladies and gentlemen, that for the sake of this small sum we cannot use forty-eight beds in that wing? The Hospital itself is in want of money, as I will prove by stating that last year the expenditure amounted to as much as £20,000, while the income was only £15,000. In order, therefore, to make up the deficiency, £5000 had to be sold out of capital. That will be the case this year, and it may be the same in future years. The capital thus diminishing, the income will naturally be smaller, and in that way this excellent Hospital, which is most admirably cared for, which has the very best surgeons and physicians—one of whom, Mr. Prescott Hewett, I know personally—will sustain a yearly diminution of its usefulness. In this way, if the public do not come forward liberally we shall see one of the most excellent and important hospitals in London becoming, year by year, in a more difficult position with regard to funds.

"I am here to state what I am not sure is known to all of you, that, with the exception of one hospital, the average cost of beds at the St. George's Hospital is less than in any other hospital in London. The authorities of the Hospital are not even satisfied with that, and, I believe, intend to appoint a committee to inquire still more closely and rigidly into the expenditure, in order to do their utmost to lessen that expenditure.

"My Lords, Ladies, and Gentlemen,—The address I have to make to you is brief. I feel convinced that the gentlemen on this platform will advocate the claims of the Hospital in longer, more detailed, and more able statements than I have made; but I am sure that none can feel more strongly than I do the importance of this meeting. I feel certain also that the public at large, if they will only take the trouble to reflect, will come to our aid. Only to-day I read an excellent leading article in the *Times* in support of the objects of this meeting. I thank you once more for the kind way in which you have received me, but let me say before I sit down that a most excellent example has been set us by a lady who has consented to give the sum of £1000 for the maintenance of a ward for the space of two years. Let this example not be lost upon us. Let us all try to follow it, and liberally open our purses for the sake of an institution of such value and importance to all of us who live in this part of London."

The Earl of Cadogan, one of the Treasurers, announced that the Prince of Wales had just handed to him a cheque for two hundred guineas. The Princess of Wales had also given a donation of fifty guineas. Miss Read had given £500, and the Marquis of Westminster a subscription of £200 a year. Mr. Prescott Hewett, the surgeon, gave a hundred guineas, and other liberal donations and subscriptions were announced, amounting to upwards of £2000.

The principal speakers at the meeting were Earl Granville, the Earl of Derby, the Earl of Carnarvon, Mr. W. H. Smith, the Marquis of Westminster, and the Rev. H. Howarth, Rector of St. George's, Hanover Square.

The Marquis of Westminster, in his admirable speech moving the thanks of the meeting to the Chairman, said that he happened to be in Milan a short time ago, and, going over a great hospital there, containing something like 3000 beds, he saw in different rooms portraits of the benefactors of the institution—some full length, others three-quarters, some half-length, and others only heads. On inquiring the reason of this distinction, he was informed that the size of the picture depended upon the amount of the sum given by the donor. One who gave, say £4000, had his portrait painted full length, while the others were represented half-length, or even by a head. . . . It might be thought a light and easy thing to come forward and make so excellent a speech as His Royal Highness had done; but he was quite sure that if any who thought thus would come forward to try, they would find themselves mistaken. In coming forward in this work of benevolence, His Royal Highness was fairly entitled to the warm and cordial thanks, not only of the governors of the hospital, but of the whole nation. He begged to include in this vote the Princess of Wales.

His Royal Highness said:—

"My Lords, Ladies, and Gentlemen,—Allow me to return you all my most cordial thanks for the kind way in which you have supported me by your presence, and to my noble friend for the way in which he proposed the resolution. Not wishing to keep you here any longer, let me only urge you to be as liberal as you can, and I hope that the excellent speeches we have heard to-day may impress you with the importance of this meeting, and with the feeling that those speeches have been made not as a mere form, but as real and earnest appeals to you to open your purses most liberally. Lord Westminster has just alluded to the hospital at Milan and to the portraits of different sizes, according to the amount of money subscribed by the originals. I have but one suggestion to make to you in that respect, and one to which I am sure you will respond—that you should all contribute very largely that circular golden portrait representative of the Queen which this Hospital so much needs."

DULWICH COLLEGE.

June 21st, 1870.

THE old corporation of "The College of God's gift" in Dulwich, in the county of Surrey, was founded in 1619, under letters patent of King James I., by Edward Alleyne, player, a contemporary and friend of Shakespeare. Those who knew Dulwich College, before its reconstitution in recent times, must remember its being spoken of as a notable instance of "the abuse of an ancient charity." In 1857 the old corporation was dissolved by Act of Parliament, and a new Governing Body was established, consisting of 19 Governors, of whom 11 were to be appointed by the Court of Chancery, and the remainder by the parishes of Camberwell, Bishopsgate, St. Luke, Finsbury, and St. Saviour's, Southwark, each appointing two Governors. A further scheme for the management of the charity was approved by Her Majesty in Council in 1882, greatly modifying the arrangement of 1857. By the latter scheme the management of the estate in its eleemosynary branch was wholly separated from the educational branch, with separate governing bodies.

The great increase in the value of the estates had allowed the establishment, in 1857, of Alleyn's School, and a large sum was then provided for the erection of school buildings, a splendid edifice being constructed by Mr. Charles Barry.

It was to open this new school that the visit of the Prince and Princess of Wales was made, on the 21st of June, 1870. By a singular coincidence this day was the anniversary of that on which the charter of the College had been first signed, on the 21st of June, 1607. The Prince of Wales distributed the prizes, after the pupils had delivered speeches, and gone through the exercises usual in public school examinations and anniversaries. The recitations were brought to a close with singing the National Anthem.

At the luncheon which followed, the Rev. W. Rogers presided, and proposed the health of the Royal visitors.

His Royal Highness, who was loudly cheered on rising to reply, said :—

"My Lords, Ladies, and Gentlemen,—I feel deeply the kind way in which you have received this toast, and I can assure you that it is with great pleasure we have to-day made so interesting a visit to a place which, for all of us, possesses an historical interest. It is hardly necessary for me to refer to the early history of the College. You all know that it was founded in the time of Queen Elizabeth, although the charter was actually signed by James I., and that Edward Alleyne was an eminent actor, and that he also held, I believe, the post of bear-keeper— I hope not bear-leader—to Queen Elizabeth. What we witness to-day is a gratifying result of that foundation. Everybody who has had the opportunity of seeing this splendid building must have derived gratification from the spectacle, and also from the proofs which have been furnished that education is by no means neglected. These proofs we have listened to in the English and French languages, and also in the ancient Greek, and we have done so with very great pleasure, in spite of the great heat which it was necessary for that purpose to encounter.

"I will not detain you with further remarks. But before I sit down let me wish thorough success and happiness to this College, and let us hope that the success which has attended the last ten years especially of its existence will continue and increase, and that year by year it will advance in standing and position and in the number of the scholars within its walls. I have now the pleasure of proposing a toast which I am sure you will all drink with enthusiasm—'The Health of the Master of Dulwich College, Dr. Carver.' From the cordial way in which his name is cheered by the boys there can be no doubt of his popularity; and to his efforts, I believe, much of the success which the school has attained is owing."

The Rev. Dr. Carver "returned his very sincere thanks for this compliment, which he took to be meant really for the institution

H

of which he was at the head. The inheritance of the last five
half-centuries was a noble one, but with it they inherited many
responsibilities, resulting from the faults and failings of their
predecessors, and there was much not only to do but to redeem.
He believed that a new era for Dulwich College had been
inaugurated, and he trusted it would hereafter win and occupy a
place among the most important and valuable institutions of the
kingdom."

Their Royal Highnesses then proceeded to the Library. Before
the ceremonies at the School, they had visited the magnificent
collection of paintings, known as the Dulwich Gallery. These
pictures were collected by Sir F. Bourgeois, R.A., bequeathed by
him to the College, owing to his friendship for Mr. Allen, the
Master of the College, at the time of his death, in 1810. Some of
the best pictures in this gallery were obtained in Poland, at the
time of the partition of that ancient kingdom by the three Great
Powers.

SCHOOLS FOR THE CHILDREN OF SEAMEN.

June 30th, 1870.

THEIR Royal Highnesses the Prince and Princess of Wales, on
the 30th of June, 1870, performed the ceremony of opening the
new schools for the children of seamen. There was a large
assembly present, including the Lord and Lady Mayoress, the
Bishop of London and Mrs. Jackson, the Sheriffs of Middlesex,
several Aldermen and public officials. The schools are situated
near the London Docks, in Wellclose Square, where for two
hundred years stood the church for Danish seamen. The site of
the buildings was the property of the Crown of Denmark, and,
with the church, was purchased from the trustees with money
granted from the Bishop of London's Fund. The newly-erected
schools afford accommodation for 600 children, and the cost was
about £5500.

An address, giving the history and purpose of the institution,
was read by the vicar of St. Paul's Church for seamen of the port
of London, to which

The Prince of Wales responded, saying "it was a source of
infinite gratification to him to be present at the completion of a
work originated by his lamented father, and to fulfil his benevolent design of providing for the education and religious welfare
of the children, after having secured a place of Divine Worship
for the parents. He trusted that the association of the site

with its former uses would bear its fruit in the success of this sacred work of education and religion."

After prayers were read by the Bishop of London, the ceremony of declaring the schools open was performed, and purses were presented, with donations to the amount of £1500, including a hundred guineas from the Prince of Wales.

A luncheon followed, at which the Bishop of London, in proposing the health of the Queen, recalled a saying of George III., who once expressed the hope that the time would come when every man in England would possess a Bible, and be able to read it. This sentiment was also felt by the old King's grand-daughter who now filled the throne, and nothing was dearer to Her Majesty's heart than the religious education of the people.

In next proposing the health of the Prince and Princess of Wales, the Bishop said that the Royal visit of this day would give a prestige to the schools which would ensure their popularity in the neighbourhood. There was a special interest for the Princess of Wales in the fact that they were on the site of the old Danish Chapel, long the only place of worship for Danish seamen in London.

The Prince of Wales, in response, said :—

"My Lord Bishop, Ladies, and Gentlemen,—Allow me in the name of the Princess of Wales and myself to tender you my warmest thanks for the kind way in which this toast has been proposed and responded to. I need not tell you that the proceedings of to-day have given us great pleasure, or that we feel a deep interest in the success of the schools which we have now opened. When we were asked to open these schools and playgrounds for the children of seamen and other persons living in this neighbourhood, we at once felt that the object was excellent, and we were anxious in coming here to-day to evince the interest we take in the schools. They have, as has already been mentioned, an especial interest for myself, because just twenty-four years ago the foundation stone of the neighbouring church for seamen was laid by my lamented father. That church, during the twenty-four years it has been in existence, has answered the purpose for which it was built, and I believe as many as 240,000 seamen, together with their wives and families, have attended divine service within its walls. Let us, then, hope that the children also may receive the benefits of a good education and religious training, and that these schools may fulfil the object for which they were built.

H 2

" In this part of London there are so many poor that good schools are especially needed, and as these schools are not intended exclusively for the children of seamen, they will probably be most beneficial to the neighbourhood at large.   Allow me to thank you for the way in which you have listened to the few remarks I have made, and to assure you that I feel deep gratification in being present to-day at the opening of these schools.   I have, before sitting down, to propose ' The Health of the Lord Bishop of London,' to whom we owe our warmest thanks for the kind way in which he has come here to take part in the proceedings of this day, when he has so many other and important duties to perform.   As I know that he has another pressing engagement in a short time, the fewer words said the better.   I therefore call upon you to drink the health of the Lord Bishop of London."

NEW GRAMMAR SCHOOL AT READING.

July 1st, 1870.

THE good people of Reading are said sometimes to have grumbled at being neglected by Royalty, their town being overshadowed by its proximity to the Royal borough of Windsor.   This notion was effaced by the splendid events of the 1st of July, 1870.   On that day the Prince and Princess of Wales, with imposing state and ceremony, visited the ancient town, in order to lay the foundation-stone of a new school, which was to be the successor of the historical Grammar School, at which Archbishop Laud was edu-cated, one of the masters of which, Julius Palmer, was martyred during the Marian persecution, and which in recent times had attained high celebrity under the scholastic reign of Dr. Valpy.

The town was in high festival for the occasion, and distin-guished company assembled to meet the Royal visitors.   When the Address had been presented by the Mayor and Town Clerk, giving a summary of the history of the school, and the purposes of the new undertaking, the Prince replied :—

" Mr. Mayor and Gentlemen,—I desire to return my cordial thanks for your address, and to assure you, on the part of the Princess and myself, of the pleasure it affords us to visit a town so conspicuous in the pages of English history.   It is most gratifying to me to co-operate with you, gentlemen, in securing for your town the benefits contemplated by the Royal founders of this ancient school. In extending to Reading and its county the advantages of a middle-class education, you are providing an education which, if conducted on sound principles, must conduce to the welfare and happiness of all who desire to profit by it; and that this result is anticipated is satisfactorily indicated by the amount of contributions already subscribed. For myself, I sincerely trust that the good work of which we are now assembled to lay the first stone may, under God's blessing, prosper and accomplish its purpose. It will at least prove to a succeeding generation that we, on our part, have striven with all our hearts and all our means to ripen the good seed sown by our fathers upwards of 300 years ago."

The ceremony of setting the stone then began, for the ceremony was to be done with masonic honours, one side of the tent having been entirely occupied by the Masons in costume. The Mayor, having received from the Provincial Grand Master the handsome silver trowel prepared for the occasion, now asked the Prince, in the name of the School Trustees, to proceed with the ceremony. The Grand Chaplain offered a prayer, the Architect presented his plans, the Grand Secretary read the inscription on the stone, and the Grand Treasurer deposited gold, silver, and copper coins of the present reign in the cavity prepared for them.

The Prince then proved and set the stone, saying :—

" May the Great Architect of the Universe enable us successfully to carry on and finish the work of which we have now laid the principal stone, and every other undertaking which may tend to the advantage of the borough of Reading and this neighbourhood, and may this school be long preserved from peril and decay, diffusing its light and influence to generations yet unborn."

To this the Masons present answered with one accord, " So mote it be." The Prince next spread corn on the stone, and from the ewers handed to him poured out wine and oil, saying :—

" May the bountiful hand of Heaven ever supply this country with abundance of corn, wine, and oil, and all the necessaries and comforts of life."

The Brethren again responded in the Masonic formula, " So mote it be." Then the Treasurer to the school presented to the Senior Master Builder (Mr. Parnell) a purse of gold, saying : " It is the pleasure of the Prince that those who have hewed the stones, and those who have laid them, and all who have assisted, should ' rejoice in the light.' "

Prayers by the Bishop of Oxford, and the Hallelujah Chorus, performed by the band and choir, closed the ceremonial, which was very quaint and impressive.

At the luncheon afterwards given in the Town Hall, the Prince, after acknowledging the usual loyal toasts, that of the Prince and Princess of Wales having been proposed by the Mayor, said :—

"My Lords, Ladies, and Gentlemen,—It gives me great pleasure to have an opportunity of expressing to all those present the gratification it has given both to the Princess and myself to be here this day. I am glad also to have the opportunity of congratulating the Mayor and Corporation and the inhabitants of Reading on the great success of all the proceedings of the day. In passing through the town we could not fail to admire the tasteful way in which all the houses and streets were decorated ; nor was it possible that the arrangements for laying the foundation stone of the new schools, and the magnificent ceremony attending it, could have gone off better. I trust we shall all take a deep interest in the school which is to be, succeeding as it does to one which has already existed for a great number of years, having been founded by my ancestor Henry VII., and receiving a Royal charter from Queen Elizabeth. I trust that the wishes expressed by the Mayor concerning the school may be realized, and that the children not only of the inhabitants of Reading but of the whole county of Berkshire will have an opportunity of receiving a thoroughly good education in it. I will not occupy your time any longer, but before sitting down it affords me great pleasure to propose a toast which I feel sure you will all receive with enthusiasm. It is ' The Health of the Mayor of Reading.' I am glad to have the opportunity of thanking him, as the representative of this ancient and loyal borough, for the kind and hearty reception it has given to us on this occasion."

After the departure of the Prince, the Mayor announced that His Royal Highness had generously handed him a cheque for a hundred guineas towards the building fund. At night the town was illuminated, and the people of Reading had good reason to be pleased with the proceedings of the day.

ALBERT GOLD MEDAL TO M. DE LESSEPS.

July 7th, 1870.

At a meeting of the Council of the Society of Arts, on the 7th of July, 1870, the Prince of Wales, as President of the Society, presented the Albert Gold Medal to M. de Lesseps. This medal is awarded for services rendered to arts, manufactures, and commerce; and no services, to commerce at least, could have been better rendered than by the realization of the Suez Canal.

The Prince addressed M. de Lesseps in a French speech, of which the following is a translation :—

"It is with sincere gratification that, as President of the Society for the Encouragement of Arts, Manufactures and Commerce, I have the honour of presenting to you to-day the gold medal which was founded after the death of my beloved father, and which bears his name. This medal is presented every year to the person who has distinguished himself most remarkably in advancing the interests of the objects for which the Society was founded, and I am fully convinced that no recipient has ever been more worthy than yourself of this honourable distinction. In presenting it, I need scarcely say that the award was unanimous, and I may perhaps be permitted to add that I stipulated for the pleasure of placing the medal myself in your hands. England will never forget that it was to you the success of that great enterprise which is so much calculated to develope the commercial interests subsisting between herself and her Eastern Empire was due ; and I trust that since your sojourn among us the English people have evinced to you their appreciation of the benefits which your great work has conferred upon this country. Allow me once more to congratulate you upon your grand achievement, and to express my sincere hope, as it is my belief, that it will fully realise the brilliant anticipations which you have from the first entertained respecting it. In conclusion, I must assure you of the pleasure I feel in presenting this medal to you, not only as President of this Society, but as a personal friend, who has, moreover, enjoyed the inestimable advantage of an inspection of the Canal under your guidance."

M. de Lesseps replied as follows :—

" Monséigneur,—I am happy in receiving from the hands of your Royal Highness the medal which has been awarded to me by the Society of Arts and Manufactures.   This medal, recalling the respected memory of your august father, has a double value in my eyes, for His Royal Highness Prince Albert, from the commencement of the enterprise of the Suez Canal, received me with that kindly feeling which was to him habitual, and which led him always to encourage everything which might be useful to social progress, to the discoveries of science, and to the development of commerce.   He received me for the first time in 1858, in his private study, where he invited me to explain to him all the details relating to the construction of the Canal, and he followed with close attention upon the map and on the working plan the course of the projected scheme as worked out by the engineers. Since that time he continued on several occasions to testify the interest which he felt in the enterprise for which the period of commencing the works had arrived. I thank your Royal Highness and the Society of Arts for having added this important manifestation to all the evidences which I have had the good fortune to receive from the Government of the Queen and from the people of Great Britain.   The words of your Royal Highness will remain engraven in my heart. I have already had the good fortune of finding myself with you, Monséigneur, when travelling in the desert, and there, where a man, however highly he may be placed, shows himself as he is, I have been able to appreciate the noble character, the lofty mind, and the elevated sentiments of your Royal Highness, and I am happy to bear this testimony in the presence of the distinguished men who surround us.   I shall ever be, as they are, the devoted partisan of your Royal Highness.   I pray you to present to Her Majesty the homage of my respect and of my gratitude, and to assure her that the Company which I have the honour to direct will be able to maintain the Suez Canal in a condition which will satisfy all the requirements of the great commerce and of the navigation of Great Britain."

It is always a pleasure to the Prince of Wales to give the Albert Medal with his own hands, sometimes at Marlborough House, as to Sir Henry Bessemer, and to M. Chevalier, the distinguished French Economist. When the award was made to Mr. Doulton, the Prince went to Lambeth to make the presentation, and said that he would have been glad to have received Mr. Doulton at Marlborough House, but thought it would be more gratifying to him to have the medal presented in his own place and among his own workpeople—an act of gracious considerateness which was well appreciated by the vast assembly who witnessed the event.

OPENING OF THE THAMES EMBANKMENT.

July 13th, 1870.

THIS great work, which, for solidity of construction, durability of material, and beauty of design, is worthy of the Metropolis of the Empire, was commenced early in 1852, but was not completed till the summer of 1870. Viewed in connection with the benefits to public health and convenience, by the improvement of the course of the Thames, and the removal of the mud banks formerly disfiguring the shores, the Embankment may be truly said to be the greatest public work undertaken in London in modern times. Portions of the footway had been previously open for passengers, and improvements have been since made in the approaches and in laying out ornamental grounds, but the completion of the roadway, from Westminster to Blackfriars, sufficiently justified the grand State ceremony with which the Embankment was opened, on the 13th of July, 1870, by the Prince of Wales.

On that day, the Prince, accompanied by the Princess Louise, and attended by the Great Officers of the Household, opened the Embankment on behalf of Her Majesty the Queen. Five Royal carriages, with an escort of the Royal Horse Guards, proceeded from Marlborough House, by the Mall, Whitehall, and Parliament Street to Westminster Bridge, where they entered the embankment. Here the procession was joined by the carriages containing the Chairman and members of the Metropolitan Board of Works. At Hungerford Bridge an address was presented by the Chairman, Sir John Thwaites. The Royal procession went as far as Blackfriars Bridge, and then returned to Westminster Bridge, when the Prince, amidst the cheers of the multitude, and the salutes of artillery, declared the Embankment to be open.

The reply to the address read by the Prince, was as follows :—

"Gentlemen,—It is a source of great regret to me, as I am sure it cannot fail to be to you, that the Queen is unable to be present, according to her original intention, at this interesting ceremony. In her name I thank you for your loyal address, and express to you the satisfaction with which she regards the completion of this great work. We must all rejoice that while the Embankment and the noble roadway, which I am happy this day to open in the name of Her Majesty, add largely to the beauty and convenience of the Metropolis, the works connected with them may be expected materially to diminish the sources of disease and suffering to the inhabitants of this bank of the Thames. In no public work of this vast capital has the liberal

and enterprising spirit of its citizens and the genius and resources
of our civil engineers been more signally displayed.   I am commanded by the Queen to congratulate you cordially on the issue
of your labours in undertakings which promise to be so enduring
and so beneficent."

Five years before this, on the 4th of April, 1865, the Prince had
visited the great works erected at Barking, in Essex, and thence
to the Erith Marshes to perform the ceremony of starting the
great engines which lift the waters of the Southern Outfall
Sewer.   In a brief speech on that occasion the Prince congratulated Mr. Thwaites, then chairman of the Metropolitan Board of
Works, and Mr. Bazalgette, the engineer, on the completion of an
important portion of the great scheme for disposing of the sewage
of London, and purifying the water of the Thames.

WORKMEN'S INTERNATIONAL EXHIBITION.

July 16th, 1870.

In the summer of 1870, while the news of impending war on the
continent stirred public feeling, preparations were being quietly
made in many a home and workshop for an international exhibition of art and industry.   The special feature of the display was
to be the encouragement of individual intelligence and skill, every
object exhibited having attached to it the name of the workman,
as well as the firm in whose employment he was, if not exercising
his art on his own account at home.

The Prince of Wales kindly consented to open the exhibition, in
the name of the Queen.   This was done on the 16th of July, 1870.
Having received an address, giving an account of the purpose of
the collection, the Prince thus replied :—

"Gentlemen,—I thank you for your address, and assure you
that it is with very great pleasure I undertake the duty imposed upon me by the Queen in opening this Exhibition.   The
objects proposed in it are such as cannot fail to meet with the
cordial approbation of all who are interested in the growth of
our arts and manufactures, and who wish to connect that growth
with a corresponding increase of sympathy and friendly relations between employers and their workmen.   In imparting to
this Exhibition an international character, you have sought to
extend the range of good which may result from it, and by
inviting competition between our workmen and those of foreign

nations, not only to afford a wholesome stimulus to both in the exercise of their various callings, but to contribute, as far as you can, to that kindly intercourse between countries which must in the end prove the principal security for the peace of the world. The allusion which you have made to my beloved father, who would doubtless have regarded this Exhibition with the liveliest interest, as the natural supplement of that first one with which his name is especially connected, will be as affecting as it must be gratifying to the Queen. It will be my agreeable duty to report to her the proceedings of to-day, and I have only now, in her name, to wish success to the undertaking."

A catalogue of the collection, and a newspaper printed in the building, were then presented to the Prince. The catalogue showed that contributions had been sent from all the chief industrial centres in England,—Sheffield, Birmingham, Coventry, Worcester,—and from Ireland, in bog-oak carvings, and articles of the linen and flax industry. The foreign contributions were from France, Austria, Italy, Holland, and other parts of the continent. A musical piece composed for the occasion was given, and the Old Hundredth psalm sung by the choir, after which the Prince declared the Exhibition open.

THE ROYAL ALBERT HALL.

March 29th, 1871.

The " Royal Albert Hall of Arts and Sciences " was opened by Her Majesty the Queen with imposing ceremony on the 29th of March, 1871. The procession from Buckingham Palace consisted of nine State carriages, in the last of which were the Queen, the Princess of Wales, and the Duke of Saxe-Coburg and Gotha. In the other carriages were the Royal Family, with the great Officers of State and the Household in waiting. The Hall was filled with nearly 8000 spectators, and the orchestra consisted of nearly 1200 musicians and singers, Sir Michael Costa being leader.

When the Queen had taken her place on the daïs, the Prince of Wales, who wore the uniform of Colonel of the 10th Hussars, advanced to Her Majesty, and, as President of the Provisional Committee, read the following address :—

" May it please your Majesty,—As President of the Provisional Committee of the Royal Albert Hall of Arts and Sciences, it is my high privilege and gratification to report to your Majesty the successful completion of this Hall, an important feature of a long-cherished design of my beloved father, for the general culture of your people, in whose improvement he was always deeply interested. Encouraged by your Majesty's sympathies, and liberally supported by your subjects, we have been enabled to carry out the work without any aid from funds derived from public taxation. I am warranted in expressing our confidence that this building will justify the conviction we expressed in the report submitted on the occasion of your Majesty's laying its first stone, that by its erection we should be meeting a great public want. Your Majesty's Commissioners for the Exhibition of 1851 in further prosecution of my father's design for the encouragement of the Arts and Sciences, an object which he always had warmly at heart, are about to commence a series of Annual International Exhibitions, to the success of which this Hall will greatly contribute by the facilities which it will afford for the display of objects and for the meeting of bodies interested in the industries which will form the subjects of successive Exhibitions. The interest shown in the Hall by the most eminent musicians and composers of Europe strengthens our belief that it will largely conduce to the revival among all classes of the nation of a taste for the cultivation of music. Your Majesty will hear with satisfaction that results have justified the original estimate of the cost of the building, and that, aided by the liberal assistance of your Exhibition Commissioners, the corporation will commence its management unfettered by pecuniary liabilities, and under conditions eminently calculated to insure success. It is my grateful duty to return to your Majesty our humble thanks for the additional mark of your Royal favour which is conferred upon us by your auspicious presence on the present occasion when our labours as a Provisional Committee are drawing to a close. We venture to hope that when we shall have resigned our functions into the hands of the governing body, which will be elected under the provisions of the Royal Charter granted to us, your Majesty will continue to the Corporation that measure of support which has been always graciously given to us."

The Queen, who had listened to the address with the utmost interest and attention, said, in a voice clearly heard in every part of the vast building : " In handing you this answer, I wish to express my great admiration of this beautiful Hall, and my earnest wishes for its complete success."

The written answer to the address was not read, but it is here given to complete the record of the day's ceremony :—

" I thank you for the loyal address which, as President of the Provisional Committee of the Hall of Arts and Sciences, you have presented to me. In opening this spacious and noble Hall, it gives me pleasure to acknowledge the generous spirit which has been manifested in the completion, by voluntary effort, of a work promising so much public usefulness. I cordially concur in the hope you have expressed, that this Hall, forming as it does part of a plan in which I must ever take a deep and personal interest, may largely and permanently contribute to the promotion among my people of the love of art, as well as to the success of the annual exhibitions, which will bring successively into instructive com-petition the choicest products of the industries of all nations. These objects could not fail to commend themselves at all times and all places to my sympathy and interest, fraught as they are with recollections of him to whose memory this Hall is dedicated. and whose dearest aim was to inspire my people with a love of all that is good and noble, and, by closer knowledge and juster appre-ciation of each other, to cultivate a spirit of goodwill and concord among the inhabitants of all regions. I gladly give the assurance of my support to the corporation to which the Hall is about to be entrusted, and I earnestly hope that their efforts to promote the objects for which it has been constructed may be rewarded by a career of abiding success."

The Bishop of London, representing the Archbishop of Canter-bury, offered a dedication prayer.

The Prince of Wales, after a minute's conference with Her Majesty, then said, " THE QUEEN DECLARES THIS HALL TO BE NOW OPENED."

The announcement was followed by immense cheering and the sound of trumpets ; and while the choir sang the National Anthem, the Park guns boomed forth a loud accompaniment.

The opening ceremony being thus accomplished, the Queen and the Royal visitors proceeded to the Royal box, where they re-mained during the performance of a selection of music. The programme included a cantata, written for the occasion by Sir Michael Costa, and the Prince Consort's *Invocazione all'Armonia,* which was first performed when Her Majesty, in 1867, laid the foundation-stone of the Hall this day opened.

THE INTERNATIONAL EXHIBITION OF 1871.

May 1st, 1871.

DURING the twenty years that had passed since the ever-memorable Exhibition of 1851, there had been many Exhibitions, one of which, that of 1862, might aspire to the title of Great, and proved fairly successful. But so numerous were the imitations of the first great example, to which, at home or abroad, none approached in romantic interest and universal popularity, that at length the idea which in 1851 charmed all the world, had come to be somewhat tiresome to the public. Inventors and manufacturers found it troublesome and expensive to exhibit, not without doubt whether there were not more disadvantages than advantages in such international displays. Some of the later Exhibitions were little better than huge bazaars or trade shows.

Having regard to these conditions, the Royal Commissioners of 1851, with the Prince of Wales as President, allowed matters to rest awhile, although still feeling under obligation to carry out the grand purposes which gave rise to the first and grandest display in Hyde Park.

It was resolved to open at South Kensington, in 1871, an " International Exhibition of the Fine Arts and of Industry ; " to be the first of a series, each with some definite aim, and mainly confined to certain arts or industries, instead of forming a miscellaneous museum of all sorts of objects. As the Queen approved of this proposal, the opening of the Exhibition of 1871 was undertaken by the Prince of Wales on Her Majesty's behalf, and was made the occasion of an imposing State pageant. In the Court Circular of May 2nd, and in the journals of the same date, a full account is given of the ceremonies of the preceding day, with lists of the illustrious and notable persons present, and other details. The Prince made formal proclamation of the opening.

In all his labours in connection with various exhibitions, at home or abroad, the Prince has had most able lieutenants, such as Sir Philip Cunliffe Owen, K.C.B., but every detail of plan and of administration has been brought before his attention, and has received the sanction of his judgment and experience. It is no exaggeration to say that to his presidency was mainly due the success of the British Department of the great Paris Exhibition of 1878. This was testified in the address presented to the Prince by Earl Granville, signed by a thousand Englishmen who had witnessed the events of that memorable season in the Place de Trocadero.

ARTISTS' ORPHAN FUND.

May 7th, 1871.

FOR the relief of distressed artists, their widows and orphans, provision is made, as far as funds allow, by the Artists' Benevolent Institution, which was established in 1814. In course of time it was found that the amount available for the support and education of the orphans of artists was very insufficient, and a separate fund was established in 1866, under the auspices of the Council of the Artists' Benevolent Institution. From time to time donations were received, and in 1871 it was resolved to make a more public appeal. The Prince of Wales cheerfully agreed to preside at a dinner in aid of the fund, which took place on the 7th of May, 1871, in the Freemasons' Hall.

The Prince was supported by a large number of artists, and of patrons and lovers of art. The usual loyal toasts were given, and the presence of members of the well-known "artist corps" led the Prince to make special reference to the Volunteers.

In giving "The Army, Navy, Militia, and Volunteers," His Royal Highness said:—

"This is a toast which is never left out at all great public dinners. By some it has been called a formal toast, but in my opinion it should never be so styled. It is a toast which we ought to drink warmly and heartily. Of that which we owe to our army and navy I shall not speak to you at length, for this is not a fitting occasion; but I may say that we are bound to those services by a deep debt of gratitude, and let us hope that we shall always have reason to be as proud of them as we are at the present moment. We must, at the same time, never forget that there is something wanting. Our army is small; smaller than those of other countries; it ought, therefore to be better in comparison. As to the navy, though a great many changes have been made in our ships, though they have been converted from wooden walls into iron batteries, I think we may confidently anticipate that the fame which attaches to our old wooden walls will be transferred to our iron fleet whenever it is called upon to meet an enemy. The Militia, too, ought never to be omitted from this toast, for I look upon it as our great army of reserve, and desire to see it honoured; while as to the Volunteers, I would remark that I think we may congratulate ourselves on the circumstance that the movement, which has now existed for eleven or twelve years, shows no sign that it is slackening. I have the more confidence in asking you to respond to this portion of the toast, because I see around me many members of the Artists' Corps, which has always maintained a high position in the Volunteer force."

The Prince, in proposing the next toast, "The Artists' Orphan Fund," said :—

" I have no doubt you will drink this toast in bumpers, particularly as this is the first dinner which has been given in aid of the Fund. I can assure you it has given me much pleasure to come here and explain to you some of the chief points connected with this excellent charity. Being a charity in aid of orphans it is, you will agree with me, worthy of peculiar sympathy. It recommends itself still more to our notice when we reflect that it proposes to help the children of those who have done so much to elevate and refine art among us, and whose beautiful pictures have so often delighted us. Many persons may imagine that it is not difficult to be a painter, but the distinguished artists whom I see around me will, I am sure, agree with me that that it is a great mistake. To be a good painter genius is by no means all that is required. Industry and perseverance must also be exercised just as much as in the case of eminent clergymen, lawyers, scientific men, philosophers, or the members of any other branch of human exertion which we can name. Again, we must remember that, although a man may have been a successful painter, although his genius may have been recognized in other countries besides his own, and although he may have accumulated money in the course of long, laborious years, yet, being laid on a bed of sickness, that money may have dwindled away, and his children may be left entirely destitute. This fund, then, is destined for the support of the orphans of such artists and for their education. No one particular school is to be set apart for education. The guardians of the children will be allowed to select the schools to which they shall go and no restrictions of any kind will be imposed upon them with respect to religion. I may add that the first idea of this fund came from a gentleman who offered to place a certain number of candidates in two schools which he himself established, and that he has since given to the charity the munificent donation of £900. My only regret is that, while we must all applaud the munificence of this gentleman, I am forbidden to mention his name. There is, however, another name with respect to which I need not be reticent, and which is well known to you all—I mean that of Sir W. Tite, who has given the large sum of £1000 to the fund. Now, I feel sure you will follow this good example, that you will support to the best of your ability this excellent charity, and that I need not urge upon you to sign freely the papers which have been placed before you. I may add that I am authorized by the Council to mention that a sum of £7000 has already been collected out of the £10,000 which are required, a result for which they beg to return their grateful thanks. But though the sum I have just named will enable them to carry out the immediate object of the fund, neither they nor any one else will have any objection to your adding considerably to that amount. I will not detain you longer, but while thanking you for your attention will again ask you to drink 'Prosperity and success to this most worthy charity.' "

The Prince of Wales then gave "Prosperity to the Royal Academy," stating that " the community at large took the greatest interest in that body of gentlemen, for to them we owe the elevated and cultivated taste with regard to painting and sculpture which now so widely prevailed in this country. The interests of the Royal Academy and of Art would, he felt sure, not suffer as long as they were confided to the care of Sir F. Grant, the distinguished President of that institution."

Sir F. Grant, in returning thanks, said the members of the Royal Academy were very glad to have it in their power to aid so excellent a charity, and that, in addition to the £500 which they had given last year to the orphanage in connection with it, they were ready to give on the present occasion a further donation of £1000. He begged, in conclusion, to propose " Prosperity to the other Art Societies." The toast was responded to by Mr. Clint, President of the Society of British Artists.

The Treasurer read a long list of subscriptions, amounting in all to £12,308, including a hundred guineas from the Royal Chairman.

ROYAL MASONIC INSTITUTION FOR GIRLS.

May 8th, 1871.

THE annual festival of the Royal Masonic Institution for Girls was held at Freemasons' Hall, Great Queen Street, on the 8th of May, 1871, His Royal Highness the Prince of Wales presiding. The whole assembly in the hall was Masonic, the ladies being limited to the gallery of the Temple. The Prince wore, besides his Royal and military Orders, the insignia of a Past Grand Master of the English craft, and around him, in full Masonic " clothing," according to their rank in the craft, were many distinguished members.

His Royal Highness the Prince of Wales, in proposing " The Queen," said :—

" The first toast which I have to give is the health of the patroness of our craft—Her Majesty the Queen, who has always identified herself so far with our Freemasonry as to extend her hand to all charities."

Sir Patrick Colquhoun, with the Grand Master's gavel, proposed the toast of " The Prince of Wales, the Princess of Wales, and the rest of the Royal Family." He referred in feeling and touching terms to the loss lately sustained by the Prince and Princess, the death of an infant son on Good Friday, April 7, and he expressed the deep thankfulness of the brotherhood that the Princess was recovering her health.

His Royal Highness the Prince of Wales, in responding for the toast, which had been received with loud applause, thanked the brethren, and said " it gave him the greatest pleasure to be there, surrounded by the brethren of the craft to which he was proud to belong. He assured them that it was a proud day indeed to him when he became a Mason, and he should always do his utmost to be a worthy brother among them. He expressed, too, on the part of the Princess, his personal thanks to Sir Patrick for his touching remarks, and his thanks to the brethren for their sympathy. He was glad to announce that the Princess was restored to her accustomed health, and in a short time would be among them. It might be fitting then to announce that the Princess had consented to be the patroness of the institution."

The toast of " Earl de Grey, the Grand Master," was then proposed by the Royal President, and Lord Clonmell proposed " The Past Grand Master, the Earl of Zetland." " The Deputy-Grand

Master's Health " was proposed by Mr. C. Sykes, M.P., who dwelt upon the great zeal and ability the Earl of Carnarvon had shown in following Masonry.

His Royal Highness the Prince of Wales, in proposing the toast of the evening, said, "in general he felt diffidence in asking for subscriptions for charities over which he sometimes presided, but he had not such a feeling on that occasion, when he looked round and saw on all sides the brethren of the craft, for he knew that one of the main principles inculcated in the minds of Free-masons was charity. He knew that the brethren composing the vast assemblage before him had come with one object, to support this excellent institution. A very full and able report had been drawn up, and therefore it was not necessary for him to address them at any length. He might say, however, that the institution was founded for the clothing, maintenance, and education of the daughters of decayed Freemasons, and it provided that the daughters of trustworthy Freemasons should not be left to the pangs of misery and ignorance. One important point was that it was supported entirely by voluntary contributions, and since its foundation in 1788 it had educated, clothed, and maintained nearly 1000 girls.

" It was specially interesting for him to be connected with that institution, as his grand-uncle, George IV., when Prince of Wales, was an earnest supporter of it, and was present at its foundation.

" It had been the great object of the committee to give the girls a good, sound, simple, and useful education—not what it had become the fashion to consider education, but an education without any 'padding.' In these days education was more thought of than it was fifty years ago, and, indeed, it was the great topic of the day. But before this time the Freemasons were among the first to set a good example, and having set this good example early, it was their duty to keep it up. The committee, in order to test the standard of education given in those schools, entered some of the names of pupils for the Cambridge Local Examinations, and, with very few exceptions, these girls so entered had passed the examinations with credit to themselves and to the institution. The institution was flourishing in every respect. During the past year 100 girls had been received into the institution, and as many had gone forth ready to take their place in the every-day life of men and women, well instructed in all the duties of the positions they would be called upon to fill.   He urged that it had become necessary to build afresh, and as he had himself found that building could not be carried out for nothing, the subscriptions of the brethren were looked for to assist the committee."

The secretary read the list of subscriptions, which included 100 guineas from His Royal Highness the Prince, and 25 guineas from the Princess, and though forty lists were not given in the subscriptions already received amounted to £5000.   On a later page will be found the record of another anniversary, when the Prince presided, and when the subscriptions were about £50,000.

The year 1888 is the centenary of the Institution, which flourishes, at St. John's Hill, Battersea Rise.   The girls are admitted at eight years of age, and maintained until sixteen. There are nearly 250 in the school.   The annual revenue, from all sources, is about £15,500.

EARLSWOOD ASYLUM FESTIVAL.

May 17th, 1871.

In the summer of 1870 the foundation-stone of a new wing to the splendid edifice of the Earlswood Asylum for Idiots, had been laid by the Prince and Princess of Wales.   The Prince further showed his interest in the institution by presiding at the anniversary festival, held at the London Tavern on the 17th of May, 1871. The Asylum, originally established at Highgate in 1847, was incorporated by Royal Charter in 1862.   Her Majesty is patroness of the charity.

On the removal of the cloth the Prince gave the toast of " Her Majesty the Queen, as the Patroness of the Institution," which was received with every mark of respect, as was also that of " The Prince and Princess of Wales, and the rest of the Royal Family," proposed by the Duke of Wellington.

His Royal Highness, in proposing the toast of " The Army, Navy, Militia, and Volunteers," expressed a hope that " the great name which the Army and Navy bore in English history would always remain unsullied in days to come. We were now at peace, thank God, but we might never know from one day to another what might occur, and, therefore, we ought always to be prepared."

Later in the evening, His Royal Highness, in proposing the toast of the evening: "Prosperity to the Earlswood Idiot Asylum," said, "he felt convinced there was no charity which had a greater demand on the public sympathy and support than it, appealing as it did on behalf of the idiot classes, afflicted by the will of Providence, and unable for the most part to help themselves. The institution was happily in a highly flourishing condition, to the great praise of those who had all along interested themselves in its prosperity. In 1853 his lamented father, who was always ready to assist the afflicted and needy, laid the foundation-stone of the present institution; in 1866 the Princess of Wales and himself interested themselves in a bazaar for raising funds for the erection of a new wing to the building, and in 1869 Her Royal Highness and himself inaugurated that new wing.

"It was a matter of satisfaction to his family and himself that they had connected themselves with an institution which aimed at so much practical good, and which was now in so flourishing a state. It was in 1847 that the late Dr. Reed brought the state of the idiot portion of the community under public notice; and from that time to this much had been done to ameliorate the condition of that most unfortunate class of our fellow creatures. Although the cases were comparatively rare in which cures had been made, still cures had been effected, and practical experience had shown that the mental state of those unfortunate beings was susceptible of manifest improvement by the exercise of care and attention well directed by intelligent and experienced persons. Many of them were taught music, and others some trade or handicraft, and in that way their hands and minds were occupied. There were cases in which patients so engaged had improved so much as to be able to return to their families, and afterwards to follow a trade which they had learnt in the institution. The Institution had been very highly praised by the Lunacy Commissioners, and he might remind the company that it was supported by voluntary contributions. This year, he believed, the contributions had exceeded those of any previous one, but an infirmary had become

necessary, although no epidemic had hitherto occurred in the
asylum; and as that would go far to exhaust the funds, he
called upon the company to do their utmost to replenish them.
His Royal Highness made a passing allusion, by way of example,
to the fact that an anonymous benefactor had thrice contributed
the sum of £1000 to the treasury of the institution, and in
conclusion he earnestly appealed to the audience to do what in
them lay towards the relief of that grievously afflicted class of
their fellow creatures."

At the close of the festival Mr. William Nicholas, the secretary,
announced that the subscriptions in the course of the evening
amounted in all to £4197 odd, including a sum of 100 guineas,
under initials, which left no doubt that it was a donation by His
Royal Highness the Chairman.

HOMES FOR LITTLE BOYS.

June 2nd, 1871.

AMONG the many institutions for homeless and orphan boys, the
Cottage Homes at Farningham are less heard of than some others
which make more clamorous appeals to the public. But they have
for many years been the scene of useful and beneficent work, and
deserve larger support. At Farningham there are 300 little boys,
homeless, and in danger of falling into evil ways, who are clothed,
fed, educated, and taught some trade by which they can earn
their own living. They are then provided with outfit, and placed
in situations, where they are looked after as Old Boys. This is a
charity which was certain to awaken the sympathy and receive
the support of the Prince of Wales, when brought under his
notice.

On the 2nd of June, 1871, His Royal Highness presided at a
festival at the Freemasons' Hall for the benefit of the charity.
He had already with the Princess of Wales visited the Homes at
Farningham, and then laid the foundation-stone of the new
buildings there. At the festival dinner, in giving the toast,
"Prosperity to the Home for Little Boys," the following is the
substance of what the Prince said :—

"The object of the promoters of this excellent charity had
been to take from the highways of this vast Metropolis those
unfortunate little beings who had been deprived of their parents,
or who had no homes, and to clothe, feed, educate, and train
them so that they might be enabled to go forth into the world

with a knowledge of some trade, and qualified, when they left this admirable home, to earn their living, by being removed from the temptations to crime, incident to the state of destitution in which they were found. What could be more dreadful than to see from day to day those wretched miserable little children, who swarmed in our streets, who knew as little as we did how or where they could live, or who were their parents and natural protectors ?

" It must be felt, then, to be the duty of every good Christian to endeavour to ameliorate the condition of that class of our fellow-creatures. He could speak from experience of the good that had been done by this charity, because he had, with the Princess, visited the institution. The asylum was erected about seven years ago near Tottenham, but as it was thought desirable to move further into the country, about 90 acres of ground were purchased near Farningham, in Kent, and the homes were established there. He then described the education received by the boys, their excellent schooling in such subjects as arithmetic and geography, besides the industrial training, which was a special feature of the institution. He found that they were taught to make clothes, boots, mats, &c. ; there was a carpenters' shop and a painters' shop, and a paper-bag shop; they had a printing establishment, a laundry, a bakehouse, a garden, a farm, and there were means for teaching the pupils a great variety of other useful occupations, so that they might go forth good and honest young men, capable of gaining their own livelihood, instead of returning to those haunts of vice from which they had been snatched. The cost of the homes was about £9000 a year, but he was sorry to say the institution was still about £5000 in debt. Mentioning the munificent donation of £1000, which had recently been received from some anonymous benefactor, His Royal Highness concluded, amid prolonged cheers, by urging those present to contribute liberally, and to try to persuade others to support this excellent institution, and so to rescue as many as possible of the poor little suffering children of the country, who had neither father nor mother living, from wretchedness and crime."

A list of subscriptions and donations during the dinner was read, amounting to the sum of £3464, including £1000 obtained from friends by Mr. Robert Hanbury, then the President of the institution, and £150 from the Royal Chairman.

Besides the Cottage Homes at Farningham, there are Orphan Homes at Swanley, where 200 orphan or fatherless boys are maintained, and receive technical education in various arts and industries, to fit them for a working life.

THE ROYAL CALEDONIAN ASYLUM.

June 28th, 1871.

THE 56th anniversary festival of this institution was held on the 28th of June, 1871, at the Freemasons' Tavern, under the presidency of the Prince of Wales, who wore the Highland costume, supported by Prince Arthur and the Duke of Cambridge. About 350 sat down to dinner, a large proportion being dressed in full Highland costume, among whom were the Duke of Buccleuch, K.G., President; the Duke of Richmond, K.G.; the Marquis of Lorne, M.P.; the Marquis of Huntly, the Earl of Fife, the Earl of Mar, and the Earl of March.

His Royal Highness the Chairman, in proposing the toast of "Her Majesty the Queen," alluded to the fact that Her Majesty was the patroness of this institution, in which she had always taken the warmest interest.

The Duke of Buccleuch proposed "The health of His Royal Highness the Chairman, the Princess of Wales, and the rest of the Royal Family." Since the foundation of this institution in 1815 the Royal Family had always responded most generously to every appeal that had been made to them on its behalf, and he trusted that in consequence of the presence of His Royal Highness on that occasion the funds of the charity would be considerably increased. He reminded his audience that among his other titles His Royal Highness possessed that of the Duke of Rothesay.

The toast was received with Highland honours, followed by the breaking of the glasses from which it had been drunk. The Gaelic verses timing the cheers were recited by Mr. Donald Mackenzie.

His Royal Highness the Chairman "expressed his sincere thanks at the enthusiastic reception which had been given to the toast, and his gratification that it had been drunk with Highland honours. He was very sensible of the kindness of the feeling that had prompted the latter act, and he begged to be regarded on that occasion rather as the Duke of Rothesay than as the Prince of Wales. This excellent institution had

been associated for so many years past with various members of
his family that he was rejoiced to be able to be there that night
to plead in its favour."

His Royal Highness in proposing " The Army, the Navy, and
the Reserve Forces," took occasion to refer to the changes that
were about to be effected in the organization of the army, and
" expressed a hope that those changes, whatever they might be,
would place the safety of the country upon a secure foundation,
and would enable us to prove that the author of the well-known
Battle of Dorking was a false prophet. The writer of that
interesting production, however, deserved our thanks, inasmuch
as he had pointed out to us the danger of being 'caught
napping.' He begged to couple with the toast the name of his
Royal Highness the Duke of Cambridge, who had already acted
as chairman of the festivals of the charity, of Sir A. Milne, and
of Colonel Loyd Lindsay, who had given such an impetus to the
Volunteer movement, and who had taken such an active part in
promoting the fund for the relief of the sick and wounded during
the late war."

His Royal Highness in proposing the toast of the evening,
" Prosperity to the Royal Caledonian Asylum," referred to " the
objects of the institution which is for supporting and educating
the children of soldiers, sailors, and marines, natives of Scotland,
who have died or been disabled in the service of their country,
and of indigent Scotch parents resident in London. The charity
had been founded in 1815, a memorable year for this country,
and from that time until his death his lamented grandfather had
presided over its interests. For his own part he could only
express the satisfaction he felt at being connected with an
institution which had received the patronage of Royalty for so
long a period. On the occasion when his grandfather had presided at one of the festivals of the institution a large sum of
money was subscribed for its support, and he trusted on that
occasion its funds would be considerably increased, so as to
enable the thirty vacancies to be filled up, in addition to providing board, lodging, clothing, and education for the 110 boys
and girls now received within the building. The children were
given a thoroughly sound education, and many of those who had
been brought up in the establishment had subsequently dis-

tinguished themselves in the Army, the Navy, and the Law. This charity, which was entirely supported by voluntary contributions, was the only one in London intended solely for the children of Scotch parents, and, therefore, he called upon all Scotchmen to contribute liberally in aid of its funds. It conferred much happiness upon our soldiers and sailors that they were able to feel assured that in the event of their death in action their children would be brought up in decency and comfort, and that they would not be allowed to fall victims to want and sin."

The toast was drunk with three times three. His Royal Highness the Chairman then briefly proposed "The Health of his Grace the Duke of Buccleuch, the President of the Institution," to which his Grace responded.

The donations announced amounted to about £2000.

During the course of the evening, the children, headed by their pipers, marched round the room.

DUBLIN AGRICULTURAL SHOW.

August 1st, 1871.

THE Royal Agricultural Society, of which the Prince of Wales is President, held its annual meeting at Dublin in 1871. The occasion was taken for a royal visit to Ireland. The Prince of Wales was accompanied by the Princess Louise, the Marquis of Lorne, and his young brother, Prince Arthur, better known in after years as the Duke of Connaught. Of all the Royal family, this son of the Queen has special relation to Ireland. One of his names he bears after the great Duke of Wellington, Arthur Wellesley, an Irishman; another of his names is after an Irish saint, and he sits in the House of Lords by an Irish title. Born in May 1850, Arthur Patrick was only a little past coming of age at this time.

The warm-hearted Irish people gave the royal Princes a truly cordial welcome. On arriving at Dublin, there was not merely official display, but the popular reception was not only friendly but enthusiastic. Flags waved everywhere, and as it was late in the evening, the city was illuminated, and *Cead mille failthe* shone out in conspicuous brilliancy. From a few knots of Fenians there were heard slight sounds of hissing, but any hostile feeling was overborne by the general rejoicing.

When the train from Kingstown arrived at Westland Row Terminus, the Lord Mayor and Corporation met the Royal visitors, and the Town Clerk read an address to which the Prince made an appropriate reply.

On the next day, August 1st, the royal visitors, having witnessed a cricket match in College Park, and had luncheon with the officers of the Grenadier Guards, went to the Show-yard in the afternoon. The Prince of Wales proceeded to the Council-room, and signed the minutes of the last meeting, in the capacity of President of the Council. The inspection of the horses, cattle, and sheep was then made. Among the awards, made by the judges of the Show in the forenoon, was a prize for the best pen of shearling ewes, exhibited by His Royal Highness.

The annual banquet was given in the evening at the Exhibition Palace. It was a brilliant and successful affair. About 450 guests were present, and the galleries were thronged with ladies. When the Prince entered and took his place at the head of the table there was tumultuous applause. After dinner the Prince rose and said :—

"My Lords and Gentlemen,—The first toast which I have the honour of proposing to you this evening is one which I am sure will be heartily received by you. It is 'The Health of Her Majesty the Queen.' In proposing this toast I am convinced that the Queen has a part in the best wishes of the Irish people. Although, unfortunately, some time has elapsed since she has been over in Ireland, still I hope the day will yet come when she may again come over. I am also convinced that the reception she has met on former occasions she will meet with again. I will not add more, but ask you to drink the health of Her Majesty the Queen."

The toast was drunk with loyal fervour. After a short interval the Prince of Wales again rose and said :—

"My Lords and Gentlemen,—I have some slight difficulty in proposing the next toast, because it relates to members of my own family ; still, as it is on the list before me, I propose 'The Health of the rest of the Royal Family.' I am sure that it has been the wish of my brothers not to be useless appendages of the State, but to do all they can to serve their country. My brother, the Duke of Edinburgh, as you are aware, has for some time past been in the Royal Navy, and has had the advantage of seeing many countries, and I may say of twice sailing round the world. On my left is my brother who is serving in the Army, and who responds to this toast. I trust that he has also a bright career before him. He has some slight claim upon you, gentlemen, as he bears the name of Patrick. Without saying more, I beg you to drink the health of the rest of the Royal Family, coupled with the name of Prince Arthur."

His Royal Highness Prince Arthur, on rising to respond to the toast, was received with loud cheers, renewed during the short but effective and well delivered speech, in which he referred to a former visit to Ireland, when he was received with much kindness and cordiality. "That visit was certainly but a short one, but it was long enough to enable me to see a good deal of the country, and to inspire in me a lasting interest in all that concerns the welfare of Ireland."

The Prince of Wales, in proposing the next toast, said :—

"Ladies and Gentlemen,—It is now my pleasing duty to propose 'The Health of His Excellency the Lord-Lieutenant, and Prosperity to Ireland.' Nothing could give me greater pleasure than having the honour of proposing this toast. I am convinced that all the Lords-Lieutenant that come over to Ireland do their utmost to fulfil their duties, and sometimes they are very arduous ones, and I feel convinced that his Excellency on my right has the goodwill of the country. The theme before me—Prosperity to Ireland—is one that might be enlarged upon greatly. Nobody wishes more sincerely than I do prosperity to this country. No one in the large assemblage which crowds this hall, and no one outside this hall, could more largely wish for the prosperity of Ireland which was so dear to them. I think I may say without fear of contradiction, that at the present moment Ireland is rich and prosperous. There has been a great decrease of pauperism and of crime, and I may say that what will do more than anything else towards making a country prosperous is the extension of its agriculture. It was with great pleasure that I accepted the position of President of the Royal Agricultural Society, and it afforded me great pleasure to be present for a short time at the Show to-day. My brother has already alluded in his speech to the fine animals we saw, and I may add that I feel sure that in no other part of the United Kingdom could a more creditable Show be held than that which was opened near Dublin this morning. During the last four years there has been a great improvement in every respect in the shows of the Royal Agricultural Societies. I believe I am not wrong in stating that in 1867 the entries in the department of horses numbered 257, and now, on this occasion, they are but one short of 600. That alone shows the interest which all classes of the community take in these Shows, and how anxious each one is to do all in his power to promote the object it has in view."

Alluding to the interest which the Earl of Pembroke had shown in the welfare of the country, and his liberality in granting a site for the Showyard, His Royal Highness said :—

"I am assured that if the many gentlemen and landlords who very often find some difficulty in leaving England, but who have large interests and large estates in this country, could contrive to come over here more frequently, it would do more good than anything else I could imagine. I am certain that they are anxious to come over, and that their relations with their tenantry and those around them should be in every respect good. I may also here refer to the great improvement made in the erection of farm buildings and cottages. Beyond doubt there has been progress in the direction of improvement there; but still I believe much yet remains to be done. Everything depends upon the well-being of the people, and if they are properly lodged it tends to cleanliness, and very possibly to moral advantage. Perhaps I may be allowed to speak of a slight personal experience in that matter. I have a small estate in Norfolk, and observed myself the greatest importance of providing suitable small cottages for those resident there, and, having done so, now reap immense advantage. I am sure that this is a question which belongs in itself to the well-being of Irish agriculture, and which will accordingly receive the best consideration of this society. There are many other topics upon which I might enlarge, but as there are still many toasts to be proposed and responded to, time will not permit. Besides, as you are aware, the excellent society under whose auspices we are assembled, while endeavouring to do as much good as possible, has no political connection whatever. You will, therefore, I am sure, forgive me if I do not enlarge more fully on other topics which might have some political bearing. I give you 'The Health of his Excellency the Lord-Lieutenant, and Prosperity to Ireland.'"

The Lord-Lieutenant, Earl Spencer, in responding, said that since they last met there had been much prosperity in the country.

It was a happy thing that they were able to mark this. The calling out of the Irish Militia had tended to encourage the confidence and loyalty of the people. His Excellency hoped that the improved relations established by recent legislation between landlord and tenant would have beneficial effects.

His Excellency then proposed "The Health of the Prince of Wales," who responded, and after several other toasts the party separated.

The Royal visitors, accompanied by the Countess Spencer and the Princess Louise, afterwards proceeded to the Lady Mayoress's ball at the Mansion House. The city was brilliantly illuminated at night.

The enthusiastic reception of the Royal Princes, and the success of this visit to Ireland gave much public satisfaction at the time, and is regarded with interest now, in the light of subsequent events. There had been some misgivings, lest the Prince might meet with an uncourteous or at least a cold and uncordial reception. But this had never been the way of Irishmen, even under what might seem unpropitious conditions. The most loyal and enthusiastic greeting ever given to a Sovereign, was that which welcomed the Queen in 1849, just after the treason of Mr. Smith O'Brien, and at the close of a long period of agitation. Still more remarkable was the welcome given to George IV. in 1821. There were neither personal nor political reasons for expecting much enthusiasm on that occasion. It was well known that the new king, like his father before him, and the brother who then stood next to the throne, were determined opponents of Catholic Emancipation. But no sooner had this king set foot on Irish soil, and left the name of Kingstown to the place where he landed, than every political grievance, penal laws and Protestant ascendency, were all for the time forgotten. The truth is that whatever agitation may be at the surface, the masses of the Irish nation, like the deep waters of the ocean, are not so disturbed as to move them to disaffection or disloyalty. There was no Irishman more loyal than Daniel O'Connell, and many of the Home Rulers of our own day are not less loyal to the British Crown. There is no fear of the Queen or any of her children being received by the mass of the Irish people without demonstrations of joy. Rather the complaint is that Ireland has so much less of the Royal sunshine than Scotland enjoys, and it might be well if the sister island became the permanent residence of a member of the reigning House.

Such thoughts have no bearing on party politics, but are naturally suggested in remembering the reception given in 1871 to the heir to the British Crown.

A succession of engagements and of entertainments took place, as on the visit of the Prince and Princess of Wales in 1868. The military display in the Phœnix Park was even more brilliant than on that occasion. One notable incident in 1871 was the installation, with great ceremony, of His Royal Highness as Grand Patron of the Masonic Institution in Ireland. A formal address of welcome having been read, His Royal Highness made the following reply :—

"Most Worshipful Sir and Brethren,—I thank you very much for your cordial and grateful address, and for the kind sentiments expressed in it towards myself. It was a source of considerable satisfaction to me when I was elected a member of the craft, and I think I may without presumption point to the different Masonic meetings which, since my initiation, I have fraternally attended. As a proof of the interest I take in all that relates to Freemasonry, I can assure you that it has afforded me great gratification to become the Patron of the Most Ancient and Honourable Society of Free and Accepted Masons in Ireland, and that an opportunity has been given to me by my visit to Ireland of being installed here to-day."

The Grand Master then clothed His Royal Highness with the collar, apron, and jewel, as Patron. The Brethren then, according to ancient custom, saluted the Prince as Patron of the Order in Ireland, the Grand Master himself giving the word. His Royal Highness then said :—

"Most Worshipful Sir and Brethren,—I have now to thank you heartily and cordially for your fraternal reception, and for the honour you have done me, and I beg to assure you of the pleasure I feel on having been invited to become the Patron of the Order of Freemasons in Ireland. It is a source of considerable satisfaction to me to know that my visit to this country has afforded this opportunity of meeting you, Brethren, in Lodge, and so interchanging these frank and hearty greetings. It is true I have not been a Mason very long. I was initiated, as you perhaps know, in London, a few years ago, after which I visited the Grand Original Lodge of Denmark, and a short time afterwards I had the signal satisfaction of being elected a Past Grand Master of the United Grand Lodge of England. Last year I had the honour of being elected Patron of the Order in Scotland; and, Brethren, though last, not least, comes the special honour you have conferred on me. I thank you for it from the bottom of my heart. I may, I think, refer with some pride to the number of Masonic meetings I have attended in England since my initiation as a proof of my deep attachment to your Order. I know, we all know, how good and holy a thing Freemasonry is, how excellent are its principles, and how perfect the doctrine it sets forth; but forgive me if I remind you that some of our friends outside are not as well acquainted with its merits as we are ourselves, and that a most mistaken idea prevails in some minds that, because we are a secret society, we meet for political purposes, or have a political bias in what we do. I am delighted, Brethren, to have this opportunity of proclaiming what I am satisfied you will agree with me in—that we have as Masons no politics; that the great object of our Order is to strengthen the bonds of fraternal affection, and to make us live in pure and Christian love with all men; that though a secret we are not a political body; and that our Masonic principles and hopes are essential parts of our attachment to the Constitution and loyalty to the Crown."

His Royal Highness's address was received with great applause. The Lodge was then closed in due form.

THE ILLNESS OF DECEMBER, 1871.

How much the Prince of Wales had endeared himself to all classes in the nation was attested by the deep anxiety and the universal sorrow when he was struck down with illness in December, 1871. Those who remember that time, can tell how, for some weeks, all thoughts were turned to the chamber of sickness at Sandringham; with what earnest anxiety the daily bulletins were looked for; and with what fervent devotion the prayers of millions ascended to the throne of grace. The "dark December" of 1861, when the good Prince Consort lay on his deathbed, increased the ominous foreboding. Touching incidents of that critical period are still told. The watchful attendance of the Princess of Wales was illustrated in no way more strikingly than in the anecdote of her request to the clergyman at Sandringham to alter the order of the morning service so as to let her, after joining in the public prayer for recovery, hasten back to her husband's side. We remember, too, the affectionate anxiety of the royal mother, and brothers and sisters; and how the Prince himself, when he recovered consciousness, asked thoughtfully about the condition of the servant, who died of the same fever which nearly proved fatal to his master.

Had the Prince been "taken" at this period of his life, history would have recorded the loss in terms of tender regret, such as had been, more than once, felt towards Princes of Wales who died before coming to the throne. The eldest son of James I., for instance, was long remembered with deepest sorrow, so much was he loved, and so large the hopes of the nation which had been centered in him. Had our Prince been lost in that illness, there would have been another instance of what inspired one of the noblest of all passages in classic literature, the " *Tu Marcellus eris* " of Virgil. Happily it was otherwise ordained, and the enthusiasm of joyful thankfulness at the recovery of the Prince was as truly national as had been the anxiety and grief at his illness. The special Thanksgiving Collect, written by the Archbishop of Canterbury, expressed well the universal feeling of the nation :—

" O Father of mercies and God of all comfort, we thank Thee that Thou hast heard the prayers of this nation in the day of our trial. We praise and magnify Thy glorious name for that Thou hast raised Thy servant Albert Edward Prince of Wales from the bed of sickness. Thou castest down and Thou liftest up, and health and strength are Thy gifts. We pray Thee to perfect the recovery of Thy servant, and to crown him day by day with more abundant blessings both for body and soul; through Jesus Christ our Lord. Amen."

When the Thanksgiving day was proclaimed, it was still doubtful whether the Prince himself would be allowed by his medical attendants to risk the winter journey for Osborne, along with the Queen. But his own desire to be present nerved him for the effort, and he obtained the assent of Sir James Paget, who had gone specially to give his opinion.

The danger had increased in the end of November and the first weeks of December. The first hopeful announcement was made on December 17th, and on January 3rd convalescence had decidedly begun. A public thanksgiving service was proclaimed for the 21st of January. On February 22nd the Letter of the Queen to the nation was published, and then followed the National Thanksgiving Service in St. Paul's on the 27th.

With regard to the Royal procession, and the display inside the Cathedral, the scene was far less imposing than on that famous day, the 23rd of April, 1789, when King George III. and Queen Charlotte went to St. Paul's to return public thanks for His Majesty's restoration to health. On that occasion there was more of heraldic pageantry, and more of official display, than accords with modern usage. But everything was done to make this assemblage as far as possible representative of all classes in social and public life. Not fewer than 13,000 persons had places allocated to them in the Cathedral. In the *Times* of Wednesday, February 28th, a full classified list of the ticket-holders will be found. About 300 Mayors and Provosts from all parts of the kingdom had places. There were 560 places for representatives of the Army and Navy. The Peers and Commons had 885 tickets for each house. The Dean of St. Paul's had nearly 1300 tickets at his disposal. The Corps Diplomatique, " distinguished foreigners," London School

Board, the Board of Works, Learned Societies, Nonconformists, and numerous other bodies figure in the catalogue. The wearers of uniform and official dress, besides the gaudy civic corporations, gave variety to the scene. The Judges, English, Scotch, and Irish, with robes and wigs, gave warm tone to the Law corner. Special state chairs were occupied by the Lord Chancellor and the Speaker, representing Parliament. The Press had 80 places, and the " General Public" made up the number 12,480 tickets—those who took part in the procession—the stewards, police, firemen, and the officials bringing up the total to about 13,000.

The crowds lining the streets, for about seven miles along which the procession passed, were innumerable; and every window and coign of vantage, with numerous scaffoldings along the line, appeared filled with spectators. Not even when the Princess of Wales entered London was there such a dense multitude seen, and it is only on rare occasions that one can see " all London in the streets." In our time we can remember some such occasions— the funeral of the Duke of Wellington, the reception of the Princess of Wales, and the entrance of Garibaldi, being among them.

It was not in the Metropolis alone, that the rejoicing was universal. Every city and town had its festivities, and its services of thanksgiving in Church and Chapel. Addresses came, by hundreds, from all quarters, and the announcement was made of holiday gatherings, of crowded meetings, of illuminations, and every form of public rejoicing. The telegraph flashed news of similar excitement throughout the whole of the Empire; and religious services were held wherever Englishmen are found on the Continent, in the Colonies, and in India. If ever a rejoicing could be called national and imperial, it was this, on the Thanksgiving Day for the recovery of the Prince of Wales.

The service commenced with the *Te Deum*, composed expressly for the occasion by Dr. Goss. The music of the anthem, from the words of Psalm 118th, verses 14–21, and 28, was by the same composer. Among other musical pieces was the choral hymn, " Gotha," by the Prince Consort. The whole of the service, devotional and musical, was most impressive, and the special prayers and thanksgivings were joined in by the vast congregation with devoutest feeling. It was noted by one who was present, with regard to the familiar " General Thanksgiving," that " the sublimity of the service culminated, and reached its highest and intensest expression, during the silent pause which followed the inserted words : " Particularly to Albert Edward, Prince of Wales, who desires now to offer up his praises and thanksgiving for Thy late mercies vouchsafed to him." The famous words which close the poem of the Seasons : " Come then expressive silence muse His praise," could be well understood in that perfect pause of a few moments, almost awful in its intensity, in the service at St. Paul's Cathedral. When the anthem had been sung, the Archbishop of Canterbury gave a short sermon or address, from Romans xii. 5 :

"Every one members one of another." This was followed by the special Thanksgiving Hymn, written by the Rev. J. S. Stone, author of "The Church's one foundation," and "Sonnets of the Sacred year." It was sung to the good and familiar tune *Aurelia*, by Dr. S. Wesley. Then the Archbishop pronounced the benediction. When the organ sounded the grand notes of the National Anthem, Her Majesty came forward and bowed twice, and the Prince bowed also. The organ continued to play variations of the anthem as the Royal procession moved down the nave. Thus ended this grand and joyful service, which will be remembered in English history.

Altogether it is with the utmost gratification we can look back upon that memorable 27th of February. A demonstration more general and spontaneous has not been recorded even in the annals of this loyal nation. Among high and low, rich and poor, there was one harmonious spirit of thankful joy, in regard to the recovery of the Prince. But apart from the special and personal aspect of the occasion, there was much to cause national gratulation. The combined feeling of religion and of loyalty showed that in this England of ours, the divine precepts : "Fear God, Honour the King," are as inseparable as they are powerful, and that their influence pervades the nation, when circumstances call them into exercise.

The words of the "Thanksgiving Hymn" well express the sentiment of the whole service of the day :—

> "O Thou our soul's salvation !
> Our Hope for earthly weal !
> We, who in tribulation
> Did for Thy mercy kneel,
> Lift up glad hearts before Thee,
> And eyes no longer dim,
> And for Thy grace adore Thee
> In eucharistic hymn.

> "Forth went the nation weeping
> With precious seed of prayer,
> Hope's awful vigil keeping
> 'Mid rumours of despair;
> Then did Thy love deliver !
> And from Thy gracious hand,
> Joy, like the southern river,
> O'erflowed the weary land.

> "Bless Thou our adoration !
> Our gladness sanctify !
> Make this rejoicing nation
> To Thee by joy more nigh;

K 2

O be this great Thanksgiving
   Throughout the land we raise,
Wrought into holier living
   In all our after days!

" Bless, Father, him Thou gavest
   Back to the loyal land,
O Saviour, him Thou savest,
   Still cover with Thine Hand :
O Spirit, the Defender,
   Be his to guard and guide,
Now in life's midday splendour
   On to the eventide ! "

What may be the depth of the duration of the feelings thus
alluded to, it it not for man to judge ; but it is not as mere forms,
that in tens of thousands of churches there are still uttered, week
by week and day by day, prayers for the Queen, and for the Prince
and Princess of Wales,—expressing the faith, and the goodwill,
and the loyalty, of the people of this empire, as truly and heartily
as on that special thanksgiving day in St. Paul's.

NORFOLK AGRICULTURAL SOCIETY.

June 19th, 1872.

THE loyal people of King's Lynn and its neighbourhood retained
pleasant remembrance of the festival time when, in 1869, the
Prince and Princess of Wales came to open the new Alexandra
Dock.   In 1872 they were gladdened by the announcement that
the Royal visitors were again coming from Sandringham, on the
19th June, to visit their ancient town, at the annual exhibition of
the Norfolk Agricultural Society. At the east gate of Lynn the
Royal carriage was met by the Mayor, who, with the Town Clerk,
and two leading citizens, asked permission to conduct the Prince
and Princess through the town.   The Earl of Leicester and Lord
Sondes were in the Royal carriage, a third carriage containing Lord
Sheffield and Lady Anne Coke. At the entrance of the Show, an
address was read, from the Norfolk Agricultural Association, to
which the Prince made the following reply :—

"Gentlemen,—I thank you sincerely for this address. It
has been a source of the greatest gratification to have had it in
my power to contribute in any degree to the success of your
association and to promote the interests of agriculture in
Norfolk. It is with these feelings that I have endeavoured to

make myself acquainted with some of the operations of farming, and to acquire some knowledge of stock, and if I have not always been successful in the path of competition, I have at least obtained prizes sufficient to encourage me to persevere, and to indulge in the hope that I shall obtain more. The Princess is always willing to come among you,—and to be present on occasions like the present. We both desire to take this opportunity of expressing the deep sense we entertain of the sympathy and interest which were manifested towards us in our late trials by yourselves and by every class in the county of Norfolk."

Then followed the inspection of the Show, and the parade of the prize animals before the Grand Stand. The Prince was a successful exhibitor, having taken a second prize in Shorthorn heifers, a second prize in the class of ponies not above thirteen hands high, a first prize for the best Southdown ram, the second prize in Southdown ewe lambs, a second prize for ten wether lambs, two prizes (second and third) in the class of Norfolk and Suffolk red-polled cattle.

In the afternoon at a banquet attended by a large number of guests, the Prince took the chair, with the Princess of Wales on his right. Grace having been said by the Bishop of Norwich, the toast of " The Queen " was received with enthusiasm, and the Earl of Leicester then gave " The Health of the Prince and Princess of Wales, and the rest of the Royal Family." He tendered the thanks of the society to the Prince of Wales for the aid which he had extended to agriculture, for his liberal assistance to the local charities, for the interest which he had displayed in county affairs, and, last but not least, for his support to the fox-hounds. The society was also still more indebted to Her Royal Highness the Princess of Wales for her gracious presence that evening. Ladies ought always to interest themselves in their husbands' pursuits, and he believed that agriculture came quite within their province. The Earl next alluded to the illness of the Prince of Wales in December last, and expressed his hope that His Royal Highness's life might long be spared, as it would be devoted to the welfare of the people of England, and the promotion of all that was good and noble. The toast was drunk with rounds of cheering, renewed when the Prince rose to reply.

His Royal Highness said that " he and the Princess were deeply thankful for the reception which they had experienced during the day. He was very glad that it had been in his power to fulfil the promise which he gave some time since that he would preside over the meeting. It had been a success, and

he should ever esteem it a high compliment to have been associated with it.   During the ten years in which he had lived in
Norfolk, he had endeavoured not to lag behind those other
county landlords who so ably fulfilled their duties.   It would
always be his earnest endeavour to promote the welfare of the
county, in which he was much interested.   He had to thank
the meeting for the kind reception which the Princess of Wales
always experienced whenever she appeared in public.   It was
most desirable that ladies should associate themselves in their
husbands' pursuits, and when the Princess did not accompany
him he always felt that there was something wanting.   With
regard to his illness, he should never forget the sympathy which
had been extended towards him.   He accepted that sympathy
as a token of the feeling of this great and enlightened country
towards himself and the Princess, the Queen, his mother, and
the Monarchical system which we had adopted."

After acknowledgment had been made by Lord Leicester, for
the toast of the Lord-Lieutenant of the county, and the Bishop
had responded for the Clergy, the Prince rose to give what he
called the toast of the evening : "Prosperity to the Norfolk
Agricultural Association."

His Royal Highness traced "the progress of the society and
especially the rapid advance which it had made since it adopted
the principle of holding its Shows periodically in all the towns
of the county, instead of limiting its meetings to Norwich and
Swaffham only.   At the present Show there were sixty more
stock entries and one hundred more implements.   Norfolk had
always been held up as a great agricultural county, and was
the home of the great nobleman, better known as 'Coke of
Norfolk.'   The fame of Coke of Norfolk had not been forgotten
by his son, the present Earl of Leicester.   The county was a
great cattle-breeding county, the home of such men as Lord
Sondes, Mr. Brown, Mr. Aylmer, and Mr. Overman.   One other
great Norfolk breeder, the late Lord Walsingham, had passed
away, but he trusted that the present Lord Walsingham would
continue to maintain the reputation of the Merton flock.

" His Royal Highness expressed his own great personal interest
in the Society and in the cause of agriculture generally.   His
late father, the Prince Consort, always felt the greatest interest

in agriculture, and used to take his children to inspect his prize animals. It might be desirable to increase the area of the Society on the model of the Bath and West of England Society, by bringing in Suffolk, Cambridgeshire, and Essex. For his own part, he supported such an extension of the Society. A landlord ought to feel a pride in having the working classes properly housed on his estate. Those who worked from morning to night should find a comfortable house, which would promote their moral and social wellbeing. He had endeavoured to improve the cottages on his own estate, and he felt pride and satisfaction in having his workmen properly housed. In conclusion, His Royal Highness strongly supported the idea of having a great county school for Norfolk, and said it would give him the greatest pleasure to support the enterprise."

After various other toasts, the last being "The Ladies," proposed by the Royal chairman, the Prince and Princess returned to Sandringham.

AT GREAT YARMOUTH.

July 5th, 1872.

THE Prince of Wales visited Yarmouth on Thursday, the 5th of July, 1872, and remained till Saturday as the guest of Mr. Cuddon at Shadingfield-lodge. The object of the visit was to open the New Grammar School, and more especially the official inspection of the Norfolk Artillery Militia, of which the Prince is Honorary Colonel. The good people of Yarmouth, however, were resolved to make the visit a general holiday, and great preparations were made for giving a loyal and enthusiastic reception. The town was gay with decorations, and the passage through the streets was like a triumphal procession. In replying to the Address of the Mayor and Corporation, the Prince said :—

"It was most gratifying to me to receive in February last the congratulations you offered me on my recovery from illness, and my gratification is increased at having it now in my power to thank you personally for your kindness and sympathy."

Reference was made to the same subject, in a feeling speech, in which the Prince responded to the toast of his health, at a banquet given by the Mayor :—

"Allow me to thank you, Mr. Mayor, for the very kind and touching manner in which you have proposed my health, and to return you all my sincere thanks for the cordial manner in which you have drunk it. I assure you it gives me more than ordinary pleasure to be here to-day. This is the first occasion since my return from abroad that I have met with an official reception, and my pleasure is increased from the fact that I regard myself as a Norfolk man. I have also to acknowledge the very high honour conferred upon me last year in my having been appointed Honorary Colonel of the Norfolk Militia Artillery, and to say how glad I am to find on coming to inspect them that they have their head-quarters at Yarmouth, for although my residence is not very near you, still you will believe me when I assure you that I entertain the same sentiments with regard to your borough of Great Yarmouth as I do towards Lynn, and all the other towns of Norfolk. I have also again to thank you for your sympathy during my illness. It is difficult for me now to speak upon that subject, but as it has pleased Almighty God to preserve me to my country I hope I may not be ungrateful for the feeling which has been shown towards me, and that I may do all that I can to be of use to my countrymen. I will not detain you much longer, but before sitting down it affords me great pleasure to propose to you a toast which I am sure you will all drink most heartily, and that is the health of the Mayor. I regard him as the representative of the people of Yarmouth, and tender to him my warmest thanks for the cordial and impressive welcome I have received. I feel convinced that, although my stay among you will unfortunately be short, it will be agreeable ; and I trust that the sun which shines so brilliantly at present will continue to favour us during the next two days."

His Royal Highness was loudly cheered throughout his speech, especially upon his declaration that he was a Norfolk man, and still more so upon referring to his recovery.

The Mayor having responded, the Prince rose and proceeded to his carriage, and drove at a slow pace by a circuitous route through the town and along the Marine Parade to the Grammar School. Here he was received by the Head Master, and an Address was presented by Sir Edmond Lacon, Chairman of the Trustees of the School, to which the Prince replied :—

" I thank you sincerely for the expressions of your kind feeling at my recovery. It is a source of the greatest satisfaction to me to have an opportunity of assisting, in whatever form it may be, in the great work of education. It is gratifying to see the schools of Edward VI. revived and devoted to the purpose for which they were founded, and those who are actively engaged in the work deserve the hearty thanks of the people to whom they extend the benefit which a practical religious education always confers. Success tells its own tale, and the numbers of the boys present in the school, together with those whom you expect to be added to it, enable me to congratulate the people of Yarmouth on your having revived an institution so calculated to promote their best interests."

His Royal Highness then declared the school open, and, with the permission of the authorities, prayed that the boys be granted an extra week's holiday at Midsummer in remembrance of his visit.

On the next day the Prince made the official inspection of the Artillery ; afterwards dining with the officers of his regiment.

THE Prince of Wales being Colonel of the Norfolk Artillery Militia, has occasion to visit Great Yarmouth more frequently than he might otherwise do. At the time of the inspection in 1887, advantage was taken of his presence for laying the foundation of the new hospital, the old one having been in use since 1838, and being too small, and unsuitable for the increased requirements of the borough. The foundation stone of the new edifice was laid with masonic ceremony on the 18th of May, 1887. The Prince was accompanied by Lord Charles Beresford, and a large muster of the brethren of the Craft assembled to meet the Grand Master. An imposing procession proceeded from the Town Hall to the site of the Hospital. The crowds in the streets were great, and the ceremony excited much interest in the town. To an address from the Corporation, the Prince replied in gracious terms ; expressing his gratification at being able again to visit the ancient borough, and to assist in so good a work ; adding, that though it was his sixth visit, he hoped it would not be the last, as he always looked forward with the greatest pleasure to coming to Great Yarmouth.

THE SCHOOL DRILL REVIEW.

July 25th, 1872.

THE Horticultural Gardens at South Kensington had seen many vicissitudes, and been turned to many uses, before it ceased to be the head-quarters of the science and art of gardening. But the ground was never turned to better use than when it was lent for the Annual Review of the thousands of boys belonging to the Training Ships and the Pauper Schools of the Metropolitan District Unions. Two of these annual reviews had been held, under the auspices of the Society of Arts, when in 1872, on the 25th of July, the Prince of Wales was asked, as President of that Society, to take the leading part in the proceedings of the day.

About 4000 boys in all mustered, each little regiment marching on the ground with its own band playing and banner flying. The Greenwich Royal Naval School, of 700 boys, were conspicuous in their neat sailor uniforms. The lads of the *Warspite, Goliath,* and *Chichester* training ships also made a good appearance. The Greenwich boys, having the advantage of more thorough training and instruction, were excluded from the competition in the drill exercises for which other schools entered.

Prince Edward of Saxe-Weimar watched each school at drill under its own inspector, and adjudged the prizes to be afterwards distributed by the Prince of Wales. A Serjeant-major of the Guards was in charge of the parade, and of the march past the saluting point. The arrangements of the day had been chiefly organized by Major Donelly, R.E., to whom great praise was due.

The boys had been at work for some hours, when at 4 P.M., the Prince and Princess of Wales arrived on the ground, accompanied by their two eldest boys in sailors' costume. The prizes were distributed in the Royal Albert Hall. The Princess went to the Royal box, but the Royal princes went with their father to the daïs, where they were welcomed with great clapping of hands, by the thousands of boys, and the thousand adult spectators of the scene. Prince Edward of Saxe-Weimar had adjudged the first prize to the boys of the *Goliath;* the second to the boys of the Shoreditch School at Brentford; and the third to the Lambeth School at Lower Norwood.

After a short address by General Sir Eardley Wilmot, speaking in the name of the Council of the Society of Arts,—

The Prince of Wales rose, and in an excellent impromptu speech "assured the members of the Council and the boys (addressing the latter in kindly way as 'you, my young friends'), of the pleasure it gave the Princess, his two sons, and himself to be present. Congratulating the schools on their excellent marching, and on the favourable report just read, His Royal Highness added that he hoped the boys had been up to the mark in their studies as well as their drill."

Two boys of each prize school came in succession to the daïs, and received the prize banners from the Prince's hand. The Prince and his sons then joined the Princess in her box, and it was a striking scene when, after some bars of prelude, the words of ' God Bless the Prince of Wales ' were taken up by a thousand young and clear voices, the Prince and Princess and the two lads standing in the front of the box while it was sung. The last of the pro-gramme was then fulfilled by the bands playing a selection of music.

The sight altogether was most gratifying. Here were 4000 boys, most of them paupers, many of them orphans, receiving an excellent education, a training in physical aptitudes and habits of obedience as well as in mental studies. The Greenwich School is composed of the children of seamen being educated for the sea, but the three thousand and more boys of the other schools must in large part be looked upon as so much material reclaimed to humanity. In fact, these three thousand and more boys may, in the words of a paper put forth by the Society of Arts, "be beheld with confident satis-faction as victims rescued from ' the bad,' and preserved for the good as honest, self-supporting producers, and worthy members of the community."

WEYMOUTH AND THE PORTLAND BREAKWATER.

August 11*th*, 1872.

On the 11th of August, 1872, the Prince of Wales went from Osborne in the Royal yacht *Victoria and Albert*, to inaugurate the completed Breakwater and Harbour of Refuge at Portland, and to pay a visit to Weymouth, the favourite resort of the Prince's great-grandfather, George III. A magnificent fleet of ironclads, headed by the *Minotaur*, bearing the flag of Admiral Hornby, and many other vessels, were in attendance for the ceremony, of which fifteen were first-rate ironclad ships of war.

The weather was stormy, and the sea had been too disturbed for the comfort of the Civil Lords of the Admiralty; but the Prince showed no signs of suffering from the rough voyage, and manfully went through the proceedings of the day. The stone being laid, prayers were said by a clergyman, plaster was spread on the sur-face on which the last of seven million tons of Portland stone was to find a firm resting-place, the usual glass bottle containing

newspapers, coins, and a chart of the island and the breakwater
was laid in the groove prepared, and, when the Prince himself had
spread some mortar, the great block was lowered into its place.
His Royal Highness then struck three blows upon it with an ivory
mallet, tested it with a silver level, and completed a very short but
sufficient ceremony, by saying, "I now declare this stone to be
well and truly laid and this great work to be complete." At the
concerted signal of a lowered colour, the guns of the fort began to
fire a salute, and the spectators raised a cheer. The inscription on
the stone read as follows, the concluding quotation having been
added, it is stated, by the Prince himself :—

"From this spot, on the 25th of July, 1849, His Royal Highness Prince Albert, Consort of Queen Victoria, deposited the
first stone of this breakwater. Upon the same spot, on the
10th of August, 1872, Albert Edward, Prince of Wales, laid this
last stone, and declared the work complete."

" ' These are imperial works, and worthy Kings.' "

At the end of the ceremony the Royal yacht steamed towards
Weymouth, and after a rather uncomfortable passage, through a
choppy sea and over the bar, in the Royal barge, the Prince landed
at the end of the pier. Here the Mayor and Corporation presented
an address, which declared that "His Royal Highness had added
one more link to the golden chain of favours already conferred by
Royalty on this ancient borough." A luncheon was given by
Mr. Hambro, the senior member for Weymouth. The streets were
gaily decorated, and the people were loud in their loyal and joyful
demonstrations. The Royal yacht returned to Osborne late in the
evening.

VISIT TO DERBY.

December 17th, 1872.

THE tidings that the Prince and Princess of Wales were coming
to Derby from Chatsworth, where they were on a visit to the
Duke of Devonshire, caused great excitement in the district.
Trains brought crowds from Birmingham, Manchester, Sheffield,
Nottingham, and Chesterfield, to swell the populace of Derby.

It was on the 17th of December, 1872, not far from the anniversary of the gloomiest time of the illness of the previous year, that
the visit to Derby was made. There were several loyal addresses
—from civic, municipal, and other bodies, including one from the
Freemasons of Derbyshire. The object of the Royal visit was
mainly to present the prizes at the Derby Grammar School, one of

the most flourishing of provincial middle-class schools. The procession of carriages passed through streets crowded with people, with brilliant escort of troops, and decorations everywhere on the route. On arriving at the school Lord Belper delivered an address referring to the foundation and history of the institution, and the high scholastic standard aimed at. The Head Master, the Rev. W. Clark, having thanked the Prince and the Princess for coming, added that His Royal Highness had kindly said he would write his name in each of the prize-books in remembrance of the occasion :—

His Royal Highness, on rising, said,—"Mr. Clark, Ladies, and Gentlemen,—I beg you to accept from the Princess, as well as myself, our cordial thanks for the very kind words that have been addressed to us. I can assure you that I have come here with feelings of the greatest pleasure, and we are glad we accepted the kind invitation of the noble duke to visit Chatsworth, and that we have had the pleasure and advantage of visiting the ancient town of Derby. I have had great pleasure in presiding to-day and distributing the prizes to the successful competitors of the Derby school. This school, as you know, is one of the oldest in the kingdom, though I am afraid one of the poorest endowed. Still it has always borne the highest reputation, which I feel convinced it will continue to maintain. To the young men to whom I have had the pleasure of distributing prizes allow me to offer my most hearty congratulations, and I trust they may continue to go on as they are doing now. If they do so they will be successful in whatever profession they enter. I will not detain you longer, but thank you once more for the kind reception you have given us this day, and also tender to the Mayor our cordial thanks for the hearty reception we have received in our progress through Derby."

It may be added that the invitation to Derby was first suggested by the Trustees of the Grammar School, who in their petition, sent to Chatsworth, represented that this school, reputed to be one of the oldest in the kingdom, was also one of the most poorly endowed. This was an appeal which at once secured the goodwill of the Prince. Nor has he forgotten the school. On the 14th of November, 1888, he went to see "the Prince of Wales's Class Rooms," erected as a memorial of his visit in 1872. In response to a petition presented by the captain of the school, the Prince obtained from the Head Master a promise of making November 14 a perpetual holiday in remembrance of this visit.

RAILWAY BENEVOLENT INSTITUTION.

March 27th, 1873.

ON the evening of March 27, 1873, His Royal Highness the Prince of Wales, who had in the morning visited several artists' studios, and in the afternoon went to the House of Lords, presided at the annual dinner in aid of the Railway Benevolent Institution, at Willis's Rooms.   After dinner and grace the Royal Chairman gave the usual first toast, the health of Her Majesty the Queen, Patroness of the Railway Benevolent Institution.   The Duke of Buckingham then proposed the health of the Prince and Princess of Wales ; and in so doing took occasion to say that it was not the first time His Royal Highness had taken interest in the Institution, and now he had done it the honour to preside at its annual festival.   The toast being duly welcomed, the Prince said :—

"My Lords and Gentlemen,—Although it is very unusual on a public occasion of this kind for the health of the Chairman to be given so early in the evening, yet mine has been proposed so kindly by the noble Duke and so well received, and has, moreover, been so kindly coupled with that of the Princess and the rest of my family, that I think it my duty to rise at once and respond to the toast.   The noble Duke has been kind enough to say that my family and myself do what we can for the support of the great charitable Institutions of the country.   I am very much flattered by those remarks.   I can only assure you—and I think I may speak for the other members of my family—that it is one of our chief objects to come forward as often as we possibly can in support of Institutions which are so beneficial and so necessary to the well-being of the country, and which are always so munificently supported by all classes of the community.   I thank you once more for the honour you have done me, and assure you that it is a great pleasure and gratification to me to take the chair here this evening."

Other toasts being proposed and acknowledged, the Prince rose and said :—

"My Lords and Gentlemen,—The toast I have now the honour to propose is a bumper toast, and I know it will be received as such.   It is that of 'Prosperity to the Railway Benevolent Institution and Board of Management.'   When I look around me this evening and see how numerous is the assemblage before me, I feel convinced that you have come here intending to do honour to that toast, and to do your utmost in every way to support the Institution which to-day has reached its fifteenth anniversary. It is difficult for me, especially before you, who are so well acquainted with the merits of the Institution, to say anything new concerning it. Still I think it my duty, as your chairman, to mention a few facts by way of an appeal to your consideration.

" The objects of the Railway Benevolent Institution may be briefly mentioned under six heads. First, it has for its object the granting of annuities of from £10 to £25 to the distressed railway officers and servants incapacitated through age, sickness, or accident; second, to grant small pensions to distressed widows; third, to educate and maintain orphan children; fourth, to grant temporary relief until permanent relief can be afforded; fifth, to induce railway officers and servants to insure their lives by dividing the payment of the premium into small periodical sums, and by granting a reversionary bonus of 10 per cent. out of the funds of the institution; sixth and lastly, to grant small sums not exceeding £10 to the families of those who are injured or killed in the performance of their duties.

" When I look at the list before me I must say it is indeed a sad one; but at the same time it must be a gratification to us, who wish well to the Institution, to see that from the 16th of November, 1871, to the 16th of November last as many as 1067 cases were relieved out of the casualty fund. I may also mention that the officers of the railway companies subscribe half a guinea and the servants 8s. a year. In fact, I may say that the railway companies give this Institution in every way their official support, and they may indeed well do so, because there is no institution which more heartily deserves our support than this.

" There is, however, one curious fact which I should like to mention. I believe I· am correct in saying that the number of officers and servants employed on railways in the United Kingdom amounts to something like 300,000, but only 35,000 of them are subscribers; and in Ireland there is not a single subscriber. I am sorry to have to make this fact known; but

all the more reason is there that we this evening should be
liberal with our purses, as I am sure we shall all be when we
consider how often we travel by railway. Not a day goes by but
most of you travel once—probably twice. In stepping into a
railway carriage, do you not think of the risks you may run?
An accident may happen to anybody, though every possible
security and guarantee may be given that no accident shall
occur.

"Well, if we as passengers run risks, how much more so the
officers and servants of the companies; and that not every day,
but every hour and minute of their lives? We may be sure it
is the earnest desire of the managers and directors—many of
whom are here this evening—to do all in their power to
guarantee the safety of the passengers and of those to whom
are entrusted the care and management of the trains. I feel
sure I cannot impress on them too strongly the necessity for
their still using every effort in their power to prevent accidents,
which are, unfortunately, too frequent. It is not for me in the
presence of so many great railway authorities to say what plan
may be best devised to lessen accidents—whether it may be
that there are too many railways, whether the immense network
which exists in this country comes too closely together at
different stations, or the trains follow each other at intervals
too short. These are questions with which I do not feel myself
competent to deal; but at the same time I feel that the question
of railways, and especially the frequency of accidents, are brought
more distinctly under our notice when we consider the claims
of the Institution we are brought together this evening to promote. This is a theme about which one might talk for a long
time; and I know, on occasions of this kind, it would be out of
place on my part to give you a long oration; yet, though I but
feebly express what others would much better have laid before
you, I hope you will believe that nobody feels more deeply for
this Institution than I do, that nobody advocates its claims more
ardently than I, and nobody will continue to take a greater
interest in everything connected with our great railways.

"To show you that I am not using mere stereotyped phrases,
I may tell you that no week elapses without my travelling once
or twice at least by train. I have therefore the opportunity of

seeing, as well as anybody can see, how admirably our railway system is worked; not only the managers and directors, but the officers and servants have my warmest admiration for doing their utmost in the execution of their duty, and also for their unvarying courtesy and attention. I will now ask you once more, in conclusion, to open your purses as freely as you can in support of the Railway Benevolent Institution."

The Secretary afterwards announced subscriptions to the handsome amount of £5000, which included a second donation by His Royal Highness of 100 guineas.

UNVEILING THE ALBERT STATUE ON HOLBORN VIADUCT.

January 9th, 1874.

ON the 9th of January, 1874, the Prince of Wales visited the City for unveiling the equestrian statue erected at the western entrance of the Holborn Viaduct, in memory of the late Prince Consort. At the site an address was read, containing a description of the memorial, and an account of its origin. The ceremony of unveiling over, the Prince was driven in the state carriage of the Lord Mayor to the Guildhall, where between 700 and 800 guests, including many distinguished persons, were invited to luncheon. After the first loyal toast, " The Queen," had been received with all honours, the Lord Mayor said: " I now raise my glass to the memory of the late Prince Consort. ' He being dead yet speaketh.' " The words were spoken with emotion, and the company rising in a body, drank the toast in silence and with every mark of respect.

The health of the Prince and Princess of Wales, and the other members of the Royal Family—including the Duke of Cambridge, who was present—having been given, the Prince responded.

He expressed his grateful sense of the cordiality of his reception, and the satisfaction he had in coming for such a purpose as the inauguration and unveiling of a statue to his lamented father. He also acknowledged the debt of thanks to the donor of the statue, whose name he knew, but who wished it not to be made public. " To the 'Corporation of London I have to express my thanks for having contributed a part of the statue—namely, the pedestal; and I am sure that the work which we have inaugurated to-day will long be an ornament to the City of London."

THE BRITISH ORPHAN ASYLUM FESTIVAL.

March 25th, 1874.

THE number of institutions for helping fatherless and orphan children is considerable, but the purpose of the British Orphan Asylum, at Slough, is distinct from most charities of the class. The orphan children here admitted are the sons and daughters of persons once in prosperous circumstances, but who have been unable to make provision for their families. Clergymen, naval and military officers, members of the legal and medical profession, are often in this position. Commercial men are also liable to sudden misfortune, and children are afterwards left in poverty, who were once accustomed to ease and prosperity. The frequency of such cases led to the establishment, in 1827, of a special Asylum for the orphans of such persons. The honorary secretary at present is the Rev. Canon James Fleming, whose name is alone sufficient guarantee for the excellent object and good management of the Asylum.

At the anniversary festival, in 1874, held at Willis's Rooms, on March 25th, the Prince of Wales presided. After the toast of " The Queen," proposed by the Chairman, the Marquis of Hertford gave the health of " The Prince of Wales, the Princess of Wales, and the rest of the Royal Family," among whom was now included the Duchess of Edinburgh. The Marquis said : " It gives us all the greatest pleasure to see His Royal Highness again among us as one of the Royal Family taking part in the sacred cause of charity. We who belong to the British Orphan Asylum have the greatest reason to be pleased and thankful to His Royal Highness for having come among us this evening." .

Other toasts having been disposed of, the Prince rose and said :—

" It is now my duty, as your Chairman, to call upon you to drink the toast of ' Prosperity to the British Orphan Asylum.' I am satisfied you will do so most heartily, when I see around me so numerous an assembly prepared to do honour to the occasion, and to assist us in our work. I feel some diffidence in proposing this toast in the presence of so many who know far better than I do the excellence of this institution, and under-stand its working. At the same time it gives me the greatest pleasure to propose the toast, and to be here this evening advocating so excellent a cause. It is always a pleasure to advocate the cause of charity, and there is no other appeal that comes so home to the hearts of all classes of the community.

" I have a special interest in this Asylum. It is now nearly eleven years since the Princess and myself visited and inaugurated the present building near Slough; and when I pass by Slough, as I frequently have to do in the course of the year, it always gives me pleasure to look at that building, and to think how many children are here provided for and educated. It is now very nearly half a century since this institution was founded, and it is different from all others in this respect, that children of parents who were once in prosperous circumstances are there educated. In it there are children of officers of the Army, of the legal, medical, and naval professions, and the proof of its usefulness is that after they have grown up they frequently write letters to the managers of the Asylum expressing their gratitude for the excellence of the practical education they have received, and which has been so profitable to them in their different avocations.

" To show how prosperous this Asylum is, I may state that in January last it contained within four of 200 children. You will perhaps ask, if this institution is in so prosperous a condition, why have this dinner? Why call so many people together? And why am I to ask you, in as civil a manner as I possibly can, to subscribe towards its support? My answer is, that the net income of the Asylum is £3000 a year, but that the increase in prices of all the necessaries of life is so enormous, that to meet the deficiency that exists as much as £1500 has been sold out of their funds; and I feel that in order to make that deficiency good, I shall not call upon you this evening in vain. There are points which I might bring before your notice, but I think that on this occasion brevity is best, for you all know what a good institution it is, and I am sure you will drink with me ' Prosperity to the Institution,' and try to make it still more prosperous for the future. I beg to couple with the toast the health of the treasurer, the directors, the hon. secretaries, and medical officers of the institution."

The subscriptions announced during the evening amounted to upwards of £2400.

BANQUET TO SIR GARNET WOLSELEY.

March 31st, 1874.

THE Lord Mayor of London, as chief magistrate of the City, has always been ready to honour men distinguished for naval and military service rendered to the country. A grand State Banquet was given on the 31st of March, 1874, to Lord Wolseley, then Major-General Sir Garnet Wolseley, on his return to England after the triumphant Ashantee Expedition. The dinner was served in the Egyptian Hall at the Mansion House. Covers were laid for 260 guests, among whom were His Royal Highness the Prince of Wales, Prince Arthur, and the Duke of Cambridge. All the officers of the Staff, and others who had taken part in the Expedition, with many eminent persons in civic or official life, were present.

The Lord Mayor, having given the usual loyal toasts, the Prince of Wales rose to respond to that of the Royal Family, saying :—

" My Lord Mayor, your Royal Highness, my Lords, Ladies, and Gentlemen,—I beg to tender you my very warmest thanks for the kind way in which the Lord Mayor proposed this toast, and for the cordial manner in which the company now assembled have received it. This is not the first time I have had the honour of an invitation to be present at the Mansion House and receive the hospitality of the Lord Mayor of the City of London. But I can assure him that however much pleased I may have been to be present on former occasions, on no occasion did it afford me greater pleasure to be here than on this evening, when he has given a banquet to welcome back those gallant officers who have so lately returned from the Gold Coast to England. The gallant officers and men of that Expedition had the opportunity yesterday of seeing the Queen, and the Queen had the opportunity of seeing them, and of expressing her approval of everything that has occurred. Yesterday afternoon, also, both Houses of Parliament unanimously accorded a vote of thanks for the manner in which that difficult though short campaign was conducted. This evening, again, the Lord Mayor takes the opportunity of welcoming those gentlemen who are here as the representatives of the troops that formed that Expedition, in the hospitable manner which is so well known in this Hall. On a question of this kind it would be unbecoming in me and out of place to make any remarks with regard to that

Expedition which has been so successfully closed. But I cannot sit down without taking the opportunity of saying how much I rejoice—if I may say so as a soldier and a comrade of those I see around me—that this Expedition has ended in so successful a manner. English officers and English troops have kept up their reputation. They have not only displayed great courage —that they have done on all occasions—but they displayed extraordinary endurance, owing to the fearful climate and country they had to contend with. I am glad to have the opportunity of welcoming home the gallant General on my right, and congratulating him on the great success of his expedition. Once more I thank you for the honour you have done me in drinking my health, and on the part of the members of my family, for the kind way in which you have spoken of them."

In responding to the toast of " The Army and Navy," the Duke of Cambridge referred to the review of the troops of the Expedition on the previous day, at Windsor, before the Queen. " The distinguished officer who conducted this war knew the task he undertook, and how to undertake it; and he was well backed by the officers and men placed at his disposal." The speech of Sir Garnet Wolseley was admirable in tone and feeling, and with clear soldier-like statement of the chief events and results of the Expedition. He thus concluded: " The military world has learnt many military lessons in recent years, but the most valuable to us as a nation that has been taught us by the Abyssinian and Ashantee Wars is that when you have to appoint an English General to command any military undertaking it is necessary to trust him; to supply him with all he asks for; and, above all things, to avoid the error of severing the military command from the diplomacy necessarily connected with the operations. I have no hesitation in saying that had my operations been encumbered by the presence with me of a Civil Governor, or of an Ambassador authorised to give me orders, I do not think I should ever have reached Coomassie. Upon my arrival at Cape Coast Castle, at the beginning of last October, I found it in a state of siege. A large Ashantee army threatened both it and Elmina; a panic and demoralisation had seized upon all classes; the people from the surrounding districts had flooded into the towns on the Coast, where they soon suffered from disease, owing to their crowded condition; trade had almost ceased altogether, and a large proportion of the people depended upon the Government for their support. When I left Cape Coast Castle, at the beginning of this month, I left there a prosperous population, enjoying the blessings of peace and the mercantile advantages attendant thereon. I found upon my arrival on the Coast the *prestige* of England at its lowest ebb, but before I departed, I left our military fame firmly established on a secure base, consequent on the victories so gallantly won by the troops under my command.   My Lord Mayor, I have to thank you most sincerely for the manner in which you have alluded to me personally and to my military services, and I have to thank you, in the name of all ranks composing the expeditionary force, for the warm reception and the noble hospitality you have accorded to us this evening."

ROYAL MEDICAL BENEVOLENT COLLEGE.

April 22nd, 1874.

THE Royal Medical Benevolent College, at Epsom, was founded in 1851, for the education of sons of medical men.   There are at present about two hundred boys, fifty of whom, on the foundation, are educated, boarded, and entirely maintained at the expense of the institution.   The education is of the highest class, and the charge, to those not on the foundation, is fifty guineas, if the pupils are above fourteen, with slight reduction for those under that age. There is accommodation in the College for twenty-four pensioners, who have comfortable quarters, and a pension of twenty guineas a year.   There are also twenty-six non-resident pensioners, with the same annuity of twenty guineas.

In support of the funds of the College, the eighteenth festival, at Willis's Rooms, was presided over by the Prince of Wales, supported by the Duke of Teck, Earl Granville, as President of the College, and a large number of the leading men of the profession.   The usual loyal and patriotic toasts having been given, the Royal Chairman gave the toast of the evening, saying : —

" My Lords and Gentlemen,—I feel both some difficulty and some diffidence in proposing the toast of ' Success to the Royal Medical College,' because, in the first place, I wish the task had fallen into abler hands than mine, and, in the second place, many of you must in any event know more upon the subject than I do.   It may not be out of place, however, on this occasion for me to give you a few statistics connected with the Royal Medical College.   No doubt many of you will be well up in the subject, but others will be reminded or informed.   This College was founded by Mr. Propert, a medical gentleman of high eminence ; and its object is, in the first place, to assist aged medical men and the widows of qualified practitioners, and, in the next place, to educate the children of such persons. In 1853 the first stone was laid at Epsom ; in 1855 the institution was opened by my lamented father, who took the deepest interest in its welfare ; and I had the opportunity, as a boy, of accompanying him on that occasion. I have therefore been acquainted with the institution, which we have come here to do honour to, for nineteen years. There were then five pensioners' houses and a school for 150 boys. There are now, including the three about to be elected, fifty pensioners, each of whom receives £21 a year, and twenty-four of whom are also resident in the College. The school contains 200 resident pupils, the sons of medical men, fifty of whom, being foundation scholars, are educated, boarded, clothed, and maintained at the expense of the institution, while the remainder are charged from £48 to £51 a year.

"A gentleman who is present (Sir Erasmus Wilson) has just built a house to hold forty more boys. I offer him our sincere thanks for the great benefit he has conferred upon the institution. The school has always been full, but we are anxious to increase its funds, and, as each foundationer costs £60 a year, you will see that we want money.

"It will not be out of place for me to remind you what a difficult profession is that of medicine—what uphill work it is to some, unlike those whom I see around. Some who would have attained high positions may be struck down by illness or by some great sorrow, and for them provision should be made. There is also the case of the eminent man making a large income, but cut off suddenly, before he has made provision for a wife and family now left destitute, though the husband and father may have led a life of usefulness in his profession. Our object is not to make long speeches, nor, I hope, to bore any of those who are assembled here, but you may be assured that, however imperfectly I may have spoken, what I have said I mean most heartily, and when I call upon you this evening to give your support—your liberal support—to this charity I feel sure I shall not call in vain. I now propose 'Success to the Royal Medical Benevolent College.'"

The subscriptions and donations announced by the secretary amounted to £1780, the list being headed by the Prince of Wales with 100 guineas.

Sir James Paget, in proposing the health of the president, officers, and members of the Council of the College, said that they were to be congratulated on the prospects of the institution, and on their having "induced His Royal Highness to leave Sandringham at this season, to add grace and dignity to the celebration of the twenty-first year of the College."

The Prince of Wales, it may be added, besides his kindly interest in all charitable institutions, has uniformly shown courtesy and respect to the medical profession, members of which he has from early life honoured with his personal friendship.

AT THE MIDDLE AND THE INNER TEMPLE.

June 11th, 1874.

ON the opening of the new Library in 1862, His Royal Highness the Prince of Wales was made a Bencher of the Middle Temple. On the 11th of June, 1874, the Treasurer and Benchers of the Middle Temple entertained the members of the Inn, and a large number of distinguished guests, at dinner, according to ancient custom, on "the great grand day" of Trinity Term. The Prince of Wales, being a Bencher, was present not as a guest, but as one of the hosts, in the grand old historical Hall. This Hall, the erection of which commenced in 1562, was completed in 1572, and is one of the most famous relics of old London. This was the second time of the Prince of Wales visiting it. On three prior occasions, at least, it has been visited by Royalty—namely, by Queen Henrietta, the consort of Charles I., Peter the Great of Russia, and William III. There is also a tradition of the Inn that Queen Elizabeth was present at a rehearsal there of the *Midsummer Night's Dream*, in which Shakespeare himself took part, and that in the course of the revel Her Majesty danced with her Chancellor, Sir Christopher Hatton. The splendid oak screen and music gallery at the eastern end were erected in 1572. The Hall is graced by one of the three genuine paintings by Vandyck of Charles I.—the other two being at Windsor and Warwick Castles—and by portraits of Charles II., James II., William III., Queen Anne, and George III. A bust of the Prince of Wales is also conspicuous, and a portrait of His Royal Highness, by Mr. Watts, R.A., has since been added.

The Treasurer, Mr. Kenyon, Q.C., presided at the dinner, when no less than 430 members of the Inn, Benchers, Barristers, or Students were present, and many illustrious guests. On the right of the chair was the Master of the Temple (the Rev. Dr. Vaughan), and next to him the Archbishop of Canterbury; on the left the Prince of Wales, and next to him the Lord Chief Justice. The Prince wore the silk gown of a Queen's Counsel, and the riband of the Garter. On his health being proposed, after that of the

Queen, it was to give "respectful and hearty welcome to Master His Royal Highness the Prince of Wales."

The Prince on rising to respond was loudly cheered, and said:—

"Master Treasurer, my Lords, and Gentlemen,—I beg to tender to you and to my brother Benchers my sincere thanks for the kind, hearty, and cordial manner in which you have received this toast. I cannot feel that I am quite a stranger among you, although it is now nearly thirteen years since I had the honour of being enrolled as a member of this Inn. My relations with you are, unfortunately, of an almost entirely honorary character, but I can assure you that I consider it a very high honour to be connected with this Inn. It is, I am sure, a good thing for the profession at large and for the public in general that I have never been called to the Bar, for I must say that I could never have been a brilliant ornament of it. I can assure you that I esteem most highly the honour of dining with you and my brother Benchers this evening, and with those distinguished men whom I see around me right and left. I entirely agree with every word that has fallen from the lips of our Master Treasurer, and I sincerely hope that this gathering may tend to much good and to bring forward those important results in legal education which you, Sir, have advocated so admirably. I thank you for the kind way in which you have received me, and I can only assure you that it has afforded me the greatest pleasure and satisfaction to meet you here this evening in this ancient Hall, where, I am told, Queen Elizabeth once danced with Chancellor Hatton. I am afraid that now-a-days the duties of the Chancellor are more arduous than they were then, and that they do not allow him much time to acquire the art of dancing. I cannot help thus reminding you of one of the great historical events which this Hall has witnessed, and I thank you once more for the great honour you have done me in proposing my health and for the cordial reception you have given me."

"The Queen" and "The Prince of Wales" were the only two toasts given at the banquet.

The Treasurer and Benchers of the Inner Temple, on the 18th of May, 1870, had entertained with much splendour His Royal Highness the Prince of Wales, His Royal Highness the Prince Christian, the Lord Chancellor, the Speaker of the House of Commons, the Lord Chief Justice of England, the Judges in Equity and at Common Law, the Queen's Counsel, the Chancellor of the Exchequer, and a very distinguished company, to celebrate the inauguration of the new Hall, which had been formally opened by Her Royal Highness the Princess Louise a few days before.

The two Royal visitors sat at the right and left hand of the Treasurer, Mr. Percival Pickering. Grace was said by the Master of the Temple, Dr. Vaughan. After due justice had been done to the dinner, the Treasurer humorously described some of the strange scenes which had been enacted in the old Hall, which had been removed to make room for the present magnificent structure. He then proposed " The Health of the Queen," which was received with loyal enthusiasm. That of " The Prince of Wales and the other members of the Royal Family " was felicitously acknowledged by the Prince of Wales. The Archbishop of York returned thanks for the Church, Sir William Codrington for the Army, and the Colonel of the " Devil's Own " for the Volunteers. Mr. Gladstone proposed " The Health of the Treasurer," whose speeches throughout the evening had been seasoned with an amount of humour which rescued even those proposing the conventional toasts from the imputation of being commonplace. " The Health of the Architect," Mr. Smirke, concluded the proceedings; and the principal portion of the company then adjourned to the drawing-room, where not only was coffee served, but—strange novelty in such an assemblage—cigars were introduced—an innovation which did not seem unwelcome.

NEW GUILDHALL AND LAW COURTS, PLYMOUTH.

August 13th, 1874.

THE new Guildhall, Municipal Offices, and Law Courts at Plymouth were opened by the Prince of Wales, on the 13th of August, 1874. On landing at the Royal Victualling Yard, the Prince proceeded in a State carriage for Plymouth. At the entrance to the borough he was received by the Mayor and Corporation; the procession proceeding through dense crowds to the Guildhall square, where the Prince was formally received as Lord High Steward of the Borough, and presented with his rod of office. An address having been read by the Recorder, the Prince made the following reply :—

" Mr. Mayor and Gentlemen,—I rejoice at again being able to renew my acquaintance with your ancient borough, and I return you my grateful thanks for the expressions of goodwill which you have paid me. The sentiments of loyalty conveyed in your address are most gratifying proofs of the feelings which animate the inhabitants of Plymouth towards Her Majesty the Queen and the members of the Royal family. I have frequently visited your borough, but never on so important an occasion as the present, when a work of no ordinary magnitude has been completed. As High Steward of the Borough, I cannot but take an especial interest in all that relates to its welfare or adds to its embellishment, and it gave me peculiar pleasure to accede to the request that was made to me that I should open this magnificent building. In conclusion, let me congratulate most heartily all those who have been concerned in the undertaking on the success which has attended their labours, and, connected as I am with your town, I feel proud to think it has been the result of local genius, perseverance, and energy."

An elegant silver key was then presented by the Mayor with which the Prince opened the new Guildhall. A banquet followed, at which, in response to the toast of the Prince and Princess of Wales, His Royal Highness spoke as follows :—

"Mr. Mayor, my Lords, Ladies, and Gentlemen,—I beg to return you, Mr. Mayor, my most cordial thanks for the manner in which you have been kind enough to propose my health, and to you, ladies and gentlemen, for the kind way in which you have been pleased to receive it. This is by no means my first visit to your ancient town. I have on frequent occasions spent some very agreeable days here; but among all the different visits that I have paid none will have been more interesting to me than the present one, nor more vividly impressed on my memory. I assure the Mayor and citizens of this town that great pleasure and gratification was afforded me in opening this magnificent hall, all the more so as my name is connected with your town as your High Steward. I esteem it a great honour to have that title, though the duties are certainly very slight; and if those duties consist only in coming here and being so kindly and cordially received by you all, I think I have every reason to congratulate myself. I congratulate those gentlemen who have built this hall, and who, I think, have every reason to feel satisfaction with its appearance and its prospects of future success. To you, Mr. Mayor, who have taken such pains during the last five years, as Chairman of the Guildhall Com-

mittee, it must be very gratifying; and allow me also to have
the pleasure of offering my sincere congratulations to the Mayor
of Devonport, as one of the architects of this Guildhall. I
again beg to thank you for the kind reception which you have
given me to-day, and, in conclusion, I beg also to thank you,
Mr. Mayor, for the kind way in which you have proposed the
Princess of Wales's health, and to assure you how deeply she
regrets that she was unable to accompany me on the present
occasion. She is now on her way to Scotland to meet her
father, the King of Denmark, who is returning that way from
his visit to Iceland."

Afterwards the Prince proposed the health of the Mayor, thanking him for his reception, congratulating him upon the good order
maintained in the streets, and requesting him to convey to the
citizens his sense of the pleasure and gratification afforded him by
the artistic decorations of the town.

VISIT TO BIRMINGHAM IN 1874.'

November 3rd, 1874.

THE Prince and Princess of Wales paid their first visit to Birmingham on the 3rd of November, 1874. When the Mayor and
Corporation of the midland capital heard of the intended visit,
they resolved to give their Royal Highnesses a right loyal and
hearty reception. Those who remember, or have read of the early
visits of the Queen and of the Prince Consort to the town, will not
be surprised at the enthusiasm with which the Prince and Princess
of Wales were welcomed on this occasion. Prince Albert came to
Birmingham for the first time in 1844. He was a guest of Sir
Robert Peel at Tamworth, and expressed a wish, as he was so near,
to see the place so famous in various arts and industries. But the
town was at that time as famous for its political independence,
to use the mildest term. In fact it was regarded as the centre and
seat of democratic radicalism, and the turbulence of Chartist times
was yet fresh in remembrance. Fears were entertained that
Prince Albert might have a cool if not hostile reception. The
result proved how groundless were these suspicions. The young
Prince was welcomed with the utmost enthusiasm, not only as the
husband of the Queen, but on account of his own moral and
intellectual excellence. He was there again in 1849, to inspect
the exhibition of arts and manufactures held in Bingley Hall; and
a third time in 1855 to lay the foundation stone of the Midland

Institute. In 1858 the Queen herself came to open the public Park and Hall at Aston. Nor was this the only visit. Few places in her dominions have been more favoured, and nowhere has there been shown more devoted loyalty.

The advanced radicalism of Birmingham was not less marked at the time of the Prince of Wales's visit, and the Mayor of that year, Mr. Joseph Chamberlain, had the reputation of holding not merely democratic but republican views. All this made the more marked the cordial reception of the Royal visitors, both by the authorities of the town, and by the masses of the people. The words of the *Times* of November 4th, in its record of the visit are worthy of being recalled, especially in what it said of the Mayor: "Whatever Mr. Chamberlain's views may be, his speeches of yesterday appear to us to have been admirably worthy of the occasion, and to have done the highest credit to himself. We have heard and chronicled a great many Mayors' speeches, but we do not know that we ever heard or chronicled speeches made before Royal personages by Mayors, whether they were Tories, or Whigs, or Liberals, or Radicals, which were couched in such a tone at once of courteous homage, manly independence, and gentlemanly feeling, which were so perfectly becoming and so much the right thing in every way as those of Mr. Chamberlain."

To the address of the Corporation, read in the Town Hall, by the Recorder, the Prince made the following reply:—

"Mr. Mayor and Gentlemen,—In the name of the Princess of Wales and in my own, I thank you for your address and for the kind terms in which you refer to our visit to your town. It has long been our wish to come to Birmingham, a city so celebrated not only in England, but throughout the world, as one of the chief centres of our manufacturing energy. It will be, I am persuaded, a source of satisfaction to the Queen to hear that the loyal inhabitants of this borough still retain so lively a recollection of the visits which with my lamented father she paid to Birmingham. Since that time the progress which has been made in the varied industries of this town has been most remarkable, and I trust that the condition of its working population, on whose exertions its prosperity so much depends, has improved in a still greater degree. In conclusion, gentlemen, I have only to express our earnest wish that Birmingham may long continue to enjoy that pre-eminence which it has so justly earned."

At the luncheon subsequently given, the Mayor proposed the health of the Queen, as "having established claims to the admiration of Her people by the loyal fulfilment of the responsible duties of her high station, and at the same time the nobility of her domestic life has endeared her to the nation. The care and solicitude she has manifested in the happiness of her subjects causes her name to be honoured at all times, and among all classes and ranks of society."

In proposing the health of the Royal guest, the Mayor said, " This town has been long distinguished, not without cause, for the independence of its citizens and the freedom and outspokenness in which all opinions are discussed, and this fact gives value to the welcome which has been offered, and stamps the sincerity of the wishes which are everywhere expressed for the continued health of their Royal Highnesses."

The replies of the Prince were confined to a few brief but appropriate sentences, and after proposing the health of the Mayor, the Royal party proceeded to visit some of the most famous manufactories of the district. The following letter was received next day by the Mayor, from the Secretary of the Prince of Wales, Sir Francis Knollys, K.C.M.G. :—

" Packington Hall, Coventry, November 4, 1874.

" Sir,—I have received the commands of the Prince and Princess of Wales to make known through you to the inhabitants of the borough of Birmingham the satisfaction they derived from their visit to that town yesterday. They can never forget the reception they met with nor the welcome given to them by all classes of the community. Their Royal Highnesses have also to thank not only the authorities who made such excellent arrangements, but likewise the people themselves, without whose cordial co-operation the good order which was preserved throughout the day in so wonderful a manner could hardly have been maintained. The opportunity which was afforded them of visiting some of the manufactures of your great town gave their Royal Highnesses sincere pleasure, and it was matter of regret to them that the time at their disposal did not allow them to make a closer inspection of works of so much interest. I may further congratulate you and the other members of the reception committee on the happy result of your labours. Nothing could have been more successful, and their Royal Highnesses will ever entertain most agreeable recollections of their visit to Birmingham. I am desired, in conclusion, to state that the Prince of Wales, being anxious to contribute £100 in aid of the funds of one of the charitable institutions of your town, requests that you will have the goodness to acquaint him with the name of the institution which you may consider to be the most deserving, and to be at the same time the most in want of support.—I have the honour to be, Sir, your most obedient servant,

" FRANCIS KNOLLYS.

" To the Mayor of Birmingham."

THE ROYAL CAMBRIDGE ASYLUM.

March 13th, 1875.

AT the seventh triennial festival of this Institution the Prince of Wales presided. The Duke of Cambridge, Prince Christian, Prince Edward of Saxe-Weimar, and the Duke of Teck were also present. The company included the Lord Mayor, the Sheriffs of London and Middlesex, and a large number of distinguished officers of nearly all ranks in the Army.

After the toast of "The Queen," proposed by the Royal chairman, the Lord Mayor, in giving the next toast, spoke of "the pride with which the nation at large regarded the Royal Family, not only on account of the admirable way in which they performed the important duties connected with their high position, but also because of their readiness on all occasions to promote and aid the various charitable institutions of the country, and to extend their sympathy to all who were in distress, not simply in this great metropolis, but in all parts of the kingdom."

The Prince of Wales, in reply, said :—

"I am sure I have every reason to be grateful to the Lord Mayor for the very kind manner in which he has proposed my health and that of the Princess of Wales and the other members of the Royal Family, and to the company here assembled for the very kind manner in which they have received the toast. Nothing is more disagreeable, I think, than to have at an early stage of the evening to rise to return thanks for one's own health; but, at the same time, I should be very ungrateful to you if I were not to thank you for the cordial manner in which you acceded to the request of the Lord Mayor. I can assure him—and I believe I can speak also for the rest of the Royal Family—that it is always our earnest endeavour to do our duty, and to assist in all good and charitable objects, which in this country are so numerous and so necessary. It will be my duty to address you again, so I will now only thank you once more for the kind manner in which you have received this toast."

The Prince of Wales, after a brief interval, again rose and said :—

"The toast I have now to offer to you is also one of those which are always given, and which are always heartily received at gatherings like the present. It is that of 'The Army and the Navy.' I find some difficulty on this occasion in proposing that toast, because when I look around me and see the Commander-in-Chief, the greater portion of the Head Quarters' Staff, and so many distinguished generals and officers, I feel it would be very presumptuous on my part were I to dilate on the subject. I think Englishmen have every reason to be proud of possessing such an Army and Navy as ours. Of course we don't pretend that they are perfection, but I am sure that every endeavour is used year after year to make our land and sea forces as efficient as possible for our defence and for the maintenance of peace both in this country and in our vast possessions abroad. In connection with the Army, it gives me the greatest pleasure to propose the health of my illustrious relative, the Commander-in-Chief. It would ill become me to make those remarks in his presence which it would afford me sincere satisfaction to offer were he absent; but I am sure that you, as brother officers, know the great interest the Commander-in-Chief takes in the Army, and I know you will drink his health most cordially on this occasion. I am not able to couple any name with the Navy, for the very sufficient reason that there is no naval officer present to respond to it. I regret that our gallant sea forces are not represented, but the toast will not on that account, I am sure, be less cordially received."

The Duke of Cambridge, who was loudly cheered, said: "I personally am much gratified by the kind reception which has been given to my name in conjunction with this toast. His Royal Highness, with a modesty which is delightful in one in his position, has expressed diffidence in proposing it; but there is no ground for such diffidence on his part, for there is no officer in the Army that I know of who takes a more lively interest in the efficiency of the service, even in its every detail, or who, whenever the opportunity offers, shows a greater aptitude than does His Royal Highness. He has proved a most worthy spokesman for the Army on this and on many other occasions, and I am sure officers of the Army are always flattered and gratified when His Royal Highness has the opportunity of speaking of them as he has done this evening. I feel particular interest in being present here, and I beg to express to His Royal Highness, who has many and constant duties to attend to, my thanks and those of my mother, who is, unfortunately, in a very suffering state, for having, on the mere expression of a wish on her part, at once consented to preside on this occasion. I beg also to thank you for the compliment which you have paid me and my family by your attendance, for I cannot forget that this institution was originally founded in memory of my father, who had many opportunities of showing the deep interest he took in the charitable institutions of the country. On that account many of his friends were anxious that some testimonial should be established to his memory, and instead of a statue I am happy to think, as I am sure he would have been glad to know, that it took the form of the useful and necessary institution we have met here to assist. But for its aid the recipients of its benefits would have to drag out a miserable existence either in the workhouse or under even still worse circumstances. We must all feel gratified that these old women are, thanks to the benevolence of yourselves and the public, enabled to pass their last days in the comparative comfort that they find in the Asylum at Kingston. As head of the Army, I may say that a higher compliment could not possibly have been paid to it than to establish an institution such as this, and I am gratified to think that the support it has received leads us to the hope that it is now established on a solid and valuable foundation. I beg again to thank you, in the name of the Army, and to say that the service feels the deepest interest in the prosperity of the Asylum."

The Prince of Wales next rose and said :—

" It is now my pleasing duty to bring before you the toast of the evening, 'Prosperity to the Royal Cambridge Asylum for Soldiers' Widows.' When I see how I am surrounded and how large a gathering is present, I feel sure I shall not call on you in vain in the interest of those whom we are concerned in benefiting on this occasion. As my illustrious relative has mentioned to you, this institution was established as a memorial to his illustrious father, the late Duke of Cambridge. The object was to provide a home for the widows of privates and non-commissioned officers of the Army. No such institution previously existed, and it is still the only one of its kind in the country. In it the widows are provided with a furnished room and an allowance of 6s. a week, besides a grant of 2s. 6d. per month for coals. While the expenditure is great, exceeding £2000, the funded income, including £50 a year, called the Princess Mary Fund for Nurses, amounts to little over £500 a year. It was originally intended to have, if possible, 130 inmates, but at the present moment there are only 57, for there is no room for more, and our great object is to make the institution a success by increasing the numbers. On philanthropic grounds alone it is almost unnecessary to say a word as

M

to its excellence. But when one thinks of the soldier, who has not only to expose his life in battle, but to run the risk of sickness and disease in a variety of different climates, away from home, often leaving his wife for many years behind him, it is impossible not to see that it must be a comfort to him, especially if ill or dying, to think there is an institution where his wife, if he succumbs, has a chance of being provided for. Among soldiers there can be but one feeling on this subject, and I am sure that on this occasion I shall not appeal to those who are present in vain.

" I regret very much that one who has taken a deep interest in this institution—its chairman, Sir Edward Cust—is not here on this occasion, and I fear on account of illness. But it is some gratification to be able to read to you an extract from a letter of his, dated the 1st of March, to Colonel Stewart, the secretary, in which he says—'I think I intimated to you last year that I should make a disposition by my will of all my copyright and interest in my military histories for the benefit of the Asylum. As I am unable to support the Prince of Wales in the chair, may I beg the favour of His Royal Highness making this donation in my name as evidence of my sympathy for the institution?' Those who are present know so thoroughly well all the merits of the institution that it would be unnecessary for me to make a lengthened speech. I will therefore wind up by once more asking you to do all in your power to assist in accomplishing the great object we have in view of extending the building so as to accommodate more widows. With the toast which I have given you, I beg, in the absence of Sir E. Cust, to couple the name of Colonel Liddell."

Colonel Liddell, who responded, said it was the desire to provide accommodation for one widow from each regiment in the service, which, of course, as there were only fifty-seven inmates, left a great deal still to be done.

The Prince of Wales : " I have now to propose a toast which, I am sure, of all those I have given none will have been received with greater cordiality, for it is that of the 'Lady Patron.' You all, I know, wish as sincerely as I do that her health— which is not good just at present—may be restored, and that she may be among us for some years yet to come. One of the reasons why this institution has prospered so much, and why so many are here to-night, is the regard which is felt for the kind and good lady who is its president. It is not surprising that she should take a deep interest in an asylum intended indirectly for the benefit of soldiers, seeing that her husband was a soldier and that her son is a soldier."

The toast having been cordially drunk, was responded to by the Duke of Cambridge, who then proposed " The Health of the Lord Mayor and the Sheriffs," thanking them for the liberality with which they had subscribed to the funds of the Asylum. The total amount of the subscriptions received was announced by the Prince of Wales to be £1635 17s. 10d.

The present number of inmates (1888) is sixty-nine. The receipts of the previous year were £2700; the invested funds nearly £23,000. The festival dinner is triennial, but additional sums have been obtained by military *fêtes* and other ways. In 1872 the Prince and Princess of Wales were present at a grand military concert in the Royal Albert Hall, when Madame Titiens and other artists volunteered their assistance, and many of the proprietors placed their boxes and stalls at the disposal of the Duke of Edinburgh, who was Chairman of the Committee for carrying out the arrangements. We trust that the Duke of Cambridge may be gratified by witnessing a large increase of the numbers benefited by an institution in which he takes so zealous and kindly interest.

AT MERCHANT TAYLORS' SCHOOL.

April 6th, 1875.

WHEN the Charterhouse School was removed from its ancient historic site to the more remote and rural site at Godalming, arrangements were made for installing Merchant Taylors' School in the Charterhouse. There was ample accommodation for the 400 or 500 boys. Portions of the old structure remain, and these with the new buildings give room for the numerous classes, with large halls, library, lecture rooms, and a magnificent assembly room, for morning and evening prayers, and on grand days for speeches and prize festivals. The poor Brethren, pensioners on the foundation, remain in their old quarters, and their chapel, with its services, continues as before.

The installation of the Merchant Taylors' School in the Charterhouse was an event of sufficient importance to justify the request for the ceremony being honoured by the presence of the Prince

M 2

and Princess of Wales, who came on 6th of April, 1875, accompanied by the Princess Mary and Duke of Teck, and other illustrious visitors. Service having been performed in the old Carthusian chapel; and an address having been read by the clerk, and presented by the Master of the Company; the Prince declared the Merchant Taylors' School open. An ode in Latin Alcaics was then declaimed by the head monitor of the School, the Archbishop of Canterbury offered a prayer for the Divine blessing, and the service closed with the Lord's Prayer and the Benediction.

Luncheon was afterwards served in the assembly hall. The Master of the Company gave a brief account of the origin and history of the School, introducing references to former Princes of Wales, who had been benefactors of the Company, from the time of Edward I., the first Prince of Wales, to that of King James I., who with his son, the Prince of Wales, dined in this hall. It was for that occasion, in 1607, that Dr. John Bull composed the music of "God Save the Queen." The Queen of James I. was Anne of Denmark. "History repeats itself," continued the Master, "for you, Sire, have entwined the flower of Denmark in the wreath of England."

The Prince, responding to the toast then given, said:—

" For the excessively kind and flattering manner in which this toast has been proposed from the chair, and received by you all, I beg to return my warmest and most sincere thanks. I need hardly assure the Master and all those assembled here to-day what pleasure it has given to the Princess and myself to be present on this occasion. The numerous guilds of the City of London are well known for their hospitality, and especially distinguished is the Merchant Taylors' Company. At the same time, although they kindly and cordially receive their guests, they do all they can to make themselves useful in this great city. I will not recapitulate what we have heard in another room, and also from the lips of the Master, of the prosperity of this School. I hope it will continue to flourish; and that the sun which is now shining will bring prosperity to a School which has so long flourished and which is now moved to other buildings. I must say we cannot but congratulate the Master and the Guild on the beautiful building in which we are assembled at the present moment. In conclusion let me propose a toast I am sure you will all drink with enthusiasm—'Success to the Merchant Taylors' School.' It affords me great pleasure to couple with it the name of the head master, the Rev. Dr. Baker."

After the luncheon the Royal visitors inspected the buildings, and walked through the playground, which is of considerable size for a city school. The cheers of the boys on the departure of the Prince and Princess were the more vehement, as they had asked and obtained from the Master an extra week's holiday.

THE GERMAN HOSPITAL.

April 16th, 1875.

THE German Hospital, at Dalston, is one of the most useful and well-managed charities in the Metropolis. It is for the reception of natives of Germany, and others speaking the German language; also for English in case of accident. There are now 125 beds for in-patients, with a sanatarium for the benefit of those who can pay a moderate sum weekly for their maintenance during illness. There is also a Convalescent Home, with about twenty beds. During the past year there were 1663 in-patients, 23,210 out-patients, and 1163 dental cases. The Hamburg Church is connected with the Hospital by a corridor. The yearly receipts average now about £10,000, and there is funded property amounting to £55,000.

The Prince of Wales presided at the thirtieth anniversary festival, at Willis's Rooms, on the 16th of April, 1875. About three hundred were present, including some Ambassadors and Consuls of Continental States, and other distinguished foreigners.

The Prince, in proposing the health of " The Queen," said that Her Majesty took the greatest interest in the welfare of the Hospital, of which she was a protector, and a donor to its funds.

Count Beust, the Austro-Hungarian Ambassador, gave the toast of " The Prince and Princess of Wales and the Royal Family." He said that he spoke the sentiments of the representatives of all German-speaking countries, when he said that the " Royal Chairman had always shown for the German Hospital a feeling German heart and an open English hand. When he brought under the notice of his Sovereign, the Emperor of Austria, that the Prince was to preside at the festival, he was immediately instructed by His Majesty to announce the donation from him of £100 to the funds. Let us, one and all, drink to our illustrious Chairman, whom the people of England know not only as a gracious and popular Prince, but also as a high-minded, generous gentleman, who takes a deep and active interest in all that contributes to the greatness and the welfare of the country, and to the relief of the sufferers among the less fortunate of the community, in the fulfilment of which noble task he is well supported by his gracious Princess."

The Prince, in reply, said :—

"I can hardly find words adequate enough to express my deep thanks to his Excellency the Austro-Hungarian Ambassador for the exceedingly kind and flattering manner in which he has proposed this toast, and to you all for the hearty way in which it was received. I can assure you that it affords me the greatest pleasure and gratification to be your chairman on the present occasion. The members of my family have now for some years taken a deep interest in this charity, and I take the same interest. This is not at all to be wondered at, considering that we have German blood running in our veins. We have the greatest sympathy with the foreigners who live in our country, and we gladly join in an attempt like this to alleviate their sufferings in every possible way. The President of the German Hospital, the Duke of Cambridge, as did his father before him, takes a warm interest in this institution, and I sincerely hope that our family will always remain connected with so excellent and admirable a charity. I thank you once more for the hearty reception you have accorded to the toast."

The Prince, again rising, proposed in cordial terms : "The Foreign Sovereigns and Princes, Protectors and Patrons of the Institution, and their Representatives who had honoured them with their presence." He stated that "the Emperor of Germany gave an annual donation of £200 to the charity, and that the Emperors of Russia and Austria, and the Kings of Würtemberg, Bavaria, Saxony, and the Netherlands, had also evinced a practical interest in the institution."

Count Münster, the German Ambassador, whose name was coupled with the toast, said he agreed with his friend and colleague, Count Beust, that it was one of the most pleasant duties of diplomatists to be present on occasions of that kind, and he felt it, indeed, a great honour to return thanks for the kind and gracious manner in which His Royal Highness had proposed the health of the foreign Sovereigns and their representatives. He was quite sure that the interest which their Majesties had taken in that fine, benevolent institution would be much strengthened when they became aware that the first gentleman in England—the heir to the British Throne—had shown his practical sympathy with it by presiding that evening. Benevolence and hospitality had always been the characteristics of the English people, but how could it be otherwise when the Royal Family invariably set them, on every possible occasion, the noblest and best example? In the name of his fellow-countrymen he tendered to His Royal Highness their most hearty thanks for the gracious part he was taking at that gathering.

The Prince of Wales next gave "The Army, Navy, and Reserve Forces," saying, in doing so, that every Englishman was proud of the land and sea forces of his country, and he always hoped they were in a highly efficient state. At the same time the Prince sincerely trusted that the occasion might never arise in which the Army and Navy might be called forth to battle with those countries so many of whose representatives were present that evening.

General Sir William Knollys made a brief reply. The Prince of Wales then gave as the toast of the evening: "Prosperity to the German Hospital." He said:—

"I can only regret that a toast of so much importance as this is has not fallen into better hands than mine, but, whatever my shortcomings, I am sure you will take the will for the deed. This toast has been given for a great many successive years, and the few remarks that I have to make to you will not be new to the great portion of the vast assembly who are gathered here this evening. At the same time, as I am your chairman, I think it my duty to make a few observations in connexion with the German Hospital.

"As most of you are doubtless aware, it has 103 beds generally full, and last year the total in- and out-patients amounted to about 18,000. Of these there were 1300 in-patients, of whom 240 were English. Besides the hospital there is a sanitarium, to which 42 persons were admitted. The rooms there are unfortunately limited in number, but the occupants are rather of a well-to-do class, such as professors, governesses, clerks, and others, who, in return for the services rendered to them, give a small sum of money towards defraying the necessary costs. Last year the expenses of the hospital were very heavy, amounting to £6500, exclusive of £600 for improvements. This, I hear, is likely to be increased considerably in the next accounts, owing to the continuous rise of prices. Fortunately, I am able to announce to you that the receipts nearly covered the expenditure. The fixed income, however, can only be put down at £1200 or £1300 a year, and the authorities of the hospital, to carry it on successfully and to keep it out of debt, have to collect annually between £4000 and £5000.

"I think every Englishman and every foreigner will agree as to the necessity for a hospital founded as this is. We who are Englishmen must all feel what a terrible position we should be in if we found ourselves weary and sick in a country where it was impossible to make ourselves understood. When, therefore, we are told that in this London of ours all who speak German are instantly admitted to this institution, we can readily imagine the enormous benefits which foreigners and Germans especially derive from it. There are, I am told, as many as 50,000 Germans living in London, many of whom have to work in unhealthy trades, such as sugar-baking. They are mostly confined indoors all day long, and, but for this hospital, they would not know where to go to find comfort and succour.

"A great merit, in my mind, of this institution is that it is a free one. It is not at all necessary to obtain a letter of recommendation before admission. Sick people have only to present themselves there and speak German to insure that the doors will be immediately thrown open to them, and that they will be tended and cared for in the most admirable manner. The nurses there are all trained in Elizabethan-stift at Darmstadt, and they do their work admirably under the care of the excellent chaplain (Dr. Walbaum), who has taken so deep an interest in the welfare of the hospital. They are thus found most important to the working of the hospital.

"As so many Englishmen derive benefit from the institution, I am sure I can appeal to my fellow-countrymen to do all in their power, and I ask the company generally to see if they cannot collect a sum larger than on any previous occasion. At the last annual dinner, at which the Duke of Cambridge presided, a sum of £500 in excess of any former collection was obtained, and I hope to-night we may even exceed the sum subscribed then. I may tell you that a distinguished guest among us to-night, Baron von Diergadt, of Bonn, sent us a few years ago the magnificent donation of £10,000. I do not ask you, gentlemen, to give quite so large a sum as the Baron, but I am sure that all that is in your power to give you will. I desire to tender our thanks to the Emperor of Austria for his munificent donation, announced by his Ambassador this evening, and I will now ask you all most cordially to assist me in supporting this excellent charity. I give you as the toast of the evening: ' Prosperity to the German Hospital.' "

The Secretary (Mr. Feldmann) afterwards announced the receipt of donations (including £105 from the Prince of Wales, £200 from the Emperor of Germany, and £100 from the Emperor of Austria) to the amount of over £5000, being £1200 in excess of any previous collection. Other toasts, including " The health of Baron von Diergadt, of Bonn," followed. During dinner, Mr. Marriott's band played a selection of operatic music, and afterward, at intervals, a choir, under the direction of Sir Julius Benedict and Herr Ganz (all of whom gave their services gratuitously), sang some German songs by Schubert, Schumann, Seidl, and other composers.

INSTALLATION AS GRAND MASTER OF ENGLISH FREEMASONS.

April 28th, 1875.

IN the history of Freemasonry there has never occurred an event more memorable, or a scene more imposing than the Installation of the Prince of Wales as Grand Master of English Freemasons, at the Royal Albert Hall, on the 28th of April, 1875. The vast Hall was filled with nearly ten thousand members of the craft, of all ranks and degrees, and in costume proper to their masonic conditions. An open space, in front of the organ, had been reserved for the Grand Officers, and for distinguished visitors, including deputations from various foreign lodges.

The Earl of Carnarvon, the Pro-Grand Master, having taken his seat on the throne, performed the ceremonies necessary for to convert the assemblage into a meeting of the Grand Lodge, and the Minute of the Prince's election as Grand Master having been read and confirmed, Garter King-at-Arms formed and headed a procession to meet His Royal Highness. The Duke of Connaught had already seated himself near the Pro-Grand Master, and had been warmly received; but when the Prince entered the Hall, the vast assemblage rose as one man, and, regardless for the moment alike of Masonic order and of the ceremonies of the craft, greeted him with such applause as even his experience at public assemblages could seldom have heard equalled. The Prince was conducted up the arena to a chair on the left of the Pro-Grand Master, and before seating himself he bowed repeatedly in response to the plaudits of the brethren. He then went through the forms prescribed by the Masonic ritual, and was duly inducted into his throne, the enthusiasm of the assembled Freemasons once again outstripping the proper order of the ceremonial, and finding vent in cheers with which the building rang again.

Garter King-at-Arms, who holds also the high Masonic office of Grand Director of Ceremonies, then proclaimed His Royal Highness in due form, and called upon the brethren to salute him in Masonic fashion. This being done, the Earl of Carnarvon rose from the seat to which he had retired, and, according to ancient custom, addressed the new Grand Master on the duties of his office. He thus concluded his address :—

"Your Royal Highness is not the first by many of your illustrious family who have sat in that chair. It is, no doubt, by the lustre of your great name and position you will reflect honour on the craft to-day; but it is also something to be at the head of such a body as is represented here. I may truly say that never in the whole history of Freemasonry has such a Grand Lodge been convened as that on which my eye rests at this moment, and there is further an inner view to be taken, that so far as my eyes can carry me over these serried ranks of white and blue, the gold and purple, I recognise in them men who have solemnly taken obligations of worth and morality—men who have undertaken the duties of citizens and the loyalty of subjects. I am expressing but very feebly the feelings and aspirations of this great assemblage when I say that I trust the connexion of your Royal Highness with the craft may be lasting, and that you may never have occasion for one moment's regret or anxiety when you look back upon the events of to-day."

The Prince, who was again greeted with loud and prolonged cheering, replied in the following terms :—

"Brethren, I am deeply grateful to the Most Worshipful the Pro-Grand Master for the excessively kind words he has just spoken to you, and for the cordial reception which you have given me. It has béen your unanimous wish that I should occupy this chair as your Grand Master, and you have this day installed me. It is difficult for me to find words adequate to express my deep thanks for the honour which has already been bestowed upon me—an honour which has, as history bears testimony, been bestowed upon several members of my family, my predecessors; and, brethren, it will always be my most ardent and sincere wish to walk in the footsteps of good men who have preceded me, and, with God's help, to fulfil the duties which I have been called upon to occupy to-day.

"The Pro-Grand Master has told you, brethren, and I feel convinced, that such an assemblage as this has never been known; and when I look round me on this vast and spacious Hall, and see those who have come from the north and south, from the east and the west, it is, I trust, an omen which will prove on this auspicious occasion an omen of good. The various duties which I have to perform will frequently, I am afraid, not permit me to attend so much to the duties of the craft as I should desire; but you may be assured that when I have the time I shall do the utmost to maintain this high position, and do my duty by the craft, and by you on every possible occasion. Brethren, it would be useless for me to recapitulate everything which has been told you by the Pro-Grand Master relative to Freemasonry. Every Englishman knows that the two great watchwords of the craft are Loyalty and Charity. These are their watchwords, and as long as Freemasons do not, as Free-masons, mix themselves up in 'politics so long I am sure this high and noble order will flourish, and will maintain the integrity of our great Empire.

"I thank you once more, brethren, for your cordial reception of me to-day, and I thank you for having come such immense distances to welcome me on this occasion. I assure you I shall never forget to-day—never!"

The Prince resumed his seat amid loud cheers, which were long continued. His Royal Highness spoke with a perfect elocu-tion which rendered every syllable audible to the whole of the vast assemblage; but when (adds the reporter of the scene) in conclusion, he uttered a manifest impromptu in saying that the reception which had been accorded to him, and the spectacle which he witnessed, were things which to the last day of his life he "should never forget—never!" there was just so much tremor of his voice as seemed to show that even the trained self-possession of Royalty was somewhat shaken, as indeed it well might be, by the magnitude and the splendour of the spectacle.

At the conclusion of the Prince's address the march from "Eli" was performed upon the organ, and then, a telegraphic address of congratulation from the Grand Lodge at Genoa having previously been read, deputations from the Grand Lodges of Scotland, Ireland, Sweden, and Denmark were successively introduced. The Grand Master next appointed the Earl of Carnarvon to be Pro-Grand Master, Lord Skelmersdale to be Deputy Grand Master, and the Marquis of Hamilton and the Lord Mayor to fill two chief offices in Grand Lodge. The nomination of the Lord Mayor appeared to give especial pleasure to the brethren, and his Lordship, as he took his official seat, was greeted by loud and prolonged applause. The other grand officers were then appointed, and at five o'clock the Lodge was formally closed. The Prince was conducted to his retiring-room by a procession of the principal brethren, and the assembly dispersed.

In the evening there was a banquet in the Freemasons' Hall, in Great Queen Street, which was thronged as it was never thronged before. The Prince of Wales, Most Worshipful Grand Master, presided; on his right being the Duke of Connaught, and on his left Lord Skelmersdale, the Deputy Grand Master. Distinguished officers and members of lodges from all parts of the United Kingdom were present.

The Grand Master proposed the health of "The Queen," in these words :—

"Brethren, the first toast I shall have the honour to propose to you this evening is one which I know will require as few words as possible, as it is always drunk with enthusiasm at all great meetings of Englishmen, more especially at meetings of the craft. I propose 'The Health of Her Majesty the Queen, the Patroness of our Order.'"

The Duke of Manchester, in proposing the health of "The Princess of Wales and the rest of the Royal Family," said: "We have for the first time among us as Most Worshipful Grand Master, the eldest son of Her Majesty, and his brother, the Duke of Connaught, whom we all highly esteem and love as the sons of a father whose memory we all so fondly cherish, and whom we so much regret."

His Royal Highness the Duke of Connaught responded, and proposed "The health of the Most Worshipful the Grand Master.'"

His Royal Highness the Prince of Wales replied :—

"Brethren, I beg to return my most sincere and my most grateful thanks to the Junior Master Mason of England for the kind way in which he has proposed my health, and to you, brethren, for the cordial manner in which you have received it. This is the first time, brethren, that I have had the honour of presiding at the grand festival. I can assure you I am very grateful for your kind reception of me this evening, and I sincerely hope that we may have the pleasure of meeting together on these festive occasions many, many long years to come. I shall never forget, brethren, the ceremony of to-day and the reception which you gave me. I only hope that you may never regret the choice you have made of your Grand Master. Brethren, I assure you on all occasions I shall do my utmost to do my duty in the position in which you have so kindly placed me.

"Before sitting down, brethren, I have a toast to propose, which I feel sure you will all drink with cordiality, and which to me is a specially gratifying toast—that is, the health of our illustrious brother the King of Sweden and Norway. It affords me especial pleasure to propose this toast, as seven years ago I became a member of this craft, initiated by the late King, the brother of the present one. Thereby I consider I have a more special interest in Sweden; and I hope that the Grand Lodges of Sweden and of England may always be bound together in goodwill and fraternal feeling. Our illustrious brother the King has been especially pleased to send over five distinguished brethren to take part in my installation. Therefore it affords me special gratification to drink to the health of one who I know is such a keen Freemason at heart, and so keen an Englishman, that he has frequently visited our shores. Most cordially and heartily do I call upon you, brethren, to drink to 'The health of our illustrious brother the Most Worshipful Grand Master of Sweden, His Majesty the King of Sweden and Norway.'"

Count Salcza responded, and, speaking in French, he passed a high eulogium on Freemasonry, and expressed his great gratification at the magnificent ceremony that had been witnessed in the afternoon, laying especial stress upon the Masonic good feeling between Sweden and Great Britain. He spoke of himself as feeling that he stood among friends and brothers, and he thanked them for their cordial reception.

His Royal Highness the Grand Master then said:—

"Brethren, we are honoured here this evening by the representatives of the Grand Lodges of Scotland, of Ireland, and of Sweden, and I feel convinced that you will all drink with me most cordially and most heartily to their health. The Grand Lodge of England is always most desirous of being on the best possible terms with the Grand Lodges of Scotland and Ireland. Although separate through having other Grand Masters, still those three Grand Lodges may consider one another more or less as one. I have great pleasure in proposing the health of my noble friend and brother, Lord Rosslyn, as representative of the Grand Lodge of Scotland, and I cannot forget the kind

reception I met with at Edinburgh some years ago when he was
Deputy Grand Master, and I received the rank of Patron of
Scotch Freemasons at the hands of the late Earl Dalhousie. It
also gives me great pleasure to propose the health of the representative of the Grand Lodge of Ireland, coupled with the name
of Brother Shekleton, Deputy Grand Master. I have also the
great privilege of being Patron of the Irish Grand Lodge, which
honour I also remember, a few years ago, receiving from the
late Duke of Leinster, who was the popular Grand Master of
Ireland at that time, and the reception I met with I shall not
easily forget. As the representative of the Grand Lodge of
Sweden it affords me great pleasure to couple with this toast
the name of the Admiral on my left. As my earliest associations in Freemasonry have been with the Grand Lodge of
Sweden, I know when I address those gentlemen I see before me
they will appreciate the pleasure it affords me in proposing this
toast. Brethren, I give you the toast of 'The Grand Lodges of
Scotland, Ireland, and Sweden, coupled with the names of Lord
Rosslyn, Brother Shekleton, and Admiral Oscar Dickson.' I
also include in this toast all the other Grand Lodges."

The toast having been drunk, Lord Rosslyn said :—

"Most Worshipful Grand Master and brethren, the honour that
your Royal Highness has done the deputation of the Grand Lodge
of Scotland is warmly appreciated by them. I am glad, indeed,
to have the opportunity after so many years' connexion with the
Grand Lodge of Scotland—no less than twenty-five years—of
congratulating the craft of England and your Royal Highness
also, upon the most magnificent scene I have ever witnessed in
my life.

"I am glad also to think that the splendour, and, I must add,
admirable management of the display to-day, does not quite efface
from your Royal Highness's recollection, the scene upon a similar
scale which we endeavoured to offer you when we had the honour
of having your name as Patron of the Scottish craft. Your Royal
Highness has been good enough to say that you have not forgotten
the occasion. I can assure your Royal Highness no Scotchman
will ever forget it, and I can speak on behalf of the Grand Lodge
of Scotland, with which I have been so long connected, having
served every office in it, from Junior Deacon up to Grand Master,
having been not quite a holiday Freemason, but worked my way
from the ranks up to the position I have the honour to hold now.

"His Royal Highness has this day told us what the duties of
Freemasonry are, and there is no doubt he has summed them up in

two words—loyalty and charity—which includes mercy, a quality
that has been described by the greatest of poets as becoming 'the
throned Monarch better than his crown.' There can be no doubt
that under the auspices of the Most Worshipful Grand Master the
Grand Lodge of England will flourish, and will continue to be a
standard for Masonry all over the world."

Brother R. W. Shekleton, Deputy Grand Master of Ireland,
spoke of the loyalty of Irish Masons, who are, he said, "remarkable for fear of God, fealty to the Sovereign, love to the brotherhood, and friendship to all classes and creeds."

Brother Admiral Oscar Dickson returned thanks in the name
of the Swedish Grand Lodge for the honour conferred upon them.

The Most Worshipful Grand Master then proposed the toast of
various Grand Officers and Brethren, according to custom. Sir
Erasmus Wilson replied for the Stewards, whose special duty it
was, with the aid of their good Brother Francatelli (the Master
Cook), to see to the humble but necessary ceremonies consequent
on our sublunary existence; or, in the beautiful words of our
Ritual: " to lead them to unite in the grand design of being happy
and communicating happiness."

As long before as the 1st of December, 1869, the Prince of
Wales had been received, at Freemasons' Hall, as a Past Grand
Master, at a meeting of the United Grand Lodge of England; and
in a brief speech replied to the address delivered by Lord Zetland,
who was at that time Grand Master.

One of the first appointments made by the Prince of Wales as
Grand Master was that of Colonel Shadwell Clerke, to the
Secretaryship of the Grand Lodge of England, an office the duties
of which he performs with great efficiency and courtesy.

ROYAL AGRICULTURAL BENEVOLENT INSTITUTION.

June 5th, 1875.

THE object of this Institution is to provide pensions for Farmers,
their wives, widows, and unmarried orphan daughters. The Queen
is patron, the Duke of Richmond is President, and the Earl of
Northbrook, Chairman of the Executive Council. At the
present time (1888), 647 persons are maintained at an annual cost of nearly
£14,000. The Prince of Wales has always been a generous friend
and supporter of the charity. At the Royal Agricultural Show at
Sandringham, in July, 1886, he called special attention to it, and
pleaded for increased support, as is necessary from the continued
and increasing depression of agriculture. At the present moment
above 400 persons, who have cultivated holdings varying from
2000 to 100 acres, are candidates for pensions, having been ruined

through the various causes of agricultural failure. During the past twenty-eight years, about 1300 persons have been granted annuities, at a total expenditure of £165,821.

At the fifteenth anniversary festival of the Institution, at Willis's Rooms, on the 5th of June, 1875, the Prince of Wales presided. After "The Queen," the patron of the charity, "The health of the Prince with that of the Princess of Wales and the Royal Family," was proposed by the Earl of Hardwicke, who said that the Prince of Wales had done them great honour in presiding that evening. "It was only another testimony of that interest which he takes in the welfare of every portion of the community. The position of the Prince of Wales was not one of the easiest. He has no definite duties, but the duty he has laid down for himself is of a very definite nature. It is to benefit to the best of his power all his fellow-creatures. He himself was not going to pass any eulogiums on the Prince of Wales, although he had intimate knowledge of his character and the privilege of his friendship. He would only say that the Prince does credit to the very high position in which he is placed, and that so long as he lays himself out to associate with English people of all classes, and to faithfully discharge duties which, if not in themselves very agreeable, are beneficial to the English race, he will be a popular and able Prince. A duty more wrapt up with sympathy than that which the Prince that evening undertook could not be conceived. He tells the whole agricultural class of this country that he places himself at their disposal to further their interests and to help them in their distress. So long as the Royal Family cling to the soil of this country, and mix with its life and its sports and amusements, they will never fail to receive the support of their countrymen in all times of trial."

The toast was received with cheers, and the Prince of Wales said :—

"It is difficult for me, gentlemen, to find words to express my gratitude for the excessively kind manner in which my noble friend has proposed this toast, and the cordial way in which you have been kind enough to receive it. I need hardly tell you that it affords me the greatest pleasure and satisfaction to occupy the chair this evening. When I know those gentlemen who have preceded me as your Chairmen, such as Mr. Disraeli, Lord Lytton, the present Lord Derby, or the Duke of Richmond, I feel some diffidence in addressing you this evening. At the same time I think the proceedings of this evening will, as I hope, be short, yet I trust they may be satisfactory to all here present.

" I sincerely say that I do take a great interest in all that is connected with agriculture. I may call myself a colleague of many of you present as a farmer on a small scale, and I only hope that I may never have occasion to be a pensioner of this institution. It is impossible, I think, for any British gentleman to live at his country place without taking an interest in agriculture, and in all those things which concern the farmers of this great country. I thank you also for the very kind way in which you have mentioned the health of the Princess of Wales and the rest of the Royal Family.

"Before I sit down I beg to propose a toast—one which is never left out at great gatherings of Englishmen, and which here ought to be brought most prominently before your notice—'The Army, Navy, Militia, and Reserve Forces.' The very backbone of the country, the best recruits of the Army and Navy, come from the agricultural districts. Since we know, also, that our commercial and agricultural interests depend upon the valour and efficiency of our land and sea forces, you will, I think, agree with me that it is a toast especially for this meeting, one most suitable for this agricultural feast. It is a toast which I feel sure you all, gentlemen, will drink most heartily. With the Army it gives me great pleasure to couple the name of General Sir W. Knollys, and with the Navy that of Sir J. Heron Maxwell."

Sir W. Knollys, in responding for the profession to which he belongs, including the Militia, the Volunteers, and the Reserve Forces, dwelt upon the habits, the physical well-being, and powers of endurance which fit the agricultural population of this country for the profession of arms. They bring with them also that contentment and discipline which till recent events particularly distinguished the agricultural labourer, and are always ready to fight for country and Queen.

Sir J. Heron Maxwell having replied for the Navy, the toastmaster, Mr. Goodchild, announced a bumper toast, and the Prince of Wales said:—

"The toast which I now have the honour of proposing to you is that of 'Success to the Royal Agricultural Benevolent Institution.' Gentlemen, this excellent and charitable institution has been only in existence for the space of fifteen years, and its object is the relief of farmers who have been reduced by failure of crops, loss of stock, bad seasons, and other reasons. It has been founded, as I say, for that purpose, but there is one thing

N

which is absolutely necessary to entitle to relief, and that is
that the recipient of the pension must have, as his exclusive
means of support, cultivated at least fifty acres, or rented land
at £100 a year at least for twenty years. And those farmers
who receive pensions must prove to the society that they do not
possess an income from other sources of more than £20 a year.
Among those, also, who are benefited by the society are the
widows and children or orphans of farmers and their unmarried
daughters.

" One main object of the managers of the institution is to
maintain in their own districts those who have not the means
of providing for themselves, so that, instead of their going to
the workhouse, or having to remove to distant parts of the
kingdom, they may be kept as much as possible in the counties
where they were born and bred. Pensions varying from £20 to
£40 a year are granted, and since the foundation of this society
as many as 432 pensioners have been elected, and 53 children
have been educated and maintained at a cost of not far from
£40,000. At present there are 302 pensioners and 41 children
on the books of the charity, and these numbers will, I understand, be augmented during the present month by the election
of 51 pensioners. The total cost of the year will be nearly
£8500, and I am sorry to say the donations and annual sums
received amount to little over £6800. Therefore, you see that
although this institution is in a highly prosperous state, at the
same time the funds are not as great as we could wish. It
is for that reason that we assemble here—to augment those funds.

" When I look around and see so large a number of gentlemen,
who have come great distances to support me on this occasion,
I feel I shall not ask them in vain to extend their support to so
excellent an institution. You were kind enough just now to
drink in a cordial manner my health, but I think if I had put
myself before you as a surgeon whose health you were going to
drink you might not have received me so cordially. On this
occasion I hope you will look upon me as a surgeon. The few
words I have to say to you are my lancet, with which I have to
bleed you—and you will all feel much the better for it.

" Many may think, ' Why should we give money to those who
possibly by their own fault may have got into distress ? ' But

that is not the object mentioned. All will agree that the cleverest agriculturists who thoroughly understand their business may, through bad seasons, failures of crops, and a variety of other causes which you know, gentlemen, far better than I do, have found themselves suddenly in the most abject want. It is a great pity that the farmers' clubs and agricultural societies do not do so much as they ought in support of so excellent an institution.

" I see by your applause it is only too true, and I must call upon you this evening to show that you have supported this charity in the most material manner. I thank you once more for the kind and attentive manner in which you have listened to the few words which I have uttered. I only regret that it has not fallen to the lot of another than myself to bring the subject before you, and I am sure that you will take the will for the deed. 'Prosperity to the Royal Agricultural Benevolent Institution !'"

The toast was drunk with all the honours, and the Secretary, Mr. C. Bousfield Shaw, read a list of subscriptions headed by the Queen with £25. The Prince of Wales gave, in addition to his annual subscription of ten guineas, a donation of 100 guineas. The largest list of collections was Mr. Naish's, of £465. The total amount was no less than £8000.

Mr. C. S. Read, M.P., then proposed the toast of "The Executive Council, the Secretary, and the Honorary Local Secretaries." In the course of his speech, he remarked that it had been well said by His Royal Highness that agriculture is exposed to more vicissitudes and difficulties than almost any other industry, and it was surprising that it should have existed so long without any benevolent institution. They must not forget in that room that they owed the fact that such an institution now exists to the kind and generous heart of their old friend, Mr. Mechi, the founder of this society; and the tenant-farmers of England would never forget the day when the Heir Apparent to the Throne of England condescended to preside at their annual banquet.

The Marquis of Huntly responded, and said as an example of the good done by active local energy, that in Cheshire they only had last year a donation of ten guineas, and subscribers of thirty-one, while from Norfolk, the Prince's county, with a smaller agricultural population, they had donations of £826.

The Prince of Wales then said :—

" The list of toasts which we all have before us has now come to an end, but I shall take the liberty of proposing one more toast, the last, but by no means the least. We have been honoured on this occasion by fair ladies, and I think it would be very wrong if we were to separate without cordially drinking their health. We see especially how much the comfort, the well-being, prosperity, and happiness of farmers and agriculturists depend upon a kind wife to cheer them by the fireside at the end of their day's work, and to lighten by female influence the load of difficulties. It affords me the most sincere pleasure to couple with this toast the name of one to whom this institution is so much indebted—Mr. Mechi. Lord Huntly has been mentioning to you the word 'energy'; and if it had not been for the energy of Mr. Mechi this society would never have existed. Let me also say, it would not be so prosperous as it is now if it were not for those energies and the assistance which he has given it. I hope the words and expressions which the noble marquis has lately made use of will not be lost by this company, and that all those who wish to further the work so worthily begun by Mr. Mechi will continue it, so that it may never decrease in funds for the excellent object for which it is designed. I beg to propose the toast of ' The Ladies,' coupled with the name of Mr. Mechi."

Mr. Mechi, in the course of his reply, said that the help of His Royal Highness would be of the greatest importance to the institution.

The way in which the Prince introduced the toast of the founder of the Institution was in his happiest vein. Mr. Mechi's death was a great loss to the agricultural community, for no one more efficiently brought their claims before the public. It may be added, that the tenant-farmers of the kingdom have no truer friend than the Prince of Wales.

THE INDIAN EMBASSY.

November 1875—May 1876.

THE visit of the Prince of Wales to India, apart from what it brought of personal information or amusement, must be regarded as one of the most important services he has yet rendered to the Empire. This is why we call it an embassy rather than a tour or a journey. It appears that as far back as the year 1858, the idea of a tour in the Eastern possessions of the Crown was suggested by Lord Canning to the Prince Consort, as part of the education of the Heir Apparent. But he was then only seventeen, and the proposal was made merely as an incident of foreign travel. A succession of events, both at home and in the East, caused the scheme to be postponed, nor was it seriously renewed till the Prince had attained an age, and acquired an experience in affairs, which would secure for the expedition high consideration for political and imperial, as well as personal, purposes.

In the beginning of the year 1875 it was rumoured that the project was seriously entertained, and on the 16th of March the Marquis of Salisbury made an official announcement to the Indian Council of the intended visit. Many arrangements, however, had to be made, and many difficulties surmounted, before actual preparations for the journey commenced. All these are recounted in detail by Dr. W. H. Russell, in the introduction to his book on the ' Prince of Wales's Tour,' a reprint in expanded and permanent form of his letters as the special correspondent of the *Times.* Dr. Russell had the advantage of accompanying the Prince as one of his personal suite, under the title of Honorary Private Secretary. It is fortunate that the journey had such a historian. The work not only gives a Diary of the tour in India, with a full record of the proceedings of the Prince, but is in itself a most interesting and instructive book of travel, full of information, conveyed in the graphic and bright style which has made the author famous as a man of letters. To this book the reader of these pages is referred for the story of the Royal expedition, both in India and in the countries through which he passed on the outward and homeward journey.*

The Prince was fortunate in the companions of his journey, even to the humbler and useful attendants. It is greatly to the credit of his judgment and his right feeling that the first to whom he expressed a wish to accompany him was Sir Bartle Frere, a wise and good man, and whose Indian experience would be of immense value. In the suite there were, of his own household, Lord Suffield, Sir Dighton Probyn, Colonel Ellis, and Sir Francis Knollys. The Duke of Sutherland, Lord Alfred Paget, Lord Aylesford, Lord Carington, Colonel Owen Williams, Lord Charles Beresford, Captain Fitz George, were invited to join the expedition. Canon Duckworth was selected as chaplain, and Sir Joseph Phayrer as physician; Mr. Albert Grey, secretary to Sir Bartle Frere, Dr. Russell, and Mr. S. P. Hall as artist, completed the list of those who formed the suite of His Royal Highness. Several of these—General Probyn, Colonel Ellis, and Dr. Phayrer —had long Indian experience; and Lord Charles Beresford had

---

* 'The Prince of Wales's Tour: a Diary in India, with some accounts of the visits to the Courts of Greece, Egypt, Spain, and Portugal.' By William Howard Russell, LL.D. With illustrations by Sydney E. Hall. Sampson Low & Co.

accompanied the Duke of Edinburgh in his Indian tour the year before.

The route to be laid down required much consultation, partly from public considerations and partly from questions of climate and care for the Prince's health. The best time of starting had also to be considered. At last all was arranged, and on the 11th of November the Prince started. The route was to be viâ Brindisi, to Greece, Egypt, Bombay, Ceylon, Madras, Calcutta, Lucknow, Delhi, Lahore, Agra, Gwalior, Nepal, Bareilly, Allahabad, Indore, Bombay, and home by Egypt, Malta, Gibraltar, Spain, Portugal. The departure from Lisbon was on the 7th of May, and on the 11th the *Serapis* anchored off the Isle of Wight, where the Princess of Wales and the children, in the *Enchantress* yacht, awaited the arrival. "The scene at the landing at Portsmouth," says Dr. Russell, "was a becoming prelude to the greeting which the whole country gave the Prince of Wales on his return from the visit to India, which will be for ever a great landmark in the history of the Empire."

The numerous and diverse events and incidents of the months in India—the sight-seeing, the adventures (some of them strange and perilous), the shooting parties and hunting expeditions, the manifold amusements and excitements of travel—all these were enjoyed by the Prince as much as if he were only the most light-hearted tourist or keenest sportsman. But at the same time, so far as official ceremony and public affairs were concerned, he bore himself all through with a thoughtfulness and dignity worthy of his high position, and of the important mission with which he was entrusted as representing Royalty and the British nation.

There was ceremonial reception at Athens, and again in Egypt in the court of the Khedive, but the first official and formal event of the Prince's mission was the investiture of Prince Tewfik, the Viceroy's eldest son, with the Order of the Star of India. This was done in the palace, with imposing ceremony.

The next official event was the reception of an address from the inhabitants of Aden, which was presented by a Parsee merchant, on behalf of the community. The address of the Parsee showed very clearly how well the object of the Prince's visit was understood throughout the East. The Prince made an appropriate reply, which no doubt was speedily wired to Bombay, and read in the native newspapers all over India.

On arriving at Bombay it was again a Parsee who headed the first deputation and read the first address to the Prince on landing in India. It was from the Corporation of Bombay, the second city in the British Empire, in population if not in wealth. The address set forth in glowing terms the historical and commercial claims of the city to distinction, and expressed the pleasure of seeing among them the heir to the Crown, whom the Queen had sent to become personally acquainted with the people of India. The Prince replied in the following words:—

" It is a great pleasure to me to begin my travels in India at a place so long associated with the Royal Family of England, and to find that during so many generations of British rule this great port has steadily prospered. Your natural advantages would have insured a large amount of commerce under any strong Government, but in your various and industrious population I gladly recognize the traces of a rule which gives shelter to all who obey the laws; which recognizes no invidious distinctions of race; which affords to all perfect liberty in matters of religious opinion and belief; and freedom in the pursuit of trade and of all lawful callings. I note with satisfaction the assurance I derive from your address, that under British rule men of varied creeds and nations live in harmony among themselves, and develop to the utmost those energies which they inherit from widely separate families of mankind, whilst all join in loyal attachment to the British Crown, and take their part, as in my native country, in the management of their own local affairs.

" I shall gladly communicate to Her Majesty what you so loyally and kindly say regarding the pleasure which the people of India derive from Her Majesty's gracious permission to me to visit this part of Her Majesty's Empire. I assure you that the Princess of Wales has never ceased to share my regret that she was unable to accompany me. She has from her earliest years taken the most lively interest in this great country, and the cordiality of your greeting this day will make her yet more regret the impossibility of her sharing in person the pleasure your welcome afforded me."

This reply, so happily conceived, and delivered with quiet earnestness, delighted all who heard it. But the echoes of it would soon reach every part of India, and the chiefs and rulers, and also the leaders of opinion in the native press, would from these words of the Prince receive a lesson of true statesmanship and constitutional government.

The greatest event at Bombay was the reception of the Rulers and Chiefs of Western India, a scene of truly Oriental magnificence, the description of which forms one of the most brilliant chapters in Dr. Russell's book. All the established forms of Indian ceremony were observed. The greatest rulers were saluted with the largest number of guns, the Maharajah of Mysore, for instance, having a salute of twenty-one guns, while others were fifteen-gun chiefs or

eleven-gun rajahs, as the case might be, according to the population
and wealth of the territories over which they ruled. Their dresses,
and jewels, and retinues, and the modes of reception, as well as
their personal characteristics, are all duly recorded. The Viceroy
of India, Lord Northbrook, was with the Prince of Wales at one
grand Durbar, and his position in regard to the Royal Envoy from
the Queen, the arrangement of which had caused some difficulty in
anticipation, was gracefully managed by the Viceroy and the
Prince themselves. The Bombay Durbar passed off admirably. It
was the Prince's birthday, the 9th of November, and no such scene
as on that day can he expect again to witness. The "Carpet," which
takes an important place in Oriental durbars, the nuzzars or gifts
of homage, and other points of ceremonial, as well as the number
of guns in the salute, had all been arranged by official notices to
the political officers attached to the native courts. But the cordial
bearing of the Prince, and his kindly words when he was told that
any visitors knew the English tongue, gave more satisfaction than
the formal ceremonials.

. A State banquet was given by the Governor in honour of the
Prince's birthday. In returning thanks for his health, proposed
by the Governor, the Prince made a short but telling speech. He
said :—

"It has long been my earnest wish—the dream of my life—
to visit India; and now that my desire has been gratified, I
can only say, Sir Philip Wodehouse, how much pleased I am to
have spent my thirty-fourth birthday under your roof in
Bombay. I shall remember with satisfaction the hospitable
reception I have had from the Governor, and all here, as long
as I live, and I believe that I may regard what I have experienced in Bombay as a guarantee of the future of my progress
through this great Empire, which forms so important a part of
the dominions of the Queen."

These last words were a true forecast of the Royal progress
throughout India. What has been said of Bombay, must serve to
give an idea of what everywhere had to be recorded. But we
must refrain from further details of what occurred at other Presi-
dencies, and only add that the crowning public event of the whole
tour, the chief ceremony of the mission of the Prince, the holding
the Chapter of the Order of the Star of India, came off, at Calcutta,
on New Year's Day, 1876, with brilliant *éclat*.

This only may be said, that no more successful embassy than
that undertaken by the Prince ever went forth from England. It
may be added that the great ends accomplished by it cost to the
British Exchequer less than £60,000 ; and this, although no expense
was spared in carrying out the mission with due display and

munificence. Nor ought it to be omitted that the Prince was most generous, as he is at home, in his gifts to useful and charitable institutions, visited by him in the course of his journey. But we must leave the fascinating story of the Indian visit, to resume the record of the humbler, but not less honourable duties, undertaken by the Prince after his return to England.

LICENSED VICTUALLERS' ASYLUM.

May 7th, 1877.

THE " Licensed Victuallers," as might be expected from so numerous, wealthy, and ancient a Corporation, possess several charitable institutions. They have a " Permanent Fund," founded as far back as 1794, and incorporated in 1836, which grants weekly allowances to about two hundred and sixty persons, at an annual outlay of £4770 ; grants £300 yearly for the maintenance of twelve children in the Society's School ; and dispenses temporary relief amounting to £500. The School just named, founded in 1803, situated in Kennington Lane, Lambeth, wholly maintains and educates 200 children of deceased or distressed members of the Incorporated Society of Licensed Victuallers. Its income from all sources averages £6000. Besides these charitable operations, there is the Licensed Victuallers' Asylum, in the Old Kent Road, founded in 1827, and incorporated in 1836, for the reception and mainten- ance of decayed aged licensed victuallers, their wives or widows, and for granting weekly allowances of money to fifty candidates, while waiting for the more substantial benefits of the Society. The Asylum comprises 170 distinct houses, with a common library, a chapel and resident chaplain. The property covers six acres of freehold land, and the annual expense is about £8500.

In support of this useful and well-managed Asylum, the Prince of Wales presided, at a special jubilee festival held on May the 7th, 1877. The Duke of Sussex was its first patron in 1827, and he was succeeded by the Prince Consort, on whose death the Prince of Wales assumed the office. A large number of influential persons accepted the invitation to be present, including Earl Granville, several members of the House of Peers, many members of the House of Commons, and three Bishops, in all about 300 supporters of the institution.

After grace by the Bishop of Winchester, in whose diocese the Asylum is situated, the Chairman rose to propose the usual opening toast of " The Queen," saying that Her Majesty had always taken deep interest in this Asylum, and had sent £50 to its funds at one of its annual festivals. Earl Granville, in a genial and humorous speech, proposed the toast of " The Prince and Princess of Wales and the rest of the Royal Family." The noble Lord said he considered it a fortunate circumstance that he was there that evening, because in the afternoon he met a friend, who said to him : " You really don't mean to say you are going to dine with those wicked people the licensed victuallers ?" Now, in arguing the case with his friend, he did not go into the abstruse question whether all persons who dealt in articles of general demand and great consumption, useful in themselves, and capable of being misapplied or abused, such as food, or drink, or money, or physic, or a great many other things which, excellent in themselves in a small quantity, might be most deleterious, when misapplied—were monsters. He satisfied himself with a much shorter answer, which was that, as a study in human nature, it would be rather interesting to see 300 monsters of iniquity assembled cordially to promote the work of genuine charity and benevolence. Having justified his presence, he ventured to say that the toast he proposed would be received with the most unfeigned and genuine pleasure, since he had to give " The Health of the Prince, of the Princess of Wales, and the rest of the Royal Family." He might recommend it on the score of the high position of the Chairman, which enabled him to influence so many for good, or on the ground that the Prince and Princess are the most popular couple in the country, and in all the vast dependencies of the British Crown. He might put it on the ground that the Prince shows that genial and cordial energy in anything which he undertakes, whether in protecting the interests of British exhibitors on the Champs de Mars at Paris, or in presiding in a work of charity and kindliness. He might also recommend it in consequence of His Royal Highness being the very best chairman of a public dinner. Instead of long speeches, His Royal Highness made addresses that were, to use a homely expression, as full of meat as an egg. But without using any arguments whatever, he would give them " The Health of the Prince and Princess, and the rest of the Royal Family," and he was sure it would be received with enthusiasm.

The band of the Grenadier Guards, under Mr. Dan Godfrey, played " God Bless the Prince of Wales," after which the Prince rose and said :—

" My Lords and Gentlemen,—I am excessively grateful to the noble Earl for the most kind and flattering—I may say far too flattering—terms in which he has been kind enough to propose my health, that of the Princess, and the other members of my family, and for the excessively cordial manner in which you have been kind enough to receive it this evening. It is, no doubt, somewhat unusual that the health of the Chairman should be given at so early a period, but I am very grateful to the noble Earl for the kind manner in which he has given it, and to you for the way in which you have received it. Lord Granville has just mentioned to you that this afternoon he was accosted by a friend, who asked him why he was coming to-night, and expressed some surprise at his doing so. Lord Granville was asked by one friend. During the last three or four days I have received as many as 200 petitions from bodies in all parts of the United Kingdom begging me on no account to be present here this evening. Of course, I do not wish in any way to disparage those temperance societies, which have, no doubt, excellent objects in view. But I think this time they have rather overshot the mark, because the object of the meeting to-night is not to encourage the love of drink, but to support a good and excellent charity. I can only say, and I am sure all those here will agree with me, that no one had the interest of all those in his adopted country more at heart than my lamented father, and I feel perfectly convinced that he would never have been the patron of the society unless he was sure that it was one that was likely to do good, and that it was deserving of his support. Lord Granville has made far too flattering allusion to me as a Chairman, but as he has been kind enough to say— giving me certainly a broad hint—that speeches of this kind should be short, I am only too happy to avail myself of it; and if brevity is the soul of wit, I shall be the wittiest of chairmen.

" Before sitting down I wish to bring to your notice a toast which is always honoured with enthusiasm at every assemblage of Englishmen. The toast is given, indeed, so often that it is difficult to vary the manner of giving it, and especially at the present moment I feel it would be unbecoming in me to dilate in any way on the Army or the Navy. But at the present moment, when the political horizon far away is so obscure, I feel sure that, whatever may happen, it is the wish of all Englishmen that our Army, though small, should be in the highest state of efficiency, and that our Navy should be, as it ought to be, the best in the world. I have lately returned from a short trip in the Mediterranean, where I had the pleasure of spending ten days in one of the finest men-of-war in Her Majesty's service; and though the captain of that vessel is my own brother, I feel I may say that there are few vessels which are in a better state of order and discipline. And I think that if all the rest of the Fleet are in the same state we shall have no cause to complain of our Naval Service. With the Army and Reserve Forces I beg to couple the name of General Sir W. Knollys, and with the Navy that of Admiral Sir A. Milne, who for so long a time has given his valuable services to the Admiralty."

Sir W. Knollys, in returning thanks, said that, in addition to intemperance in drink, there was such a thing as intemperance of the brain and pen, and he had observed marks of that in some of the communications which, as a member of the Prince's household, he had had under his notice during the last few days. Sir Alexander Milne also returned thanks. The Prince of Wales then rose and said :—

"My Lords and Gentlemen,—The toast which I now give you is the toast of the evening—'Renewed Prosperity to the Licensed Victuallers' Asylum.' We are met here together to-night for the purpose of doing honour to its 50th anniversary, and when I look round me and see so numerous an assembly, I feel sure that we shall have in every respect reason to be grateful for the bounty of these gentlemen, who are prepared to do much towards benefiting this excellent charitable institution. As everybody is aware, it was founded as a refuge for the aged and decayed members of the trade, so that they might be spared from dying of hunger, or being thrown on the poor-rates as recipients of parish relief.

" The first stone of this Asylum was laid by my grand uncle, the Duke of Sussex, and forty-three houses were then erected. Up to the year 1835 lodging only was provided ; but the Board of Management then originated a fund which enabled them to maintain the inmates as well. A weekly allowance in money and coals was granted to these poor people.

" In the year 1849 the applicants had become so numerous that it was determined to erect an additional building. The first stone of that building was laid by my lamented father, who again performed a similar service when it was found necessary, nineteen years ago, to enlarge still further this Asylum. In the year 1866 my brother, the Duke of Edinburgh, laid the foundation stone of another wing.

" In the year 1863 I had the pleasure of becoming the Patron of this Society, although in sad circumstances, in succession to my father. I had great satisfaction also in assisting in the ceremony of unveiling the statue which has been erected to the memory of my father in the grounds of the Asylum. I believe I am correct in stating that the institution now consists of about 170 separate habitations. The number of inmates is about 210, who receive, the married couples, 10s., and the others, 8s. per week, besides coals, medical assistance, &c. The annual expenses are very large, as they amount to upwards of £8000, and as for the greater amount of that expenditure the Asylum is dependent upon voluntary contributions, the Governors are most anxious to collect now a sum which may be added to their capital in order that they may feel that they have more certain sources of income. I feel sure you will aid them, and I call upon you once more to give most liberally all that is in your power to give, and to show that you are anxious by pecuniary means as well as by your presence here this evening to benefit the institution. I will not weary you with any more words, because no doubt at many other dinners the main facts of the case have been brought before your notice. I will only say that it has given me the greatest pleasure to take the chair this evening. I thank you again for the cordial support which you have been kind enough to give me, and I feel that now again I may call upon you once more to do all in your power for the prosperity of the Licensed Victuallers' Asylum."

Lord G. Hamilton, M.P., proposed the toast of " The Stewards," Mr. E. N. Buxton, M.P., in acknowledging the toast, said they had no desire to claim from His Royal Highness in any sense any appearance of taking sides on a question by his presence there that night. The kind words he had spoken only showed his approval of the great principle that every trade should provide for its poor and disabled members.

The Secretary of the Institution read a list of subscriptions, headed with an additional donation of 100 guineas from His Royal Highness, which was followed by large subscriptions from Messrs. Bass, Allsopp, Huggins, Mr. C. Sykes, M.P., and other gentlemen. The whole list amounted to £5000.

In recent years the subject of intemperance has attracted more attention, and the crime and poverty resulting from drink has led to a general consent of opinion that some greater regulation of the trade is necessary.

UNVEILING ALBERT STATUE AT CAMBRIDGE.

January 22nd, 1878.

THE election of His Royal Highness Prince Albert to the Chancellorship of the University of Cambridge, was one of the honours of which he was most justly proud. He was only twenty-eight years of age, and had not yet been eight years in England. But during these years he had won the respect and admiration of all that was highest and best in the nation. When the Chancellorship of Cambridge became vacant by the death of the Duke of Northumberland, on the 12th of February, 1847, application was made to the Prince, on the next day, by Dr. Whewell, the Master of Trinity, to allow himself to be put in nomination for the office. The request was separately made by the Marquis of Lansdowne on the same day. A letter from the Bishop of London (Blomfield) conveyed the assurance that the Prince's acceptance of the office would be regarded by many of the leading members of the University, with whom he had conferred, as " honourable and advantageous to the University." The Prince replied, through Mr. Anson, to whom the bishop's letter was addressed, that he would be gratified by such a distinction, if it was the unanimous desire of the University.

Unfortunately there was another candidate proposed, and an election took place, the Prince obtaining a large majority. Of 24 Professors who voted, 16 gave their votes for the Prince; of 30 Senior Wranglers, 19 were on his side; while of the resident members 3 to 1 voted for him. Notwithstanding this strong expression of opinion, the Prince felt inclined to refuse the office, but was induced to accept it, on the reasons of the opposition being explained to him, and on the assurance that the contest would be forgotten after a few months, and that he might then count on the confidence and goodwill of the whole Academical body.

Fortunately he accepted, and the assurances of his supporters were more than verified. On the 24th of March the ceremony of inauguration was gone through at Buckingham Palace, when the Letters-Patent were presented to the Prince by the Vice-Chancellor, accompanied by the most distinguished officials, and about one hundred and thirty members of the University. How soon and how powerfully his influence was felt in advancing education at Cambridge, is matter of history. The following simple entry in his Diary, on the 1st of November, 1848, shows the result of his first efforts : " My plan for a reform of the studies at Cambridge is carried by a large majority." To the enlightened and judicious plans of the Prince the subsequent advances and extension of education in England have been largely due. Nowhere was this more gratefully acknowledged than at Cambridge.

During his life he was honoured, and after his death a statue was erected to his memory, chiefly by subscriptions from the University. The site chosen was in the FitzWilliam Museum, a memorial worthy of the noble benefactor, who bequeathed to the University his valuable collection of pictures and books, with a sum of £100,000 to be spent in providing a building suitable for their reception. The statue of Prince Albert was here fittingly placed. It was one of the best works of Mr. Foley, in his later years, and is universally admired as a striking and worthy representation of the illustrious Chancellor.

It was for the ceremony of unveiling this statue that the Prince of Wales visited Cambridge on the 22nd of January, 1878. He was met at the gate of the Museum by the Chancellor, the Duke of Devonshire, the Lord High Steward, the Vice-Chancellor, and a distinguished company. On entering the vestibule an address was read by the Chancellor, seting forth the services to the University of the Prince Consort, during his fifteen years' tenure of office. The address thus concluded :—

" This memorial of the Prince Consort cannot but serve to remind us also as Englishmen of the signal benefits conferred by His Royal Highness upon our Queen and country by his wise and far-seeing counsels, his never-wearying vigilance and attention to the public welfare, and his entire devotion to the duties of his exalted station at the sacrifice of all personal interests and objects.

" We thank your Royal Highness for the distinguished honour conferred upon the University by your presence among us this day. It remains only for us to prefer our request that your Royal Highness will now be graciously pleased to uncover the statue. To no one does this honourable office more appropriately belong."

The Prince of Wales returned the following reply :—

" My Lord Duke, Mr. Vice-Chancellor, Members of the Senate, and Gentlemen,—I thank you for your address. I feel that it is hardly necessary for me to assure you what pleasure it affords me to be present on this occasion for the purpose of unveiling the statue of my illustrious father and your late Chancellor, in compliance with the special desire and invitation of the Chancellor and the Members of the Senate of the University. But, apart from the performance of this duty, I must express my great satisfaction at having an opportunity of revisiting Cambridge as a member of your University, and recalling to my mind the agreeable recollections which I have always retained of my undergraduate's days. The interest which the Prince Consort took in everything relating to the welfare of the University is well known to us all, and it is a source of deep gratification to me to witness the respect which the members of the

University show to his memory by the erection of this fine
statue. I will now proceed to execute the task imposed upon
me of unveiling the statue."

The Prince then walked up to the Statue, and having pulled a
string, it stood unveiled before the assembly, who contemplated it
for a few moments in silence.

The Chancellor again addressing the Prince, thanked him for
the honour which he had done the University in being present on
so interesting an occasion. It was, however, a source of regret to
him that so many had passed away who had the best means of
becoming acquainted with the views and thoughts of the Prince
Consort—such as Professor Sedgwick and Dr. Whewell—who, if
they were alive, would gladly have borne testimony to his great
virtues that day. There were, however, many now in that hall
who, he had no doubt, entertained the liveliest recollections of the
deep interest which was taken by His Royal Highness in the work
in which the University was engaged.

The Earl of Powis also bore testimony to the unwearied interest
which was taken by the Prince Consort in the development of new
studies in the University, even amid the weighty cares of State.

Dr. G. Paget, Regius Professor of Physic, spoke in highly
eulogistic terms of the Prince Consort's love of science and art,
observing that it was under his auspices that the Moral and
Natural Science Triposes had been established, to the great advantage of teaching in the University.

The ceremony in the entrance-hall was thus brought to a close,
and the Prince of Wales, the Chancellor, and their respective
suites proceeded to the picture gallery, where His Royal Highness
held a *levée*, which was very numerously attended. After the *levée*
he returned to Trinity College. It was several years since the
Prince of Wales had paid a visit to Cambridge of any duration. He
spent some time there as an under-graduate, and made with the
Princess of Wales a stay of three days in 1864, when he had the
degree of LL.D. conferred upon him.

Another memorable visit was paid on the 9th of June, 1888,
when the Prince of Wales, accompanied by the Princess and their
three daughters, witnessed the conferring of an honorary degree
on Prince Albert Victor. Other notable graduates *honoris causâ*
were on the list that day, including the Marquis of Salisbury, the
Earl of Rosebery, Lord Selborne, Mr. Balfour, Mr. Goschen, and
Professor Stokes. At the luncheon afterwards given in the Fitzwilliam Museum, the Prince of Wales said it was seven and
twenty years since he was first connected with the University.
"They were happy days," he added, "and I always look back to
them with the greatest pleasure and satisfaction."

INFANT ORPHAN ASYLUM, WANSTEAD.

June 28th, 1878.

THIS institution maintains and educates the orphans of persons once in prosperity, from earliest infancy till fourteen or fifteen years of age. About 60 children are now (1888) annually elected. Nearly the whole of the income depends on voluntary contributions. Subscribers have votes, according to the amount of their subscriptions. There are now nearly 600 in the Asylum, which is open to children from all parts of the British dominions. The Asylum stands in beautifully wooded grounds, at Wanstead, on the outskirts of Epping Forest.

The Prince, accompanied by the Princess of Wales, presided at the anniversary festival, on June 28th, 1878. They drove to Wanstead, and were received at the Asylum by the Bishop of St. Albans, in whose diocese it is, and by the officers of the institution. They were conducted to the Examination Room, where, Dagmar Mary Petersen, a little orphan girl, eight years old, daughter of a Dane, who settled in London as a commercial clerk, herself admitted just eighteen months ago by the loyalty of a lady of the Society of Friends, who wished thus to honour the Princess, commenced the proceedings with a pretty speech which she had got perfectly by heart and recited very clearly. In her childish voice she gave those assembled a distinct account of the asylum. " She had been told that it was the largest of the kind in England. When the boys, girls, officers, and servants are all there, 700 persons sleep in the building. The schools are in three divisions, senior, infants, and nursery children. In the two large senior schools there are about 400 boys and girls. They learn grammar, history, geography, arithmetic, French, music, and drawing, and the girls learn needlework besides. In the two infant schools they do not learn quite so much. In the nursery they learn just a very little and play a good deal. And being little children they learn about the Bible." The little girl who spoke this simple address presented a bouquet to the gracious Princess after the ceremony, and was kissed, praised, and otherwise gratified.

"God bless the Prince of Wales " was excellently sung at the conclusion of the speech; the children came up to the Princess and took their prizes from her hands; and marched out of the room, keeping time to lively music. The Royal party inspected the school-rooms, play-rooms, and dormitories, cheerful and well-ventilated halls; and the Princess carried toys to the children in the nursery.

The Prince of Wales took the chair at luncheon, supported by the Princess of Wales, and their suite, the Duke and Duchess of Manchester, the Bishop of St. Albans and Hon. Mrs. Claughton,

O

and a large assembly. After grace the Prince of Wales rose and proposed " The Health of Her Majesty the Queen." The toast-master next announced a bumper toast, and the Duke of Manchester gave " The Health of His Royal Highness the Prince of Wales, and the Princess of Wales," "a toast which is never more heartily honoured than on these fortunately frequent occasions, when their Royal Highnesses patronize and encourage well-organized charitable institutions, among which this was perhaps one of the best he knew."

The Prince of Wales said, in reply :—

" Ladies and Gentlemen,—On the part of the Princess and myself, we beg to return our warmest thanks to the noble duke for the kind way in which he has proposed this toast, and to you, ladies and gentlemen, for the cordial manner in which you have received it. It has afforded both the Princess and myself the greatest possible pleasure and the greatest possible gratification to come here to-day and to inaugurate the fifty-first anniversary of this excellent and commendable institution. What we have seen ourselves, and what the most part of the company have witnessed on their own part, I think will do more than anything I can say to show you what an excellent institution this is, and how worthy it is of support in every way. The manner in which the children sang, the discipline under which they are evidently kept, the clean and healthy appearance of all of them, is a matter of sincere congratulation to all those who take interest in this institution or have the trouble of its management. I may say that there is one little girl who perfectly astonished us by the elocution which she possessed—well worthy of many a distinguished member of Parliament.

" It was highly interesting to the Princess, as well as to myself, to have been here to-day, the fortieth anniversary of the Queen's Coronation. The first stone of the building in which we are now was laid by my lamented father a few months before I was born ; and I hold in my hand the mallet which was used by him on that occasion, and which has been sent to me by Sir Charles Reed, the chairman of the London School Board, whose father, Dr. Andrew Reed, was, I understand, one of the promoters of this institution, and always took the warmest interest in its welfare. This day seventeen years ago the Prince Consort visited this institution, and this day exactly twelve years ago was the last time the Princess and I were here.

" I am sure there is but little more for me to say in commend-
ing so admirable an institution to you, which has now existed
for half a century, which maintains 600 children during the
course of the year, and has educated and sent forth into the
world as many as 3000 up to the present time.   But a well-
managed institution like this, with the spacious rooms which
we have seen, will naturally convince you that it must cost a
considerable sum, and I believe I am not incorrect in stating
that it requires at least £18,000 a year to maintain this asylum.
And as it is almost entirely supported by voluntary contributions I feel sure that all those present will do all they can to
support this institution, and to tell their friends when they go
home how worthy it is of support.   I have now, in conclusion,
only to propose—a toast which I give most heartily—' Prosperity to the Infant Orphan Asylum.' "

The Prince of Wales then left the chair, resigning it to the
Bishop of St. Albans, who gave the other usual toasts.

The secretary read a list of subscriptions.   The Queen had sent
her annual donation of 10 guineas; the Prince of Wales before
leaving placed in the hands of the secretary a cheque for 100
guineas; the Duke of Edinburgh gave 10 guineas; H. S. C. (who
had long been an anonymous benefactress), 100 guineas; country
friends, £462.   In all, about £1600.

This concluded the formal proceedings, but the summer weather
tempted many of the visitors to prolong their stay in the pleasant
gardens of the asylum.

THE TRAINING SHIP 'BRITANNIA.'

July 24th, 1878.

In the autumn of 1877, the Prince of Wales went to Dartmouth, to
place his sons, Prince Edward (as he was then usually called) and
Prince George, on the training ship *Britannia*, under the care of
Captain Fairfax, R.N.   At the end of the summer term, in the
following year, the Prince consented to preside at the distribution
of prizes on the *Britannia*, and graciously announced that the
successful pupils should receive their medals and books from the
hands of the Princess of Wales.

The Mayor and Corporation of the ancient borough of Dartmouth
took advantage of the occasion to give official welcome to the

Royal visitors, and to present an address, which the Prince
signified his readiness to receive on board the Royal yacht, *Osborne.*
Thither the magistrates repaired in the forenoon. The picturesque
estuary of the river Dart never had displayed so festive an appearance. The *Britannia*, and her attendant yacht the *Sirius*, the Royal
yacht, the Admiralty yacht, which had brought the Lords of the
Admiralty, several ships of the Plymouth fleet, under Admiral Sir
Thomas Symonds, besides a large flotilla of yachts, steam launches,
and all sorts of boats, were covered with gay bunting, while flags
floated from every point of the shore and the town.

The Town Clerk having read the Address from the ancient
borough, which was first incorporated by a charter of Edward III.,
in 1342, and had figured in subsequent history, especially at the
time of the Spanish Armada, the Prince, in reply, said :—

" On behalf of the Princess of Wales, as well as on my own
behalf, I offer my sincere thanks to you for your address and
for your cordial welcome to us on our visit to this ancient and
beautiful town.   The salubrity of the climate of Dartmouth and
the excellence of your sanitary arrangements have long been
known to me, and I can appeal to no better proof of my entire
confidence in them than that afforded by the step I have taken
in sending our two sons to be educated on board the *Britannia.*
I beg to assure you that with that step both the Princess and
myself are perfectly satisfied.   I trust you will continue to
devote your attention as you have done in the past to the improvement of the sanitary arrangements of the town.   I thank
you again for the kind wishes you have expressed towards the
Princess, myself, and our family."

The Prince also congratulated the Mayor, Sir Henry Seale, on
the splendid effect of the illuminations of the previous evening.
Accompanied by the Municipal authorities, and by the Duke of
Connaught, Prince Louis of Battenberg, and a numerous retinue,
the Prince and Princess then proceeded to the *Britannia* for the
distribution of the prizes. They were received by Mr. W. H. Smith,
then First Lord of the Admiralty, and the other Lords ; by the
Commander-in-Chief of the Plymouth division of the Channel
Fleet ; and Captain Fairfax of the *Britannia.* Between 500 and
600 of the friends or relatives of the cadets, and other invited
guests, among whom were Lord and Lady Charles Beresford, Sir
Samuel and Lady Baker, were assembled on the quarter-deck,
sheltered from the sun by a canopy of flags, surmounted by the
flag of Denmark, and the white ensign of England.

The distribution of the prizes took place, a report on the state of
the training having been previously read by Dr. Hirst, director of

studies at the Greenwich Naval College, who had superintended the examination of the cadets.

After the distribution, the Prince of Wales, standing on the deck in the uniform of a captain of the Royal Naval Reserve, said :—

"My Lords, Ladies, and Gentlemen,—Permit me to express to you the great pleasure it has given the Princess to present the cadets who are about to leave the *Britannia* the prizes which they have so successfully won, and to express to you on my own part as well as on that of the Princess the very great pleasure it has given us to be here to witness and take part in these interesting proceedings. From Dr. Hirst we heard a most interesting and exhaustive speech regarding the studies of the cadets and their merits. I can only wish those who are about to leave the *Britannia*, and who have now fairly entered that noble service for which they have been trained, all possible success. Let me hope that the tuition they have received here will not be thrown away upon them, and that they may all emulate those bright examples to be found in English history and of which every naval officer must be proud. To those cadets who still remain on board this ship I can only recommend strict assiduity to their studies and strict obedience to discipline, and all of them to try to pass out of the *Britannia* as highly as they can, remembering, above all, that saying which one of our greatest admirals has handed down to posterity—'England expects every man will do his duty.' A personal interest which the Princess and myself take in this ship and the confidence we have of its being an excellent practical school for boys have been testified by the fact that we have sent our two sons among you to be educated. For myself, my only hope and trust is that they may do credit to the ship and to their country."

Mr. W. H. Smith, M.P., First Lord of the Admiralty, thanked their Royal Highnesses for their welcome presence, and called upon the cadets to give three cheers for the Prince and Princess of Wales. The cheers were prolonged to three times three, caught up in row-boats around, and echoed by the high banks of the Dart. The chief captains of the cadets, who are mainly responsible for discipline and occupy a place of honour in the ship's mess-room on the main deck, were presented to the Prince and Princess, and the proceedings came to an end. Captain and Mrs. Fairfax had the honour of entertaining the Royal personages and a select party at luncheon. Later in the day the Prince of Wales paid a visit to Captain Zirzow, on the German Imperial frigate *Niobe*, and drank a glass of wine to the health of the Emperor of Germany. Captain Zirzow telegraphed at once to the Emperor that the Prince of Wales had called a health to him.

When the Prince and Princess arrived at Dartmouth on Tuesday they were rowed to the *Britannia*, one of their sons steering and the other pulling the second bow oar. They left the ship in a boat rowed by full-grown sailors, and with their two sons, who were going home for their holidays, sitting in the stern sheets. From the *Britannia* to the landing-place, which was brightly draped with crimson cloth, hawsers were stretched and thus a clear lane was kept among the crowd of craft for the passage of the Royal boat. The cadets of the *Britannia* sat in their blue coats with tossed oars, and cheers were raised by those on the boats, yachts, the many little steam launches, and the shore. Little girls threw flowers before the Princess as she stepped upon the landing stage. A special train was waiting to meet the ordinary mail from Penzance and Plymouth.

So ended a visit which formed an interesting incident in the family life of the Prince, and the events of which will long be remembered in South Devon.

CABDRIVERS' BENEVOLENT ASSOCIATION.

May 5th, 1879.

THE objects of the Cabdrivers' Benevolent Association are : 1, to give annuities of £20 a year; 2, to grant small loans; 3, to give temporary assistance in cases of urgent distress; 4, to assist the widows and orphans of cabmen. This is an institution the benefits of which are so obvious, and for the help of a class of men so hard-worked, so uncertainly paid, and so useful to the public, that we are not surprised at the readiness with which the Prince of Wales assented to preside at one of its annual festivals, and at the hearty earnestness in which he made an appeal on its behalf. It was at the festival dinner on the 5th of May, 1879. On coming to the toast of the evening His Royal Highness said :—

"There is, I think, no class of our fellow-countrymen that deserve more of our consideration than the cabdrivers of this great city, and it has already been truly expressed to you that one cannot think without pity of these poor men sitting on their cabs in the cold east winds with which we are, alas! so well acquainted, and in the rain and snow which have been our lot now for so many months.

"They are as a rule, I believe, a class honest, persevering, and industrious. For them I have to plead to-night, and for this excellent institution, which has for the last nine years rendered to them such great benefits.

"The objects of this Cabdrivers' Benevolent Association are, as you are aware, threefold—first, to give annuities at the rate of £12 each to aged cabdrivers or to those who from infirmity are unable to earn their living; secondly, to grant loans without interest to members requiring such aid, and to give temporary assistance to those who may be in distress through unavoidable causes; and, thirdly, to give legal assistance to members who may be unjustly summoned to the police courts. It is hardly possible to conceive that any benevolent institution of this kind is more deserving of support, not only by the large assembly who are gathered here, but by the inhabitants generally of our great Metropolis. There are a thousand cabmen who are members of this Association, and they pay 5s. a year. Pensions of £12 are granted now to old and indigent cabdrivers, but it is our great wish to augment that sum to £16 " (now £20). "The system of loans seems to have answered admirably in every respect; £600 has been granted to the members without interest, and these loans have, I understand, been always most regularly and most punctually repaid. Two hundred and thirty-three cabmen or their families have been assisted by this society in various years since its formation, and its existing capital is more than £3000; but this we hope to augment still further.

"One statement I may make which may be of interest to those present here this evening. I mentioned that as a class the cabmen are thoroughly honest. As a proof of that I have statistics here before me which state that last year there were between 16,000 and 17,000 articles left in cabs, amounting in value to about £20,000, which have been punctually returned. I believe, at least it is the popular belief, that there is only one article a cabman never returns, and this is an umbrella, and I think that is, we may consider, quite fair. A gentleman having an umbrella may not want a cab, but without an umbrella he will be compelled to take a cab if the rain comes on!

" There are now between 11,000 and 12,000 cabmen, and the amount of the expense in cab fares comes to a most colossal sum, something between £4,000,000 and £5,000,000 sterling. With regard to the remark I made as to the honesty of cabmen, it may perhaps be not out of place if I mention an anecdote which was told me to-day.   A gentleman drove in a cab to a shop, left the cab, and entered the shop.   On coming out of the shop, he was not in so quiet a frame of mind as when he entered it ; it was evident to the passers-by that he was dissatisfied with the shopman ; he left the shop and went away.   The shopman threw a case into the cab.   The gentleman had forgotten it.   But the cabman immediately drove to Scotland Yard and delivered the case, which was found to contain jewellery worth £2300.   This will give you some idea of the honesty of these men, for whom we are endeavouring to do much.   Some considerable good was done only four years ago by a philanthropic and noble lord whose name is known to you, who started cabmen's shelters.   There are now twenty of these, and they shelter 2000 cabmen, doing much to alleviate the discomfort of the men, who sit so many hours of the night suffering from the inclemency of the seasons.

" When I see this large assemblage I feel I shall not call in vain, and I call upon you to augment the capital which already exists.   With this toast I have great pleasure in associating one who is treasurer of the Association, Lord Richard Grosvenor (now Lord Stalbridge), member of a family well known in works of charity and philanthropy.   I thank you for the kind way in which you have listened to my imperfect remarks, and now I must ask you to drink with enthusiasm 'Success to the Cab-drivers' Benevolent Association !' "

It is pleasant to find from the latest published report that the Institution, which the Prince of Wales so warmly commended, is in a prosperous condition.   The annuities have been raised to £20, and there, are 40 annuitants now on the books.   The receipts in 1887 were £2191, and the funded property was £10,000.   Temporary relief was given to upwards of 200 cabmen.   Upwards of 1200 members contribute 5s. annually, but this is a small proportion of the whole number of cabdrivers, more of whom ought to be persuaded to join as members, as they alone receive the benefits of the Association.   The applicants for loans, on the prescribed terms, were 89.   The cabmen have been fortunate in the chairmen at the festivals and annual general meetings. The Prince of Wales is patron of the Association. The honorary secretary is G. Stormont Murphy, Esq., and the office is at 15, Soho Square.

THE PRINCESS HELENA COLLEGE.

May 23rd, 1880.

THE Prince of Wales presided at Willis's Rooms at a dinner in aid of the funds of the Princess Helena College, on the 23rd of May, 1880.

After the customary proceedings and toasts of the evening, and speeches by the Duke of Cambridge and Lord Sydney, the Prince rose and proposed the toast of "Prosperity to the Princess Helena College." He said:—

"At many of the dinners at which I have the pleasure of taking the chair, the charities in support of which they are given require more words to bring them to the notice of those who attend than the present one does. But though the specific nature of this institution relieves me from the necessity of entering upon any lengthened advocacy of its claims, it is not the less deserving of your hearty support in every respect. As you are aware, the Princess Helena College was formerly called the Adult Orphan Institution, and it has for its object the bringing up of daughters of officers of the Army and Navy and of clergymen. Its first meeting took place as far back as 1818, and in 1820 the institution was built. As Lord Sydney told you, it originated with a relative of his own. It was founded by her, and by my grand-aunt, Princess Augusta of Gloucester. King George IV. also took great interest in its welfare, allotting the plot of ground in the Regent's Park where the College now stands.

"The object of the institution is not only to provide a thoroughly good education for the daughters of officers and clergymen, but to send them forth into the world in a useful capacity; and I think you will agree with me that in the capacity of well-qualified governesses they go forth in the most useful manner. In the days when it was first instituted so much attention was not given to education as in our time, and you can therefore easily understand that as more highly efficient education is needed now for these young ladies there is a proportionate increase of expense. Like many other institutions, its expenditure has been greater than its receipts, and, as a consequence, it has been found necessary to somewhat alter its rules by admitting a certain number of paying students as boarders, and also by establishing day classes for the daughters of gentlemen. In order to fit the institution for this new sphere of operations it has been necessary to enlarge the building, and though, no doubt, the effect of this arrangement will be to increase receipts, the enlargement of the building has naturally entailed great cost, and in order to meet that charge I have to call upon you, gentlemen, to do all you can, by a most liberal contribution to-night, to enable the committee to meet their pecuniary difficulties. The best proof you can give me of the real interest you take in the welfare of this excellent institution will be to subscribe as handsomely as it is in your power to do. I am informed that a distinguished naval officer is acting as steward here to-night in gratitude for the benefit his daughters have derived in their education from a governess who was brought up at the Princess Helena College. I have mentioned before that the Queen is its patron. Her Majesty subscribes £50 a year to its funds, and on this special occasion she presents 100 guineas. The interest taken by my sister, the Princess, in its welfare is sufficiently proved by the fact that she is President of the Council of the College, and I have great pleasure in stating to you that it is by her express wish and recommendation that I am here to-night. I will, in conclusion, again ask you to let me feel by the liberality of your contributions that I have not failed in my duty as your Chairman."

The Secretary then read a list of donations and subscriptions, which, including those from the Queen and 100 guineas from the Prince of Wales, amounted to over £2060.

The College still flourishes at Ealing. a populous district, where day boarders are also admitted to the classes of the institution.

NEW HARBOUR AT HOLYHEAD.

June 17th, 1880.

To possess the best possible packet service between England and Ireland is a matter of national importance. In the old days of sailing ships the perils and uncertainties of the passage across the Channel were notorious. When steamships carried mails and passengers, and when the bridging of the Menai Straits for railway traffic had been achieved, it was necessary to provide improved harbour accommodation, and other works, both for convenience and safety, at Holyhead. These works included a spacious harbour, and a breakwater securing the additional space of a sheltered roadstead. The length of the North Breakwater is nearly 8000 feet. The harbour and deep-water sheltered roadstead are together between six and seven hundred acres in extent. It took twenty-five years to carry out the design, at a cost of about £1,500,000. This outlay included the works and buildings for Government use in the postal service. The engineer-in-chief was Mr. James Rennel, and on his death, in 1856, Mr. afterwards Sir John Hawkshaw.

To celebrate the completion of the works, the Prince of Wales visited Holyhead on the 19th of August, 1873, when he declared the Breakwater complete and the Harbour of Refuge open. The Duke of Edinburgh, Master of the Trinity House, Sir Frederick Arrow, Deputy Master, and many distinguished representatives of various departments of the public service assisted at the ceremony. Near the Lighthouse a gun-metal plate records the fact that the Breakwater, "commenced in 1845, was on August 19th, 1873, declared complete, by Albert Edward, Prince of Wales," in whose public life the proceedings of the day form a memorable event.

But there was yet much to be done for the Anglo-Irish route, viâ Holyhead. The communication had so increased that the North Western Railway Company found enlarged harbour accommodation a necessity for the benefit of their own traffic.

It is not often that Royal sanction is given to the undertakings of shareholding companies; but the new harbour at Holyhead, while it was constructed at the cost and for the benefit of the London and North Western Railway Company, has so much importance for commerce and traffic, as to make it a national object. The Prince of Wales was accordingly asked to inaugurate the new harbour, and a large number of distinguished and official persons were invited by the Directors to be present on the occasion. At the luncheon, the Chairman of the Company proposed the usual loyal toasts, and the Prince of Wales responded in the following terms :—

"Mr. Chairman, Ladies, and Gentlemen, — I am deeply flattered by the kind manner in which this toast has been proposed and received in this large and distinguished assemblage. I feel it a matter of the greatest pleasure, and at the same time the greatest pride, to be among you here to-day. It is a matter of pride, ladies and gentlemen, to be connected with this Principality, and it has afforded me the greatest pleasure to accept the invitation of the Chairman and Directors of the London and North Western Company to inaugurate this new harbour. It is not the first time, as you are aware, that I have had occasion to come to Holyhead. Seven years ago I had the pleasure of inaugurating your breakwater, which I am glad to see is now successfully terminated and is of the greatest possible utility. The sunshine we have enjoyed to-day may be taken as a good augury for the success of the London and North Western Railway Company in their new undertaking. This undertaking has cost them a very large sum of money, but it will, I am sure, be of the greatest benefit to commerce, and will tend to make the Holyhead route still more than it is a connecting link between England and Ireland. Before sitting down I have a toast to propose, which I feel sure you will drink with the greatest pleasure; it is 'The Health of the Chairman, Mr. Moon, and Success and Prosperity to the London and North Western Railway Company.' I also desire to declare the new harbour open."

Both on land and water there were many loyal demonstrations; and gentlemen representing all the leading railway companies, French and Irish, as well as English and Welsh, were entertained by the Directors of the London and North Western.

The opening sentences of a leading article in the *Times* on the following day, form a tribute due to the Prince for his part in the ceremony:—

"The representative duties of Royalty in this country are heavier than the private functions the hardest-worked Englishman has to perform. Only the other day we were recording the part played by the Prince of Wales in an ecclesiastical pageant in Cornwall. On Wednesday he was introducing a foreign Sovereign to the Corporation of London. Straight from that ceremonial he had to take flight across the island to open formally the new harbour at Holyhead. In these scenes and a hundred like them a Prince's functions cannot be discharged satisfactorily unless he be at once an impersonation of Royal State and, what is harder still, his own individual self. He must act his public character as if he enjoyed the festival as much as any of the spectators. He must be able to stamp a national impress upon the solemnity, yet mark its local and particular significance. In presenting a King of the Hellenes to the citizens at the Guildhall the Prince of Wales had to remember that his guest and the guest of the City was both a near and dear relative and the embodiment of an illustrious cause. In laying the first stone of a cathedral at Truro he had to be both Duke of Cornwall and the Heir of England. In presiding yesterday at Holyhead he had to recollect the provincial associations connected with the title he bears, and not forget the imperial importance of a work which creates a new link between two great divisions of the United Kingdom. That he achieved his task successfully was a matter of course. No apprehension ever touches those who are present at a scene of which the Prince of Wales is the centre, that he may chance to chill by lack of interest, to choose his words of admiration inopportunely, or to praise without sympathy. The work he came, as it were, to sanction by national approbation is a grand engineering undertaking, and is grander yet in its probable moral consequences. The Prince of Wales understood and expressed its significance from both aspects."

NEW COLOURS TO THE ROYAL WELSH FUSILIERS.

August 16th, 1880.

THE Royal Welsh Fusiliers (or Twenty-third Regiment of Foot in the old Army Lists) received the more familiar name from having been first raised in Wales in 1714, and in honour of the Prince of Wales of that day. Their nationality is further betokened by the Prince of Wales's plume, with the motto "Ich Dien," which, together with the Rising Sun, the Red Dragon, the White Horse, and the Sphinx, they bear on their colours. The regiment is one of the oldest and most famous in the Army, and the proud words, "Nec aspera terrent," which are emblazoned on its regimental silk, it has amply justified by its gallant conduct from the Battle of the Boyne, in 1690, to the Indian Mutiny, in 1858, including Egypt, Corunna, Martinique, Albuera, Badajoz, Salamanca, the Pyrenees, Nivelle, Orthes, Toulouse, Waterloo, Alma, Inkerman, Sebastopol, and nearly fifty other engagements which are not recorded on its colours.

It was peculiarly fitting that the duty of presenting new colours to this brave and distinguished Welsh regiment should be undertaken by the Prince of Wales. This he did on the 16th of August, 1880, coming from Osborne for the purpose, when the 1st Battalion

of the Welsh Fusiliers, above nine hundred strong, including
officers, was embarking for India from Portsmouth.

The colours, exchanged for new ones on that day, had been presented in 1849 by the late Prince Consort, the battalion at the
same time receiving from the Queen the first of those Royal goats,
which have always since marched at the head of the regiment.
When the gallant " Nanny Goats," as the Twenty-third are nick-
named, first had the regimental pet is not exactly known, but
since 1849 a Royal goat has been received from Windsor whenever
a vacancy occurs.

The colours replaced by the new ones in 1880 had a history of
their own, and the regiment took pride in them, although in such
a tattered condition that they could not be unfurled. The Queen's
colour was that which was carried by Lieutenant Anstruther, who
was killed when planting it on the Great Redoubt at Sebastopol.
Twelve officers and half the rank and file fell in that terrible rush,
but the Royal Welsh had the honour of first entering the enemy's
stronghold. No fewer than seventy-five bullets passed through the
colours, and the pole of one of them was shot in two, and had to
be tied up with a cord. Sergeant O'Connor, though dangerously
wounded, carried the Queen's colours till the end of the battle, and
was rewarded by a commission in the regiment, receiving the
Victoria Cross at the close of the war. He rose to be Colonel of
the 2nd Battalion, and was present, with his breast covered with
well-earned decorations, when the Prince of Wales came to
present the new colours at Portsmouth. The colours were afterwards carried through the Indian Mutiny, where Colonel Elgee
and several of the officers had the honour of serving under them.
The ragged relics were relegated to the honourable obscurity of
Wrexham Church.

The ceremony of removing the old colours and presenting the
new was an imposing spectacle, witnessed by an immense assemblage, and amidst great enthusiasm. The old colours having been
placed in front of the saluting post, were afterwards sent to the
rear, the band playing " Auld Lang Syne."   Then the new colours
were presented by the Prince, with whom was the Princess of
Wales, the Duke of Edinburgh, and Prince Edward of Saxe-Weimar.
Having received the colours from the Majors, the Prince presented
them separately to the Lieutenants, and then turning to the
Colonel, spoke as follows :—

" Colonel Elgee, officers, and non-commissioned officers and
men of the Royal Welsh Fusiliers,—I consider it a very great
privilege to have been asked to present your regiment with new
colours on the eve of its departure for India. It occurs to me
in presenting these colours that they are to replace those which
were given to you about thirty-one years ago by my lamented
father, and which through three campaigns your regiment has

carried with honour and success. You will in a few years celebrate your 200th anniversary, and during that time your regiment has served in nearly every quarter of the globe, and seen as much or more service than any regiment in the Army. You have served at Corunna, Salamanca, the Peninsula, Waterloo, Alma, Inkerman, Sebastopol, Lucknow, and, coming down to more recent times, Ashantee. I feel sure that there will always be the same emulation among those who serve in your ranks as there has been in the past, and that the good name of your regiment will always be maintained as prominently as it is now. You are now on the eve of departure for India, and nobody wishes you 'God-speed' more sincerely than I do. I feel sure that, whatever your services may be, they will be such as will bring credit to your regiment, and will add additional proofs of the valour for which it is so justly celebrated."

Colonel Elgee made a suitable and soldierly reply, thus concluding : "I am sure that wherever the colours are carried—whether before an enemy or in the performance of our duties at home in times of peace—the regiment will always maintain the high reputation it has won. On the eve of our departure for India, we beg to express our heartiest wishes for the health and happiness of Her Most Gracious Majesty the Queen, your Royal Highness, the Princess of Wales, and the remainder of the Royal Family."

The line having been reformed, His Royal Highness had the whole of the officers drawn up on each side of the drums, and as they saluted and passed to their posts, each was individually presented to the Prince and Princess by the Colonel. A few more movements, and the ranks were closed, the line broke into columns to the right, and marched past to the jetty, where they embarked on board the *Malabar*. After luncheon, the whole party from the Royal yacht, including the Princess Beatrice, who had arrived in the *Alberta* to receive the Empress Eugénie and take her to Osborne on a visit to the Queen, proceeded on board the *Malabar*, where they stayed three-quarters of an hour and made a thorough inspection of the ship, where they were welcomed with much enthusiasm. When at length the ship drew away into the stream, followed by the Royal yacht *Osborne*, the band of the Royal Marines ashore played " The March of the Men of Harlech," and " Cheer, Boys, Cheer," while the troops responded by singing " Auld Lang Syne."

THE ROYAL HOSPITAL FOR WOMEN AND CHILDREN.

May 24th, 1881.

THIS Hospital, which is the oldest of its kind in London, is situated in Waterloo Bridge Road, in a populous and poor district. It contains now about 50 beds. The number of out-patient attendances averages 3000 a month, and upwards of 250 visits each month are paid by the house-surgeon to sick children at their own homes. The ordinary receipts are about £3000, and the funded property £6500. It is a well-managed and useful charity, and just such a one as would gain the good will of the Prince of Wales, who presided at the festival dinner, in Willis's Rooms, on the Queen's Birthday, May 24th, 1881.

After the customary loyal and patriotic toasts, the Royal Chairman briefly but earnestly pleaded the cause of the charity. He said that—

The largeness of the gathering on that occasion was evidence of the interest taken in this great and important charity. During the last few years, he remarked, we had suffered from both agricultural and commercial depression, and institutions of a charitable kind, especially those which owed their existence and maintenance to voluntary contributions, must naturally feel a depression, which prevented many persons from coming forward to their support; but still he did not despair of the results of the appeal which he had to make that evening. This institution had now been in existence for seventy-one years. It was situated in a very populous and very poor district, its object being the cure of sick children and women. He might remark that many of his family had taken considerable interest in this hospital. His grandfather, the Duke of Kent, presided at the first anniversary dinner, and his great-uncle, the Duke of Sussex, took a deep interest in it. Only four years ago his sister, the Princess Louise, visited the institution, and, being much gratified with what she saw, gave her name to one of the wards. Unfortunately, the institution was not so flourishing financially as it ought to be. The ordinary income was £2000 a year less than was required to meet the expenditure. It was also most important that the hospital should be enlarged. The freehold of the surrounding property had been obtained from the Duchy of Cornwall at an expense of £3000. Several years ago that great philanthropist, Lord Shaftesbury, presided at a dinner in aid of this charity, when a sum of nearly £3000 was raised. If the same amount could be made up that evening all who were interested in the institution would be deeply gratified. Mentioning that since the foundation of the Hospital as many as 400,000 children had been relieved, His Royal Highness said that patients were received not only from all parts of this country, but also from the Continent, and medical and surgical treatment was afforded them gratuitously. The report of the Hospital Saturday Fund stated that the institution stood among the first for efficiency and economy.

Before concluding his speech the Prince of Wales proposed the health of the Lord Mayor, who is by virtue of his office President of the institution. Mr. Kestin, the Secretary, read a list of donations and subscriptions which, including 100 guineas from the chairman, exceeded £2000.

AT KING'S COLLEGE.

July 2nd, 1881.

THE Prince of Wales, accompanied by the Princess, distributed the principal prizes of the year at King's College, London, on the 2nd of July, 1881. The Rev. Canon Barry, D.D., the Principal, received the Royal visitors, and at the opening of the proceedings, said : "it will always be a day in the annals of the College to be marked with a white stone, when the Prince and Princess of Wales had come for the first time among them, and on the jubilee day of the institution." After the distribution of the prizes and decorations, the Prince acknowledging a vote of thanks for his presence, proposed by the Duke of Cambridge, and seconded by the Bishop of Gloucester, said :—

" Mr. Principal Barry, Ladies and Gentlemen,—For the very kind words in which the illustrious Duke has proposed the vote of thanks, the kind way in which it has been seconded by the Bishop of Gloucester and Bristol, and the cordial manner in which you have all been good enough to receive this vote, I ask you to accept my most sincere thanks, and also the thanks of the Princess of Wales for the kind way in which her name has been alluded to to-day.

P

"It would have been a gratification to me on any day to come to this college and present the prizes to the successful competitors, but as this day is your jubilee day, your fiftieth anniversary, it makes it still more interesting to me to come here to-day and give away the prizes. After all that has fallen from the lips of your Principal, and after perusing, though I admit somewhat cursorily, the annual report, but little is left for me to say; but all those who take an interest in the success of this college will have every reason to be satisfied with the state of the college, and with the report which I hold in my hands. Everything connected with this institution is on a most satisfactory and excellent footing.

"In these days, when education is so much thought of, and when meetings in every part of the kingdom are continually taking place for the purpose of getting still higher standards of education, it is naturally difficult for institutions of old date to keep up with the times; but I do not think or fear that this college will have any reason to fear competition from others, as it already stands as one of the second or third great educational colleges in the kingdom. The prizes which have been given to-day for the different subjects in this list embrace nearly every possible subject of education which may be of use to those young men who are going out into the world.

"This college justly claims to be one which has done very much for the higher education of men; and it affords me, and I know it affords also the Princess of Wales, great gratification to learn that it will be extended also towards the education of women. This year, since the Principal and the Council received a memorial signed by various distinguished persons, they have very wisely adopted that memorial, by enabling women already to receive education by way of listening to lectures from distinguished teachers and professors in this college.

"It has been already stated that some of our children have received education from some of the professors of this college. It is very gratifying to us that such has been the case, and we have every hope that they will derive benefit from the instruction they have received.

"Before concluding I wish to congratulate those young gentlemen to whom I have presented these prizes to-day on having received these proofs that the education they have received here has not been thrown away. As most of them are about to leave the college, I sincerely hope they will allow me to offer them my best wishes, and to trust that in their future career they will continue to do credit to themselves and those by whom they have been educated. I again express the pleasure which both the Princess and myself have felt in coming here to-day, and say that we most cordially wish continued and lasting prosperity to King's College."

COLONIAL BANQUET AT THE MANSION HOUSE.

July 16*th*, 1881.

THE Lord Mayor of London entertained the Prince of Wales, President of the Colonial Institute, and a large company of representatives of the Colonies, with other distinguished guests, at dinner, at the Mansion House, on July the 16th, 1881. Seldom has there been such an assemblage in the Capital of the British Empire. Governors, Premiers, and Administrators of so many countries were present, that one might almost wonder how affairs went on in their absence. But rulers as well as subjects must have holiday rest, and the facility and rapidity of travel allow easy access from all parts of the world to "the mother country."

The Lord Mayor (Sir William McArthur, M.P.), after the toast of "The Queen," said that they were honoured with the presence of an unexpected but very distinguished guest, the King of the Sandwich Islands. It was the first time that His Majesty had visited Europe, and he naturally wished to visit the land which first made known to the world the islands of the Pacific. "Having once visited the Sandwich Islands," said the Lord Mayor, "I was charmed not only with the beauty of the scenery and the fertility of the soil, but with the good order which everywhere prevailed. His Majesty reigns over a very prosperous and a very happy people."

The toast being duly honoured, the King of the Sandwich Islands expressed his high sense of the graciousness of the Queen, the Prince of Wales, and the other Royal and distinguished persons he had met, and would carry back to his country the most grateful and pleasant recollections of his visit.

The Lord Mayor next gave "The health of the Prince of Wales, the Princess of Wales, and the other members of the Royal Family." In response to the toast, the Prince arose amidst great cheering, and said :—

"My Lord Mayor, your Majesty, my Lords and Gentlemen,—
For the kind and remarkably flattering way in which you, my
Lord Mayor, have been good enough to propose this toast, and
you, my lords and gentlemen, for the kind and hearty way in
which you have received it, I beg to offer you my most sincere
thanks. It is a peculiar pleasure to me to come to the City,
because I have the honour of being one of its freemen. But this
is, indeed, a very special dinner, one of a kind that I do not
suppose has ever been given before; for we have here this
evening representatives of probably every Colony in the Empire.
We have not only the Secretary of the Colonies, but Governors
past and present, ministers, administrators, and agents, are all,
I think, to be found here this evening, I regret that it has not
been possible for me to see half or one-third of the colonies
which it has been the good fortune of my brother the Duke of
Edinburgh to visit. In his voyages round the world he has had
opportunities more than once of seeing all our great colonies.
Though I have not been able personally to see them, or only a
small portion of them, you may rest assured it does not diminish
in any way the interest I take in them.

"It is, I am sorry to say, now going on for twenty-one years
since I visited our large North American colonies. Still, though
I was very young at the time, the remembrance of that visit is
as deeply imprinted on my memory now as it was at that time.
I shall never forget the public receptions which were accorded
to me in Canada, New Brunswick, Nova Scotia, and Prince
Edward Island, and if it were possible for me at any time to
repeat that visit, I need not tell you, gentlemen, who now represent here those great North American colonies, of the great
pleasure it would give me to do so. It affords me great gratification to see an old friend, Sir John Macdonald, the Premier of
Canada, here this evening.

"It was a most pressing invitation, certainly, that I received
two years ago to visit the great Australasian Colonies, and
though at the time I was unable to give an answer, in the
affirmative or in the negative, still it soon became apparent that
my many duties here in England would prevent my accomplishing what would have been a long, though a most interesting
voyage. I regret that such has been the case, and that I was

not able to accept the kind invitation I received to visit the Exhibitions at Sydney and at Melbourne. I am glad, however, to know that they have proved a great success, as has been testified to me only this evening by the noble Duke (Manchester) by my side, who has so lately returned. Though, my lords and gentlemen, I have, as I have said before, not had the opportunity of seeing these great Australasian Colonies, which every day and every year are making such immense development, still, at the International Exhibitions of London, Paris, and Vienna, I had not only an opportunity of seeing their various products there exhibited, but I had the pleasure of making the personal acquaintance of many colonists—a fact which has been a matter of great importance and great benefit to myself.

" It is now thirty years since the first International Exhibition took place in London, and then for the first time colonial exhibits were shown to the world. Since that time, from the Exhibitions which have followed our first great gathering in 1851, the improvements that have been made are manifest. That in itself is a clear proof of the way in which the colonies have been exerting themselves to make their vast territories of the great importance that they are at the present moment. But though, my Lord Mayor, I have not been to Australasia, as you have mentioned, I have sent my two sons on a visit there ; and it has been a matter of great gratification, not only to myself and to the Princess, but to the Queen, to hear of the kindly reception they have met with everywhere. They are but young, but I feel confident that their visit to the Antipodes will do them an incalculable amount of good. On their way out they visited a colony in which, unfortunately, the condition of affairs was not quite as satisfactory as we could wish, and as a consequence they did not extend their visits in that part of South Africa quite so far inland as might otherwise have been the case. I must thank you once more, my Lord Mayor, for the kind way in which you have proposed this toast.

" I thank you, in the name of the Princess and the other members of the Royal Family, for the kind reception their names have met with from all here to-night, and I beg again to assure you most cordially and heartily of the great pleasure it

has given me to be present here among so many distinguished
colonists and gentlemen connected with the colonies, and to
have had an opportunity of meeting your distinguished guest,
the King of the Sandwich Islands. If your lordship's visit to
his dominions remains impressed on your mind, I think your
lordship's kindly reception of His Majesty here to-night is not
likely soon to be forgotten by him."

The Duke of Manchester, in responding to the toast of " The
House of Lords," said that he took much less part in the proceedings of that august body than many of its members. He had,
however, lately visited some of our colonies—and that was, perhaps,
the reason why he was called upon to respond to that toast.
Having given some remarkable statistics of progress in Australia,
he said, " It was calculated that Australians and New Zealanders, per
head, man, woman, and child, consumed £8 10s.-worth of British
goods, while France only rated at 7s. 8d. per head, and the United
States at 7s. per head. These were facts showing that, if for no
other reason, there were very forcible financial reasons why we
should consolidate, encourage, and promote in every way the
prosperity of the British Colonies."

The Speaker, in returning thanks on behalf of the House of
Commons, said he was one of those who had a great faith in the future
of the English people throughout the world. Wherever Englishmen set their foot they grew and prospered; they had learnt the
habit of self-government, and were well acquainted with the forms
of government, and they carried with them English customs,
English habits, English institutions. Thus we had a great Colonial
Empire firmly compacted together of colonists from the old country,
all loyal subjects of the Crown. He trusted and believed that that
state of things would long continue, and he hoped that the bonds
between those colonies and the mother country would become
closer and closer from generation to generation.

The Lord Mayor then proposed the toast of the evening, " The
British Colonies," to which the Earl of Kimberley replied, concluding with these words : " This is a representative assembly,
and one of the most remarkable ever gathered together in this
Metropolis. I congratulate you, my Lord Mayor, on the happy
notion of bringing together this assembly, which must have an
equally happy effect in promoting good feeling both here and in
the Colonies, inasmuch as it is a type of the union which ought to
bind us together."

The Prince of Wales then proposed the Lord Mayor's health
in a brief speech, in the course of which he said that it must
be especially gratifying to his lordship to preside at such a
dinner, seeing that he was well acquainted with the colonies,

being a colonial merchant of high repute, and having visited, if not all, at any rate most of our great colonies.

The Lord Mayor briefly acknowledged the compliment, and said this meeting was one of the most gratifying incidents of his year of office.

CITY AND GUILDS OF LONDON INSTITUTE.

July 18th, 1881.

OF many movements originated by the late Prince Consort, and carried forward by the Prince of Wales, the advancement of technical education is one of the highest national importance. Without going into past history, it is sufficient to say that of late years some of the Guilds of the City of London have been awakened to a sense of their duties in training artisans, for which purpose they were at first mainly founded. The Corporation of London has aided the movement, but in a more limited way. At first the efforts were directed to the encouragement of technical education in existing schools and colleges by pecuniary grants. But subsequently the Institute has been enabled to establish schools of its own, and to assist in development of technical instruction, not in London only, but in many large provincial towns.

The Institute had been incorporated in 1880, and in May of that year the late Duke of Albany laid the foundation stone of the Finsbury Technical College, the first building in the Metropolis exclusively devoted to this practical training. In Lambeth and other districts similar schools have been instituted; but it was thought advisable to found a Central Institute for systematic teaching the practical applications of science and art to the trades and industries of the country. Hitherto the training of artisans has been mainly dependent on the customs of apprenticeship in the various handicrafts; upwards of twenty of the City Companies, including nine out of the twelve greater Guilds, had subscribed largely, and had entered the associated Institute, when the Prince of Wales was invited to become the President. By the influence of the Prince, as President of the Royal Commissioners of 1851, a site for the proposed central College was granted at a nominal rent, on the estate at South Kensington. To lay the foundation stone of this building, the Prince, accompanied by the Princess of Wales, came on the 18th of July, 1881.

An address having been delivered by the Lord Chancellor, Lord Selborne, Chairman of the Committee of the Institute, the Prince of Wales delivered the following speech, which more clearly presents the whole subject, and brings out its national importance:—

"My Lord Chancellor, my Lords, Ladies, and Gentlemen,—I thank you for your address, and beg leave to assure you that it gives me much satisfaction to attend here to-day to lay the foundation stone of an institution which gives such forcible expression to one of the most important needs in the education of persons who are destined to take part in the productive history of this country.

"Hitherto English teaching has chiefly relied on training the intellectual faculties, so as to adapt men to apply their intelligence in any occupation of life to which they may be called; and this general discipline of the mind has on the whole been found sufficient until recent times; but during the last thirty years the competition of other nations, even in manufactures which once were exclusively carried on in this kingdom, has been very severe. The great progress that has been made in the means of locomotion as well as in the application of steam for the purposes of life has distributed the raw materials of industry all over the world, and has economized time and labour in their conversion to objects of utility. Other nations which did not possess in such abundance as Great Britain coal, the source of power, and iron, the essence of strength, compensated for the want of raw material by the technical education of their industrial classes, and this country has, therefore, seen manufactures springing up everywhere, guided by the trained intelligence thus created. Both in Europe and in America technical colleges for teaching, not the practice, but the principles of science and art involved in particular industries, had been organized in all the leading centres of industry.

"England is now thoroughly aware of the necessity for supplementing her educational institutions by colleges of a like nature. Most of our great manufacturing towns have either started or have already erected their colleges of science and art. In only a few instances, however, have they become developed into schools for systematic technical instruction. This building, which is to be erected by the City and Guilds of London, will be of considerable benefit to the whole kingdom, not only as an example of the institute devoting itself to technical training, but as a focus likewise for uniting the different technical schools in the Metropolis already in existence, and a central establishment also to which promising students from the provinces may, by the aid of scholarships, he brought to benefit by the superior instruction which London can command. While studying at your institution, they will have the further advantages that the treasures of the South Kensington Museum and the numerous collections in the City may bring to bear on the artistic and scientific education of future manufacturers.

" Let me remind you that the realization of this idea was one of the most cherished objects which my lamented father had in view. After the Exhibition of 1851, he recognized the need of technical education in the future, and he foresaw how difficult it would be in London to find space for such museums and colleges as those which now surround the spot on which we stand. It is, therefore, to me a peculiar pleasure that the Commissioners of the Exhibition, of which I am the President, have been able to contribute to your present important undertaking, by giving to you the ground upon which the present college is to be erected, with a sufficient reserve of land to insure its future development.

"Allow me, in conclusion, to express the great satisfaction which I experience in seeing the ancient guilds of the City of London so warmly co-operating in the advancement of technical instruction. I am aware that several of them have for some time past in various ways separately encouraged the study of science and art in the Metropolis, as well as in the provinces ; and it is a noble effort on their part when they join together to establish a united institute with the view of making still greater and more systematic endeavours for the promotion of this branch of special education. By consenting at your request to become the President of this Institute I hope it may be in my power to benefit the good work, and that our joint exertions, aided, I trust, by the continued liberality of the City and Guilds of London, may prove to be an example to the rest of the country to train the intelligence of industrial communities, so that, with the increasing competition of the world, England may retain her proud pre-eminence as a manufacturing nation."

After this address, the ceremony of laying the foundation stone was completed. A medal to commemorate the event had previously been struck at the Royal Mint.

It is stated in the *Times* of October 20th, 1888, that "in the last ten years several of the Companies, in conjunction with the City Corporation, have together given something like a quarter of a million to the City Guilds of London Institute — the amount including gifts of £46,000 from the Goldsmiths, of £43,000 from the Drapers, of £37,000 from the Clothworkers, of £34,000 from the Fishmongers, of £22,000 from the Mercers, of £10,000 from the Grocers, and of £11,000 from the City Corporation. Besides this, to mention the more salient examples, the Drapers have given some £60,000 to the People's Palace, the Goldsmiths have promised an annuity of £2,500, equivalent to a capital sum of £85,000, to the New Cross Technical Institute, the Mercers propose to devote £60,000 to the establishment of an agricultural college in Wiltshire, and the Shipwrights' Company is taking the lead in a movement for the formation of a college of shipbuilding in connection with a Technical Institute at the East-end."

Besides all this, the people of South London are preparing to establish three Technical Institutes, with the help of the Charity Commissioners; and, if possible, to secure the Albert Palace for a Battersea Institute. A similar movement has begun in North London. These local Technical Schools are independent of the City Guilds of London Institute at Kensington, but the impulse was given by its establishment.

THE INTERNATIONAL MEDICAL CONGRESS.

August 3rd, 1881.

THE seventh meeting of the International Medical Congress was formally opened by the Prince of Wales, on the 3rd of August, 1881. It was the first time the Congress had been held in England. The great room of St. James's Hall was nearly filled, 3000 members being present. No lady practitioners were admitted, although at least 25 women, practising medicine, were then on the English Medical Register, and a protest against the decision of the Council had been signed by 43 duly qualified medical women. At previous meetings of the Congress in foreign countries women were not excluded.

The Prince of Wales, on his arrival, was received by Sir W. Jenner, Sir William Gull, Sir James Paget, Sir J. Risdon Bennett, and other members of the Committee. The Honorary Secretary having read the report of the Executive Committee, the Prince of Wales, who was accompanied by the Crown Prince of Prussia, the late Emperor " Frederick the Noble," rose and said :—

" Your Imperial Highness and Gentlemen,—I gladly complied with the request that I should be patron of the International Medical Congress of 1881, and among many reasons for so doing was my conviction that few things can tend more to the welfare of mankind than that educated men of all nations should from time to time meet together for the promotion of the branches of knowledge to which they devote themselves. The intercourse and the mutual esteem of nations have often been advanced by great international exhibitions, and I look back with pleasure to those with which I have been connected ; but when conferences are held among those who in all parts of the world apply themselves to the study of science, even greater international benefits may, I think, be confidently anticipated, more especially in the study of medicine and surgery, for in these the effects of climate and of national habits must give to the practitioners of each nation opportunities, not only of acquiring knowledge, but of imparting knowledge to those of their *confrères* whom they meet in Congress.

" I venture to think, gentlemen, that the Executive Committee have acted wisely in instituting sections for the discussion of a very wide range of subjects, including not only the sciences on which medical knowledge is founded, but many of its most practical applications, and I am very happy to see that so great scope will be granted for the discussion of important questions relating to the public health, to the cure of the sick in hospitals and in the houses of the poor, and to the welfare of the Army and Navy. The devotion with which many members of the medical profession readily share the dangers of climate and the fatigues and dangers of war, and the many risks which must be encountered in the study of means, not only for the remedy, but for the prevention of disease, deserves the warmest acknowledgment from the public.

" I have great satisfaction in believing, in seeing this crowded hall, that I may already regard the Congress as successful in having attracted a number never hitherto equalled of medical men from all parts of this kingdom, as well as from every country in Europe, from the United States, and from other parts of the world. The list of officers of the Congress, including as it does the names of those distinguished in every branch of medical science, shows how heartily the proposal to hold the meeting in London has been received. I think it speaks well for the good feeling of the profession that there should have been so warm a response to the invitations. How cordially the proposal has been received may be seen not only in the large number of visitors, but in the fact that they include a large proportion of those who enjoy a high reputation not only in their own countries, but throughout the world. I sincerely congratulate the reception committee on this good promise of complete success, and I trust that at the close of the Congress they will feel rewarded for the labour they have bestowed upon it. The report which the secretary-general, Mr. MacCormack, has read will have explained how great have been his labours. He will hereafter be well repaid, and I am sure Mr. MacCormack is sensible that he will be recompensed even for his great exertions by the assurance that the progress of the important science of medicine has been materially promoted, for any addition to the knowledge of medicine must always be followed by an increase in the happiness of mankind."

There was general cheering at the close of the speech, and Sir James Paget, as President of the Congress, then read the inaugural address ; after which the meeting resolved itself into sections for special subjects. Professor Virchow, of Berlin, delivered an address in German at one of the sections.

MEMORIAL TO DEAN STANLEY.

December 13th, 1881.

In the ancient Chapter-house, Westminster Abbey, a meeting was held on the 13th of December, 1881, for promoting a scheme for raising a fitting memorial to the lamented Dean Stanley. The Very Rev. Dr. Bradley, the new Dean, presided, and was supported by the Prince of Wales, the Archbishop of Canterbury, the Marquis of Salisbury, Earl Granville, the Duke of Westminster, and many eminent persons in Church and State. There were also some ladies, and the representatives of Working Men's Clubs and Institutes, the purpose being to honour the memory of Dean Stanley, not merely as a high ecclesiastic, but as the helper of many good and beneficent objects in social life. The proposed tribute was to take the form first of a monumental memorial in the Abbey to the

Dean, and also to his wife, Lady Augusta Stanley, and to establish a Home for Training Nurses at Westminster, an object in which Lady Augusta had taken deep interest. The present meeting, however, was only to set on foot the movement, and the first resolution was: "That the genius, the character, and the public services of the late Dean of Westminster eminently entitle him to a national memorial." This was moved by the Prince of Wales, who said :—

"Mr. Dean, my Lords, and Gentlemen,—In proposing the first resolution, which has been committed to my care, I desire to express the very sincere pleasure, though I must call it the sad pleasure, which I feel in being asked to move this resolution. I do so with feelings of sorrow, owing to the long friendship and acquaintance which I had with the late Dean of Westminster; and yet with pleasure, as I have the satisfaction of proposing to you a national memorial to which I am convinced the late Dean was so thoroughly entitled. The loss which the death of that eminent man has caused to this, and, I may say also, to other countries, is indeed great. That loss was deeply felt by my beloved mother the Queen, who bore for the late Dean the greatest possible friendship and affection, and also by all the members of her family.

"If I may be allowed to speak about myself, I had the great advantage of knowing most intimately Arthur Stanley for a period of twenty-two years. Not only had I the advantage of being his pupil during my residence at the University of Oxford, but I was also his fellow-traveller in the East when we visited Egypt and the Holy Land together; and I am not likely to forget the charm of his companionship and all the knowledge that he imparted to me during that tour. The many virtues and many great qualities of the Dean are so well known to all of you, and are so well appreciated throughout the length and breadth of the land, that it is almost superfluous in me, and would be almost out of taste, were I now to go through the long list of all that he has done from the day in which his name came into prominence. Still, as the churchman, as the scholar, as the man of letters, as the philanthropist, and, above all, as the true friend, his name must always go down to posterity as a great and good man, and as one who will have made his mark on the chapter of his country's history. To all classes he felt alike—to rich and poor, to high and low—he was, I may say, the friend of all; and it is most gratifying on this occasion to see here present the representatives of all classes of the community, and especially of the great labouring class to whom he was so devoted, and who, I think, owe him so much.

"It is also deeply gratifying, I am sure, to the Dean and those who take a deep interest in this meeting that we have the advantage of the presence to-day of the Minister of the United States. As I was saying, not only was the late Dean appreciated and looked up to in this country and in Europe, but also by that kindred country across the Atlantic to which he so lately paid a visit, and where we know that he received so much kindness and hospitality. I heard from his own lips on his return from America the expression of the great gratification he derived from his visit, and of the hope—of what, alas! was not to be—that he might on some future occasion be able to repeat it.

"There is much more that I should wish to say in regard to one whom I so deeply deplore, and to whom I bore so great an affection. But I am sure it is not the object of this meeting to make long speeches, and as many speakers have to follow me, I will only again express the gratification I feel in being here to propose the resolution which I now have the honour of bringing before you."

The resolution was seconded by Earl Granville. The Hon. J. Russell Lowell bore testimony to the honour in which the memory of Dean Stanley was held in America, and said he felt sure that many of his countrymen would be delighted, as some already had done, to share the privilege of helping this memorial.

The Archbishop of Canterbury (Dr. Tait) moved the next resolution, as to the placing of the recumbent statue in the Abbey, and also completing the windows in the Chapter-house, in accordance with plans proposed and partly executed by the Dean. After speeches by the Marquis of Salisbury, Mr. S. Morley, M.P., the Marquis of Lorne, and Lord Chief Justice Coleridge, Mr. Gardiner, representing the Working Men's Club and Institute Union, spoke of the constant efforts of the late Dean to help and elevate the classes who lived by manual labour. He was President of their Union, and he was honoured by the working men of Westminster and London.

RIFLE VOLUNTEERS.

March 1st, 1882.

The 21st anniversary dinner of the Civil Service Volunteers, on the 1st of March, 1882, at Willis's Rooms, was presided over by the Prince of Wales, honorary Colonel of the Corps. In replying to the toast of his health, proposed by the Duke of Manchester, the Prince said :—

"My Lords and Gentlemen and Brother Volunteers,—For the kind manner in which the Duke of Manchester has proposed this toast, and for the cordial welcome given to it by you, gentlemen and brother Volunteers, allow me to return you my most sincere thanks. I can assure you that it affords me great satisfaction to preside here to-night on what I may call the twenty-second anniversary of the existence of this regiment. The twenty-first anniversary of the Rifle Volunteers was celebrated last year, and it will, I am sure, not be forgotten through the length and breadth of the land that the Queen reviewed the English Volunteers in Windsor Park in the summer, and the Scotch Volunteers afterwards at Edinburgh.

"I remember, gentlemen, as though it were only yesterday, when I was an undergraduate at the University of Oxford in 1859, the commencement of the Volunteer movement. I remember the interest which all the townspeople of Oxford took in that movement, and also the interest it excited among the undergraduates. I confess I thought at that time, and many others shared my opinion, that to a certain extent the commencement of that movement was an inclination on the part of the citizens of our country to play at soldiers. Many thought that the movement would not last. However, I am glad to find, as you all will have been equally glad to find, that we were entirely mistaken in that opinion. Twenty-two years ago, when, I may say, the movement had begun to ripen, I am not wrong, I think, in stating that the number of Volunteers was very nearly 100,000 men. The force has since gone through certain vicissitudes, but I think I may say that at the present moment it never was in a more flourishing condition, and it now numbers not far short of 200,000 men. Most sincerely do

I hope that the occasion may not arise when their services might be required for the defence of their country, but I feel convinced that, should that occasion ever arise, the Rifle Volunteers of the United Kingdom will go to the front and stand to their guns in every sense of the word.

" One great inducement to join the force has been, I think, the Wimbledon camp and rifle shooting, and I feel convinced that in no country are there better rifle shots than in this, and few better than in the Volunteer force.   No doubt a great stimulus has been given to that force by their being called on to take part in manœuvres, reviews, and sham fights, and of late years from their being frequently brigaded with regular troops.   I am sure there is nothing they like better, and I am sure that for the Regular Army, as well as for the Militia, it is most desirable this should continue.

" With regard to this regiment with which my name has been now associated for twenty-two years, I can only say that from all the accounts I have heard it is in a high state of efficiency. Since the time of their formation in 1860, 2177 men have passed through their ranks, and last year the regiment had a strength of 518 men.   Nearly all their officers, I believe, have passed through the school, and attained the distinction of the letter P in the Army List—a distinction of which I know they are justly proud.   I had an opportunity of reviewing them in 1863 in London, and again at Wimbledon in 1870 ; I saw them at the Review at Windsor last year, and I sincerely hope, if it may not be inconvenient to those members of the corps who have so many avocations, to see them before many weeks are over at the Review at Portsmouth.

" Gentlemen, let me thank you also for the kind way in which you have received the name of the Princess of Wales and the names of my brothers and my sons.   I am happy to be able to announce to you that I received a telegram just before dinner informing me of the arrival of the *Bacchante* at Suez.   My sons are now, therefore, rapidly approaching the termination of their cruise, which has been round the world.   I thank you once more for your kind reception of me to-night, and it affords me the greatest pleasure now to propose the toast of ' Prosperity to the Civil Service Rifle Volunteers,' coupled with the name of your Colonel, Lieutenant-Colonel Lord Bury. I know that in his presence it would be disagreeable to him if I were to mete out any praise which I feel is his due, but I know how much he has at heart the prosperity and the efficiency of his regiment, and, being now the oldest serving Lieutenant-Colonel in the Volunteer force, that you would all deeply regret the day when he should leave you. I call upon you, and upon the distinguished guests here to-night, to drink prosperity to the regiment, and couple the toast with the name of Lord Bury."

Viscount Bury, in responding to the toast, said that'in looking at the first list of the officers of the regiment, he found only three names of those now in active service, those of His Royal Highness, of himself, and Major Mills. About 350 members of the corps sat down to dinner on this, its 21st anniversary. The Duke of Portland, Lord Elcho, now the Earl of Wemyss, Colonel Loyd-Lindsay, Colonel Grenfell, Governor of the Bank of England, Colonel Du Plat Taylor, and many veterans of the Force, were present.

BRITISH GRAVES IN THE CRIMEA.

March 10*th*, 1883.

ATTENTION had from time to time been directed, by reports of travellers and others, to the neglected state of the burial-places in the Crimea, and the ruinous condition of monumental memorials over the graves. An allowance of £90 a year had been made by the Government for maintaining the different cemeteries, but this was utterly insufficient for the purpose. The Consul-General at Odessa had recently reported that there were at least eleven graveyards or cemeteries scattered between Balaclava and Sebastopol, and there were many others in different places where the dead had been laid. The scandal of neglect was so great that the Duke of Cambridge called a meeting at the United Service Institution, Whitehall, to consider what ought to be done. A large number of distinguished men, including many of those who had passed through the Crimean War, responded to the invitation, and letters were received from others throughout the country who were unable to be present.

The Duke of Cambridge made a clear statement of the condition of affairs, and mentioned various suggestions for putting a stop to the desecration of the burial-places, and for preserving the memorials from further injury. The Prince of Wales had come to

Q

the meeting, and as he had seen the places referred to, during his Eastern travels, he was asked by the Chairman to move the first resolution, which was to the effect that immediate steps should be taken to remedy the existing state of the Crimean graves.

The Prince, who was warmly received, rose, and said :

"Your Royal Highness, my Lords, and Gentlemen,—I was not aware until I arrived in this room that I should be called upon to move the first resolution.   But I need hardly tell you the great interest the subject we are discussing here to-day has for me, and the great pleasure it gives me to propose the following resolution :—' That the present condition of the British cemeteries in the Crimea is not creditable to this country, and that endeavours should be made to raise the necessary funds to have them restored, and to preserve them from further desecration.'   In 1869 I had occasion to visit the Crimea, and to go over all those spots so familiar to most of the gentlemen I see opposite me, who took a part in the campaign.   And it was a matter of particular interest to me to visit those different spots where our brave soldiers were buried. I confess that it was with deep regret that I saw the manner in which the tombs were kept.   The condition of the graves was not creditable to us, and not creditable to a great country like ours, for I am sure we are the very first to do honour to the dead who fought in the name of their country.

" It struck me at the time that one of the great faults lay in there being so many different cemeteries.   The French had a much simpler and a better system—that which they call the *ossuaire.*   I was told at the time that to the feelings of Englishmen—on religious, and possibly, I may also say, on sentimental grounds—it was repugnant to disturb the remains of those who were interred in the Crimea as was done by the French, and that to collect them and put them into one large building was not what was consonant with our feelings generally.   But I cannot help thinking, as considerable time has elapsed since our comrades fell, and also as we are, in every sense of the word, a thoroughly practical nation—I feel myself strongly, although I cannot say how far that feeling may be shared by the meeting to-day—that it would be far better, and in the long run far cheaper, if we were to build a kind of mausoleum, collecting the remains of our comrades who fell in the Crimean War, and putting them into such a mausoleum. It was really sad to see the neglected condition of the tombs. There was one especially with which I was struck—that of Sir Robert Newman, who was in the Grenadier Guards, and fell in the Battle of Inkerman. His tomb was a most elaborate and expensive one, and was built with a dark stone, a kind of porphyry. This was broken almost entirely to pieces. Upon inquiry of some Russian authorities who accompanied me on that occasion, I discovered a curious fact. The idea was not merely that of disturbing and breaking open the tombs; but, as most of you are aware, the Crim Tartars—who are Mahomedans by religion—had an idea that treasures were to be found in the tombs. Therefore, the disturbing of them was not merely for the sake of disturbing the dead, but with the hope of finding some treasures there. It is needless to say that their investigations were not satisfied in that respect.

"Of course, gentlemen, with regard to the pecuniary part of the question, it is not for me to go into that; but I hope that, as so many distinguished military and naval men are present, they cannot but have a strong feeling with me that it will ever be a living disgrace to us unless we adopt some means to-day by which the tombs of our comrades who fell in the Crimea are kept in a proper state of preservation. I have merely suggested the idea of an *ossuaire*, because it seems to me the simplest form to adopt. But it would involve, what many object to, disturbing the remains of some who fell. I only hope that before the meeting separates to-day we may have arrived at some satisfactory conclusion that the graves of our comrades shall in some way be respected and maintained in a manner creditable to ourselves and to our country. Therefore, it is with the greatest pleasure that I move the first resolution."

The resolution was seconded by General Sir W. Codrington, who said that the Russian Government had given additional land at Cathcart's Hill; and that the grave-stones and other memorials should be removed there. He did not think there should be any removal of the remains of the dead.

The Prince of Wales again rose, and said—

"I wish to add that when I went over the different places of interest in the Crimea, and inspected all our burial-places, I was accompanied by one of the most courteous gentlemen,

General Kotzebue, the Governor-General of Odessa; and I need only say that, as far as the Russian Government represented by him was concerned, everything was done to keep the graves from desecration. But he told me that, unfortunately, they were powerless to prevent it; and it was his opinion, and he strongly advised me, that the only way in which to prevent a repetition of a desecration of the tombs would be, as I mentioned before, to collect the remains and place them in a mausoleum— in the same way, in fact, as the French had done. I wish also to say that, on my return in the summer from my visit to the Crimea, I brought the whole matter most strongly before the late Lord Clarendon, who was then Secretary of State for Foreign Affairs."

After conversation and remarks by Admiral Sir H. Keppel, General Sir L. A. Simmons, Lord Wolseley, and others, resolutions were carried for the concentration of the memorials in one central place, without removing the remains of the dead; and for applying to the Government and to the nation for larger funds to pay additional guardians of the cemeteries. The Duke of Cambridge was warmly commended for having called the meeting, which was justified by the large attendance, and the Prince of Wales for his advocacy of the object in view. The interest of their Royal Highnesses was practically attested by the gift of £50 from the Prince of Wales and £25 from the Duke of Cambridge toward the necessary funds. It was stated in the course of the proceedings that the French Government granted yearly more than double what the British Government did, for protecting the Crimean graves.

THE FISHERIES EXHIBITION.

1883.

IN the preface to the Official Catalogue of the International Fisheries Exhibition, the compiler, Mr. Trendell, gives an interesting account of the origin and gradual development of that successful undertaking. It was not till some years after the great Exhibition of 1851 that attention was given to this special department of industry and commerce. At Boulogne, Havre, and other maritime places, there were local expositions; but the first international exhibition on a large scale was that of Berlin in 1880. Norwich was the first town in England to follow the Continental example. The local character of the undertaking soon expanded into a national enterprise, the Corporation of London and the

Fishmongers' Company lending their influence. Chiefly through the agency of Mr. Birkbeck, one of the Norfolk County members, the official sanction of the Government was obtained, with permission to grant medals and diplomas of merit, as in other national exhibitions. The Prince of Wales took a lively interest in the success of this Norwich project, and he secured the co-operation of Mr. Birkbeck for holding an International Exhibition in London.

In July 1881 a meeting was held at the Hall of the Fishmongers' Company, when a formal resolution was passed for carrying out the proposal, and a Committee formed for arranging the general plan of the Exhibition. In February 1882 a second meeting was held at Willis's Rooms, when the Duke of Richmond read the report of the proceedings of the Committee formed in the previous year. The sanction of the Queen was obtained as Patron, and the Prince of Wales as President, the Duke of Edinburgh and the other Royal Dukes being named Vice-Presidents, with the Duke of Richmond as Chairman of the General Committee. The sentiments and motives of the promoters of the undertaking were well expressed in words spoken by the Prince of Wales at the inaugural banquet at Norwich. He said :—

" It is particularly gratifying to see that at last an interest is being taken not only in our fisheries, but in our fishermen, whose lives are so frequently exposed to risk through the severity of weather and the dangerous character of the Eastern coast. Among a very interesting display of specimens, I especially observed the apparatus for saving life, and a variety of models of lifeboats, which cannot fail to bring before the public generally their duty in regard to the protection of the fishing interests of our country. Whilst thinking over the probable results that may attend this Exhibition, I could not fail to reflect upon the labour it has cost more minds than one ; and I do trust, having regard to the importance of our national fishing interest, and the value of our fishermen's lives, that a sort of National Society may be instituted which will maintain those who are unfortunately in want, and help to assuage the grief and misery of the widows and orphans of those who perish at sea. I believe it is only necessary to throw out the hint to see established in this country a National Fishermen's Aid Society, which shall command the support not only of those living upon the line of our fishing coast here, but of all concerned in fishery throughout our dominions."

It thus appears that at the time of the Norwich Exhibition, and much more after the greater show at South Kensington, the Prince of Wales had in view the welfare of the fishing folk as well as the benefit of the fisheries. What is an exhibition—with its display of exhibits, its prizes, awards, conferences, and its whole visible organisation—compared with the safety of our fishermen's lives, and the improvement of their homes? For some departments of this beneficent work there are special agencies at work—such as the Lifeboat Association, the Deep-Sea Mission, Sailors' Homes, and Seamen's Hospitals—but the idea of the Prince was that a great central society, analogous to the Royal Agricultural Society for the cultivation of the soil, might be established, attending to all matters bearing on the social and moral, as well as the material, benefits of the fishing population of these islands. It is said that the Government has resolved tardily to have a Department of Agriculture; it is equally needful to have a Department for all matters connected with the "harvests of the sea."

OPENING OF FISHERIES EXHIBITION.

May 12th, 1883.

THE International Fisheries Exhibition was opened with great ceremony on the 12th of May, 1883, by the Prince of Wales, "by command of Her Majesty, and on Her Majesty's behalf." Most of the members of the Royal Family were present, the Foreign Ambassadors and Ministers, Her Majesty's Ministers, and other distinguished persons. The Prince was accompanied by the Princess of Wales, Prince Albert Victor, and Prince George of Wales. The Duke of Richmond, Chairman of the General Committee, having read a statement of the object and the contents of the Exhibition, the Prince replied:—

"My Lord Duke, my Lords, and Gentlemen,—It gives me great pleasure to open this International Fisheries Exhibition on behalf of the Queen, although I feel assured that it is a matter of sincere regret to all present that Her Majesty finds herself unable to undertake a duty which it would have afforded her much gratification to have performed. In view of the rapid increase of the population in all civilized countries, and especially in these sea-girt kingdoms, a profound interest attaches to every industry which affects the supply of food; and, in this respect, the harvest of the sea is hardly less important than that of the land. I share your hope that the Exhibition now about to open may afford the means of enabling practical fishermen to acquaint themselves with the latest improvements which have been made in their craft in all parts of the world; so that without needless destruction, or avoidable waste of any kind, mankind may derive the fullest possible advantage from the bounty of the waters. I am glad to hear that your attention has been directed to the condition of the fishing population. It is a subject in which my brother, the Duke of Edinburgh, was led to take a particular interest during his tenure of office as Admiral Superintendent of the Naval Reserve; and, as he is compelled to be absent during the sittings of the Congress to which you allude, I shall have the pleasure of reading a paper on this topic which he has prepared at its first meeting. Lifeboats and life-saving apparatus undoubtedly fall strictly within the province of a fishery exhibition; but I may congratulate you on the circumstance that, without overstepping your proper limits, you have been able to confer a benefit, not only on all fishermen and all sailors by profession, but also on all who travel by sea; and in these days of rapid and extensive locomotion this means a large proportion of civilized mankind. On behalf of the Queen, I add my thanks to those which you tender to the Governments of foreign nations and of our colonies for their generous co-operation. And to their representatives whose untiring exertions you so justly acknowledge, I offer not only thanks, but an English welcome."

The Archbishop of Canterbury having offered a prayer, the Prince declared the Exhibition open.

CLOSING OF FISHERIES EXHIBITION.

October 31st, 1883.

If there ever had been any doubt as to the success of the International Fisheries Exhibition, it had been thoroughly removed long before the end of the season drew near. The popular interest had been shown from the beginning, and the number of visitors exceeded all expectations. The total number of visitors was 2,703,051. The daily average of visitors, including Wednesday, when half-a-crown was the price of admission, was 18,388. The financial result was sure to be satisfactory when such vast numbers had been attracted.

On the 31st of October, the day appointed for closing, Mr. Edward Birkbeck, M.P., Chairman of the Executive Committee, read to His Royal Highness the President an address, presenting the chief statistical and other official reports of the undertaking. One novel feature was the report on "the fish dinners" supplied with the co-operation of the National School of Cookery. No less than 209,673 dinners were supplied, at sixpence a head, and with satisfactory pecuniary results.

A Report as to the work of the Juries having been presented by the Duke of Edinburgh, the Prince of Wales thus replied to the address of the Executive Committee:—

"I have listened with great pleasure to the Report of the Executive Committee.

"Her Majesty has followed with much interest the success which has so signally attended this Exhibition, and I have had the gratification of receiving, this morning, a telegram from the Queen, begging me to inform you of these sentiments, and likewise to express Her Majesty's fervent hope that lasting benefit to the fishing population may be the reward of those who have shown so much interest in the welfare of this Exhibition. And it is as much a matter of satisfaction to my brothers as to myself to have contributed towards the success of an enterprise, respecting which, at the outset, nothing was certain but the heavy responsibility of those who had engaged in it.

"I am well aware that Her Majesty's Government, the Governments of Foreign Countries, and of our Colonies, through their respective Commissioners, and the various public bodies and private persons to whom you have alluded, have afforded most valuable and indeed indispensable aid to our undertaking; and I desire to add my own thanks to yours for their very important assistance.

"But it is just that I should supply the only deficiency which I observe in your Report, by pointing out that without the administrative capacity and unremitting toil of the Members of the Executive Committee, and especially of its Chairman, the eminently satisfactory results which you have reported to me could not have been attained.

"I learn with much pleasure that, after all expenses are defrayed, a substantial surplus will remain in your hands.

"The best method of disposing of that surplus is a matter which will need careful consideration. It would be premature to allude to any of the various suggestions which have already been put forward ; but I am of opinion that no proposal will be satisfactory to the public, unless it is immediately directed towards the carrying out of the objects of the Exhibition from which the fund is derived ; namely, the promotion of the welfare of Fishermen, Fisheries, and the Fishing Industry in general.

"And I think our duty towards the supporters of the Exhibition will not be discharged until we have done something towards the alleviation of the calamities fatally incidental to the Fisherman's calling; and until we have also done something towards the promotion of that application of Science to practice from which the Fishing Industry, like all other industries, can alone look for improvement.

"I believe, that apart from what may be effected by the judicious use of the Surplus Fund, the latter end may best be attained by the formation of a Society, having for its object the collection of statistics and other information relative to Fisheries; the diffusion among the fishing population of a knowledge of all improvements in the methods and appliances of their calling; the discussion of questions bearing upon Fishing Interests; and the elucidation of those problems of Natural History which bear upon the subject. Such a Society, as the representative of the interests of the Fisheries, would naturally take charge of the scientific investigations which bear upon those interests, and would, no doubt, be brought into relation with the Aquarium which you wisely propose to offer to the Government, and with the already existing Fishery Museum of the Department of Science and Art, which is founded on the Collection bequeathed to the nation by the late Mr. Buckland, but which has been immensely enlarged and enriched by the liberality of many of our exhibitors.

"You have rightly divined that it is a source of great gratification to me to be able to continue the work commenced by my father in 1851 ; and, by giving scope for the peaceful emulation of the leaders of industry of all nationalities in public Exhibitions, to divert the minds of men from those international rivalries by which all suffer, to those by which all gain.

"The evidence of the public interest in such Exhibitions, afforded by the vast concourse of visitors from all parts of the realm to that which is now closed, has led me to hope that the buildings which have been erected at so much cost, and which have so admirably served their purpose, shall continue for the next three years to be employed for Exhibitions of a similarly comprehensive character.

"In considering what shall be the subject-matter of these Exhibitions, three topics of paramount interest to our community have presented themselves to my mind. These are Health, both bodily and mental; Industrial Inventions; and the rapidly-growing resources of our Colonies and of our Indian Empire.

"I have expressed a desire that the Exhibition of 1884 will embrace the conditions of health, in so far as, like food, clothes, and dwellings, they fall under the head of Hygiene, or, like appliances for general and technical teaching, gymnasia and schools, under that of Education.

"The question of the Patent Laws has for many years engaged the attention of all those interested in the progress of invention and the just reward of the inventor. I am advised that the Patent Act of last Session will afford a satisfactory solution of the difficulties which beset this subject, and will be especially useful to the poor inventor by enabling him to obtain protection for his invention at a considerably reduced rate, and in a manner which will be more advantageous to him.

"Under these circumstances, it has appeared to me that much good may result from an Exhibition in the year 1885, showing the Progress of Invention, especially in labour-saving machinery, since 1862; that is to say, since the last great International Exhibition held in this country.

"At the close of the Paris Exhibition of 1868, I had the satisfaction of receiving from the Colonial Commissioners an address, in which great stress was laid on the desirability of establishing a permanent Colonial Museum in London, as a powerful means of diffusing throughout the Mother Country a better knowledge of the nature and importance of the several Dependencies of the Empire, of facilitating commercial relations, marking progress, and aiding the researches of men of science, and also of affording valuable information to intending emigrants.

"At that time I was able to do little more than to assure the Commissioners of my readiness to promote such a scheme, and to recommend the respective Governments to give it their full consideration.

"I trust that the British Colonial Exhibition which I propose to hold in 1886, may result in the foundation of such a Museum —the institution of which would secure for the people of this country a permanent record of the resources and development of Her Majesty's Colonies; and I hope that an important section of the proposed Exhibition of that year may result from the co-operation of our fellow-subjects, the people of India, in a suitable representation of the industrial arts of that Empire.

"In conclusion, I desire, as President of these Exhibitions, to thank the Special Commissioners, the Members of the General Committee, and the Jurors, for the time and labour they have devoted to the business of the Exhibition; and to express my high approbation of the cheerfulness and assiduity with which the members of the Executive Staff have discharged their very onerous duties.

"And I must finally signalize, as especially deserving of our gratitude, my brother, the Duke of Edinburgh, and the other foreign and English gentlemen, to whom we are indebted for the bestowal of much time and thought upon the papers which have been brought before those Conferences, which have formed so interesting and so useful a feature of the Exhibition. I am glad to hear that the value of the contribution to Fishery Literature, effected by the publication of these papers and the discussions to which they gave rise, has received authoritative recognition."

FINANCIAL RESULTS OF FISHERIES EXHIBITION, AND DISPOSAL OF SURPLUS.

AFTER all the affairs of the Exhibition of 1883 had been wound up, including the financial accounts, a meeting of the General Committee was held on Saturday, March 22nd, 1884, to receive the Report of the Executive Committee. Details of receipts and outlay were presented. Reference was made to the wide interest awakened by the Exhibition, the attendance of fishermen from many lands, as well as from all parts of the United Kingdom, and the success of the attempt to sell fish at prices hitherto unknown in our great towns.   The Report and Balance Sheet having been presented, the Prince of Wales thus spoke:—

" You have all listened, I am sure, with great interest to the report that has been read to you by the Chairman of the Executive Committee.   From what we have heard, I think it is patent to all that the late Fisheries Exhibition has in every point of view been a success.   It has been a financial success, and it has also been a success as regards the enormous number of people who have visited it, not only of our own countrymen and those from our colonies, but from every part of the globe. It is unnecessary for me on an occasion of this kind to enumerate the objects of this Exhibition, but I maintain that its two salient objects—viz., the scientific and practical ones— have fully justified its existence : its scientific object by the display of every possible kind of modern appliance, thus showing the great improvements that have been made in the fishing industry of the world ; and its practical object because it not only showed to our own countrymen, but to all the world, what a valuable means of subsistence fish is.   Many, I believe, had no idea of its value ; while the existence of varieties of fish was made known which had not even been heard of by the great majority of people.   Well, gentlemen, you have all heard that there is a surplus amounting to £15,243, and the question is naturally how to employ that sum.   In the address that I read to you at the closing of the Exhibition I held out some hope that this might be applied in a useful and practical manner, and I would therefore now suggest to the General Committee that one of the best objects by which to perpetuate the results of this successful Exhibition would be to appropriate, say, about £10,000 to alleviate the distress of widows and orphans of sea fishermen.   I use the words ' alleviate the distress ' because I do not wish to bind any of you to our erecting an orphanage. That would cost a great deal of money, and, I think, would possibly be a mistake.   If we were to embark in any great building enterprise of that kind, and in future find ourselves in debt, we should have frustrated the very object we have in view, viz., supporting the widows and orphans of those brave men who peril their lives at sea. I would also suggest that £3000 should be given as an endowment to a society, which might be called the Royal Fisheries Society. What shape that might take will be for your future consideration; but possibly some society might be founded under such a name or character, similar to the Royal Agricultural Society. We shall then have a surplus of about £2000 left, which, I think you will all agree, will be a good thing to keep in reserve. It would be for the general public in future to show their interest in this scheme by supporting it to the best of their ability. I beg, therefore, to move the following resolution :—'That a sum of £10,000 be invested, with a view to applying the proceeds to the assistance of families who have suffered the loss of a father or husband in the prosecution of his calling as a sea fisherman; and that a further sum of £3000 be applied to the formation of a Fisheries Society, such as was suggested by His Royal Highness the President in his reply to the report of the Executive Committee on the 31st of October, 1883.' "

That suggestion was that a society should be formed, having for its object the collection of statistics and other information relative to Fisheries; the diffusing among the fishing population of a knowledge of all improvements in the methods and appliances of their calling; the discussion of questions bearing upon fishing interests: we wish we could add, "the interests of the public," in obtaining more and cheaper fish !

NEW CITY OF LONDON SCHOOL.

December 12th, 1882.

THE large and commodious building on the Embankment, which is the new seat of the old "City of London School," was formally opened by the Prince of Wales, accompanied by the Princess of Wales, on the 12th of December, 1882. The Lord Mayor, in state, the masters of the principal City Companies, and a large assembly of civic and educational notables were present. The Lord Mayor having given an address on the history of the school, and the work done by the Corporation in connection with it, asked the Prince to declare the new building open.

The Prince, after expressing the gratification it gave to himself and the Princess to take part in the proceedings of the day, and, having thanked the Lord Mayor for the historical address, said :—

"After what you have all heard with regard to the existence of this school, it will be hardly necessary for me to add more than a very few words. I also express my fervent hope that a school such as this one, which has flourished for a space of between forty and fifty years, will continue ever to do so. It is a palpable fact that many pupils have gone up to the Universities, and taken high degrees, both in Classics at Oxford and in Mathematics at Cambridge. The present Head Master is one of those who took high honours at Cambridge. Last, but not least, the Lord Mayor himself was educated in this school, and is the first boy who has reached that high position.

"I must congratulate the architect, and all those who have designed and built this school. I feel convinced from what we have seen that it is an admirably suited building for all educational purposes. Its site, close to the Thames, where it will get fresh air, and the admirable manner in which all the rooms are constructed, promise well for the future. Let me once again express a fervent hope that, under the blessing of God, it will continue to flourish and prosper. I now declare the new buildings open."

The announcement was received with great cheering, with a flourish of trumpets. The present Head Master, Dr. Abbott, worthily sustains the reputation which the school held under Dr. Mortimer.

THE NORTHBROOK CLUB.

May 21st, 1883.

THE opening of the club, in Whitehall Gardens, named after the Earl of Northbrook, for the use of native gentlemen from the East Indies and their friends, attracted a large and influential assemblage. By the request of Lord Northbrook the Prince of Wales declared the club open. He said that, after the clear and full statement by Lord Northbrook, he had little to say about the objects and advantages of the club. After expressing his gratification at being invited to be present, he said :—

"I have not forgotten—and I address this especially to those gentlemen who come from India—nor am I likely ever to forget, the magnificent reception I met with in India, not only from the Native Princes, but from every class in India; and the interest I take in all that concerns Her Majesty's Indian empire I assure you will ever continue. I think it highly desirable that a club of this nature should have been formed, so as to bring natives of India into direct communication with our own countrymen, and that facilities should be afforded them to find a comfortable place where they can meet together for the interchange of ideas, and where they can seek relaxation after their labours in the professions which they have come here to study. That it will be found in every respect desirable, I am sure, and I have not the smallest doubt that it will be successful. I am glad to hear from Lord Northbrook of the money which has come from India. It is gratifying to know that the Indian Princes have been magnanimous in their subscriptions, and have shown the great interest they take in the success of the undertaking. I heartily wish prosperity to the Northbrook Club."

Some letters from India having been read, and several native gentlemen having been presented, the Prince made a tour of the club with the committee.

CITY OF LONDON COLLEGE IN MOORFIELDS.

July 8th, 1883.

THE City of London College, which has spacious premises in White Street, Moorfields, is intended for giving educational advantages to young men, chiefly by means of evening classes for those engaged in business or work during the day. It was originally established, in 1848, at Crosby Hall, moving from there to Sussex Hall, Leadenhall Street, and finally settled in the new building in Moorfields, the cost of which was £16,000. To inaugurate this new College, the Prince of Wales, accompanied by the Princess, went to the City. After being shown over the building their Royal Highnesses were conducted by the Lord Mayor to the great hall, which is capable of holding about 1000 persons, and which was densely filled.

The Reverend Prebendary Whittington, Principal of the College, read an address thanking the Prince for his presence, and stating the objects of the College. He mentioned that in 1858 the

Prince Consort paid a visit to Crosby Hall, and testified his approval of the work done for the intellectual, social, and moral improvement of the young men of London, by consenting to become the first patron, an office which had since his death been filled by the Queen. Her Majesty had testified her continued approval by a generous donation to the new building fund.

The Prince of Wales, in reply, said :—

" Ladies and Gentlemen,—It is with sincere pleasure that I thank you on behalf of the Princess of Wales, as well as on my own, for the loyal address of welcome which has just been presented to us, and for being given this opportuntity of expressing to you our approval of your efforts for the improvement of the intellectual, social, moral, and spiritual condition of the young men of this vast metropolis. Such occasions are always fraught with the deepest interest to me, recalling as they do the memory of my beloved father, the Prince Consort, who devoted his time, his experience, and his great abilities to the promotion of undertakings such as the one you now have in hand, to which he lent his countenance by becoming its first patron, and which the Queen still encourages by her patronage. We sincerely trust our presence here to-day may encourage others to take an interest in this great undertaking, and we rejoice to be able to declare your new building open."

A prayer for the continued success of the institution was then offered up by Bishop Claughton, and the Old Hundredth Psalm was sung.

The Secretary then read a list of subscriptions, including fifty guineas from the Prince of Wales. The Lord Mayor said that the Prince always showed his interest in education, and he had lately been present at the opening of the City of London School. This College gave more advanced and practical teaching than was given at that School.

Mr. Clarke, Q.C., M.P., said he had been a student of the College twenty-six or twenty-seven years ago, and the education he there received had been most valuable to him. Mr. Prebendary Mackenzie having supported the resolution of a vote of thanks to their Royal Highnesses, the Prince returned his warm thanks and added :—

" So much has been said with regard to this College that I should only be taking up your time if I were to allude to it further than to say that I feel convinced—and it is our earnest hope—that this College, which has been so successful hitherto, will continue to prosper in the new building. Most cordially do we wish it all success. A greater proof cannot be given of the excellent character of the education which the students here receive than that given by the seconder of the resolution, Mr. Clarke, who has not only attained a high position in the profession he has adopted, but who has also become a member of Parliament. I thank you again for your kind reception of us ·to-day, and for the pleasure it has given us to inaugurate this very handsome building."

HOUSING OF THE POOR AND THE WORKING CLASSES.

February 22nd, 1884.

His Royal Highness the Prince of Wales is not infrequent in his attendance in the House of Lords, but he has very rarely addressed the House. It is natural that he should avoid even the appearance of being mixed up with political controversies, or touching points that might bear a party construction. But on questions of a social or patriotic bearing to which he is known to have given personal attention, the voice of the Prince would be always heard with pleasure, and his opinions carry due weight. It was so in the matter of the Housing of the Poor, which was brought before the House on the 22nd of February, 1884.

The Marquis of Salisbury moved an Address to Her Majesty for the appointment of a Royal Commission to inquire into the housing of the working classes. Lord Carington seconded the motion, after which the Prince of Wales rose, amidst cheers from both sides of the House. He said :—

" My Lords,—The speeches which have fallen from the lips of the noble Marquis who introduced this subject, and from the noble Lord who has just sat down, cannot fail to have been heard with the deepest interest by your Lordships. I feel also convinced that your Lordships, in common with all classes of Her Majesty's subjects, will be gratified to learn that the noble Marquis has asked for a searching inquiry to be made into that great and momentous question with regard to the housing, and the amelioration of the dwellings, of the poor and the working classes, and that Her Majesty's Government have already appointed a Commission for that purpose.

R

"My Lords, it is not my intention to trouble your Lordships with many remarks, though I take the keenest and liveliest interest in this great question. Still, I confess I have not gone sufficiently into the matter for me to venture on giving an opinion, especially after what has fallen from the noble Marquis and the noble Lord. At the same time, I can assure you, my Lords, that I am deeply flattered at having been appointed a member of the Royal Commission. The subject of the housing of the poor is not entirely unknown to me, as having acquired a property in Norfolk now for twenty years, I have had something to do in building fresh dwellings for the poor and working classes. On arriving there I found the dwellings in the most deplorable condition, but I hope now that there is hardly one on the estate who can complain of not being adequately housed.

"I quite endorse what has fallen from the noble Marquis and the quotation which he made from the letter of Mr. Williams which appeared in to-day's newspapers. A few days ago I visited two of the poorest courts in the district of St. Pancras and Holborn, where, I can assure you, my Lords, that the condition of the people, or rather of their dwellings, was perfectly disgraceful. This in itself proves to me how important it is that there should be a thoroughly searching inquiry. As your Lordships are aware, there have existed now for some short space of time several private societies organised for the purpose of inquiring into this very question. I am sure that we ought all to be grateful to these gentlemen for giving up their time to so important a subject, and I feel that the Royal Commission can in nowise clash with the efforts of these private individuals.

"In conclusion, my Lords, I wish to say that I cherish an earnest hope, which I feel will be shared by your Lordships, that the result of this Royal Commission will be a recommendation to Parliament of measures of a drastic and thorough kind, which may be the means of not only improving the dwellings of the poor, but of ameliorating their condition generally."

His Royal Highness was followed by Lord Shaftesbury, the Bishop of London, and others, but nothing was added in the debate of a practical nature, and the motion of Lord Salisbury was unanimously carried.

THE GUARDS' INDUSTRIAL HOME AT CHELSEA BARRACKS.

February 25th, 1884.

THE Prince and Princess of Wales, accompanied by the Princess Louise, Marchioness of Lorne, and the Princesses Louise, Victoria, and Maude of Wales, visited Chelsea Baracks on Monday, the 25th of February, 1884, for the distribution of prizes to the girls at the Guards' Industrial Home. It is very honourable to the officers of the Guards, that they provide as far as they can for the welfare of the wives and families of the soldiers, as well as of the men of their regiments. The boys educated in the regimental schools were easily provided for, but for the training of the girls for useful occupations it had been advisable to establish this Industrial Home in the neighbourhood of the barracks. This was explained by General Higginson, commanding the brigade of Guards in the Home district, and a report of the state of the institution during the past year was read by Colonel Cockran, the honorary secretary.

The Prince of Wales then distributed the prizes to the girls, in his usual kindly manner. General Higginson, in the name of the brigade, thanked their Royal Highnesses for the proof they had given of their favour and good will. The Prince replied—

" General Higginson, Ladies, and Gentlemen,—The Princess begs me to return her warmest thanks for the very kind words in which you have expressed your thanks to her on behalf of the brigade for taking part in the ceremony which we have just witnessed. I know I am only expressing her views when I state that it has given her sincere pleasure to be here, and that she shares with me an interest in everything which concerns the brigade of Guards. After what has fallen from you, General Higginson, and after the reading of the report, there is little left for me to say beyond congratulating those who founded this institution and those who so ably maintain it, upon the highly satisfactory way in which it is managed and upon the creditable manner in which, as we know, every detail connected with its working is conducted. We sincerely hope that those young ladies who have to-day received prizes will go forth to pursue their avocations in life with credit both to themselves and to the instruction they have received in this institution. We trust that having reached its 21st anniversary—the coming of age of the Guards' Industrial Home—the institution will ever continue to flourish.   For my own part, I may say, General Higginson, that I think all the officers, non-commissioned officers, and men of the Household Brigade are aware of the deep feeling which I entertain towards them, and that I have not forgotten my association with them three-and-twenty years ago.   That feeling of kindliness towards them, and of interest in all that concerns them, will continue to the day of my death."

After the ceremony was over, there was an amateur theatrical performance, to the great amusement not only of the young folk, but of the crowd of spectators who filled the hall.

¦ROYAL NATIONAL LIFEBOAT INSTITUTION.

March 15th, 1884.

THE Prince of Wales presided, not for the first time, at the annual meeting of the Lifeboat Institution, which was held at Willis's Rooms on the 15th of March, 1884.   The Secretary, Mr. C. Dibdin, having read the report, the Prince of Wales said :—

"Ladies and Gentlemen,— Before calling upon the noble duke (the Duke of Argyll) to move the first resolution, I wish to say a few words.   You have all of you, I feel convinced, heard with the greatest interest the report which has just been read by the secretary, and I think we must all be unanimous in the opinion that that report is highly satisfactory as regards everything connected with this institution.

"The National Lifeboat Institution, having been founded in 1824, has now reached its sixtieth anniversary, and I think you will all agree with me that there is no institution throughout our country which is of greater importance or more demands our sympathy and assistance.   From our geographical position as a sea-girt isle, and from the immense colonies which we have acquired, the mass of ships that travel to and fro and reach our islands is almost too vast to enable us even to realize what their number can actually be.   Those vessels naturally encounter tempests, the results of which are shipwrecks and loss of life.   The risks especially which that valuable and important community, the fishermen on our coasts, have to run from the beginning to the end of the year must be well known to you all. It is especially to save their lives, and not only theirs, but the lives of all who travel on the sea, that this great national institution has been founded. Strange to say that notwithstanding the great improvements which have been effected in navigation and in the different scientific inventions which have been made, there is no doubt that an increase of shipwrecks annually occurs.

"I may mention that it must have been of interest to those of you who visited the Fisheries Exhibition last year to notice all the models of boats, contrivances for fishing, and apparatus for saving life which were there shown to you. It must be patent to everybody that a society of this kind is an absolute necessity. Look at what it has done. Since its foundation nearly 31,000 lives have been saved by its instrumentality. Already this year up to now—the middle of March—300 lives have been saved, and last year the total number was nearly 1000. The institution has now 274 lifeboats, and no doubt you are fully aware, through the medium of the Press, of the gallantry which has been displayed by the coxswains and crews of those boats. This is so well known to you, I am sure, that I need not engross your attention by dwelling upon the topic. Of one thing, however, I must remind you. I must impress upon your minds the fact that, although we admit this to be a national and most important institution, it is at the same time entirely supported by voluntary contributions. Therefore I most urgently ask you to ponder well over this fact, and impress upon you the great necessity which exists for keeping it up and maintaining it in a state of efficiency with adequate funds. A large annual income is, of course, required for this purpose. To maintain a lifeboat station in a good state £70 per annum is needed.

"Allusion has been made in the report to the fact that the Princess of Wales has become a vice-patroness of this institution, and I need hardly tell you that she shares with me all the views that I hold in relation to it. It was a great gratification to her quite recently to present medals to two of the most deserving coxswains who had distinguished themselves in saving lives. Upon the utility and merits of this institution one might speak for hours, but our meeting to-day is for business, and not merely for the purpose of delivering addresses ; so I will now call upon the Duke of Argyll to move the first resolution."

Speeches having been made by the Duke of Argyll, Admiral Sir H. Keppell, Lord Charles Beresford, and the Lord Mayor (Fowler), and resolutions passed, the Duke of Northumberland proposed a vote of thanks to the Prince of Wales for presiding, who in responding said :—

" I assure you it has been a source of sincere gratification to me to take the chair on this occasion. I assure you also that nobody more cordially wishes this institution continued success and prosperity than I do. It is a thoroughly national and useful institution, and if it is only as ably managed and conducted in the future as it has been in the past, I feel convinced it will continue to flourish. I know how much we ought to feel grateful to those who have undertaken the arduous duty of managing this institution, for giving their valuable time and assistance, and how much our hearts ought always to go with those brave and gallant men who seek to rescue the lives of their fellow-countrymen in all weathers, and in all times by day or night."

THE HEALTH EXHIBITION.

June 17th, 1884.

THE lamented death of the Duke of Albany on the 28th of March, 1884, prevented the Prince of Wales from taking active part in the preparations for the Health Exhibition of that summer. He had before arranged, along with the Executive Council, of which the Duke of Buckingham was Chairman, the general plan of the Exhibition, in the designs of which Prince Leopold had taken deep interest. On the 17th of June the Prince formally inaugurated the work of the international juries, a necessary and important part of the whole undertaking. It was the first occasion in which His Royal Highness had taken part in public affairs since the death of his brother. The meeting took place in the Albert Hall, and a great assembly had gathered, including many distinguished foreigners.

The Duke of Buckingham, on behalf of the Executive Council, expressed the great gratification they felt at the appearance of His Royal Highness among them, as to him was due the inception of the undertaking. Sir James Paget, the Vice-Chairman of the Council, delivered an elaborate and eloquent address on the purposes and the importance of the Exhibition. He was followed by Sir Lyon Playfair. After these addresses Lord Reay presented to His Royal Highness, the Foreign Commissioners, and the Chairmen and Jurors for the different sections. The Prince then said :—

" Your Excellencies, Ladies, and Gentlemen,—Owing to a very sad cause I was unable to open the Health Exhibition. But I am particularly glad to have had this opportunity of being present to preside here to-day on the occasion of the assembling of the international juries. It has given me great pleasure to have made the personal acquaintance of all those distinguished gentlemen who have come from the Continent, and who, no doubt at considerable inconvenience to themselves, have so kindly consented to come over here to decide on matters appertaining to the Health Exhibition. It is particularly gratifying to me to have been here to receive them, and I sincerely hope that their labours will be crowned with success. That the Exhibition has up to the present time been successful so far as numbers are concerned we have evidence to show, but I hope at the same time that for scientific and educational purposes the public at large may derive even greater benefit from it than they can get by merely coming here to enjoy the Exhibition as a place of recreation.

" After the address from the Duke of Buckingham, and the long, able, and most interesting one from Sir James Paget, which was commented upon by Sir Lyon Playfair, it would be perfectly superfluous for me to detain you but for a few moments on any subject relating to health. These addresses, which you have all listened to with such great interest, will, I trust, have proved to you what an important consideration the matter of health is. This Exhibition, under the able chairmanship of the Duke of Buckingham and those gentlemen of the Executive Council who have worked under him, has, I think, been brought to a remarkable degree of perfection. They have done everything they can do to make it pleasing to the eye; but still I hope that those who visit the Exhibition will remember that there are greater and more important objects at stake—that they will go home impressed by the study of those objects as well as by the pleasure they may have derived from the wonderful inventions and methods of showing them. I wish to tender my thanks to the Lord Mayor and the great City Companies for their kind co-operation in this Exhibition, and I am sure we are all much gratified at the success of what is called Old London. Before concluding I would beg to ask the Chairmen and Jurors at the close of the proceedings to constitute their juries and select their secretaries."

The French Ambassador, in moving a vote of thanks to the Prince of Wales for presiding, referred to His Royal Highness's readiness on all occasions to give his time and to devote his energies to any cause which might advance the welfare of the people of this country. He called on them to thank His Royal Highness, not only in the name of those present and of the foreigners who had contributed to the Exhibition, and more particularly those of France, but in the name of thousands upon thousands of the poor and disinherited of the earth, of children and the helpless, whose benefit would ultimately be promoted by this Exhibition.

The Lord Mayor seconded the motion, which was agreed to with acclamation. The Prince, in closing the proceedings, tendered his warmest thanks to the French Ambassador and his colleagues for their presence on that occasion and for their continued co-operation in the Exhibitions with which he had been connected. His Royal Highness, in concluding, thanked the Lord Mayor, as representative of the City of London, for all that the City and the Guilds of London had done to promote the success of the Exhibition.

———————————— .

OPENING OF GUILDS OF LONDON INSTITUTE.

June 25th, 1884.

THE building, of which the foundation was laid nearly three years before, was completed within the time originally contracted for, and the Prince of Wales came to open it on the 25th of June, 1884. Again the Lord Chancellor read the report, and on behalf of the Governors and Council of the City and Guilds of London Institute, thanked His Royal Highness for his continued interest, and his presence that day. Touching allusion was made to the death of the Duke of Albany, who had laid the foundation stone of the Finsbury Technical College in May 1881. "As years roll by, and when the connection between the technical education of the people and the commercial prosperity of the country becomes as well understood and appreciated here as it is abroad, the year 1880, in which the City and Guilds of London Institute was incorporated, and the year 1884, in which this central institution was opened, will stand out as epochs in what we hope may be an unbroken record of industrial progress; and we sincerely trust that the remembrance of this day's proceedings may ever furnish to your Royal Highness a pleasing and satisfactory thought, enabling you to associate the endeavours of your illustrious father, dating back more than thirty years, to improve the arts and manufactures of the country, with the work of this Technical Institute, over which your Royal Highness so graciously presides."

The Prince of Wales, in reply, said :—

" My Lord Chancellor, my Lords, and Gentlemen,—I have listened with attention to your address, and I assure you it gives me great pleasure to be able to preside at the opening of this important institution, the first pillar of which, in company with her Royal Highness the Princess of Wales, I set nearly three years since. I thank you for your very feeling reference to the severe loss which the Queen, and each member of Her Majesty's family, has sustained by the untimely death of my late brother. His interest in every movement calculated to humanize and to elevate the people of this country will, I am quite sure, cause his loss to be felt far beyond the circle of his immediate friends.

" I have been gratified that the City and the Livery Companies of London have so generously responded to the letter which, as President of the Institute, I addressed some few months since to the Lord Mayor and to the Worshipful Masters of the Livery Companies of London. This Institute, which owes its origin to the liberality of the City and of the Guilds of London, is an illustration of the excellent work that may be done by united action, which could not possibly be accomplished by individual efforts. Conformably with the traditions of these ancient Guilds, there is, perhaps, no purpose to which they could more appropriately devote their surplus funds, and none which would be of more practical advantage to the country at large than the promotion of technical education. The altered conditions of apprenticeship, and the almost general substitution of machine for hand labour have made the teaching of science, in its

application to productive industry, a necessary part of the
training of all classes of persons engaged in manufacturing
pursuits.

"There never was a time, perhaps, when the importance of
technical education was more generally recognized than now,
and I am gratified to learn from the report of the Royal Commissioners appointed to inquire into the subject to which your
lordship has referred, that, although we are still behind many
of our foreign neighbours in the provision of technical schools
of different grades, the encouragement afforded by the State to
the teaching of science and of art, supplemented as it now is by
the Institute's assistance to the teaching of technology, has placed
within reach of our artizan population facilities for technical
instruction which have already influenced, and which promise
to influence still more in the future, the progress of our manufacturing industry.

"As president of this Institute, I have noted with much
satisfaction the rapid development of the work which the
Council have initiated, and which they so successfully control.
I am anxious to take this opportunity of expressing in public
what is already known to you, my Lord Chancellor, and to the
members of the Council, the obligations which we are all under
to Mr. Philip Magnus, our able director and secretary, for his
unwearied exertions in having so successfully accomplished the
organization of the practical work of the institution. I have no
doubt that the opportunities for advanced instruction, which
will be afforded in the well-arranged laboratories and workshops
of this building, will enable the managers and superintendents
of our manufacturing works to obtain more readily than hitherto
that higher technical instruction which is so essential to the
development of our trade and commerce.

"But it is especially as a training college for teachers that
this institution will occupy an important place in the educational
establishments of this country. The demand for technical
instruction has increased so rapidly during the last few years
that the supply of teachers has not kept pace with it, and I have
noticed with satisfaction that in the scheme for the organization
of this school due prominence is given to the provision of
gratuitous courses of instruction for technical teachers from all

parts of the kingdom. I shall be glad to see other corporations and individuals follow the example of the Clothworkers' Company, by establishing scholarships which shall serve to connect the elementary schools of this country with this institution. Hitherto, all schools have led up to the Universities, and literary training has been encouraged to the disadvantage of scientific instruction. Manufacturing industry has, consequently, not been able to attract to its pursuits its fair proportion of the best intellect of the country. The foundation of scholarships in connection with this institution will enable selected pupils from elementary schools to enter schools of a higher grade, and to complete their education within these walls.

"As president of the International Health Exhibition, I am glad that the Council of this Institute have been able to place at the disposal of the Council of the Health Exhibition a portion of this building for the exhibition of apparatus and appliances used in technical and other schools. I have no doubt that we shall find in that exhibition, which I hope to be able presently to visit, much that is generally instructive, and that the foreign sections will contain exhibits which will prove of great interest to the educational authorities of this country. To the Corporation and to the Livery Companies of London, the Council of the International Health Exhibition are indebted for much valuable assistance, and I thank them for it.

"It now only remains for me to declare the Central Institution of the City and Guilds of London Institute to be open, and to express the warmest hope that the important educational work to be carried on in this great national school of technical science and art will help to promote the development of our leading industries, and that the City and Guilds of London, which have so liberally subscribed funds for the erection and equipment of this institution, will maintain it with efficiency, and will at the same time continue their support to all other parts of the Institute's operations."

After short speeches by Lord Carlingford, Mr. Mundella, and the Lord Mayor, the Prince inspected the various parts of the Institute, including the rooms where specimens of the work of students of the Finsbury College, and where exhibits from foreign technical schools were displayed.

ANTI-SLAVERY SOCIETY MEETING IN GUILDHALL.

August 1st, 1884.

ONE of the most important meetings presided over by the Prince
of Wales, and one of the most memorable gatherings for many a
year past seen in the City of London, was that held in the Guildhall, on the 1st of August, 1884.   The object was to celebrate the
Jubilee of the Abolition of Slavery in the British Colonies, to
recall the work of the British and Foreign Anti-Slavery Society
during the last half-century, and to consider the position and
prospects of the slavery question at the present time throughout
the world.

It was in every respect a most remarkable meeting.   The great
Hall was densely crowded from end to end.   On the platform
were assembled large numbers of distinguished persons, of different
creeds, and opposite political parties, but all united in the cause
which had brought them together that day.   The names of a few
of those present will show how various were the classes thus
represented.   The Lord Mayor (Alderman Fowler, M.P.), and the
Chief Magistrates of London, the Archbishop of Canterbury and
Cardinal Manning, Earl Granville and the Earl of Derby, Sir
Stafford Northcote and Mr. W. E. Forster, Mr. Sergeant Simon,
Sir Wilfrid Lawson, Mr. T. R. Potter, Mr. Henry Richard, and
many other leading members of Parliament, sat together on the
same platform.   There were present a few of the veterans who
had taken part in the anti-slavery struggles fifty years before,
such as Joseph Sturge and Sir Harry Verney, M.P.   Descendants
of the early champions of the cause, bearing the honoured names
of Wilberforce, Lushington, Buxton, Pease, Forster, showed that
the spirit of their fathers was maintained in a new generation.
Among the ladies on the platform were the Baroness Burdett-
Coutts, Miss Gordon, the sister of General Gordon, of Khartoum,
and some members of the Society of Friends, always abounding in
good works.

The Secretary of the Society read a list of names of those
unable to be present, but expressing warm sympathy with the
purpose of the meeting.   There were letters from the Chief Rabbi,
from Lord Salisbury, the Duke of Norfolk, the Duke of Sutherland, the Duke of Argyll, Lord Carnarvon, and other men of
distinction.   The most touching communication was from the
venerated Earl of Shaftesbury, who had promised to attend, but
was obliged to dictate a letter from a sick-bed, in which he
expressed the satisfaction he felt in having lived to see such
changes in regard to slavery during the past fifty years.   On the
dais behind the platform were busts of Granville Sharp, and of

Clarkson, decorated with flowers, and in front were exhibited massive wooden yokes and iron chains, such as are used for the gangs of slaves in the journey to the coast of Africa.

Well might Lord Granville express his delight on "looking at this assembly of eminent men in all the walks of life in this country, of different professions, of different pursuits, of different religious denominations, of different political parties, all absorbed by one philanthropic idea, and presided over by the illustrious Prince, the Heir-Apparent to the Throne." How the Prince came to occupy this position, it may interest many readers to know. Mr. Allen, the Secretary of the Society, and Mr. W. E. Forster, went to ask him to preside at the meeting. Mr. Forster, for whom the Prince had high personal esteem, reminded him that his father had made his first public appearance as chairman of a meeting of the Anti-Slavery Society. The Prince did not need to be reminded of this, but at once most cordially assented to preside from his own interest in the subject, and if Mr. Allen would give a few necessary dates and facts he would do the best he could. With this assurance the success of the meeting was secured.

The Lord Mayor, according to civic custom, having taken the chair for an instant, then vacated it, and invited His Royal Highness to preside over the meeting. The Prince then rose, amidst enthusiastic cheers, and said :—

"My Lords, Ladies, and Gentlemen,—At the express wish of the Lord Mayor I am asked to preside on this auspicious occasion. I need hardly tell you that in such a cause it gives me more than ordinary pleasure to occupy the chair at so great and influential a meeting as this. I confess I had some reluctance in presiding to-day, feeling that others could accomplish the task far better than I should. But I also felt that possibly I might have some slight claim to occupy the chair on such an occasion, as so many members of my family have presided over former meetings in connection with Anti-Slavery movements. In the years 1825 and 1828, my uncle the late Duke of Gloucester presided at meetings of the Society, which were numerously attended. The Duke of Sussex did so in 1840; and you are well aware of the interest they took in promoting the objects of the Society by bringing forward questions concerning it in Parliament. In the same year my lamented father occupied the chair at a very large and crowded meeting at Exeter Hall; and I believe that occasion was the very first on which he occupied the chair at any public meeting in this country. Let me say that my excuse for standing before you to-day may be given in words used by him forty-four years ago. They were these—'I have been induced to preside at the meeting of this Society from the conviction of its paramount importance to the greatest interests of humanity and justice.'

"This is a great and important anniversary. To-day we celebrate the jubilee of the emancipation of Slavery throughout our colonies; and it is also a day which has been looked forward to with pleasure and satisfaction by this excellent Society, which has worked so hard in this great cause of humanity.

"We may be all proud, ladies and gentlemen, that England was the first country which abolished negro Slavery. Parliament voted, and the nation paid, twenty million pounds to facilitate this object. Our example was followed by many other countries, though I regret to say that in Brazil and Cuba slavery still exists, as well as in Mohammedan and heathen countries. It is a very natural temptation that, in newly-peopled countries, and especially when the climate prevents Europeans from working, forced labour should be introduced. The Duke of Gloucester very properly said that 'The Slave-trade can only be thoroughly abolished by the abolition of Slavery; that while there is a demand, there will be a supply; this is the keynote of the Society during its existence.'

"Principally owing to the indefatigable exertions of the undaunted Thomas Clarkson and his great Parliamentary coadjutor, William Wilberforce, the Slave-trade and the untold horrors of the Middle Passage were, as far as Great Britain was concerned, put an end to in the year 1807. The majority, therefore, of the Slaves in the West Indian Islands who received the benefit of the Emancipation Act were descendants of those Africans who had been originally torn from the forests of Africa. Speaking of the proclamation of the emancipation of the Slaves in the colonies, Mr. Buxton said:—'Throughout the colonies the churches and chapels had been thrown open, and the Slaves had crowded into them on the evening of the 31st of July, 1834. As the hour of midnight approached they fell upon their knees, and awaited the solemn moment, all hushed, silent, and prepared. When twelve o'clock sounded from the chapel bells they sprang upon their feet, and through every island rang glad sounds of thanksgiving to the Father of all, for the chains were broken and the Slaves were free.'

" I may mention that I have within a short time ago received a telegram from the President of the Wesleyan Methodist Conference in session at Burslem, congratulating me and you on the meeting of to-day, and stating that it was during the session of the Conference in 1834 that the abolition of Slavery in the West Indian Colonies became an accomplished fact—a consummation for which, as Wesleyan Methodists, they had universally prayed and laboured. They cannot therefore, but profoundly rejoice at the jubilee of the great event, with its incalculable benefits, not only to the West Indies, but to all other peoples throughout the world.

" It may not, perhaps, be generally known to you that Slavery was abolished in India in 1843 by the simple passing of an Act destroying its legal status, and putting the freeman and Slave on the same footing before the law. The natural result took place, and millions of Slaves gratuitously procured their own freedom without any sudden dislocation of the rights claimed by their masters. A plan similar to this would be found a most effectual one in Egypt and other Mohammedan countries. This example was followed by Lord Carnarvon in 1874 on the Gold Coast of Western Africa, where he was able to abolish Slavery without any serious interference with the habits and customs of the people. Under the influence of England, the Bey of Tunis issued a decree in 1846, abolishing Slavery and the Slave-trade throughout his dominions, which concluded in the following simple and forcible terms:—' Know that all Slaves that shall touch our territory by sea or by land shall become free.'

" In connection with this there are two names which I cannot do otherwise than allude to to-day—that of Sir Samuel Baker, and one which is on everybody's lips—that of General Gordon. You are well aware that during the term of five or six years that they were governors of the Soudan their great object was to put down the Slave-trade on the White Nile. They were successful to a great extent, but I fear they had great difficulties to contend with, and when their backs were turned much of the evil came out again which they had found on their arrival.

"I will now turn to Europe. The great Republic of France in 1848, under the guidance of the veteran Abolitionist M. Victor Schœlcher and his colleagues, passed a short Act abolishing Slavery throughout the French dominions: 'La République n'admet plus d'esclaves sur le territoire Français.' In Russia the emancipation of twenty millions of serfs in 1861 by the late Emperor of Russia must not pass unchronicled in a review of the history of emancipation, although, strictly speaking, this form of Slavery can scarcely be classed with that resulting from the African Slave-trade. In the United States of America in 1865 the fetters of six millions of Slaves in the Southern States were melted in the hot fires of the most terrible civil war of modern times. Passing on to South America, and looking to Brazil, it may be noted with satisfaction that all of the small republics formerly under the rule of Spain put an end to Slavery at the time they threw off the yoke of the mother country. The great Empire of Brazil has alone, I regret to say, retained the curse which she inherited from her Portuguese rulers. At the present moment she possesses nearly a million and a half of Slaves on her vast plantations, but arrangements are made for their gradual emancipation.

"Now, having taken this glance at the condition of Slavery to-day, I will add, in the words of the Society, that 'the chief object of this jubilee meeting is to rekindle the enthusiasm of England, and to assist her to carry on this civilising torch of freedom until its beneficent light shall be shed over all the earth.' The place in which this meeting is held, the character of this great meeting, and the reception these words have received, assure me that I have not done wrong in stating freely these objects. One of the objects of the Society is to circulate at home and abroad accurate information on the enormities of the Slave-trade and of Slavery, to give evidence—if evidence, indeed, be wanting—to the inhabitants of Slave-holding countries of the pecuniary advantages of free labour, and to diffuse authentic information respecting the beneficial result to the countries of emancipation. The late Duke of Gloucester, in the course of a speech made by him in 1825, said that 'his family had been brought to this country for the protection of the rights and liberties of its subjects, and as a member of that family he should not be discharging his duty towards them if he did not recommend the sacred principles of freedom by every means in his power.' Most heartily and most cordially do I endorse his words.

"I rejoice that we have on the platform the eminent sons of two eminent fathers in the work of abolishing the Slave-trade and Slavery. Lord Derby and Mr. Forster, whom I rejoice to see here, have a hereditary connection with emancipation. The late Lord Derby, then Mr. Stanley, was Colonial Secretary to the Liberal Government of that day, which had set before it the task of carrying through Parliament a measure which was to put a term to Slavery in all the dependencies of the United Kingdom. Mr. Forster's father, having taken his full share of the agitation which led to the abolition of colonial Slavery, went to Tennessee on an Anti-Slavery errand and died in that State. There are glimpses, ladies and gentlemen, in Mr. Trevelyan's 'Life of Macaulay,' of the devotion with which this great movement was carried on. Zachary Macaulay, father of our great historian, was one of the chief workers in the cause, and it is said of him that for forty years he was ever burdened with the thought that he was called upon to wage war with this gigantic evil. In some of the West India islands the apprentice-ship system produced worse evils than the servitude of the Slave. The negroes were theoretically free, but practically Slaves. The masters had been paid for their emancipation, but still held them to service. In a year or two the term of apprenticeship was shortened, and soon afterwards public opinion at home demanded and effected its complete abolition. There were four years of disappointment, trouble, dispute, and suffering in all the West Indies, except the island of Antigua, where the planters had preferred to make the change from Slavery to freedom at a single step. Full emancipation of the colonies had to be enforced in 1838 by another Act, which abolished the transition stage, and proclaimed universal and complete emancipation. This Act only completed the work which 1833 began. The battle in which so many noble spirits had been engaged was practically won when the name of Slavery was abolished. The negroes of the West Indies look back to the 1st August, 1834, as the birthday of their race. The Emancipation Act,

s

which on that day came into force, spoke the doom of Slavery all round the world.

" I have ventured on this occasion to touch on different topics and dates which I thought would be of interest, but it is not my wish to weary you with longer details. Allow me to thank you for the kind way in which you have listened to the remarks I have made, and to assure you how deeply I am with you on this occasion, both heart and soul."

It was no formal compliment when Earl Granville, who followed the President, said, that "the illustrious Prince, following the example of his noble father, and of other members of the Royal Family, not only presided on this occasion with dignity and grace, but had spoken with earnestness and power on this great question." He also paid a generous tribute to the memory of Lord Palmerston, under whom he had begun his own official life, and who had laboured long and zealously in the anti-slavery cause.

The speakers who succeeded, without exception, rose to the height of the great argument. Sir Stafford Northcote, the Lord Iddesleigh of after years, closed his speech with a noble peroration : " They had deep reason to be thankful for the position which England had been allowed to take in this great controversy. They knew what that great position was ; they knew how it astonished the world, and how it astonished ourselves, that this island had spread itself in its intentions and designs over so large a portion of the world's surface, and what responsibility it had taken upon itself in consequence. This position had brought us into communication with every portion of the globe where Slavery prevailed. It gave us great opportunities, and we must see that they are not neglected. England's mission was not to magnify herself and speak of the greatness she had achieved : it was rather to look to the happiness and the advancement of the world. There were lines written by a great poet which were originally applied to the great Empire of Rome, but which were applicable to England. They spoke of that which became an Imperial race, and of the aptitude of other nations for other arts and pursuits. It was the Imperial position and the boast of England to release the captive, and set free the Slave ; and, in the words of the poet to whom he had referred, he would say : ' These are Imperial arts, and worthy thee.' "

The Archbishop of Canterbury spoke of the duty of the clergy to promote and direct public feeling on this question. Lord Derby, then Foreign Secretary, in referring to direct action by England, said that international diplomacy set limits to carrying out all that they might wish in regard to foreign slavery. "The English Act of 1834 had practically given the death-blow to slavery throughout the world. I do not think this is saying too much, for we know the force of public opinion." He concluded by saying that " the slave trade, although somewhat checked, will never be thoroughly got rid of till Slavery dies out in Asia, and in partially civilized countries. How this is to be effected, when it can be done, and through what agencies, are questions not to be settled by an off-hand sentence at a public meeting. But that it ought to be done—that it can be done, and that in time it will be done— are matters about which I entertain no doubt; and, that being so, I have much pleasure in proposing this resolution."

The resolution ran as follows :—" That this meeting, while fully recognising the great steps made by nearly all civilised nations in the path of human freedom, has yet to contemplate with feelings of the deepest sorrow the vast extent of Slavery still maintained among Mohammedan and heathen nations, producing, as its consequence, the indescribable horrors of the Central and East African Slave-trade, as fatal to human life on shore as the dreadful Middle Passage formerly was at sea; in view of this appalling state of things, this meeting pledges itself to support the British and Foreign Anti-Slavery Society in its efforts to urge the Governments of all Slave-holding countries to put an end to Slavery as the only certain method of stopping the Slave-trade."

Mr. Forster said that this resolution had been drawn with a temperance of language which he feared he would not have been able to command. He thought that the services which England had rendered to some nations still encouraging Slavery and the Slave-trade, entitled her voice to be raised with great authority. But he recognised the difficulties, which should nerve them to greater earnestness in strengthening public opinion in this country on the subject. " I greatly rejoice," said Mr. Forster, " to see this meeting, and I believe this means a new departure, and a determination to carry on the work, and to strengthen the hands of this Society for what it has yet to do."

Cardinal Manning, in an earnest and eloquent appeal, also urged the claims of the Society. " The reports published by it, as to the actual state of Slavery and the Slave-trade, are too sadly true. We are told that Livingstone, whose name cannot be mentioned in this hall or anywhere without awaking the sympathy of all Christian men, has left it on record as his belief that half-a-million of human lives are annually sacrificed by this African Slave-trade. This horrible traffic runs in three tracks, marked by skeletons, from the centre of Africa towards Madagascar, towards Zanzibar, and towards the Red Sea. Also, we are told, that of those who are carried away by force, some are so worn by fatigue as to die, others falling by the way are slaughtered by the sword, so that of this great multitude only one-third ever reaches the end of their horrible destination. It would seem to me that never in the Middle Passage was murder and misery so great."

What was thus said by Cardinal Manning has been since confirmed by his Eminence Cardinal Lavigerie, Archbishop of Algiers and Carthage, when recently in London, engaged in a righteous crusade to be preached by him in all the Capitals of Europe. This African prelate, from his own knowledge, during the last thirty years, as missionary and as prelate, gave terrible details of the slave trade, as the curse of that dark continent. The Cardinal says that the traffic can never be stopped, except by force, and if the Governments of Europe cannot effect this, he advocates a voluntary crusade of men, ready to form armed colonies of blacks to protect the missionaries of religion and civilization, and to defend the slave regions from the murderous raiders who invade them. The success of Emin Pasha who has for ten years kept the whole of his great Equatorial province free from the ravages of the slave-hunters shows what can be done. But for the shameful abandonment of Gordon at Khartoum, the slave trade would at this time have been almost at an end, and the grand desires of Livingstone for the peace and welfare of Africa would have been accomplished. Let us' hope that Cardinal Lavigerie's visit may not be in vain so far as England is concerned. He came quietly and went quietly, only paying two visits after his public appearance at Prince's Hall, one to the Marquis of Salisbury, and the other to the Prince of Wales.

To return to the Guildhall, the loyal and hearty thanks of the meeting were offered to His Royal Highness, on the motion of the Lord Mayor, seconded by Sir Thomas Fowell Buxton, and carried by acclamation. The Prince, in reply, said :—

" I am not likely to forget this important day, and most sincerely do I hope that important results may accrue from it. We have to-day celebrated the past, but we have the future to look to, as many speakers have said, and I cannot do better than agree with my right hon. friend on my left (Mr. Forster) that we must act with caution. But with due caution, and with the advice and good example which have been set, I feel sure that in time all countries will follow in the footsteps of England. The best chance of a complete abolition of Slavery will lie in civilisation, in opening up those great countries, Asia and Africa, many parts of which are now known to but few Europeans, and in disseminating education. In time people will see that they have derived no benefit from having Slaves, that the freeman will do his work far better than the one who is forced to labour. I mentioned, in first speaking, the names of many men connected with the subject on which we have met to-day. I will now add the name of one who was taken from us a few months ago, and who always had the deepest interest in this Society—I allude to the eminent and much regretted statesman, Sir Bartle Frere. And on this occasion his widow, Lady Frere, has sent to us these slave irons [pointing to the chains in front], which were brought some years ago from Zanzibar by Sir Bartle Frere, and you will, by looking at these implements of the slavers, be convinced more, perhaps, than by anything else, of the cruelty and hardships which slaves in this part of Africa had to undergo. I will not detain you longer, but I must thank you once more for the kind support you have given me to-day, and also those gentlemen, many of them old and valued friends of my own, who have addressed you in such eloquent and exhaustive speeches."

The Prince vacated the chair, which was then taken by the Lord Mayor, and His Royal Highness left, amid loud cheers. His Royal Highness afterwards graciously consented to become Patron of the British and Foreign Anti-Slavery Society.

VISIT TO IRELAND IN 1885.

April 9th–17th.

SEVENTEEN years had passed since the Prince and Princess of Wales had been in Ireland, and had been received with generous and loyal enthusiasm. It was feared by many that the spirit of loyalty in the Irish people had died away and could never be revived. The selfish and treasonable agitators who had long stirred up hostile and disloyal feelings were vexed and angry when they heard of another Royal visit. They used every means that a malign ingenuity could suggest to repress the generous impulses of the Irish race, and did all in their power to prepare for the Prince and Princess of Wales a reception different from that which had been given on their former visits. When they found that the mass of the people looked forward with joyful anticipation to the coming of the Prince and Princess among them, they recommended, on the part of what they called the national party, to maintain a "dignified neutrality," and to abstain from joining in the loyal demonstration with which it was evident the Royal visitors would be welcomed. The design proved a failure. From the moment of landing at Kingstown to the day of their departure, not in Dublin only, but in the progress through the south of Ireland, the feeling of disaffection and disloyalty was overborne by the spontaneous and hearty enthusiasm of the people.

The first manifestation of loyal feeling was displayed at Kingstown, when an address was presented by the Commissioners of the township.   The reply of the Prince shows how the spirit of the address was appreciated :—

" Mr. Chairman and Town Commissioners of Kingstown,—It has given me great pleasure to receive the address with which you have greeted me on my first landing in Ireland after some absence from your shores, and I am grateful to you for the welcome which you have accorded to the Princess of Wales and myself.   I value, I can assure you, very highly the expression of loyalty and attachment to the Crown which your address contains, and I will not fail to communicate to the Queen the sentiments of loyalty and of devotion which you express towards Her Majesty.   Most certainly do I hope that this may not be the last visit which we shall pay to a country where we have always been welcomed by kindness, and where the hospitality which we have invariably received on all former occasions has left so many pleasant recollections impressed on our minds."

On arriving at Dublin the first address was presented by the City Reception Committee, the citizens having, with the hearty co-operation of all classes, undertaken to pay the common courtesies of welcome, which rightly should have been done, and on former occasions were done, by the Lord Mayor and Corporation. An address was at the same time presented by the Chamber of Commerce.   To both addresses the Prince thus replied :—

" Mr. Martin, Mr. Guinness, and Gentlemen,—On behalf of the Princess of Wales and myself, I thank you heartily for the address you have read to me, and I am very grateful to the citizens of Dublin who through you have welcomed me to their city.   It gives the Princess and myself much gratification once more to visit a country where we have received so much kindness, and I regret the length of the interval which has elapsed since we last were in Ireland, and fully appreciate your sentiments of loyalty to the Throne and Constitution, and I will take care to communicate to the Queen your expressions of devotion and attachment to Her Majesty.   It will give me much pleasure to renew my acquaintance with Dublin and see the results of the civic and private enterprise to which you refer.   The furtherance of the welfare of all classes of the realm is an object which is dear to me, and I trust that the efforts of the Commission of which I am a member will tend to the improvement of the dwellings of those who contribute by their labour to the prosperity of our great towns, and will thus add to their public utility as citizens as well as to their private and domestic happiness. I hope to visit many parts of Ireland and see much of the work, as well as share some of the amusements, of the Irish people. The kindness with which you have greeted me encourages me to look forward with pleasure to my visit to a country where courtesy and hospitality have ever been the characteristics of the people."

One passage in the address of the Chamber of Commerce the Prince did not refer to, but it is of great importance. After the warm expressions of loyalty to the Throne and the Constitution, and of devotion to the Queen and the Royal Family, the address continued, " We earnestly desire that your present visit may bo productive of so much pleasure to your Royal Highnesses that you may feel encouraged to honour Ireland hereafter by visits of more frequent occurrence and of longer duration. We venture to assure you that it would be a great gratification to Her Majesty's loyal subjects in Ireland if a permanent Royal residence should be established in our country, and if some members of the Royal Family should see fit to make their home among us for some part of every year." About the permanent Royal residence in Ireland, the Prince kept a judicious silence, for it is a point which involves financial as well as political questions. But the opinion of the best Irish, of all classes, may well be considered, if the proposal is brought before Parliament.

The address of the Royal Dublin Society when the Royal party visited the Agricultural Show elicited another appropriate speech from the Prince. After acknowledging the expressions of loyalty to the Throne, and of personal kindness in the welcome given, the Prince said :—

" The proceedings of your society have ever been a matter of deep interest to me, as they were to my lamented father ; and, having been fortunate enough on many occasions to be a successful exhibitor at agricultural shows, I am able to appreciate the service rendered to agriculture generally, and to the rearing of cattle and horses especially, by your labours. In your attitude towards the geographical survey I rejoice to see a determination which proves to me that the promotion of those objects which you consider to be for the best interests of your country is paramount in your minds. I most sincerely trust that success may attend each and all of your important undertakings, for they are designed to promote the prosperity of a people who, quick to grapple with the difficulties of science and always ready to take advantage of the benefits of commerce, are necessarily dependent to a large extent on highly taught and scientific agriculture."

Later in the day the Prince went to see for himself the condition of some of the poorest parts of the city. His kindly sympathetic manners towards the poor, and the minute acquaintance which he showed with the whole subject of the housing of the labouring classes, in all the details of construction and sanitation, were the theme of universal surprise and admiration. Of this inspection of the "slums" a reporter at the time said, "The visit of the Prince to these parts of the city was not publicly announced. But the people were not long in discovering who their visitor was. He had come among them with his eldest son, unattended by any guard, and the event showed that his confidence was not misplaced. Cheers and welcomes and every outward demonstration of loyal good feeling attended him along his whole course. It was a reception which had been well earned, and it will certainly not be the least pleasant recollection which the Prince will carry back when his Irish visit is at an end."

The proceedings on the 10th of April were as many and as laborious as those of the preceding day. The first duty was the reception of addresses from various public bodies. There were no fewer than thirty different addresses, presented by deputations of five persons for each. They were received by the Prince, who wore the Order of St. Patrick. The Princess of Wales was on his left, and Prince Albert Victor on her left. All the addresses were handed in succession to the Prince, without being read, which would have occupied too much time, and then the deputations were requested to approach the daïs, when the Prince, in clear expressive tones, read the following reply :—

"Your Graces, my Lords, and Gentlemen,—I have thought it more for your convenience, as well as more within the compass of my ability, that I should, with your permission, make a general reply to the many kind addresses with which you have honoured me, and copies of which have already by your courtesy been before me, than that I should attempt a separate reply to each. I feel myself highly honoured by having been welcomed in this historic hall by so many bodies representing so many and so varied interests as you do. Leaders of local administrations, heads of religious communities, representatives of learning and art, philanthropy and education, you have one and all greeted me with the kindness and good will which has made a deep impression upon me, and which I never shall forget. You have alluded in terms of loyalty, which have much gratified me, to your attachment to the Constitution, and have expressed in a manner which I will not fail to communicate to the Queen your devotion to Her Majesty.

" In varied capacities, and by widely different paths, you pursue those great objects which, dear to you, are, believe me, dear also to me—the prosperity and progress of Ireland, the welfare and happiness of her people. That many difficulties from time to time impede you I can well understand. Such is the natural course of events. But I am glad to be able to gather from your addresses that you are advancing steadily towards the goal which you have in view. From my heart I wish you success, and I would that time and my own powers would permit me to explain fully and in detail the deep interest which I feel not only in the welfare of this great Empire at large, but in the true happiness of those several classes of the community on whose behalf you have come here to-day. You have referred to the Princess of Wales, who has accompanied me on this occasion, and for her I thank you for your welcome to a country, of the past visits to which we have pleasant recollections, and where we hope in future, as we have in the past, to spend happy days."

The several deputations listened with great interest to the reply, and at the close gave expression to their pleasure in cordial acclamations.

The next event set down in the programme of the day was one to which great national importance is attached—namely, that of laying the foundation stone of the new Museum of Science and Art in connection with South Kensington. Elaborate preparations had been made for it, and the grounds at each side of Leinster House, which is to be the central building, were adorned with gay flags and fitted up with stands, from which the entry of the Royal party and the ceremonial itself could be seen. A guard of honour, contributed by the Cornwall Regiment, with their band, was stationed on Leinster Lawn, opening upon Merrion Square, through which the Royal party entered. On the route from the Castle to Leinster House, the streets were everywhere densely crowded, and the houses decorated. An open passage for the procession was kept by the police without any difficulty, the populace behaving with exemplary decorum. The Prince and Princess acknowledged most graciously the enthusiastic greetings of the crowds, which were largely composed of the working classes. The first stone having been duly laid, and a statement having been made by Professor Ball of the objects of the new " Museum of Science and Art, and of the National Library of Ireland," the Prince replied :—

"Mr. Ball, my Lords, and Gentlemen,—I thank you heartily on behalf of the Princess of Wales and myself for the very cordial welcome which you have given us to-day. It is peculiarly satisfactory to me to have been able to take part in the interesting ceremony of laying the foundation stone upon which the superstructure of the new museum will, I hope, before long be built. It gratified me to learn of the action which the Science and Art Department had taken in reference to this museum, and to observe the support which that action received both from the Royal Dublin Society and from the Royal Irish Academy. It is by a united movement such as this that difficulties are overcome and success made possible of attainment. I am glad to think that the two great societies I have named have combined to smooth the way for an institute which will, I trust, be useful to a large number of the people of Ireland. I hope some day to see in full working order the institution of which the first stone has been laid this afternoon. When this is so, the magnificent collections, which have obtained a wide reputation, will be open to a public thoroughly capable of appreciating their merit and deriving advantages from their amalgamation under one roof. The Museum will worthily face the great library, where the efforts of a State Department have been successfully combined with a movement originated by the the citizens, and supported out of the rates, the object of which is to give free facilities for reading and study to the people of this metropolis. I am glad to have been assisted to-day by the councils of the great societies to which I have referred. To them, as well as to the visitors of the Museum, and the trustees of the National Library, I offer my warm thanks for the kindness of their reception, as well as for the opportunity they have given me for sharing in a movement calculated to make Leinster House even more worthy than heretofore of the pride of the Irish nation, and the admiration of literary and scientific bodies throughout the world."

After leaving the Leinster House the Royal and Viceregal parties drove to the Royal University, where another interesting

ceremony was performed. The hall of the University was crowded
with a brilliant concourse of graduates and spectators. Their
Royal Highnesses and the Lord Lieutenant and Countess Spencer
were met by the Chancellor, the Duke of Abercorn, and the Vice-
Chancellor, Lord Emly. After their Royal Highnesses had robed
they were conducted to the hall. After all had taken their seats
in the hall, a formal announcement was made by Dr. Meredith
that the Senate had resolved to confer the degree of Doctor of Laws
honoris causâ upon His Royal Highness Albert Edward Prince of
Wales, and also the degree of Doctor of Music *honoris causâ* upon
Her Royal Highness Alexandra Princess of Wales, and that their
Royal Highnesses had been graciously pleased to intimate that
they would accept those degrees. The announcement was received
with loud applause by the assembly. The Chancellor then read
and presented an address to the Prince, offering a respectful
welcome and homage to His Royal Highness and his august
consort. It also referred to the success of the University.

The degrees having been conferred, the Prince rose and
said :—

"My Lord Duke, my Lords, and Gentlemen of the Senate of
the Royal University,—I am very grateful to you for the
manner in which you have received us in this hall, and on
behalf of the Princess of Wales and myself I thank you for the
kind welcome with which you have greeted us. The higher
education of the people is a subject in which I learnt from my
lamented father to take a great interest. It is a question to
the solution of which your labours, I am happy to think, have
contributed much. Though no considerable time has elapsed
since the foundation of the Royal University, it has already had
a marked effect among those people of this country who are
especially open to the influence of a University career. I shall
value the degree which you have conferred upon me, and I am
proud to rank myself among the graduates of a University, the
advantages of which I am happy to hear from you that all
classes of the community avail themselves of.

"By the admission of women to your degrees you have supported the view that the gentler sex are capable, not only of
severe competition in science, but of enjoying the benefits and
using the power which a well-considered scientific education
bestows. It gratified me to learn that you were willing to
confer upon the Princess of Wales the degree of Doctor of
Music, which, Her Royal Highness wishes me to state on her

behalf, she has received with pleasure not only because she felt that it was an honour to herself, but because she wished to show her approval of her action of the ladies of Ireland in accepting the facilities and advantages which you have offered to them. In Her Royal Highness's name and in my own, I thank you for the honour you have done me, and for the kindness with which you have received us to-day."

The Prince's speech was received with great cheering. The proceedings concluded with the National Anthem. The Royal and Viceregal parties returned to Dublin Castle amid renewed greetings from the citizens who still waited in the streets to see them.

Some of the incidents of the Royal visit must be passed over with simple mention, the Levée held by the Prince, the Drawing-room held by the Princess, and the State Ball given by the Lord Lieutenant, of which it was said at the time that "no scene so animated and attractive has been witnessed in Dublin Castle since the former visit of their Royal Highnesses to Ireland." The opening of the new dock at the extremity of the North Wall attested the progress that has been made in the Port of Dublin, accommodation being now provided for shipping of the largest class. The Prince congratulated the "Port and Docks Board" on the completion of this work, and the Princess performed the ceremony of opening and christening the new basin, which is called the Alexandra Basin in commemoration of the event.

This took place on Saturday, the 11th of April. On the same day the Royal visitors inspected the Artane Industrial School, with its workshops and farms, and its probationary institution for the very young, a truly beneficent work carried on by the Christian Brothers. The Artane institution is one of the best of its class. The Government contribute 5s. a week for each boy trained there, the rest of the cost being provided by charitable donations, and the profits of the workshops.

Having described the visit to the Royal University, that to Trinity College must not be omitted. The reception was one of most enthusiastic loyalty. In the hall a vast assembly awaited the entrance of their Royal Highnesses, consisting of the members of the Senate, Fellows, Professors, and invited visitors. An address was read by the Vice-Chancellor, in which reference was made to the former visit of the Prince, when his name was enrolled among those of adopted sons of the *alma mater*. The Prince made appropriate reply for himself and for the Princess, and at the close of his speech asked the Provost, Dr. Jellett, to grant the under-graduates a term. "I cannot," added the Prince, "ask for the degree examination, but perhaps you will grant the college examination." To the request so graciously made, the Provost

said that the Board of Trinity College acceded. The cheers from
the undergraduates as the Royal visitors passed into the hall had
been enthusiastic, and were if possible more fervent as they
left the College.

The last function performed by the Prince before leaving
Dublin was presenting new colours to the Cornwall Regiment,
then in garrison at Dublin. The ceremony took place in the
Castle Gardens. The corps mustered 800 strong, under Colonel
Stabb, the commanding officer. The Prince wore his Field
Marshal's uniform, and his son that of the Norfolk Artillery
Volunteers. The usual routine on such occasions was followed,
after which the Prince addressed the regiment which had formed
up close around the group of officers among whom he stood.

"Colonel Stabb, Officers, Non-commissioned Officers, and
Men of the Duke of Cornwall's Light Infantry,—I consider it
a high honour to be permitted to present new colours to such a
distinguished regiment as that under your command—one which
ever since it was raised in 1704 has had as brilliant a record of
services in the field as any regiment in Her Majesty's service.
You first served with the great Duke of Marlborough in
Flanders, and then in America. Dettingen is the first name
inscribed on your colours. In the great Peninsular War you
especially distinguished yourselves, and suffered heavy losses
at Corunna and Salamanca. At Quatre Bras and Waterloo
you lost more than any other corps engaged, and the gallant
Sir Thomas Picton was killed at the head of your regiment.
Your next service was in India, where you took part in the
Punjab campaign. Later, in 1857, you gallantly distinguished
yourselves in the suppression of the Indian Mutiny, and
gallantly held the Residency of Lucknow during its defence
from June till November. You were on that occasion commanded by Brigadier-General Inglis, who for those services was
created a Major-General and a Knight Commander of the Bath,
while you received the honour of being made Light Infantry.
You, Colonel Stabb, are, I believe, the only officer of the regiment
present who served during the Mutiny. When some years ago
I visited the remains of the Residency of Lucknow, my attention
was especially called to the services of this regiment. On your
return the Queen and my father inspected the regiment and
personally thanked the officers, non-commissioned officers and
men for their gallant conduct at Lucknow, and I feel doubly

proud as their son to have the honour of presenting these new colours to you to-day. The latest records on your colours are Egypt and Tel-el-Kebir. A second battalion, at this moment serving in the Soudan, has recently been added to you, which, with the Royal Cornwall Rangers Militia, of which I am the honorary Colonel, and the two Volunteer battalions, make up the Duke of Cornwall's Light Infantry. From the title I bear I am simply proud to be thus connected with this fine regiment. In confiding these colours to your care I feel that the honour of your Sovereign and your country will ever be before you as on former occasions, and that in the future, as in the past, the roll of honourable distinction of your colours will ever increase."

Colonel Stabb, in the name of all the officers and men of the regiment, thanked His Royal Highness for the great honour he had done them in presenting the colours, and said he could not do better than express a fervent hope, which he did with a great deal of confidence, that the regiment would as faithfully defend the new colours as they did their colours at Waterloo and Lucknow. He was sure the honour would be appreciated by the battalions of the regiment, and he tendered to His Royal Highness their grateful thanks.

On the afternoon of the 13th the Prince and Princess started from the Kingsbridge Station for Cork. At Mallow there were signs that the visit to the South might not be without unpleasant incidents. A loyal address was presented at the station, but Mr. O'Brien and other Home Rule leaders had brought a number of Nationalists with bands, to disturb the unanimity of welcome. The rioters had to be ejected by the Constabulary. At Cork there were similar attempts at hostile demonstration, but it was shown only by the lowest rabble, and at the instigation of the political agitators. The patriots of the present time are of immeasurably lower type than Daniel O'Connell, even when he was most zealous for Repeal of the Union. He was always loyal as well as patriotic, and however bitter in words, he was always a gentleman in his actions. Whatever may be the views as to politics, the men who could incite their followers to insult the Prince and Princess of Wales, whose hearts are full of sympathy and love for Ireland, are unworthy the name of Irishmen. At Cork, several of the Home Rule members urged the people to resent the visit of the Royal party as a degradation to their city. At Dundalk on the same day, Mr. Redmond, M.P., addressing a meeting of the National League, "expressed his joy at the difficulty of England with the Soudan and Afghanistan. He hoped that the Russian bear would soon stick his claw into the British lion. He was sorry that the

Prince of Wales was not there to see what the real feeling of the Irish people was, instead of scampering about the country attended by military and police and bloody Earl Spencer."

In spite of a few jarring notes of this kind, the reception of the Prince and Princess in Ireland was worthy of the warm and hospitable character of the Irish Nation. Another proof was given that the disaffection is only temporary and partial, and due to the malignant influence of those who delude the ignorant with false representations. No one understands this better than the Prince of Wales, than whom the people of Ireland have no truer friend.

THE DARWIN MEMORIAL.

June 9th, 1885.

As one of the Trustees of the British Museum, the Prince of Wales was requested to represent them on the occasion of the unveiling of the statue of Charles Darwin, in the entrance-hall of the Museum of Natural History, now at South Kensington. The ceremony of unveiling was performed by Professor Huxley, whose address, after brief reference to the high claims of the author of ' The Origin of Species,' and other works of enduring fame, gave a statement as to the history of the memorial statue. Then addressing the Prince as representing the Trustees, he was requested to accept the statue from the Darwin Memorial Committee.

The Prince, in reply, said :—

" I consider it to be a high privilege to have been deputed by the unanimous wish of my colleagues, the Trustees of the British Museum, to accept, in their names, the gift which you have offered us on behalf of the Committee of the Darwin Memorial. The Committee and subscribers may rest assured that we have most willingly assigned this honourable place to the statue of the great Englishman who has exerted so vast an influence upon the progress of those branches of natural knowledge, the advancement of which is the object of the vast collection gathered here. It has given me much pleasure to learn that the memorial has received so much support in foreign countries, and it may be regarded as cosmopolitan rather than merely national ; while the fact that persons of every condition of life have contributed to it affords remarkable evidence of the popular interest in the discussion of scientific problems. A memorial to which all nations and all classes of society have contributed cannot be more fitly lodged than in our Museum, which though national is open to all the world, and the resources of which are at the disposal of every student of Nature, whatever his condition or his country, who enters our doors."

THE BIRKBECK INSTITUTION.*

July 4th, 1885.

THIS institution was founded in 1825, by Dr. Birkbeck, a zealous educationist of that time, for promoting learning, chiefly among the middle and working classes, by opening evening classes, and establishing lectures and other means of instruction.   The old building having become insufficient in its accommodation, a new edifice was erected near Chancery Lane, of which the foundation stone was laid, in 1883, by the late Duke of Albany.   To open this new building the Prince and Princess of Wales came, on the 4th of July, 1885.

A loyal address having been presented by Mr. Birkbeck, M.P., one of the trustees, the Prince thus replied :—

" I thank you for the loyal address which you have presented to me, and would express the heartfelt satisfaction which I experience in visiting an institution with which my lamented brother's name will ever be associated.   You have referred to his touching words when laying the foundation stone of this building, and I am reminded that on that memorable occasion he stated that he had lent his aid to an enterprise on the accomplishment of which he would be able to look back with feelings of satisfaction and pride !   It was not permitted to him to see this noble structure in its finished state, but I rejoice to know that prior to the great calamity which befell us he had received an intimation that the building was approaching completion.

" I observe with pleasure the names of the distinguished contributors to the building fund, and I rejoice that the Queen has shown her interest in an institution which met with the warm support of my revered father.   Sixty years ago the Duke of Sussex performed the inaugural ceremony of your old building ; and it speaks much for the vitality of your institution that after so lengthened a period a member of my family should be again invited to declare a building open so extensive as this one, the erection of which has been absolutely demanded by the expansion of your work. An institution in which provision is made for 6000 students, and to which both sexes are invited, must exert a very beneficial influence on the young men and women of the Metropolis, for whose mental advancement it has been erected. Many of the students in the old building have worthily distinguished themselves, and it behoves those who partake of the greater advantages of the new institution to emulate the noble examples which have been set by their predecessors.

"The movement initiated by Dr. George Birkbeck was a very remarkable one, and the foundation of the old institution was an event of historic importance. We are informed that this movement has spread not only throughout the Kingdom, but that its ramifications have extended to different parts of the world, and the presence to-day of representatives of our Colonies is to me one of the most interesting features of the proceedings. The success of Dr. Birkbeck's work is to be traced in the fact that, in the words of Professor Tyndall, ' it responded at the proper time to a national need, and to a need of human nature.'

"This institution has anticipated some of the beneficent movements of the age, and by its technical instruction, and the admission of both sexes to its advantages, has exerted a very powerful influence for good. With a vitality so potent we may look forward to the time when even this extensive building will be insufficient for your needs. It is a subject for congratulation that the institutions which by the establishment of the Birkbeck Institution have been called into existence are being so wisely adapted to the requirements of the age, and are exerting by their development such a beneficent influence among the people at large. I desire to thank you most heartily for the kind welcome you have given us here this afternoon, and I earnestly hope that this great institution will continue to flourish, and that we may hear from time to time of its increasing prosperity.

" This building, which will be regarded as a memorial of my dear brother's devotion to the great cause of education, I have

T

now the gratification to declare open, and, in his words, 'to dedicate it to those noble uses which it is intended to serve.' "

The thanks of the audience to the Prince were proposed by the Lord Mayor, and seconded by Sir Charles Tupper, High Commissioner for Canada.

RAILWAY GUARDS' FRIENDLY SOCIETY.

July 5th, 1884.

AT the ninth triennial festival of the Railway Guards' Universal Friendly Society, held at Willis's Rooms, July 5th, 1884, the Prince of Wales presided. A large number of directors and leading men connected with the railway companies were among the company. In giving or responding to the usual loyal toasts, His Royal Highness, in a very grateful and gracious way, took the opportunity of expressing his warm sense of the uniform attention shown to the Queen, and also to himself and the Princess of Wales, during their very frequent journeys, by the directors and all the officials and servants of the various railway companies. Everything was done for their safety and comfort, and he wished thus publicly to acknowledge his appreciation of what was done.

In giving the toast of the evening, "Prosperity to the Railway Guards' Universal Friendly Society," the Prince said :—

"We are to-day celebrating the ninth triennial festival of this Society, in aid of the 'Permanent Sick and Injured, and Widows and Orphans' Fund,' and I think all will agree with me that there is no charity which better deserves the attention and support of the public than this one. That it has already received such support is apparent to us from the length of time it has existed, but like all other great institutions of the kind in our country, the money which is required is, also, greatly in excess of that which is at their disposal to meet the actual necessities which arise.

"No public servants, I think, more deserve our sincere sympathy and support than the guards of our railway trains. It is obvious to all of us who have to travel constantly on railways how much our safety depends on their industry, their vigilance, their sobriety, and their discipline; and it is very gratifying to know that we may confidently rely on finding these qualities in them. Knowing what they have to go through, their exposure to all weathers and to risks of all kinds; remembering how much they have to be away from their homes and their families, it seems to me that we have hardly the right to expect to obtain from them their valuable services unless we in some measure mitigate their sufferings in sickness and from accident, and unless in case of death we do something for the maintenance of their widows and orphans. The Society was founded in June, 1849, and is one of the oldest societies in existence designed for the benefit of railway *employés*, and may be said to represent every line in the United Kingdom. It consists of forty-eight districts at the present time, situated at the principal railway stations throughout the country, from London to Inverness. In addition to the usual advantages offered by friendly societies—the ordinary sick and death benefits—this society possesses two special features adapted to the requirements of railway guards, who are exposed to very great risks from accidents. These objects are: 1st, a liberal provision for life for all those members who may become permanently disabled, either from injuries or constitutional causes; 2nd, annuities for the widows and orphans of deceased members. Other institutions, if they attempt to provide these exceptional benefits, only do so to a limited extent, and the members to whom they are granted are elected as vacancies occur; but the policy of this society has always been to provide these great blessings for all who are so unfortunate as to require them; and, notwithstanding that statistics show that guards run greater risks than other classes of railway servants, the contributions of the members themselves have been so largely supplemented by the generous support accorded by the public generally, that the society up to the present time has been able to carry out this fundamental principle."

The greater portion of the speech of His Royal Highness consisted of statistics of a most interesting kind, both as to the vast extent of railway travelling, the number of trains, of passengers, of railway *employés*, at that time numbering 357,650. All these statistics, as obtained from the returns of the Board of Trade, and also the number of persons killed or injured, especially those employed on the lines, were presented with admirable clearness to the audience, and were heard with great interest; but the statistics are not the same now, and are therefore not here given.

T 2

The Prince concluded with an earnest appeal for help to the institution for which he pleaded. The appeal was liberally responded to, the subscriptions amounting to £3383, including a hundred guineas from the Royal Chairman, which has been his generous custom at the close of most of the charitable meetings for objects which have had the advantage of his support and advocacy.

It ought to be added that the Prince had already presided at a festival of the "Railway Benevolent Association," where he spoke with equal warmth and sympathy for all classes of railway servants. There are now other institutions with similar objects, partly provident and partly benevolent, and it is an excellent kind of charity. The directors of companies do their part, and, where there is any just cause, can be made to do more, under the Employers' Liability Act. For unavoidable accidents the men themselves contribute their money, on the principle of mutual insurance, but there is need also for more of the benevolent gifts of those who travel by rail.

CONVALESCENT HOME AT SWANLEY.

July 13th, 1885.

On the 8th of July, 1872, the Prince of Wales, as President of St. Bartholomew's Hospital, formally opened a new Convalescent Home, in connection with that Hospital. This was an institution much needed at the time, and its advantages had long been urged on the Governors by Mr. Foster White, the Treasurer. At several existing Homes, such as at Walton-on-Thames, and Bognor, patients from St. Bartholomew's had been received, but it was desirable to have an establishment of its own, and conducted by its own officers. The carrying out of this scheme would require large expenditure, and a suitable building could not be provided for a considerable time. A temporary home was obtained at Highgate, through the generous munificence of Sir Sydney Waterlow, one of the Governors of the Hospital. He presented as a free gift the lease, for several years, of Lauderdale House, a mansion with many historical associations, somewhat old, but with every convenience for use as a temporary home for convalescent patients, and so it continued for thirteen years. On the 13th of July, 1885, the Prince, accompanied by the Princess of Wales, and the Princesses Louise, Victoria, and Maude, visited Swanley, in Kent, to open the permanent Home, erected through the generosity of Mr. Charles T. Kettlewell, one of the Governors of the Hospital. It is a spacious building, with accommodation for forty-five male and twenty-five female patients, standing in the middle of beautiful grounds, comprising an area of fifteen acres.

Their Royal Highnesses having taken their places on the daïs at the end of a tent, Sir Sydney Waterlow, who had for several years given the use of Lauderdale House at Highgate, read an address, which gave a summary of the facts relating to the new institution. Besides the gift of £15,000 by Mr. Kettlewell for the building, an anonymous donor, a governor of the Hospital, contributed £500 for the site; Mr. Homan, another governor, and Mrs. Homan had built a chapel and provided its furniture and communion plate; and Sir James Tyler had given an organ to the chapel, and built the lodge at the entrance of the grounds.

Sir Sydney having finished his address, the Prince of Wales said :—

" Sir Sydney Waterlow, Ladies, and Gentlemen,—You have given us a most interesting account of the history of the institution you wish me to open. I can only say on behalf of the Princess of Wales and myself that we are extremely happy to have an opportunity of assisting at the inauguration of an institution such as this, where the patients ought to feel very grateful for the manner in which every plan for their comfort has been carried out through the munificence of Mr. Kettlewell. Nothing can be of greater importance than that convalescent homes such as this should exist, especially in connection with large hospitals such as St. Bartholomew's. The spot now chosen, with its healthy aspect and beautiful scenery, will, I am sure, meet all requirements. It affords me great pleasure to be here to-day, and I feel proud to be the president of such an institution as St. Bartholomew's, and to be able to assist Sir Sydney Waterlow, who takes such interest in, and devotes so much of his time and energies to, the prosperity of the hospital. I have great satisfaction in declaring the home to be now open."

The ceremony over, the Rev. S. Kettlewell, who had offered the dedicatory prayer, and his son, Mr. C. T. Kettlewell, donor of the building, were presented to the Prince of Wales by Sir Sydney Waterlow. Before leaving, the Royal party visited the home, and also inspected the adjacent laundry buildings which have been erected for use as a washing establishment for St. Bartholomew's Hospital.

THE YORKSHIRE COLLEGE AT LEEDS.

July 15th, 1885.

THE Yorkshire College at Leeds is one of the most important and useful of the educational institutions that have in recent times been established. Commencing in 1874 on a comparatively small scale, it has gradually grown to be a great school, not for technical and scientific training only, but for all departments of study. The staff of the College includes professors of mathematics, physics, chemistry, engineering, and various branches of industrial teaching; and also of classics, history, and modern literature, and languages. The celebrated Leeds School of Medicine has been affiliated to the College. For special departments of practical instruction provision has been made, the Clothworkers' Company of London undertaking to support that which pertains to textile industries, and the Drapers' Company that of colliery management and mining engineering. Workshops, laboratories, lecture rooms, and other premises, are connected with the College, the buildings of which were designed by Mr. Alfred Waterhouse, and commenced in 1877, when the foundation stone was laid by the Archbishop of York. The friends of the College have contributed not less than £200,000 to bring it to its present condition. To inaugurate this great institution the Prince and Princess of Wales visited Leeds on the 15th of July, 1885.

On arriving at Leeds from Studley, the seat of Lord Ripon, their Royal Highnesses were received by the Mayor and Corporation, and conducted to the Town Hall, which was opened by the Queen and the Prince Consort in 1858. An address being read by the Town Clerk, the Prince replied :—

" Mr. Mayor and Gentlemen,—I receive with the greatest pleasure the address which you have just presented to me, and the Princess of Wales joins me in thanking you most sincerely for your kind words of welcome. Coming from the civic authorities of one of our greatest industrial centres these expressions are a proof, if any were required, that the population of this country remains true in its appreciation of the value of our time-honoured institutions, in devotion to the Queen, and in attachment to the Royal Family. I rejoice to learn from your address that the visits of the members of my family at various times to this great city have been attended with beneficial results, and have contributed in some degree to its welfare and prosperity, and to the development of the many useful institutions for which Leeds is so justly famous. Although it has pleased the Almighty to remove some of my dearest and most gifted relations from the scene of their labours, I can assure you that their survivors will always be ready to encourage by their presence and assistance the foundation and advancement of such institutions as the one which we are brought together to-day to inaugurate. It will be a source of sincere gratification to me to convey to the Queen your expressions of loyal devotion, and I can assure you that they will be highly appreciated by Her Majesty."

An address from the Leeds Masonic lodges was also received and responded to, after which their Royal Highnesses proceeded to the Yorkshire College. Here they were received, in the Clothworkers' Court, by the Marquis of Ripon, President of the College and Chairman of the Council, Sir Edward Baines, Sir Andrew Fairbairn, Mr. Beckett Denison, and other distinguished persons. Deputations of the London Companies, the Mayors of several Yorkshire boroughs, and Yorkshire Members of Parliament; the Principal and Professors of the College; and a numerous company had assembled. Prayer was offered by the Archbishop of York; an address was read by Professor Bodington, the Principal. Sir Edward Baines made a statement as to the origin and growth of the College, in which he said that he must mention a feature of the College which, so far as he knew, was original and highly useful. Their professors had always been ready to deliver popular scientific lectures on extremely moderate terms, and those lectures had proved very attractive, but recently they had undertaken, in addition, to give scientific instruction to the numerous teachers of elementary schools on Saturdays and several evenings of the week, and thus they not only conferred a boon on the teachers, but qualified them to impart the elements of science to their scholars. A double advantage was realized to several hundreds of teachers and to thousands of scholars of elementary schools. The scholars were by these means introduced to such a knowledge of the elements of science as would qualify them to become useful members of mechanics' institutes, and might in many cases implant a taste for higher attainments than had been looked for either in the school or the institute.

The Prince of Wales replied as follows to the address read by the Principal :—

"My Lords and Gentlemen,—We have received your addresses with feelings of extreme gratification, and it affords us sincere pleasure to be present here to-day, and to be able to take a part in the inaugural ceremony in connection with this important and useful institution. I have for a long time been deeply impressed with the advisability of establishing in our great centres of population colleges and schools, not only for promoting the intellectual advancement of the people, but also, as you have very justly observed, for increasing their prosperity by furthering the application of scientific knowledge to the industrial arts. I rejoice to hear that your laudable endeavours have been duly appreciated, and have received liberal support from various quarters, and I beg to offer my most hearty congratulations to the great company of the Clothworkers of the City of London for their judicious and liberal encouragement of your College—an example which, I trust, will ere long find many ready followers. We have inspected with considerable interest the various lecture-rooms and laboratories over which you have conducted us, and we have had much satisfaction in acceding to your request to declare this valuable addition to the science and art of the country open. I thank you, in conclusion, for your expressions of loyalty and devotion to the Queen, which I will not fail to communicate to Her Majesty. I declare the Yorkshire College now open."

This concluded the proceedings in this part of the day's programme, and the company then dispersed. The Royal visitors accepted an invitation from the authorities of the College to luncheon in the Coliseum, which is a newly-erected edifice affording much larger and better accommodation than any other building in the town for great public gatherings. Besides the invited guests, the two tiers of galleries were overcrowded with spectators. The Marquis of Ripon, who presided, having proposed the usual loyal toasts, the Prince replied as follows:—

" In the name of the Princess and in my own, I beg to tender to you, Lord Ripon, our warmest thanks and acknowledgments for the very kind terms in which you have proposed this toast, and to you, ladies and gentlemen, for the way in which you have received it. I am anxious to tender to the mayor, as the representative of the citizens of this large and important town, our thanks also for the magnificent and cordial reception we have met with to-day, one which we are not likely to forget. This is certainly not the first visit I have paid to Leeds, as I did so some seventeen years ago, but the pleasure on this occasion is enhanced in my eyes as the Princess has been able to accompany me. The mayor also alluded to the fact that the visit of the Queen and of my lamented father had not been forgotten, and we were glad to visit that very Town Hall which they opened some twenty-six or twenty-seven years ago. I consider that the object of our visit here is connected in some respects with the visit of the Queen and my lamented father, as he alluded at that time to the great importance of scientific and technical education, and of a great town like this if possible taking up the matter. In opening to-day that important and useful building, the Yorkshire College, I feel I may in some way have followed in his footsteps, by having been the means of promoting what is of the greatest importance to our country, and what is also of the greatest importance to the success of our great commercial enterprises—viz., technical and scientific education.

" The building which we have visited to-day will always be in our recollection one of great interest, and we feel sure that it is likely to flourish and be of the greatest importance, and to set an example to all the other great towns of the kingdom. The rooms we visited, and all the arrangements for learning in a scientific and technical manner not only the industries themselves, but their scientific principles, cannot but be productive of the greatest good not only now, but in years to come. The College has received many great and munificent donations, which will be read out later on, but I may mention the names of Sir Andrew Fairbairn, the Duke of Devonshire, and Lord Ripon, your President, as having contributed largely to the funds of the institution. I must say also that those who are interested in the College owe a deep debt of gratitude to the Clothworkers' Company of the City of London, for the magnificent donations which they have given are a proof of the importance of this institution. They have also shown their interest in it, and their belief that it is certain to be successful."

His Royal Highness then referred to the importance attached to music in Yorkshire, and to the great interest he had taken in the Royal College of Music. He remarked that he thought the promotion of that art would materially benefit all classes in this country. Towards that College he knew nearly £1000 was collected in Leeds, but that unfortunately was insufficient to endow a scholarship, but if the president and directors of the Yorkshire College could see their way at some future time to add music to the list of subjects taught he felt sure they would not in years to come regret it, and that it would be of great benefit to the people of Leeds.

Before proceeding with the toast he had the privilege to propose, " Prosperity to the Yorkshire College," with which he could not help feeling that he must associate the health of Lord Ripon. He felt that they would wish him to say a word with regard to its former president, one who was distinguished and lovable in every sense of the word, and who was carried off by the hand of the assassin in the midst of health and life. That was indeed matter for thought and reflection, and he felt sure that every Yorkshireman deeply regretted the death of Lord Frederick ·Cavendish. In his successor, however, they had found one who had occupied some of the most important offices which could be held under the Crown, and who, having himself been President of the Council on Education, was well fitted to hold the high office which he now did. He therefore called on them to drink with him, " Prosperity to the Yorkshire College," with which he had the greatest pleasure in coupling the name of their president, Lord Ripon.

The Chairman, in acknowledging the warmth with which the toast was honoured, alluded with pride to the position the College had in ten years won. He hoped they would place the crown upon their work by coming into union with the Victoria University at Manchester.

THE GORDON BOYS' HOME.

January 12th, 1886.

AFTER the sad tidings of the death of General Gordon at Khartoum had been confirmed, there was a universal desire to connect his name with some national memorial. Tributes of honour were paid to him by the leaders of both parties in Parliament, and a grant was voted for a public monument, in the form of a statue, which is now seen in Trafalgar Square. But a desire was felt for some other memorial, and after much consideration the most suitable was thought to be an institution for training boys of the class in whose welfare he took deep personal interest. This was the origin of the Gordon Boys' Home, first located at Fort Wallington, Fareham, and now having its permanent site at West End, Chobham.

From the time of the first suggestion of a memorial the Prince of Wales took the most active interest in the matter. He attended the early meetings of the committee formed to carry out the proposal, and moved the first resolution for a memorial at the Mansion House on May 30th, 1885. At that time the idea was to found a hospital at Port Said, but this scheme was not carried out. There seemed to be difficulty in agreeing about some fitter memorial, but the committee finally resolved on the establishment of the Boys' Home, and the War Office granted the use of Fort Wallington to commence the undertaking, for which the funds had to be provided by public subscription. In support of this fund the Prince of Wales summoned a meeting at Marlborough House on the 12th of January, 1886. At this meeting he said that "having had the honour of presiding at the meeting of the Gordon Memorial Committee in the summer of 1885, he thought it desirable, at the beginning of another year, to summon a meeting to hear what progress had been made." He told of the appointment of Major-General Tyndall, C.B., as commandant, and of his commencing the work with a few boys at Fort Wallington, the number gradually rising to fifty. The Prince called on Lord Napier of Magdala to say a few words in addition to the formal report which was read.

Lord Napier of Magdala, as Chairman of the Executive Committee, then presented the report of the progress made in the establishment of the Gordon Memorial Home. He said that on visiting the institution a few days ago he found the boys on parade in a neat and appropriate uniform. They looked clean, smart, and steady. The dormitories were like soldiers' barrack-rooms, in perfect order. The lavatories gave every facility for cleanliness. In the kitchen the boys all took a turn in cooking. In the workshops the pupil teachers were undergoing instruction in carpentry work. The school was well arranged and the teaching effective. In short, the progress of the institution was remarkable, considering the short time it had been established, and this was due to the organization of General Higginson and the administration of General Tyndall and his staff. Nor had the necessity for amusement been left unprovided for. The work was done in the spirit of the great soldier and Christian whom the institution commemorated, and the results were most gratifying.

The Prince of Wales said :—

"I feel sure it must be gratifying to all of us to hear the statements made by Lord Napier of Magdala of the satisfactory manner in which the Gordon Boys' Home is progressing. I may also say that all of us are indebted to the great energy which Generals Higginson and Tyndall have displayed."

His Royal Highness then called on General Higginson, who pointed out the special advantages to be obtained by the institution, where the training would fit the boys for any calling which they might choose, if they do not go into the army. He said that "this was a national memorial to a great man. It would be more than pitiful if an institution like this were allowed to languish or to be cramped in its development. That would lead the world to believe that Gordon's memory was forgotten. The one great object Gordon had was to help the distressed, and he could not imagine that when it was known what work was being done the institution would fail for want of funds."

The Duke of Cambridge made a very earnest and generous appeal, and ended by telling the meeting that it was to the Prince of Wales that the success of the movement would be mainly due. " Gentlemen," said the Duke, " we have had great praise bestowed, and justly bestowed, upon my gallant friend Field-Marshal Lord Napier of Magdala and upon General Higginson, who have taken up this interesting charge; but allow me to remark that there is nobody to whom we owe so much as His Royal Highness the Prince of Wales. I do not wish to flatter him, but I must say that when the Prince takes up a subject he always does so thoroughly and well. I do not think there has ever been a subject which he has taken up more feelingly and thoroughly than he has taken up this Gordon Memorial, and having done honour to those who have assisted in the way they have, I think we should do equal honour to His Royal Highness, and I therefore beg to move a vote of thanks to him for the kind and gracious manner in which he has taken up this subject and has presided at this and other meetings."

The Prince of Wales said :—

" After the kind and flattering remarks which have fallen from my illustrious relative I regret to be under the painful necessity of calling him to order, but there is a motion which has not yet been put to the meeting. At the same time I thank him beforehand most sincerely for what he has been good enough to say. You all know the very great interest I take in this important matter, and I feel sure it is right we should bring before the public as much as possible the name of that great and distinguished officer and Englishman who is now no more. He is not forgotten, but as months and years go by so many important events come before the public that sometimes other matters naturally are considered more prominent, and even a name like General Gordon's might be forgotten for a time. I am inclined to think there is nothing that could perpetuate his memory in a more satisfactory form in regard to his own relations, and what they think he would have wished, than this boys' home. I cannot help thinking 'The Gordon Boys' Home' will be ever associated with the name of General Charles Gordon.

" To obtain money is always a difficulty. I do not doubt the willingness of the public to give money, but their ability is not always so great, and I have a suggestion to make to you which may find favour in your eyes. If it is thought desirable that we should have a public dinner, I should be happy to take the chair. We could invite many to attend and give as much as they were able, and I have great hopes that in that way, and from speeches that may be made, the subject will be brought still more prominently before the public, and that we may do more good than by advertising." The resolution "That the Institution cannot be developed without larger funds, and it is resolved that further effort be made to obtain them," was then put to the meeting by His Royal Highness and carried.

The Duke of Cambridge said : " Having made my speech, I will not repeat it. I admit I was out of order, but I now beg to move a vote of thanks to His Royal Highness for his kindness in presiding on this occasion." The motion was seconded by the Duke of Norfolk.

The leading article in the *Times* on the following day thus closed : " There are few benevolent institutions which offer fairer promise of good results than the Gordon Boys' Home. But the care with which it has been organized and the special sphere which it seeks to fill enable us to press with greater confidence its peculiar claim to the support of the English public, founded upon the fact that it forms a national monument to the memory of a great Englishman. The heroism of General Gordon, his betrayal by those who utilized his rare personal qualities in the hour of their need, and the tragic end of a life of simple devotion to duty have been somewhat obscured by the ephemeral contests of the passing hour. Looking back over the records of the last few months, we are almost reduced to the sad and savage mood of Hamlet—' then there's hope a great man's memory may outlive his life half a year.' But the memory of Gordon's life and death will be a point of light in the history of the Victorian age long after the strenuous trifling of our politicians has sunk into forgetfulness. In honouring this man of antique mould, this Englishman who in a somewhat tricky and small-minded age 'could do and dared not lie,' we shall far more honour ourselves; and in munificently endowing a work such as he loved to carry out the nation will find itself twice blessed."

The London office of the Gordon Boys' Home is at 20, Cockspur Street, within sight of the statue in Trafalgar Square.

OPENING OF THE MERSEY TUNNEL.

January 20th, 1886.

FOR more than half a century, in fact ever since the opening of the first English railway, it has been the dream of engineers to obtain direct communication between Liverpool and Birkenhead, and the Welsh lines. The ferry-boat traffic had been enormous and ever increasing, but it little helped the transit of minerals and heavy goods. Even since the construction of the great Runcorn bridge the land route had been found long and troublesome. It was not till 1870 that parliamentary sanction could be obtained to make a direct route by tunnelling under the Mersey, but attempts to carry out the scheme were not then successful. At length, towards the close of 1879, an arrangement was made with Major Isaac, and from that time the work was unceasing, above 3000 men having been constantly employed. In 1886 the work was completed. The importance of the undertaking was recognized, and the Prince of Wales was invited to open "The Mersey Tunnel." The Princess of Wales was unable to be present, but on the 20th of January, 1886, the Prince, with his sons Prince Albert Victor and Prince George, came from Eaton Hall, where they were the guests of the Duke of Westminster.

On his arrival at Birkenhead the Prince was escorted to a daïs, and an address was read by Mr. Knight, the secretary, on behalf of the chairman, Mr. Cecil Raikes, M.P., and the directors, engineers, contractors, and officers of "The Mersey Railway Company." In reply His Royal Highness said :—

"Mr. Raikes and Gentlemen,—I thank you for your address and for the cordial and loyal terms in which you have welcomed me here to-day. I experience at all times sincere pleasure when circumstances permit me to associate my name with any undertaking tending to advance the welfare and convenience of the community, and I accepted, therefore, with much satisfaction your invitation to be present on this interesting occasion to assist in the inauguration of a national work of such vast importance. An enterprise of this nature is always deserving

of the warmest support and encouragement, as it not only completes the railway system of the district, and thus provides
constant and easy means of communication between towns of
such prominence as Liverpool and Birkenhead, but it cannot
fail also before long to afford material benefit to the millions of
hands in the neighbouring industrial centres by aiding the more
rapid development of commercial intercourse. The heartiest
commendation should, therefore, be bestowed on all engaged in
the promotion of so great and worthy an object. I fervently
trust that well-merited success may be the result of your
labours, and that an ever-increasing prosperity may be your
reward for the difficulties which you have encountered, and
which have been mainly overcome by the admirable skill, the
indomitable patience, and the unceasing and unwearied energy
which have been displayed by all those who have contributed to
bring this work to a happy and a triumphant termination. Let
me convey to you, in conclusion, gentlemen, at the special
request of the Princess of Wales, the expression of her deep and
unfeigned regret at having been unavoidably prevented from
accompanying me here to-day. She begs me to assure you that
nothing but the imperative orders of the physicians would have
precluded her from sharing the gratification which I experience
at taking part in the proceedings which celebrate the consummation of your most arduous task."

When the cheers which greeted the Prince's speech had
subsided, the Mayor of Birkenhead, Mr. John Laird, was introduced to His Royal Highness, whom he asked to receive an
address from the Corporation of that town. The Recorder then
read the address, which remarked—" The communication between
Birkenhead and Liverpool has hitherto been by a ferry, one of the
most ancient and important in the kingdom, first established at a
very early period, and conferred by King Edward III., in the year
1332, on the Prior and Convent of Birkenhead. It is a happy
coincidence that your Royal Highness should be present to open
this new connecting link between the county from which your
Royal Highness derives the title of Earl of Chester and the Royal
Duchy of Lancaster."

His Royal Highness made an appropriate reply, in which he
said :—

"Mr. Mayor and Gentlemen,—It has given me, I assure you,
unfeigned pleasure to have been able to comply with your

request to receive an address from the Mayor, Aldermen, and Burgesses of the borough of Birkenhead, and I am confident that though you may be one of the youngest of the corporate bodies, you equal the oldest in loyalty and in devotion to the Queen and the Royal Family. The completion of the work which I am about to declare open will mark an important era in the history of this district, for it will not only afford an improved line of communication between two towns of so much consequence and increasing prosperity as Birkenhead and Liverpool, but it will likewise supply the means of easy and ready access to the principality of Wales, with its places of picturesque beauty and interest, and its numerous health resorts. The utility of the undertaking cannot therefore be over-estimated."

The Royal party then re-entered the train, and after inspecting the works at the station the train entered the tunnel, and in four minutes reached the James Street Station on the Liverpool side. They were raised to the street level by a hydraulic lift, and the Prince being conducted to a daïs in the waiting hall, said, " I declare this station opened." Prolonged cheering greeted the announcement, which was continued throughout the route as the Princes drove to the Town Hall. In the Council-chamber an address was read by the Town Clerk from the Corporation, to which the Prince replied, acknowledging cordially the welcome given to him, and the kind references to his family, adding :—

" You rightly observe that I am deeply interested in every movement that is calculated to tend to the advantage and well-being of the people of this country, and it is a great satisfaction to me to think that my name will be associated with the memorable enterprise which by completing a connecting link in our railway system supplies a want that has been long felt in this part of the kingdom."

At the luncheon afterwards given in the ball-room, where about 250 guests had been invited, responding to the toast of his health, the Prince said that he had received, since his arrival in Liverpool, a telegram from the Princess, regretting her absence, and saying how deeply she was interested in the purpose of his visit. He also expressed his thanks for the reference to his sons, who were much gratified by the opportunity of visiting this great town.

" I have been engaged to-day, Mr. Mayor, on an interesting and important work, which I feel convinced will be a very great benefit, not only to the town of Liverpool, but to the vast commercial resources of this and surrounding towns. The difficulties in making a subterranean or subaqueous railway are only too clear. You have hitherto had means of taking passengers and goods over the river by steam ferries. I am aware that this right has existed a long time—I believe as far back as the 11th century. But it is a remarkable fact that in the last year you conveyed across the Mersey, from Birkenhead to Liverpool, on the steam ferries 26,000,000 passengers, and 750,000 tons of goods. You may say, such being the case, why do you require to have this tunnel, and to have your railway to connect Liverpool and Birkenhead ? The answer is that you have to encounter storms, you have to encounter fogs, and you have to encounter ice. Both your passengers and your goods are very frequently imperilled. Therefore, a great engineering scheme of this kind, which will be a very great boon, is one deserving of encouragement. Not only will it benefit the commerce of the north-west of England, but it will also open up a railway system to Wales and that beautiful picturesque country with all its health-giving resorts. Great praise is due to Major Isaac for the indefatigable manner in which he has carried out this work and has found the capital, and we have also to recognize the indomitable energies of Mr. Brunlees and Mr. Fox, the engineers, and I must not forget to mention the name of Mr. Waddell, the contractor. At the head of this company we find my right hon. friend, Mr. Cecil Raikes, who has had a long experience in railways. Before sitting down, as I know there is no time for long speeches, I wish most cordially to drink ' Prosperity to the Mersey Railway,' which I am sure you will drink most heartily, and to connect with the toast the name of its chairman, Mr. Cecil Raikes."

Mr. Raikes, in responding, said he held it as a most happy omen for that great undertaking whose completion they celebrated, that the heir to the throne should have come there to take part in completing an enterprise which would, he believed, be reckoned as one of the most important and interesting of Her Majesty's reign. His Royal Highness had been good enough to refer especially to the connection which was now to be established between Liverpool and his principality of Wales. As a resident in that principality he could assure His Royal Highness that the ex-

U

pression of interest would be cordially appreciated and treasured
by the people of Wales.

The Prince of Wales said :—

" Ladies and Gentlemen,—Although the toast list is closed, I
have the permission of the Mayor to propose one more toast,
and I feel sure it is one which will recommend itself to you all,
as it is the health of the chairman of this entertainment, the
Mayor.   You are aware of the Mayor's great popularity, and
his deserved popularity ; for have you not re-elected him for a
second term of office as your Mayor ?   I feel that it is difficult
to praise him in his presence, but at the same time he will
forgive me if I say that I know how the inhabitants of Liverpool have been grateful to him for the great kindness, generosity,
and philanthropy he lately evinced at Christmas, when he gave
that well-known and popular Lancashire dish, the hotchpotch,
to the poor inhabitants of your town.   That kindness will not
be forgotten by them, and it will be gratifying to him to know
the good he did and the pleasure he gave on that occasion.   As
for myself, this is not my first visit to Liverpool, and I hope by
no means it may be my last.   I have always been received here
with the greatest kindness, and I have always looked back to
my different visits with the greatest pleasure and satisfaction.
The fact that 100 years ago this town numbered only 40,000
people, and now, with its suburbs, numbers close upon 700,000,
speaks for its prosperity.   Most cordially do I propose this
toast, Mr. Mayor, and most sincerely do I wish long life to you,
and prosperity to your town."

The Mayor briefly replied, and the proceedings terminated ; the
Prince and his sons drove in an open carriage to the station, great
crowds in the streets cheering them, and returned to London.

INSTITUTION OF CIVIL ENGINEERS.

March 27th, 1886.

NOT for the first, nor the second time, the Prince of Wales was
entertained at the Annual Dinner of the Institution of Civil
Engineers, on the 27th of March, 1886.   The banquet was held on
this occasion in the hall of Lincoln's Inn, the use of which was
kindly granted by the Benchers.   The Prince was accompanied by

Prince Albert Victor and the Duke of Cambridge. A very large company of distinguished men in various walks of life, as well as the leading engineers of the day, were present, about two hundred in all.

The President, Sir Frederick Bramwell (the President of the British Association at Bath in 1888), in giving the usual loyal toasts, took occasion to mention that of the Royal guests, two, the Prince of Wales and the Duke of Cambridge, were honorary members of the Institution of Civil Engineers, and he hoped that the third would before long be added to the list.

In responding to the toast of " The Prince and Princess of Wales and the rest of the Royal Family," after expressing his grateful thanks, the Prince said :—

" In coming here this evening among you I feel that I am not a stranger, as you have paid me the high compliment of enrolling me as an honorary member of your Institution. At the same time I consider it a high privilege, and I may say a high honour, to dine here at this your annual banquet, as I am sure no one will gainsay me when I assert that an Institution like this is one of the most important in this country, and one for which we have the highest respect. I do not know what we should do without the civil engineers. How could we cross rivers? How could we go under them? Where would be the roads? Where would be the railways? And, perhaps, most important of all, where would be those great works of sanitation, which are of such vital concern to all countries and to all towns? For all these things are left in your hands.

" Some years have elapsed since I last had the pleasure of dining here, and in the interval I well know that civil engineers have not been idle. I may just mention a few works which have come under my own observation, not only in this country but in India, works which have been carried out by civil engineers, though all may not, perhaps, be members of this Institution. The first that occurs to me is the new Eddystone Lighthouse, of which I myself had the pleasure to assist in placing the first stone. Then there are those great works which will be handed down to posterity and of which civil engineers will ever be proud—I refer to the Mersey and Severn Tunnels. The former work I had the great pleasure of opening two months ago. Then comes the Forth Bridge, not yet completed ; I visited the works two years ago, and I hope in two, or at most three years we may see the great bridge in working order. While

referring to these great works, which will always remain me-
mentoes of the ability of the civil engineers of our time, I must
not forget to allude to a more distant evidence of engineering
skill—viz., the Alexandra Bridge in India, which was built
over the River Chenab, and which I had the good fortune to
open now ten years ago.

"I might speak for a long time if I detailed all the important
works constructed by civil engineers that I have seen, and
especially if I were to mention also a string of illustrious names
familiar to every one. But I shall abstain from doing so now,
first because, as you hear, my voice is not very good, and in the
second place because it has been agreed upon that there are not
to be any very long speeches. It is my satisfaction now before
sitting down to propose a toast which I am sure will be most
gratefully and sympathetically received by the company, and
that is ' The Health of your President, Sir Frederick Bramwell.'
I cannot allude to him in the manner I should like, or enumerate all the distinguished services which he has rendered to his
country ; but one thing I will venture to say, and that is that
his name will always be honourably connected with the advancement of technical education. The interest he has taken
in that great subject, and the labour he has bestowed on it,
have gained for him the high honour, conferred by his Sovereign,
of the order of knighthood, and I am sure he will still continue
to devote his time and energies to a measure which is of the
greatest importance to this country. For myself I may say
that I also owe him a deep debt of gratitude for the services he
has rendered as chairman of the executive committee of the
recent Inventions Exhibition. I have now the great pleasure
of proposing the toast of ' Prosperity to the Institution of Civil
Engineers,' coupled with the name of your President Sir
Frederick Bramwell."

Sir Frederick Bramwell made an amusing speech, in which he
highly magnified the office of the Civil Engineer as contrasted with
every other profession. The Duke of Cambridge spoke well, as
usual, for the Army, and Lord Charles Beresford gave a supple-
mentary speech, in response to loud calls, after Admiral Le Hunte
Ward had responded for the Navy. The improvements in both
military and naval armaments due to civil engineers were duly
recognized by all the speakers.

AT THE COLONIAL OFFICE.

April 29th, 1886.

SIR HENRY HOLLAND (now Lord Knutsford), as Secretary of State
for the Colonies, entertained the representatives at the Colonial
Conference, and various gentlemen connected with the Crown
Colonies, at a dinner at the Colonial Office, on the 29th of April,
1886. The Prince of Wales, the Duke of Abercorn, the Marquis of
Lorne, the Earl of Carnarvon, and the Earl of Rosebery were
among those present. The loyal toasts being given, Sir Henry
Holland said that to the hard work and warm sympathy of the
Prince of Wales the success of the Colonial Exhibition was largely
due. The Prince, in acknowledging the toast, said :—

"Sir Henry Holland, my Lords, and Gentlemen,—When Sir
Henry Holland was kind enough to invite me here this evening
to meet the colonial delegates I was under the impression that it
was a private dinner, in so far that I should not be called upon
to make a speech. In this respect he has sprung a mine upon me.
But, notwithstanding, I beg to thank him for the very kind way
in which he has proposed this toast, and to thank you for the
cordial manner in which you have received it. I can only
assure him and you of the very great pleasure it gives me to
meet you here this evening.

"In this large gathering there are many gentlemen connected
with the colonies whom I have had the pleasure of knowing
personally, and it affords me especial pleasure to make the
acquaintance of others who have come over in connection with
this occasion. I am aware that the proceedings of the conferences which have taken place have been kept secret from the
public in a most marvellous way, which is not an easy matter
in these days. But from the words which have fallen from Sir
Henry Holland I am glad to hear that everything has been so
prosperous, and I hope that the important and difficult questions
which have been discussed during the last few weeks will bear
fruit. Nobody wishes more sincerely than I do that the good
feeling, or, as the French say, the *entente cordiale*, between the
mother country and our great colonies may be established on a
still firmer basis. Far be it from us, and far distant may the
day be, when we shall see the colonies separated from us in
any way.

"You have been kind enough to allude to the Colonial Exhibition, which is. now a matter of the past. I feel sure that in that Exhibition, during the few months that it lasted, our own countrymen learnt perhaps more of the colonies than they could in any other way except by visiting them. No better means could have been adopted for bringing the colonies more prominently before us. Most sincerely do I hope that that Exhibition may bear fruit. I most sincerely trust that the end of the Conference may also be successful, and that it may realise all that we could wish. It is true, as you have observed, that I have not yet had an opportunity of visiting the distant colonies, especially the Australian colonies and those of the Cape. Much as I may desire to go out to those distant colonies, I fear that my duties at home may prevent my doing so. However, I assure you that it is my wish to do so, and though I am unable, it is through circumstances over which I have no control."

Lord Rosebery, in giving the toast of their Colonial guests, said, that whatever questions of home policy divided Englishmen, party feeling never interfered in those greater Imperial questions. It was a happy innovation to invite representatives of the colonies to meet in conference, and he trusted that the result of that meeting would hasten the welding and uniting of the Empire.

INSTALLATION AS GRAND MASTER OF MARK MASONS.

July 1st, 1886.

A LARGE and most imposing gathering, held in connexion with the Grand Lodge of Mark Master Masons, took place at the Freemasons' Hall on the 1st of July, 1886. His Royal Highness the Prince of Wales, whose installation as Grand Master of English Freemasons, at the Albert Hall, in April 1875, has been already narrated, was now installed as Grand Mark Master. There were upwards of 1000 Grand, Past, and Provincial Grand Officers present, including many distinguished representatives from India and the Colonies, as well as from all parts of the United Kingdom. The Earl of Kintore, Grand Master, presided at the ceremony.

When the Prince entered the Grand Lodge, which had been opened by Lord Kintore, he was accompanied by a large and representative body of Mark Masons deputed to conduct His Roya

Highness to the throne. He then took the customary obligation, having been proclaimed and saluted on the throne, to which he was conducted by Lord Kintore. Addressing the Prince, Lord Kintore expressed the feelings of loyal devotion felt by every Mark Mason in Great Britain, and in the Greater Britain beyond the seas, at the step which the Prince was pleased to take that day. He then gave a few statistics to show the progress of Mark Masonry. In 1876 there were but 5 time-immemorial lodges, and 18 Provincial Grand Lodges. In 1886 there were 13 time-immemorial lodges, and 375 warranted lodges, divided into 44 Provincial Grand Lodges, including those in New Zealand, South Africa, Australia, India, and other parts of the globe. The consent of the Prince of Wales to be Grand Mark Master was proof of his zealous personal efforts to unite the Colonies and Dependencies of the empire with the mother country. The Prince, in his reply, said that—

He thanked the Past Grand Master most heartily and sincerely for the address he had just delivered. He feared that Lord Kintore had referred to him in terms far too kind and flattering. He assured the brethren he considered it a high honour and compliment which had been paid him that day, and he accepted the distinguished position of Grand Master of Mark Master Masons with a deep feeling of gratitude, and as a high honour to himself. He assured the brethren that anything he could do to further the interest and welfare of the Mark Degree would be done with sincere pleasure. He was most thankful and grateful for the kind feeling the brethren had manifested towards him, and he appreciated very highly the compliment which had been paid by the Mark Masons who had attended from distant parts of the kingdom. Lord Kintore had spoken in kind and feeling terms of his beloved mother the Queen. It would afford Her Majesty sincere gratification to know the kind terms in which her name had been mentioned, and the hearty manner in which it was invariably received, especially in a meeting of this description. Personally he thanked them from his heart, and he desired to assure them that all he could do for the welfare of Mark Masonry would always be done with very great pleasure.

The Grand Master then appointed the Grand Officers for the ensuing year, beginning with Lord Kintore as Pro-Grand Master, Lord Egerton of Tatton Deputy Grand Master, the Duke of Connaught Senior Grand Warden, and numerous others to the usual offices. The Pro-Grand Master presented the Prince with a jewel, which he accepted with pleasure, and said it would be a gratifying memento of the pleasant proceedings of the day.

After the conclusion of the Grand Lodge proceedings, there was a luncheon at the Holborn Restaurant, at which the Prince presided. After the customary loyal toasts had been proposed, the Prince regretted that he had to leave, having to fulfil an engagement at the East-end of London.

FOUNDATION STONE OF THE PEOPLE'S PALACE.

June 28th, 1886.

THERE are few who do not know the history, and have not rejoiced in the success of the People's Palace for East London. The magnificent spectacle when the Queen went in state, on the 14th of May, 1887, to open "The Queen's Hall" at the Palace, will long be remembered by the multitudes who witnessed the ceremony, or who saw the Royal progress through the crowded streets.

The foundation stone had been laid, with almost equal pomp, and amidst as great popular enthusiasm, by the Prince and Princess of Wales on the 28th of June in the previous year. On that occasion nearly 10,000 people were assembled within the space set apart for the ceremony, including 1000 delegates from the various trade, friendly, and temperance societies in East London, with 2000 or 3000 school-children.

The Lord Mayor in his robes of office, and attended by the officers and many members of the Corporation, and a vast number of distinguished persons—among whom were the Chief Rabbi, Dr. Adler, the Bishop of Bedford, and many of the Clergy of the neighbouring districts, Cardinal Manning, and Mr. Walter Besant—awaited the arrival of the Royal visitors. This was announced by a salute by the guard of honour of the Tower Hamlets Engineers and the 24th Middlesex Volunteers. They were received by Sir Edmund Hay Currie and the Beaumont Trustees, the Master and Wardens of the Drapers' Company, and delegates from various Committees. From the old and well-known "Beaumont Trust," and the munificent donations of the Drapers' Company, supplemented by public contributions, the large funds necessary for the People's Palace had been derived.

The ceremony began by the Archbishop of Canterbury offering a special prayer, followed by the Lord's Prayer, and the singing of the Old Hundredth Psalm. Sir E. H. Currie, Chairman of the Committee, then read and presented an address, to which the Prince replied as follows:—

"Sir Edmund Hay Currie and Gentlemen,—I thank you, on behalf of the Princess of Wales and myself, for your address, and I can assure you that we heartily rejoice that an opportunity has been afforded us of again visiting this important district of the Metropolis. We thoroughly appreciate the endeavour of the trustees to promote a scheme which, from the comprehensiveness and liberality of its scope, should not fail to prove advantageous to the population of the near neighbourhood in which the Palace is to be erected, and to the inhabitants of the Metropolis at large. We do not doubt that the opportunities for healthy recreation so essential in a population that is comprised mainly of artisans and mechanics and their families will be promptly and properly appreciated by those for whom the People's Palace had been provided. The facilities which will be afforded for continuous education of all kinds will, we are convinced, materially tend to still further develop and perfect the various handicrafts of this neighbourhood, and should therefore prove of the greatest importance, not only to the inhabitants of East London, but to the nation at large, and should enable Englishmen to continue to maintain in the future, as they have in the past, that supremacy in the arts of peace at home which, among civilized nations, must be the invariable and necessary accompaniment of power and prosperity abroad. We congratulate the trustees upon the success which has already attended their efforts in having secured £75,000 of the £100,000 required, and we sincerely trust that the munificent donations of the Drapers' Company, Mr. Dyer Edwardes, Lord Rosebery, and the Duke of Westminster will influence others to follow so excellent an example. The 'Queen's Hall,' of which I am about to lay the first stone, will, I understand from the architect, Mr. Robson, be capable of accommodating more than 3000 persons, and will be so constructed as to serve the purpose of a winter garden, affording a resort for social intercourse and entertainment at a period of the year when the summer garden will not be available. We humbly join in the prayer of the Archbishop of Canterbury that God's blessing may rest upon this great work, and that, in the years to come, benefits both material and moral will result to the thousands who, we trust, will not fail to avail themselves of the facilities which the scheme will afford."

The stone was then laid with the usual ceremonies, the Prince's declaration that it was "well and truly" laid being received with general cheers. The proceedings were concluded with the benediction, pronounced by the Archbishop.

Long before the time of the People's Palace, visits to the East of London had not unfrequently been made by members of the Royal Family. On the 24th of June, 1880, the Prince and Princess of Wales, accompanied by their sons, Prince Albert Victor and Prince George, went to open a Recreation Ground in Whitechapel, for the benefit of the people of that parish, and of Bethnal Green, Spitalfields, and other adjacent districts. The ground, above an acre in extent, had formerly been a burial-ground of the Society of Friends, some of the members of which had contributed towards its being laid out as a pleasure-garden. The Rev. J. F. Kitto and the Rev. S. A. Barnett, whose names have long been associated with good deeds in East London, hoped that the presence of the Prince and Princess of Wales that day would give new impetus to the movement for obtaining open spaces in crowded parts of the Metropolis. The Prince expressed his gratification at being present, and said he was desired by the Princess to say that she declared the Recreation Ground now open.

SALE OF SHORTHORNS AND SOUTHDOWNS AT SANDRINGHAM.

July 15th, 1886.

To be "President of the Royal Agricultural Society of England" is an honour which the Prince of Wales gained not merely from his high position, but from his genuine love and practical knowledge of agriculture. Old King George III. was proud to be known as "Farmer George," but his great-grandson, the "Norfolk farmer," knows vastly more about the subject, and turns his knowledge to more profitable account. This was shown at the great sale of Shorthorn cattle and Southdown sheep which the Prince held at Sandringham, at the time of the Royal Agricultural Show at Norwich, in July 1886.

The idea of holding the sale at that time was a fortunate one, for the Show had brought to Norwich breeders of stock from every part of the kingdom, and some from foreign countries. Many of the leading members of the Royal Agricultural Society were the guests of the Prince at Sandringham during the week of the Show. Special trains were run to Wolferton Station from Norwich, so that there had never been seen such crowds at Sandringham, as on Thursday, the 15th of July, the day of the sale. Ample provision had been made for their reception, a large marquee capable of seating 1500 persons being erected in a field adjacent to the homestead. Among those who sat down to the luncheon were almost all the agricultural celebrities of England, and some of the most noted breeders of cattle and sheep in France. The entrance of the Prince and his family to the tent was received with immense enthusiasm.

After luncheon the Prince proposed the health of the Queen, which was duly honoured, and then the Duke of Richmond and Gordon gave the toast of "The Prince and Princess of Wales." He said that two days before it had fallen to his lot to move a vote of thanks to the Prince in his capacity as President of the Royal Agricultural Society of England, which might be deemed the Royal Academy of farming. Now he had to speak of him in his capacity of a Norfolk farmer. Amid much cheering, the Duke went on to say that it would be well for Norfolk farmers if all of them had such a wife as it was the good fortune of the Prince to possess, and that the high qualities of the Princess had endeared her not less to the people of Norfolk than to the other inhabitants of her future realm. In speaking of the sale itself, the Duke said that the quality of the stock, all of which he had personally examined, was remarkably level and good, and that the Prince was conferring a distinct benefit upon the agricultural community in the eastern counties by giving them an opportunity of obtaining such grand strains of blood as were to be found in the Sandringham Shorthorns and Southdowns. It is needless to add that this toast was received with the most enthusiastic cheering, and the plaudits were so sustained that the Prince had to wait some time before beginning his reply. He said :—

"Your Grace, my Lords, Ladies, and Gentlemen,—The kind way in which this toast has been proposed by the Duke of Richmond and Gordon and received by you all cannot but give the greatest possible pleasure both to the Princess and myself. We derive the most genuine satisfaction at seeing so many of the inhabitants of Norfolk here in our country home, for I can assure you that we take the deepest interest in all that concerns the welfare of this county. This has been a week of great agricultural interest for the county of Norfolk, and we have among us many men eminent as breeders and farmers from other parts of the kingdom, and to them also I extend a cordial welcome. As we have a busy afternoon before us, I will not detain you long, but before sitting down I should like to say a few words with respect to the Royal Agricultural Benevolent Institution, which has urgent need of support, as, owing to the recent depression in agriculture, the demands upon it have been so heavy that it is unable to do as much as it could a few years ago. In conclusion, let me bid you heartily welcome to Sandringham, and ask you to bid well at the sale."

This genial speech was received with applause, and its closing words with cheerful laughter. The Duke of Manchester next proposed the health of Mr. John Thornton, the auctioneer, who may be regarded as the Tattersall of the Shorthorn world, and who, in responding, said that he was more anxious to hear others than others would be to hear him. The company then broke up, the Prince and Princess of Wales leading the way to the sale-ring, which had been pitched close to the homestead, with three covered stands for the Royal party, the auctioneer and his chief customers, and for the county people, who mustered in great force.

The auctioneer gave much interesting information as to the establishment of the herd of Shorthorns and the flock of Southdowns at Sandringham. Since the herd of Shorthorns was formed the Prince of Wales has been in the habit of exhibiting at the Royal and other shows held within easy reach of home, and the animals selected for exhibition, but not forced into extreme condition, as is so often done, have been very successful, for they have taken sixteen first prizes, twelve seconds, four thirds, and four special prizes, while it is interesting to note that at the Royal Agricultural Show at York three years ago the Prince obtained what is generally regarded as the highest honour of the showyard —viz., the prize for a family group consisting of mother and several daughters.

The Prince has been not less conspicuously successful with his Southdown sheep, as this flock, first formed in 1886 by the selection of sheep from the flocks of the Duke of Richmond at Goodwood, Lord Walsingham at Merton, Mr. Webb at Babraham, and Mr. Gorringe at Kingston, has won sixty-eight first and sixty-two second prizes, to say nothing of minor distinctions, bringing the total of prizes up to 183, while at the Smithfield Show last winter three Southdowns from Sandringham won the £50 champion cup and the gold medal as the best pen of sheep in the hall. These facts being well known to all those who attended the sale, while they had the further assurance that all the lots offered would be sold without any of those reservations which mar so many auctions, the bidding was very brisk; but in spite of this the number of lots was so great that the sale, commencing at two o'clock, lasted until nearly six.

The detail of the sale only concern those who have to do with buying or breeding; and the records of the pedigree stock, and the prices obtained, and other particulars, will be found in the reports of the meeting. To the general reader of this book the whole proceedings are full of interest, as being a scene of genuine

English country life, and the Prince of Wales was thoroughly in his element as the centre of the grand agricultural assemblage. How Washington Irving would have rejoiced to be there, and what a description he would have given of the scene!

SION COLLEGE.

December 15th, 1886.

SION COLLEGE was founded by the Rev. Dr. White, Vicar of St. Dunstan's in the West, in the time of Charles 1. He held several other preferments, but we forgive him for being a notable pluralist because he made such good use of his money. By his will he left £3000 for the purchase of a site in the City of London, for erecting a hospital, consisting of twenty almshouses, and a college, which he endowed, with an annual revenue, not large, but sufficient in those times. Dr. White's intention was to enable the clergy of the City of London, and the incumbents of outlying parishes, to obtain corporate existence, like other crafts and professions, and so be legally qualified to hold and to administer property. This was well carried out by the Rev. Dr. Simpson, Rector of St. Olave's, Hart Street, one of the executors, who gave special attention to the library, now so important a feature of the College.

The College was established by Charter in 1630, and confirmed in 1664 by Charles II. The site selected was that of the Priory of Elsing Spital, London Wall, where a spacious building was afterwards erected, and continued in use till our own day. The library gradually became an important one, especially after 1710, when the Government conferred upon it the privilege of being one of the libraries entitled to receive copies of all books entered at Stationers' Hall. In 1843 this privilege was commuted for an annual grant, which barely sufficed for the maintenance of the library and other expenses. At length it was determined to sell the site in London Wall, the value of which was great for business purposes, and to remove to a better site, on which more commodious buildings might be erected. By Acts of Parliament authority was obtained to sell the old site, which realized thirty-three times the amount given for it in 1627. Another Act of Parliament authorized the purchase of a site on the Thames Embankment, the freehold of which cost £31,625, and on this, at a cost of £25,000, the present magnificent building, designed by Mr. A. W. Blomfield, was erected. To open this new Sion College, the Prince of Wales, accompanied by the Princess of Wales, went to the City on the 15th of December, 1886.

The Archbishop of Canterbury, and several Bishops, the Lord

Mayor and Sheriffs of London, the Lord Chancellor, and many distinguished persons were present, and a numerous body of the Clergy. The President of the College (who is elected annually by the Fellows), the Rev. Richard Whittington, a name of good omen, read an address, the Archbishop having previously conducted a short religious service. To the address the Prince replied :—

" Mr. President and Gentlemen,—I thank you for your address, and for the kind terms in which you allude to the Princess of Wales and my children. I experience the greatest satisfaction at being present on this interesting occasion, when your ancient corporation may be said to take a new departure. I am grati- fied to learn that the words of advice which I uttered two or three years ago have borne good fruit and have helped on the removal of your College from the comparative obscurity of London Wall to this central and eligible spot. I congratulate you on the completion without any serious drawback of a work which from its nature could not but be surrounded by many administrative and financial difficulties, only to be overcome by much tenacity of purpose, energy, and hard work. Many of you will probably look back with some feeling of lingering regret upon a spot hallowed by the memories of two centuries and a half, and by the recollection that in the same place, for many years before Sion College existed, the Augustinian canons devoted themselves to the alleviation of suffering, and provid- ing a refuge for the homeless and the outcast. Yet, if Sion College was to continue its work in the future as it has carried it on in the past, such a change as I inaugurate to-day was essential. On this site and with this building, upon the beauty and convenience of which your architect may well come in for his share of congratulation and praise, Sion College may become more than ever a centre where the London clergy may meet together to exchange experiences and learn by personal inter- course how substantial is the tie which results from devotion to one high purpose. Of your library I need say little. The high place which it occupies among similar institutions is well known, and the extent and excellence of its contents are universally acknowledged. I have to congratulate the clergy of London upon having at their command such a varied collection of the best literature of all ages to stimulate their studies and enrich their minds. I will only add an expression of my satisfaction

at learning that those poor persons for whose temporal wants
your benevolent founder, Dr. Thomas White, made provision
have reason to claim a full share in the gratification which
attends the proceedings to-day."

The Lord Mayor said it was a great privilege for him to be
called on, as Lord Mayor, to say a few words on that most
interesting occasion. He congratulated the President and Fellows
that Sion College was rebuilt under such favourable auspices and
so happily placed between those seminaries of the law, the ancient
and honourable societies of the Temple, of which His Royal
Highness was so distinguished a member, and the more modern
institution, on which he thought the Corporation might justly
pride itself, the City of London School for the classical and
commercial training of our younger citizens, which His Royal
Highness graciously inaugurated just four years ago.

The Lord Chancellor said there were no words of his which
would adequately express the gratitude and affection which all
those present felt towards His Royal Highness and the Princess.
This was only one of a series of acts by which their Royal Highnesses had exhibited their sympathy with the people, and there
was nothing good, high, and noble that was not from time to time
graced by their presence.

The Prince of Wales then, amid loud cheers, declared the library
to be open.

The procession, having been re-formed, left the library and
descended to the hall, which was also filled with spectators. Here
the President pointed out the ancient panels, the pictures,
including portrait of the founder, and other treasures removed from
the old building. The Prince declared the Hall open, and their
Royal Highnesses signed their names in the Register of Benefactors.

It may be added that it was a hint from the Prince of Wales
that hastened the decision to remove from London Wall. He was
viewing from the roof of the old library the fire in Wood Street,
Cheapside, when he said to the Rev. W. H. Milman (the librarian,
son of Dean Milman) that he thought it was the duty of the
Governors to remove their valuable library to a safer locality.

COLONIAL AND INDIAN EXHIBITION OF 1886.

On the 10th of November, 1884, the Queen issued a Royal Com-
mission to arrange for holding an Exhibition of the products,
manufactures, and arts of Her Majesty's Colonial and Indian
Dominions, in the year 1886. Of this Commission the Prince of
Wales was President, and Sir Philip Cunliffe-Owen Secretary.
The first meeting took place at Marlborough House on the 30th of

March, 1885. In opening the proceedings His Royal Highness said :—

"In addressing you for the first time, I would remind you that the objects for which Her Majesty has been pleased to appoint this Commission are, briefly, to organise and carry out an Exhibition by which the reproductive resources of our Colonies and of the Indian Empire may be brought before the people of Great Britain, and by which also the distant portions of Her Majesty's Dominions may be enabled to compare the advance made by each other in trade, manufactures, and general material progress.

"This project, to the realisation of which I have looked forward for some years, is essentially one of a National and Imperial character, differing in this respect from former Exhibitions, in which the elements of trade rivalry and profit largely existed.

"No such opportunity of becoming practically acquainted with the economic condition of our Colonies and the Indian Empire has ever been afforded in this country. The attractive display in the Indian and Colonial Courts at the Paris Exhibition of 1878 could only be witnessed by a comparatively small number of the population of these Islands, millions of whom may be expected to view and profit by the evidence which the Exhibition of 1886 will afford of the marvellous progress made by their fellow-countrymen beyond the seas.

"I also trust that this gathering may serve even a higher purpose, and be the means not only of giving a stimulus to commercial interests and intercourse, but of strengthening that Bond of Union between Her Majesty's subjects in all parts of the Empire, the growth and manifestation of which are most sincerely appreciated by us all.

"Whilst Her Majesty's Government have given their hearty approval to the objects for which the Commission has been appointed, they have not so far found it desirable to make any definite grant towards it. The Commission have, therefore, to rely entirely upon the public support of the great purposes which the Exhibition is intended to promote; and on the attractive form which it will be the endeavour of all concerned to give to it.

" I cannot doubt but that, under such conditions, should no untoward events occur, the project will be more than self-sustaining.

" At the same time, it has been thought prudent not to dispense with the usual provision of a Guarantee Fund, though I trust no circumstances may arise rendering it necessary to make any call on the guarantors. To this Fund the Indian and Colonial Governments have made liberal contributions, amounting to £51,000."

The Prince then gave detailed announcements of the responses made to appeals addressed to corporations, firms, and individuals in Great Britain, and in the Colonies and India. He also explained the arrangements for administrative and financial affairs, and for the reception of foreign representatives.

" In conclusion, let me express the hope that this great undertaking, and the many occasions for friendly intercourse with our fellow-subjects from India and the Colonies which it will afford, may convey to them the assurance that, while we are deeply moved by the spirit of patriotism they have lately shown in desiring to bear their share in the graver trials of the country, we on our part wish to participate in every effort to further and develop their material interests—interests which we feel to be inseparably bound up with the prosperity of the Empire. We must remember that, as regards the Colonies, they are the legitimate and natural homes, in future, of the more adventurous and energetic portion of the population of these Islands. Their progress, and their power of providing all that makes life comfortable and attractive, cannot, therefore, but be a matter of serious concern to us all. And, as regards India, the increasing knowledge of that vast Empire and the rapid and easy means of communication to all parts of it which now exist, render its remarkable and varied products and its social and political condition a source of yearly increasing interest and importance to us.

" For the attainment of the purposes I have indicated, I am sure I may rely on your friendly co-operation and assistance, in your several localities, and within the sphere of your individual influence. Although it has been impossible from the pressure of their duties elsewhere for some members of the

x

Commission to be present at this meeting, I am gratified by the assurance from them that we may none the less rely on their practical and earnest assistance on every occasion in furthering the work which has been entrusted to us, and achieving the important ends which I trust may flow from its successful accomplishment."

May 3rd, 1886.

A meeting of the Royal Commission was again held on the 3rd of May, in the Durbar Hall of the Indian Palace, when the Prince of Wales, as the Executive President, addressed the audience. He gave an interesting report on all the chief matters that had engaged the attention of the Royal Commissioners ; and referred to the co-operation received from the Colonies and India. He stated that the guarantee fund had reached the amount of £218,430, of which the City of London had voted £10,000. A vote of thanks was proposed by the Duke of Cambridge, seconded by Lord Granville, to the Prince of Wales for the able and energetic manner in which he acted on behalf of the Commission as their President. "It is not the first time that His Royal Highness has acted as President in undertakings of this nature, and it is very difficult for any individual to praise him in his presence without appearing fulsome, but it is not fulsome to say that he has always devoted his whole energies to bringing everything to a successful issue with which he is connected."

The Prince, in his reply, said :—

He hoped that the Exhibition would be not only entertaining to the eye, and that it will prove of material benefit to our own countrymen, but that it will also tend to strengthen the bond of brotherly love between ourselves and the rest of Her Majesty's subjects.

April 30th, 1887.

At the final meeting of the Royal Commission, held at Marlborough House on the 30th of April, 1887, the minutes of the previous meeting, held on the 3rd of May, 1886, having been read, the Prince of Wales addressed the meeting :—

"Your Royal Highness, my Lords and Gentlemen,—I have asked you to meet me to-day, in order that I might submit for your approval a Report which I have drawn up upon the work of the Royal Commission for the Colonial and Indian Exhibition, a draft of which has already been forwarded to each of you for consideration.

" The contents of this Report are so exhaustive, and the information afforded so full and complete, that it seems scarcely necessary that I should detain you with many explanatory remarks.

" You will remember that the last occasion on which I had the pleasure of meeting you was on the eve of the opening of the Exhibition by Her Majesty the Queen. You are all aware of the success of that opening, and you, I am sure, appreciated the keen interest which the Queen took in the Exhibition, both by performing that imposing ceremony, and by the frequent visits which Her Majesty afterwards paid to the various Sections.

" The great importance attached to the objects of this Exhibition was evidenced by the striking manner in which it was visited by the public. You will have seen by the Report that it was attended by no fewer than 5,550,745 persons. Of this number, a large proportion were admitted under schemes in which I took a deep personal interest, by means of which admission was granted to provincial and metropolitan artisans, with their wives and families, at greatly reduced rates.

" It may safely be asserted that a vast amount of public good has arisen from the holding of this Exhibition. No one can have failed to notice the earnest attention paid by all classes of the visitors to the contents of the Exhibition; and the instruction which was derived from an examination of the varied objects displayed therein cannot but tend to a better knowledge of the outlying portions of the Empire, among the inhabitants of the mother country.

" At a previous Meeting I referred to the appointment of the Finance Committee, to its enlargement, and to the manner in which its labours were being conducted, and I would now specially draw your attention to the Report they have presented to me. The accounts now before you, which have been circulated for your information, have been subject to a continuous and careful audit. They have been made up at the earliest possible day consistent with the proper realization of the assets belonging to the Royal Commission, and with the

settlement of the many and varied claims presented after the
close of the Exhibition, and which the Finance Committee had
necessarily to adjust. You will see that the fullest information
in ample detail is given under appropriate heads of the entire
receipts and expenditure of the Royal Commission up to the
23rd April, and I am sure that you will share my satisfaction
at the gratifying result of a substantial surplus of £35,235 7s. 8d.
remaining in the hands of the Royal Commission.

" I am anxious that the appropriation of this surplus, and the
objects to which it should be devoted, should be in harmony
with the wishes of the entire body of the Royal Commission.
I desire, therefore, to draw your attention to a paragraph in the
Report of the Finance Committee, to the effect that in view of
the fact that this Exhibition, and those which preceded it, have
to a certain extent been considered as one series, consideration
might be given to the requirements of any former Exhibition,
the financial results of which have been less satisfactory than
those of the present undertaking.   In this recommendation
I entirely concur, and a Resolution in that sense will be
submitted for your approval.

" I would also suggest to you the advisability of retaining
for the present a certain sum for the purpose of meeting any
unforeseen contingencies ; which sum should for the next few
years remain vested in the names of trustees, but should
ultimately be applied to the same purpose as that to which the
residue is devoted.

" As regards the balance of the surplus, I would commend to
your consideration the propriety of transferring it to the funds
of the Imperial Institute of the United Kingdom, the Colonies,
and India (in the promotion of which the Queen and I both
take so warm an interest), the more especially as we may
regard the Institute, to a certain extent, as the outcome of the
Exhibition which was closed in November last.

" Before moving resolutions to this effect, I would wish to
express to you my deep gratitude for the support which you
have at all times given to me in the duties which I, as your
Executive President, have had so much pleasure in performing ;
and I am sure you will join with me at this our last Meeting in
expressing most heartily our appreciation of the co-operation

which the Royal Commission received from the Colonies and India, and of the exertions of the gentlemen representing these Governments, which tended in so marked a degree to the success of the past Exhibition.

" The enthusiastic manner in which the proposal for holding this Exhibition was received in all portions of Her Majesty's Empire, the energy displayed in realising the views of the Royal Commission, and the continued support rendered to us by the Colonial and Indian Governments and their representatives in London, resulted in the achievement of a work of which all those who participated in it may be justly proud, and which formed a fitting prelude to an undertaking intended to commemorate the Jubilee of Her Majesty's reign, by permanently gathering together in one building the varied productions of the whole of the British Empire, in the interchange of which its past prosperity is so much due, and by which its future development may be promoted.

" In closing these observations, I would desire to convey to the gentlemen composing the Finance Committee, my warm personal acknowledgments for their unremitting attention, and the great services they have rendered, at so much sacrifice to their time and convenience. I equally desire to acknowledge the admirable and efficient arrangements made throughout by the Executive Secretary, and to return my thanks to the whole staff employed on the Exhibition. Their zeal and readiness at all times to promote its success demand special recognition at our hands. In all this, I feel assured I give expression to the sentiments of every member of the Royal Commission."

In the speeches of those who moved and seconded the resolutions submitted to the meeting, reference was repeatedly made to the permanent Imperial Institute, of which the Indo-Colonial Exhibition seemed the precursor. The Prince, in acknowledging the vote of thanks at the conclusion of the meeting, said :—
" I most truly hope that the words which fell from Lord Derby and Lord Kimberley with respect to the Imperial Institute may come true. If I may use the allegory, now that we have, as it were, burnt the late Exhibition to-day, I hope the Imperial Institute may be a Phœnix arising out of its ashes. I trust that it may be a lasting memorial, not only of that but of the Jubilee of Her Majesty the Queen."
The Exhibition was opened by Her Majesty on the 4th of May,

and those who were present will not readily forget the impressive nature of the proceedings on that memorable day. The Official Report of the Royal Commission (printed and published, as all the Exhibition Reports have been, by W. Clowes & Sons) is a most valuable manual on all matters relating to the Exhibition—the most imposing and interesting of any since that of 1851. It was also the most successful as to finance, there being a surplus of no less than £35,285 7s. 8d. Of this £25,000 was voted to the Imperial Institute fund, and the remainder applied to liquidate the debt remaining from the Inventions Exhibition, and the formation of a reserve fund connected with other Exhibitions.

THE IMPERIAL INSTITUTE.

January 12th, 1887.

The Imperial Institute, while it will be the grandest and most enduring memorial of the Queen's Jubilee, will also be associated in history with the name of the Prince of Wales. It was by him that the idea was first entertained, and the proposal first made; and to his zealous and persevering efforts the successful carrying out of the project is due. There had been various circumstances preparing this way for the great undertaking, but it was the success of the Indo-Colonial Exhibition, held in 1886, that led to the proposal of a permanent Imperial Institute. It would be a visible emblem of the unity of the Empire, and a place for illustrating its vast resources; a museum for exhibiting its manifold products and industries; a centre of information and communication for all the countries throughout the world under the British sovereignty; and be helpful to the increase and the distribution of the wealth of the nation. It would co-operate and not conflict with older institutions of tried utility, such as Colonial museums and exchanges, emigration societies, technical colleges, and other organizations for the welfare of the people. The scheme was worthy of being adopted as a national memorial of the Jubilee of the Queen's reign, and was fittingly inaugurated by the heir apparent to the throne.

Of the progress of the movement, and of the home for the Institute at South Kensington, it is not necessary here to speak, but the following speech of the Prince of Wales, at St. James's Palace, on the 12th of January, 1887, gives the best summary of all that is designed and expected in regard to the Imperial Institute.

Letters had been sent out inviting many influential persons to meet His Royal Highness as chairman, and the members of the organizing committee of the Institute. The banqueting room at the old Palace was filled with an audience such as has rarely been brought together on any occasion in recent years. Many of the most distinguished men in all departments of public life, the Lord Mayors of London and York, with nearly 200 Mayors, Provosts, and Chief Magistrates of English and Scottish boroughs, Masters and Wardens of City Companies, and Directors of great corporate bodies and societies were present. The Prince of Wales, on entering the room, accompanied by Prince Albert Victor, was warmly received; and thus he addressed the meeting :—

"My Lords and Gentlemen,—You are doubtless aware of the general feeling on the part of the public that some signal proof of the love and loyalty of Her Majesty's subjects throughout her widely extended Empire should be given to the Queen when she celebrates the fiftieth year of her happy reign. In order to afford to the Queen the fullest satisfaction, the proposed memorial should not be merely personal in its character, but should tend to serve the interests of the entire Empire and to promote a feeling of unity among the whole of Her Majesty's subjects. The desire to find fitting means of drawing our colonies and India into closer bonds with the mother country, a desire which of late has been clearly expressed, meets, I am sure, with the Queen's warmest sympathy. It occurred to me that the recent Colonial and Indian Exhibition, which presented a most successful display of the material resources of the colonies and India, might suggest the basis for an institute which should afford a permanent representation of the products and manufactures of the whole of the Queen's dominions. I therefore appointed a committee of eminent men to consider and report to me upon the best means of carrying out this idea.

"Upon the report of the committee being submitted to me, and after giving every clause my full consideration, it so entirely met with my approval that I accepted all its suggestions, and I therefore directed that a copy of that report should be sent to each of you. As I trust you have mastered the suggestions of that report, I do not purpose re-stating them to you in detail, but I would remind you that I propose that the memorial should bear the name of the Imperial Institute of the United Kingdom, the Colonies, and India, and that it must find its home within buildings of a character worthy to commemorate the Jubilee year of the Queen's reign.

"My proposals also are that the Imperial Institute should be an emblem of the unity of the Empire, and should illustrate the resources and capabilities of every section of Her Majesty's dominions. By these means every one may become acquainted with the marvellous growth of the Queen's colonial and Indian possessions during her reign, and will be enabled to mark by the opportunities afforded for contrast how steadily these possessions have advanced in manufacturing skill and enterprise step by step with the mother country. A representative institute of this kind must necessarily be situated in London, but its organization will, I trust, be such that benefits will be equally conferred upon our provincial communities as well as upon the colonial and Indian subjects of the Crown. It is my hope that the institute will form a practical means of communication between our colonial settlers and those persons at home who may benefit by emigration. Much information and even instruction may beneficially be imparted to those who need guidance in respect to emigration.

"You are aware that the competition of industry all over the world has become keen, while commerce and manufactures have been profoundly affected by the recent rapid progress of science and the increased facilities of inter-communication offered by steam and the electric telegraph. In consequence of these changes all nations are using strenuous efforts to produce a trained intelligence among their people. The working classes of this country have not been slow to show their desire for improvement in this direction. They wish to place themselves in a position of intellectual power by using all opportunities offered to them to secure an understanding of the principles as well as of the practice of the work in which they are engaged. No less than 16,000,000 persons from all parts of the kingdom have attended the four exhibitions over which I presided, representing fisheries, public health, inventions, and the colonies and India, and I assure you I would not have undertaken the labour attending their administration had I not felt a deep conviction that such exhibitions added to the knowledge of the people and stimulated the industries of the country.

"I have on more than one occasion expressed my own views, founded upon those so often enunciated by my lamented father, that it is of the greatest importance to do everything within our power to advance the knowledge as well as the practical skill of the productive classes of the Empire. I therefore commend to you as the leading idea I entertain that the institute should be regarded as a centre for extending knowledge in relation to the industrial resources and commerce of the Queen's dominions. With this view it should be in constant touch, not only with the chief manufacturing districts of this country, but also with all the colonies and India. Such objects are large in their scope, and must necessarily be so, if this institute is worthily to represent the unity of the Empire.

" To some minds the scheme may not be sufficiently comprehensive, because it does not provide for systematic courses of technical instruction in connection with the collections and libraries of the proposed institute. I would be the last person to undervalue this suggestion. I am well aware that the advantages we have enjoyed in the competition of the world by the possession of fuel, combined with large mineral resources and by the maritime habits of our people, are now becoming of less importance, as trained intellect has in other countries been more and more applied to productive industry. But I know that this truth has already penetrated our centres of manufacturing activity, for many of the large towns have founded colleges and schools of science and art to increase the intellectual factor of production. London, also, has taken important steps in the same direction. The Imperial Institute should be a supplement to, and not a competitor with, other institutions for technical education in science and art both at home and in the colonies. At the same time, I trust that the institute will be able to stimulate and aid local efforts by directing scholarships for the working-classes into suitable channels, and by other similar means.

" Though the institute does not engage in the direct object of systematic technical education, it may well be the means of promoting it, as its purpose is to extend an exact knowledge of the industrial resources of the Empire. It will be a place of study and resort for producers and consumers from the colonies and India when they visit this country for business or pleasure, and they, as well as the merchants and manufacturers of the

United Kingdom, will find in its collections, libraries, conference and intelligence rooms, the means of extending the commerce and of improving the manufacturing industries of the Empire. I trust, too, that colonial and Indian subjects visiting this country will find some sort of social welcome within the proposed building. This institute will thus be an emblem, as well as a practical exponent, of the community of interests and the unity of feeling throughout the extended dominions of the Queen.

"From the close relation in which I stand to the Queen, there can be no impropriety in my stating that if her subjects desire, on the occasion of the celebration of her fiftieth year as Sovereign of this great Empire, to offer her a memorial of their love and loyalty, she would specially value one which would promote the industrial and commercial resources of her dominions in various parts of the world, and which would be expressive of that unity and co-operation which Her Majesty desires should prevail among all classes and races of her extended Empire.

" My lords and gentlemen, I have invited you to meet on this occasion in order that I may appeal to you to give me your assistance in establishing and maintaining the Imperial Institute. If you approve of the views I have expressed, I am certain I may rely upon your strenuous co-operation to carry them into effect. I admit that it has not been without anxiety that I resolved to make the propositions I submitted to you, but confidence and support have come to me in the knowledge that I can appeal to you, and through you to the whole country, to give your aid to a work which I believe will be of lasting benefit to this and future generations."

Resolutions were proposed and speeches made by Earl Spencer, the Lord Provost of Edinburgh, Viscount Hampden, the Lord Mayor of London, the Mayor of Newcastle, and the Marquis of Lorne, approving the scheme, and promising hearty support. The Lord Mayor proposed a vote of thanks to the Prince, who tendered his thanks for the attendance at the meeting, and the approval given to the proposal.

" I am glad, gentlemen, to have this opportunity of expressing to you collectively and individually my deep feelings of gratitude, in seeing you all here to-day at a time of year when travelling is neither easy nor pleasant, considering the distances which you have had to come; and also for the kind response which you have made to my appeal. It augurs well for the future, and I feel convinced you will do all in your power to assist me in making this Imperial Institute worthy of the name of our Queen and of her Empire. The promotion of this scheme is with me a labour of love, and it must, I am sure, strike you all that, apart from wishing to do honour to the name of my beloved mother, nobody is more desirous than I am that a monument, if I may use the term, may be erected worthy of her Empire."

A public meeting was held the same day at the Mansion House, attended by a large number of the most influential men in the City. The Lord Mayor (Sir Reginald Hanson), Earl Granville, Mr. Plunket, M.P., Mr. Mundella, M.P., Mr. Goschen, M.P., and Lord Rothschild, were among the speakers, and resolutions were passed with an enthusiasm which gave good augury for the success of the Imperial Institute.

THE LONDON ORPHAN ASYLUM.

March 12th, 1887.

THE London Orphan Asylum, for the maintenance, clothing, and education of Fatherless Children, is one of the oldest and best charities of its class. The Prince of Wales presided at the Jubilee Festival, at the Hôtel Métropole, on the 12th of March, 1887. Among the numerous friends of the charity present were the Duke of Abercorn, the Earl of Clarendon, Sir Donald Stewart, Sir Dighton Probyn, and many distinguished men. The Prince, in giving the toast of "The Queen," said it was the first public dinner at which he had presided in the Jubilee year of the Queen, and this was also the jubilee of her connection with the London Orphan Asylum, of which she had been for fifty years its patron. The toast was received with more than usual enthusiasm.

Alderman Sir R. N. Fowler, M.P., in giving the next loyal toast said that the charity had been already deeply indebted to the Prince of Wales, who had, along with the Princess of Wales, laid the foundation stone of this Asylum at Watford.

Other loyal and patriotic toasts having been given, the Prince rose to propose the toast of the evening. He said:—

"My Lords and Gentlemen,—The London Orphan Asylum is an old institution; it was founded in 1813, two years before the battle of Waterloo; and it owed its origin to a distinguished philanthropist of the time, Dr. Andrew Reed. Of course it began on a very small scale, for the old proverb applied in this as in so many other cases that you must cut your coat according to your cloth. It commenced in the first year of its organization with only three children; but in 1822 there were as many as 126 children in the school. Twenty years later there were as many as 326; twenty years later still there were 414; and now it affords me the greatest pleasure to announce to you that we have upwards of 500 children.

"The first subscription list contained the names of 255 subscribers, and among them was my grandfather. He was the first patron and headed the list with 50 guineas; and in 1823 my grand-uncle, the late Duke of York, laid the foundation stone of the institution at Clapton; while two years later the late Duke of Cambridge, who was always foremost in all great charitable undertakings in this country, presided at its annual festival. The institution continued to grow and more children had to be admitted, until at last there was not sufficient room in the old home. A new one was, therefore, instituted at Watford, and in 1869 the Princess and myself were asked to lay the foundation stone of your present home. Having taken part in that ceremony, it gives me much gratification to learn in what a flourishing condition the institution now is, which is exemplified by the presence of upwards of 500 in the home. And when I look at the young ladies and the boys before us I think you will come to the conclusion that the management of the institution is thoroughly good. During the 74 years of the existence of the asylum something over 5000 orphan children have been maintained, clothed, and educated.

"The great Duke of Wellington took very great interest in the institution, and I believe I am not wrong in stating that he presided at its festivals on five different occasions. A remarkable and very important fact in connection with the institution is that those who have received education and aid from the society are those who do all they can to give it support at the present time, and part of the institution at Watford was built by subscriptions of the old scholars, and I am told that there are as many as ten old pupils of the institution in one commercial house in the City, while many are present here to-night who are prepared to give liberal donations. The education they receive is a thoroughly sound and practical one, and when they leave every effort is made to find them situations, and they are sent out with proper clothing. As a proof that it is managed on economical principles I need only say that the cost per head in the past year amounted to little over £30. The amount disbursed in the 74 years since its foundation has reached the large sum of £700,000—all of this large sum, with the exception of £1000 a year which you can rely upon, having been derived from voluntary contributions.

"This year being the Jubilee of Her Majesty's reign the managers are most anxious to mark the epoch in some manner which will benefit the institution, and they have resolved to add 100 scholars, of whom 50 were admitted in January and 50 more will be admitted in June. The cost of this will, undoubtedly, be very great, the ultimate amount being between £18,000 and £20,000. I am here, therefore, as your chairman, to ask you to contribute as liberally as you can for the maintenance of this ancient and most creditable institution. I am well aware that now and for some years past there has been both agricultural and commercial depression, but I feel convinced that in the cause of charity—and what greater charity can there be than providing for orphan children?—I shall not appeal in vain to my countrymen to do all in their power as philanthropists to support an institution which has been carried out on the best and most economical principles."

The toast was drunk with much enthusiasm, and acknowledged by Mr. Capell (the treasurer). The total amount of the subscriptions announced during the evening was £5000, including an annual subscription of 20 guineas from the Queen and 100 guineas from the Prince of Wales.

When the foundation-stone was laid by the Prince and Princess of Wales, in 1869, 250 purses were laid on it, containing in all about £8000. For the chapel £5000 was given by one whose early days were spent in the Asylum. The Grocers' Company contributed £3000 to build one house; the Countess of Verulam and the Countess of Essex raised another sum of £3000, as a kind of welcome to the county. The income in 1887 was £15,000, but the invested funds give little more than £1000, so that there is constant need of new "voluntary contributions," to maintain the 550 orphans now in the houses.

THE COLLEGE OF PRECEPTORS.

March 30th, 1887.

THE associated teachers who, under the name of the College of Preceptors, have for above forty years laboured to raise the standard of middle-class education, deserve praise and honour for what they have accomplished. Without Government aid or grant, and unpatronized by dignitaries of Church or State, these learned and patriotic men have succeeded, by training teachers, establishing examinations, and granting certificates, in acquiring a reputation and influence now very generally recognized. Their work is truly of national importance, and this His Royal Highness the Prince of Wales declared when he readily assented to formally open the new building of the College, in Bloomsbury Square, on the 30th of March, 1887. This College is self-supporting, and the cost of the erection and equipment of the new building was defrayed out of savings that had accumulated in the hands of the treasurer during the previous seven years.

A very large number of persons interested in education assembled in the lecture-hall to witness the ceremony, among whom were Sir Lyon Playfair, Sir Richard Temple, Mr. Lyulph Stanley, the Dowager Lady Stanley of Alderley, the Presidents of several societies, and the Head Masters of Harrow, Charterhouse, and Merchant Taylors' Schools, of Marlborough and Dulwich Colleges, and of Christ's Hospital.

On the arrival of the Prince of Wales, accompanied by the Princess of Wales, and their daughters Princesses Victoria and Maud, an address was presented by the Rev. Dr. T. W. Jex-Blake, President of the Council. The Prince, in replying, said :—

" Dr. Jex-Blake, Ladies, and Gentlemen,—It gives the Princess of Wales and myself great satisfaction to have been able to accede to the request of the council, and to open the new building of the College of Preceptors. I am reminded, by your reference to the circumstances that this building is opened during the year of the Queen's jubilee, of the many and important improvements that have taken place in Her Majesty's dominions during the last fifty years, and especially in the advancement of education among all classes of the people, a share of which progress is due to the excellent work undertaken by this self-supported institution.

" For over forty years the College of Preceptors has exercised a marked and growing influence for good upon the education given in some of our endowed schools, and more particularly in the numerous private schools for boys and girls which are an important feature in the educational system of this country. The value of your work is sufficiently shown by the high reputation of your examinations and by the constantly increasing number of your candidates, and I sincerely congratulate you on the results you have achieved. In the further development of the work of training teachers you have before you a future of great usefulness, for there can be no doubt that the provision of properly-trained teachers for middle and higher schools is almost, if not quite, as necessary as for our public elementary schools.

"The key of the building which you have presented to me I shall retain as a memento of this ceremony, and in declaring this building open I fervently hope that the influence and teaching which will go forth from it may tend to improve and to raise to a yet higher standard the education given in the private and secondary schools of our country. I declare this building now open."

The Royal party were afterwards conducted through the building, the arrangements of which are justly admired. The entrance corridor is wide and lofty. On one side of it there is a club-room for members, and on the other the secretary's and clerks' offices. The council-room is large and handsome, and the lecture-room occupies the whole of the second story, and is surrounded by book-cases capable of holding 10,000 volumes.

THE MANCHESTER EXHIBITION.

May 3rd, 1887.

THE great Exhibition at Manchester during the Queen's Jubilee year is too recent an event to need any remark prefatory to the statement that it was opened by the Prince and Princess of Wales on the 3rd of May, 1887. Their Royal Highnesses, who were guests at Tatton Hall, drove with Lord Egerton through the park to Knutsford, where they stopped to witness the crowning of the May Queen, and other old English May Day customs which have been revived in that quaint little town. The Prince gave the permission asked by the Committee to add the title of Royal to the Knutsford May Day Sports. They then travelled in a saloon

carriage to Manchester, accompanied by Lady Sefton and Lord
Egerton.

On arriving at the Town Hall an address was presented, to
which the Prince read the following reply:—

" It gives me sincere pleasure to be permitted on behalf of the
Queen, my dear mother, to visit the city of Manchester for the
purpose of opening the extensive and interesting Exhibition
which the inhabitants of Manchester have organized with such
admirable zeal and energy, particularly as it is associated with
your congratulations on Her Majesty's attaining the fiftieth
year of her reign.   In her name I thank you for your loyal and
dutiful address.   It has been a source of much gratification to
the Queen to receive assurance of unfaltering attachment to her
throne and person from all parts of the Empire on the occasion.
The Princess of Wales and I desire to express our admiration
of the noble building which you have provided for the conduct
of your municipal affairs, and we think it worthy of the vast
wealth and importance of the city of Manchester.   It gives us
great satisfaction to be able to promote and encourage all
charitable works and institutions designed for the social and
educational improvement of the community.   We thank you
for your good wishes for the welfare of ourselves and our
children, and we hope that prosperity and happiness may ever
attend on the labours of the loyal and industrious inhabitants
of this great city."

The route of the procession from the Town Hall to the Exhibition was a very long one, being chosen by the Prince in preference
to a shorter one submitted to him, on the ground that he would
rather afford pleasure to a larger number of people than see the
finer edifices' on the shorter route.   In the Palm House of the
gardens luncheon was served, and then the opening ceremony
took place in the nave of the building, in the position known as
the Music Room.   Mr. Hallé's orchestra was in front of the organ,
and the National Anthem was performed with fine effect, the vocal
rendering being also given by Madame Albani and the full chorus.
The Bishop of Manchester offered prayer, and the choir sang the
Old Hundredth Psalm.   To the address read by Sir Joseph Lee,
the Prince replied:—

" I receive with great satisfaction your address on the
opening of this large and instructive Exhibition.   On behalf
of Her Majesty I declare it open from this day.   The illustra-

tions which you have collected on engineering and chemical industry, and the products of manufacture and useful toil, afford ample testimony to the skill and ingenuity and steady perseverance of the inhabitants of this district, and prove how justly they hold a high and an honourable place in the industrial ranks of the Empire. The collection of natural products and manufactures of Ireland, and the gratifying display of English works of art, add much to the interest and value of this Exhibition, in which I recognise a worthy mark of your desire to do honour to an occasion so auspicious as the celebration of the fiftieth year of Her Majesty's reign. The Princess and I desire to thank you heartily for your good wishes on our behalf, and for the cordial welcome which you have given us."

The Prince, in the name of the Queen, declared the Exhibition open. A fanfare of trumpets was then given and a *feu de joie* fired. The proceedings closed with a procession through the different departments, while the "Lobgesang" or "Hymn of Praise" was rendered by the full orchestra and chorus. At the Exhibition station a special train was waiting to take the Royal party back to Tatton Hall.

THE LONDON HOSPITAL NEW BUILDINGS.

May 22nd, 1887.

THE London Hospital has many and special claims on public sympathy and support. Its position, in Whitechapel, surrounded by poor and crowded parts of East London; its small endowments compared with some of the other great hospitals; the vast number of patients annually relieved, both in the house and as out-patients; and its being virtually a "free" hospital, nearly three-fourths of the in-patients being received without letter or recommendation; all these circumstances appeal to liberal charity. In 1887 there were 8863 in-patients admitted, of which 6019 were freely received, without letters of subscribers. There are children's wards where, during the same time, 1717 were admitted; and Hebrew wards, where 623 received treatment. The total number of out-patients, treated either at the Hospital or at their homes, was nearly 100,000, including relief given in less serious and protracted illness. The income from endowments is little more than £15,000 a year, while the annual cost of maintenance is

Y

£50,000. The Medical School is supported by the fees of pupils, but for the general maintenance of the Hospital appeal must be made to the public for voluntary subscriptions and contributions.

A Nursing Home, to accommodate 100 nurses, a new Library, and other buildings having been recently added, the Prince and Princess of Wales were invited by the Governors, of whom the Duke of Cambridge is President, to inaugurate these additions to the institution. This was done, with suitable ceremony, on Saturday, the 21st of May, 1887. The Princesses Louise and Victoria of Wales, and the Crown Prince of Denmark were also present. The Governors and officers of the Hospital, with many distinguished persons, were in attendance, and great interest was shown by the crowds of people who thronged the streets on the occasion. The Royal party visited several of the wards, where the Princess of Wales showed kindly sympathy with many of the poor patients, especially in the children's wards. On arriving at the dining-hall of the nurses and sisters, who wear a plain and tasteful uniform, a hymn was sung, and a prayer offered by the Bishop of Bedford, after which, at the request of the Duke of Cambridge, the Princess of Wales formally declared the Nursing Home to be open.

The Medical College was then visited, and in the new library an address was presented by the President. The Prince of Wales, in acknowledging the address, said:—

" Your Royal Highness and Gentlemen,—The Princess and myself thank you for your address, and can assure you that we have much pleasure in coming here to-day to open the nursing home and college buildings of this important institution. The Hospital, which is the largest civil one in the United Kingdom, which contains 800 beds and which supplied medical and surgical assistance to 80,000 out-patients last year, may be regarded almost in the light of a national institution, as every description of case, excepting those of an infectious or incurable nature, is admitted. Such a Hospital cannot fail to be of inestimable value to the population of over a million persons residing in its vicinity, and especially to the labouring class, who are so extensively employed in connection with the railways and docks. But it has other and additional claims upon public sympathy and assistance. First, although its annual expenditure amounts to nearly £50,000, it is mainly supported by voluntary contributions; secondly, it has undertaken the difficult task of improving the system of nursing and of providing a higher class of nurses, with better discipline and superior training and instruction. To effect this object house accommodation was essential, and instead of closely-packed dormitories the new home provides separate rooms, a cheerful dining hall, and other advantages, all tending to brighten the lives of the inmates, while reserving for them the necessary quiet and rest.

"The new library and buildings which I am now about to declare open belong to a college over 100 years old. It was the first in the Metropolis in which a complete curriculum was established, and being attached to the largest Hospital in the country, and situated in the midst of the most populous artisan neighbourhood in London, it offers greater facilities for the acquirement of medical and surgical knowledge than perhaps any other college of a scientific character. I understand that among the important duties which the students perform are those of dressers, clinical clerks, maternity pupils, and other assistants, and from their number the resident officers are selected after having become qualified practitioners. The Princess and I most earnestly pray that every blessing may attend the labours and efforts of all those who are working among the sufferers in the Hospital, and you may rest assured that we shall always take the warmest interest in the welfare and prosperity of your noble institution."

Dr. Langdon Down, the senior physician, in thanking His Royal Highness on behalf of his colleagues and the students, explained that the new buildings did not diminish the funds of the Hospital, as a rent was paid for them by the teaching staff of the medical school. The Prince then declared the new buildings and the library to be open. The Duke of Cambridge then called for three cheers for the Prince and Princess, which were given with great heartiness, followed by "one cheer more for the Duke," who has always been a zealous and generous friend of the London Hospital.

DEACONESSES' INSTITUTION AND HOSPITAL AT TOTTENHAM.

May 28th, 1887.

THE object of the Deaconesses' Institution at Tottenham is " the training of Christian women to serve as deaconesses "—that is to say, as sisters trained for working, teaching, and nursing, without being subject to any obligation or vow of celibacy, as is usual in the sisterhoods of Roman Catholic communities. The training of nurses is one of the chief purposes sought, following in this the example of the celebrated institution of Kaiserwerth, where, under Pastor Fliedner, Florence Nightingale and other English as well as German nurses were trained. In fact the full title of the establishment at the Green, Tottenham, is the " Evangelical Protestant Deaconesses' Institution and Training Hospital." The Hospital contains 100 beds for the sick poor, and there are also a few private rooms for paying patients. Thousands of the poor are also attended every year in the neighbourhood.

From the commencement of the work, in 1867, the late Samuel Morley, M.P., took warm interest in it, and at his death two of his sons, Howard and Charles Morley, erected a new wing to the building, as a memorial of their father. It was to open the " Samuel Morley " memorial wing that the Princess of Wales, accompanied by the Prince and their three daughters, visited Tottenham on the 29th of May, 1887. A large number of persons were assembled, including deputations from foreign countries, Pastor Fliedner from Kaiserwerth, Pastor Nehmitz from Berlin, and other Pastors, Lady Superintendents, and Deaconesses from German and Danish institutions.

When the Royal party had been conducted to the marquee where the ceremony was to take place an address was read to the Princess of Wales by Dr. Laseron, the medical director. The Prince, in replying on behalf of the Princess, said :—

" Dr. Laseron, Ladies, and Gentlemen, — The Princess of Wales desires me to express her sincerest thanks for the address which has just been read to her, and to express to all who take an interest in this institution the great pleasure and gratification it affords her to take part in to-day's proceedings. There can be, I am sure, nothing more noble or more praiseworthy than an institution like this, in which women give up their lives to the object of philanthropy in order to heal and mitigate the sufferings of the sick. An institution like the Deaconesses' Institution is one well worthy of the support of all. I am sure that the proceeding of to-day, in opening a fresh wing of this hospital, is a sincere gratification to the Princess, and especially that it should be called after the name of one whom I have had the privilege of knowing, and whom you all knew, at any rate by name, and whose loss we must all deeply deplore—the late Samuel Morley. I am sure no more fitting name could be given to the new wing than that it should be called after him who, with the members of his family—one of whom I am glad to see here to-day—has contributed so much to the prosperity of this institution. In the name of the Princess I beg to express to you the pleasure it gives us to be present here to-day."

Purses were then presented to the Princess by many girls, as gifts to the funds, and Dr. Laseron handed to her Royal Highness a key to unlock the new wing. The Royal party were then conducted to the hall, where the Princess unveiled the "Samuel Morley Tablet," bearing an inscription commemorative of the occasion.

THE FREEMASONS AND THE QUEEN'S JUBILEE.

June 13th, 1887.

HER GRACIOUS MAJESTY being the chief patroness of the Order of Freemasons, and of the Masonic charities, it was deemed fitting that an address should be presented to her on the occasion of her Jubilee. Accordingly, the Prince of Wales, with the Duke of Connaught and Prince Albert Victor, and a vast company of officers and members of the Order, representatives chosen by lodges in different parts of the empire, assembled in the Royal Albert Hall on the 13th of June, 1887. The number present was about 7000. No such scene has been witnessed since that day, twelve years before, when the Prince was installed as Grand Master of English Freemasons. The procession which received the Grand Master and conducted him to the throne was a magnificent affair. The assemblage, we are told, although "tyled," was not held as a lodge. The business of the meeting being opened, his Royal Highness the Grand Master said :—

"Brethren,—This is, I think, one of the greatest gatherings of Freemasons I have ever seen, with the exception of the occasion when, after election by the craft, I received the honour of installation as your Grand Master. It is most gratifying to me, as I feel sure it will be to the Queen, that so large a gathering has assembled here to-day to do her honour on the fiftieth anniversary of her reign—the Jubilee of her accession. This gathering will be a proof to her, as it is also to me, of the great devotion and loyalty of the craft to the Throne—a devotion and loyalty which have ever animated the Free and Accepted Masons of England. We are here, brethren, as you are aware, for the purpose of moving an address to the Queen, congratulating her upon having attained the fiftieth anniversary of her reign. You are well aware that my ancestors—some of them former Sovereigns of this nation—did much in support of Freemasonry, and, though they well knew it to be a secret society, they were well assured that it was in no wise a dangerous one. Among our tenets of motives 'loyalty' and 'philanthropy' stand out prominently, and we are proud of the fact. I assure you, brethren, that it is most gratifying to me to receive so large, important, and influential a gathering as this to-day, and I am rejoiced that in the many events which are to be the signs of the people's rejoicing at the Jubilee of the Queen, this meeting, at the Royal Albert Hall, of the Free and Accepted Masons of England will be first on the list. I will now call upon Grand Secretary, Colonel Shadwell E. Clerke, to read the proposed address, and then our worshipful brother the Earl of Carnarvon will move its adoption."

The Address and the Speech were on the same lines as most of the Jubilee addresses, but of course with special reference to the loyalty and the devotion of Freemasons. The great company having chanted the National Anthem, the ceremony of giving Jubilee honours was performed, among the numerous recipients of which were the Maharajah of Kuch-Behar, the Lord Mayor of London, Sir Francis Knollys, Sir Philip Cunliffe Owen, and Sir Charles Warren.

The Grand Master announced that the amount paid by the members that day amounted to upwards of £6000, the whole of which would go to the Masonic charities for children and the aged, under the rules of the Order.

THE SHAFTESBURY HOUSE.

THE Prince and Princess of Wales, accompanied by Prince George and Princess Louise of Wales, went on the 17th of June, 1887, to lay the foundation stone of a central building for the "National Refuges for Homeless and Destitute Children." There are many institutions in London for similar objects, but this charity is one of old standing, and one of the most important and best. It was established in 1843 under the patronage of Lord Shaftesbury, in Great Queen Street. The income of the Society was only £180 in the first year, and all that could be attempted was to shelter and teach a few poor children in a "Ragged School," open two evenings a week. The efforts of Mr. W. Williams, the Secretary, and zealous coadjutors, were successful in gradually increasing the operations of the Society, till, in the year of the Queen's Jubilee, the Committee had the satisfaction of managing seven industrial homes, in town and country, with more than 1000 children, and two training ships, the *Chichester* and the *Arethusa*, with an annual income of about £20,000. The good work in its various departments continues to prosper. All this and more was stated in an address by the Earl of Jersey, Chairman of the Reception Committee. Among the friends of the Society who had witnessed its progress, and helped it from the beginning, was Mr. John MacGregor, the founder of the Shoe-black Brigade, and the chief helper of the Secretary in bringing the *Chichester* to its high excellence as a training-ship.

The ceremony was performed in a tent erected on the site of the new Home, in Shaftesbury Avenue, close to the once notorious Seven Dials. The building is intended to provide shelter for 100 homeless boys, a home for 35 working lads, a club for "old boys" trained in the institution, and the central offices of the Society. After the address had been read, the Prince of Wales thus spoke :—

"Lord Jersey, Ladies, and Gentlemen,—In thanking you for the address which you have just read, allow me to express to you, and to this great assemblage, the very great gratification it gives both the Princess and myself to be here to-day, to take part in so interesting and what I may also call a most important ceremony. You are well aware of the deep interest and solicitude we take with regard to all classes of the community in this great Metropolis, but we claim that we take especial interest in what concerns the well-being and the welfare of the working classes and of the poor of London. It is therefore a great gratification to us that I should be afforded the opportunity to-day of laying the foundation stone of a home to be called 'The Jubilee Memorial Home,' in commemoration of the fiftieth year of the Queen's reign, and, at the same time, I rejoice to think that this building is to be named 'The Shaftesbury House,' as a memorial of the great and distinguished philanthropist whose loss we must always and shall ever deeply deplore. Most sincerely do we hope that this home may be the means of bringing many of those waifs and strays always existing in so great a metropolis as ours; we trust, too, that they may have such an education and training that, as they grow older, they may be able to go out into the world honest and respectable citizens, and have an opportunity of gaining their livelihood. I thank you again, Lord Jersey, for this address, and assure you that it gives us the greatest pleasure to be here to-day."

The stone was then well and truly laid, and his Royal Highness was presented with the trowel. A paper was laid by the Prince upon the stone, and Lord Jersey announced the gift of £50 from his Royal Highness, £30 from Sir Robert Carden, and other donations. " God bless the Prince of Wales," and the " National Anthem " were then chanted. The Royal party left amidst enthusiastic cheering. A large number of the boys from the country homes were present, and from the training-ships in their sailor costumes.

CONSECRATION OF TRURO CATHEDRAL.

November 3rd, 1887.

THE foundation stone of Truro Cathedral was laid in 1879 by the Prince of Wales, with Masonic ceremony. He was accompanied by the Princess of Wales, Prince Albert Victor, and Prince George. The Prince was again asked to be present at the Consecration, when the building was completed. The ceremony took place on the 3rd of November, 1887. On arriving at the station, the Mayor of Truro presented an Address, to which the Prince thus replied :—

" I thank you for your loyal address and for the kind words with which you receive me on this memorable occasion. It affords me the most unfeigned satisfaction to be able to attend the great religious service which is held here to-day, and to be present at the consummation of the important ceremony in which I took a leading part more than seven years ago. The interest which the Duchess of Cornwall and I have felt in the progress of the work has continued unabated since that period, and she commissions me to assure you how deep is her regret and disappointment that unavoidable causes prevent her from accompanying me to the consecration of the first Protestant cathedral erected in England since St. Paul's in London. I join most heartily in the expression of your hopes that the western part of the building may ere long be completed, and I trust that circumstances will then allow me once more to visit a town which can boast of having been mentioned in Domesday Book 800 years ago. Let me in conclusion, gentlemen, express my warm acknowledgments to you for the loyal and cordial terms in which you allude to the Queen and the Duchess of Cornwall."

The Archbishop of Canterbury, the predecessor of the present Bishop, and a large number of the Episcopal body, with many of the clergy and laity of the diocese, were present in the Cathedral. The service, including the administration of the Holy Communion, occupied nearly four hours. After the service the Prince drove to the Truro Public Rooms, where about four hundred of the principal residents of Cornwall assembled for luncheon, Lord St. Germans, Lord Lieutenant of the County, presiding.

The noble Chairman, after proposing the toast of "The Queen," gave that of "Their Royal Guest," who, he trusted, felt at home in his ancient Duchy. The Prince, in reply, said:—

"Lord Mount-Edgcumbe, Ladies, and Gentlemen,—I am deeply touched by the very kind manner in which this toast has been proposed by our Lord Lieutenant and by the way in which it has been received. Although it has not been my good fortune to come as often to this ancient Duchy as I could have wished, still among the different visits which I have been able to pay you none has given me greater pleasure and satisfaction than that which I am paying at the present moment. You may rest assured that I feel proud of the ancient title that I bear. The interest that I take in the welfare of the county will never be diminished. Seven years and a half ago I was enabled to lay the foundation stone of this cathedral with Masonic honours. To-day I have been present at its consecration. The most interesting service and religious ceremony at which we have assisted to-day are not likely to be forgotten by me, nor by any of you. It is the event of a lifetime, and I congratulate you, the Duchy, the county, and all connected with it, on the erection of so noble an edifice, and I trust that before long we may see the completion of the building. It is a real sorrow to me that the Princess of Wales and some of my children should not have accompanied me on this occasion as they did when the foundation stone was laid. Although they are far away, you may feel sure that they take a great interest in what is being done here to-day. Time is short and we have to leave. If, therefore, the words I have uttered to you to-day are few, you must not question their sincerity and heartiness. I thank you for the kind reception that you always give me when I come among you. Before sitting down I wish to give one toast, which I am sure you will drink with pleasure. It is 'The Health of our Lord Lieutenant.' You know how much is due to him and to your Bishop. I am sure that it is a source of great satisfaction to them to see so many distinguished prelates around them on this great occasion and so large a body of the laity."

The toast was received with enthusiasm, and the company would have remained standing while the air "God bless the Prince of Wales" was being played upon the organ, had not the Prince motioned to them to resume their seats.

NEW COLOURS TO THE OLD 46TH REGIMENT.

November 4th, 1887.

THE visit of the Prince of Wales to the West of England closed with the ceremony of presenting new colours to the 2nd Battalion Duke of Cornwall's Light Infantry at Devonport. On his arrival, an address was presented by the Corporation. The Prince replied:—

"I have had much satisfaction in receiving your address, and I thank you for your kind welcome to a borough in which on more than one occasion I have experienced a very cordial reception. I have a perfect recollection of the circumstances of my departure for Canada to which you allude. It is hardly necessary for me to remind you of the many important events which have occurred in the history of this kingdom, and in my own life, since the day on which I embarked for North America from your port, twenty-seven years ago.   Let me express to you my warm acknowledgments for your gratifying recognition of my earnest endeavours to encourage all undertakings tending to promote the welfare of this great country.   I am well aware that the position which I occupy as the eldest son of the Sovereign entails upon me the performance of duties which it always has been my most earnest desire to fulfil to the utmost of my ability, and I can assure my fellow-countrymen that in the future, as in the past, they will at all times find me anxious to respond to any call which they may make upon me to aid them in the advancement of any object either of charity or of public utility."

The Prince then drove to the Raglan Barracks, where the regiment awaited his arrival.

The usual ceremonies on such occasions were proceeded with, and the old colours, which had been borne by the 46th, or South Devon Regiment, as it was formerly called, through the Crimean War and in Egypt, were taken to the rear to the music of "Auld Lang Syne."   The new colours, after the prayer of consecration by the chaplain of the garrison, were presented to the lieutenants. The Prince then addressed the troops:—

"Colonel Grieve, Officers, Non-Commissioned Officers, and Men of the 2nd Battalion Duke of Cornwall's Light Infantry,— You have conferred a great pleasure and satisfaction upon me in having asked me to give your efficient regiment new colours. I do so with the greatest pleasure, because I know that, in giving these new colours, I intrust them to the care of a regiment which has distinguished itself for many years in every part of the globe, and that they are certain to be in safe hands, and will continue to do honour to their Sovereign and country as heretofore.   I am proud to be associated with your regiment as Honorary Colonel of the 3rd Battalion.   I am aware that, perhaps, the old name of the 46th is more dear to you; but I feel sure that, whether under that name or under the present one, you will continue to bear the high state of efficiency which has always existed ever since the regiment was raised.

Your regiment was raised, as I am aware, in 1741, and you distinguished yourselves in the War of Independence.   In consequence, in 1777, of your Light Company at Dominica having gallantly defended General Wayns, you were awarded the privilege of wearing red feathers, a distinction which you still bear in the shape of red cloth on your helmets, and of which you feel very proud. I am also aware that your regiment served with distinction in the Crimea, and these old colours, which are to be carried by the old regiment no more, were given to you on board ship, prior to landing in the Crimea, and have been used for many years. You have since served in different parts of the Empire, and especially in the recent campaign in Egypt and in the Nile Expedition, under the command of the late gallant and lamented General Earle. There is much more that I could say in connection with your distinguished services, but, owing to the want of time and the unfortunate inclemency of the weather, I do not wish to detain the regiment longer than is necessary on parade. Let me congratulate you, Colonel Grieve, on the smart appearance of your regiment and the admirable way in which they look. I sincerely hope the regiment, as opportunities offer, though I hope they may not, whether in the defensive or offensive, will continue as it always has to distinguish itself. I can congratulate you, Colonel Grieve, upon the honour of commanding so fine and efficient a regiment."

THE GLASGOW EXHIBITION OF 1888.

May 8th, 1888.

ON the 8th of May, 1888, the Exhibition at Glasgow was opened by the Prince and Princess of Wales. There have been many Exhibitions, international and national, since the famous " World's Fair " of 1851, but few of them have surpassed, in variety of interest, that which the Glasgow people have successfully carried out, in the spacious and picturesque building in Kelvin Grove Park. Certainly, not one of the national Exhibitions has offered so wonderful a display of the wealth, enterprise, and versatility in productive industry, of the subjects of the British Crown. There was at Manchester an unrivalled collection of art-treasures, and at other places there have been special features of distinction. But, on the whole, the Exhibition at Glasgow has been one of most varied excellence, worthy of the Queen's Jubilee year, when the preparations were made for it, and worthy of the silver-wedding year of the Prince and Princess, whose presence was welcomed on the opening day.　The experience of other Exhibitions has not been lost, and one of the most interesting portions of the show has been the antiquarian and historical collection displayed in the Old " Bishop's Palace," after the manner of the artificial constructions first made familiar in the streets of " Old London " at South Kensington.

Before opening the Exhibition, the Prince and Princess were received in the Corporation Chambers by the Lord Provost, magistrates, and a distinguished assembly.　An address of welcome was read by Dr. Marwick, the Town Clerk, some of the points of which may be gathered from the reply of the Prince, which was as follows :—

" My Lord Provost and Gentlemen,—I have received your address with feelings of sincere satisfaction, and I thank you on behalf of the Princess of Wales and myself for your cordial words of welcome and your kind reference to our Silver Wedding. We have come here to-day to celebrate, in one of the most prosperous cities of the United Kingdom, the inauguration of a great national work of the highest and most varied interest, and one altogether worthy of your important city.　I can assure you I thoroughly understand and appreciate the anxious desire which has prevailed among you that an Industrial Exhibition should be held this year in Glasgow, and I consider that with the commercial, manufacturing, and mercantile eminence which she enjoys, such a desire is not only right and proper in the highest degree, but natural and commendable.　We warmly sympathise with you in this feeling, and I would that my lamented father were alive now to witness the development of the general idea of which he was the originator.　The relations of this city with all the markets of the civilised world have long been well known, but they have been immensely extended during the present century by the energy and enterprise of those merchants and citizens, who, by deepening the Clyde and providing the extensive harbour and dock accommodation which now exists, have overcome the natural disadvantages of its position, and given it a permanent place among the shipping ports and commercial centres of the Kingdom.　Let me, my Lord Provost and Gentlemen, sincerely thank you for the loyal terms in which you alluded to the Queen.　I shall have much pleasure in communicating to Her Majesty the hope that you have expressed that she will visit your magnificent Exhibition, and I will not fail to acquaint her likewise with your words of devotion to her throne and person."

The Royal party left the Council Chamber for the Lord Provost's residence, where they partook of luncheon. After the luncheon the Royal party passed under a triumphal arch at the West-end Park main entrance, and over the Prince of Wales Bridge, opposite the Exhibition gate. Sir Archibald Campbell, President of the Executive Committee, here met the Prince, and a number of gentlemen who have been instrumental in promoting the Exhibition were introduced to his Royal Highness. Sir A. Campbell handed to the Prince a gold key, and his Royal Highness, amidst cheers, opened the east door of the vestibule, and entered the Exhibition. The Prince and Princess walked to the front of the platform of the Grand Hall, the Glasgow Choral Union meanwhile singing the National Anthem, and the Artillery on the neighbouring heights firing a salute of twenty-one guns. After their Royal Highnesses were seated and prayers had been read by the Rev. Dr. D. M'Leod, Sir A. Campbell presented an address.

The Prince of Wales, accepting the address, said :—

" Sir Archibald Campbell, my Lords and Gentlemen,—I thank you for your address, and I can assure you that it affords the Princess of Wales and myself very sincere pleasure to be present on this important occasion. That gratification is increased by the sense of the connection which you have recognised as existing between this International Exhibition and that in which my revered father took so deep an interest and so active a part. The various Exhibitions which have been held since 1851 have undoubtedly done much, not only to enlist the sympathy of the nations of the world and to engage them in friendly rivalries of industrial competition, but largely to extend our knowledge of every branch of manufacture, and to afford pleasure to all ranks and classes of society in every country in which these Exhibitions have been held. Recognising the benefits which they have thus conferred, such Exhibitions can never fail to enlist the sympathy of the Queen and command the support of the Princess and myself. We are here to-day to give personal testimony to that feeling, and to express our satisfaction not only with the public spirit with which the undertaking has been supported financially, but with the enthusiasm with which exhibitors from all parts of the world have enriched the collections of science, art, and industry gathered within these buildings.

"Nor is it possible to overlook the special appropriateness of such an Exhibition in this city, in which the researches and discoveries of Black, of Watt, and, in our own day, of Thomson, have been productive of world-wide benefits to mankind. In the application of science also, Glasgow can point with just pride to Bell, whose 'Comet' is still preserved as a memorial of the first attempt to apply the forces of steam to the propulsion of ships, and to the multifarious industries which have here found a home. To the widely different character of these industries, which secure to the population of this district immunity from many of the risks which necessarily attend devotion to one special department of labour, it is only possible to allude in general terms. Here there exist and flourish side by side great establishments for shipbuilding, the production of marine machinery, locomotives, mill machinery, and mechanical appliances for the working of iron and coal for the production of mineral oil, the manufacture of thread, glass, and pottery, carpet-weaving, dyeing and printing. It must not likewise be overlooked that Glasgow was the cradle of the steam-carrying trade with America and the great mercantile centres of the world. It is gratifying to me to learn that, in the comprehensive collection to be found here, due regard has been paid to the exhibition of works of art, and that the walls of your galleries are enriched by many and valuable paintings and works of sculpture. Here, as in the Exhibition at Manchester, are to be found evidences of the fact that the successful prosecution of trade, manufacture, and commerce afford not only the means of gratifying, but of developing the taste for art.

"Not the least interesting of all is the section in which an honourable place has been given to the works of artisan exhibitors. In every industrial community, and nowhere more so than in Glasgow, the development of the taste, skill, and handicraft of its operatives must always command a respectful consideration and interest. To the Women's Industry Section we shall also look with special sympathy, recognising the importance of encouraging every means by which women's work may be made productive.

"It is also a gratification to us to observe that the artistic building in which the Exhibition is contained occupies an appropriate position within, I may almost say, the shadow of the University of Glasgow, the second in antiquity of the old Universities of Scotland. The site of the University is no doubt modern; but it is satisfactory to see the Institution which was founded through the influence of King James II. in 1450 in a more flourishing state at present than at any previous period of its history. It only remains now for the Princess and myself to express our earnest hope that this great Exhibition may prove an immense success, and that the thousands who, we trust, will visit it may derive such instruction from an examination of its various sections as will prove of material advantage to them for years to come."

After an Inauguration Ode had been sung, the Prince declared the Exhibition open, amid much enthusiasm. The Hallelujah Chorus was then given by the choir. The Royal party spent considerable time in inspecting various parts of the Exhibition, the Princess being specially interested in the " Women's Industries " Section; after which they returned to the Central Railway Station, *en route* to Hamilton Palace.

On the same day, May 8, the Queen, accompanied by the Princess Christian, and other members of the Royal family, honoured by her presence the performance of Sir Arthur Sullivan's *Golden Legend*, given by command at the Royal Albert Hall. Later in the year, on the 22nd August, she gratified the citizens of Glasgow by visiting the Exhibition. in response to the loyal invitation from the Corporation and the Committee given to the Prince on the opening day. The Queen honoured Sir Archibald Campbell, of Blythswood, Chairman of the Committee, by being his guest on that occasion. The opportunity of this Royal visit was taken for opening the new municipal buildings in George Square. It was nearly forty years since Her Majesty, along with the lamented Prince Consort, had visited the western capital of Scotland. No city in her Majesty's dominions has made more wonderful progress than Glasgow, or made more eager use of its natural advantages. The visit of the Prince of Wales at the opening of the Exhibition, and the subsequent visit of the Queen will make the year 1888 ever memorable in the annals of Glasgow.

SIR BARTLE FRERE'S STATUE.

June 5th, 1888.

AMONG the memorials of illustrious men in the gardens of the Thames Embankment, no one will be honoured more than the statue to Sir Bartle Frere. It was erected by public subscription, in memory of his private virtues and of his public services. The grand bronze figure of the patriotic Englishman is much admired. The likeness is good, and the whole monument, with its pedestal of Cornish granite, imposing. Many distinguished men were present to witness the unveiling of the statue by the Prince of Wales on the 5th of June, 1888. He was accompanied by the Princess, and their two daughters, the Princesses Maud and Victoria. Among the company were the Duke of Cambridge, the Archbishop of Canterbury, Lord Napier of Magdala, and Sir Richard Temple, M.P., who asked the Prince of Wales to perform the ceremony. The Prince said :—

"Sir Richard Temple, Ladies, and Gentlemen,—It gave me great pleasure, after the lamented death of Sir Bartle Frere, to accept the post of President of the Committee, especially when we found that a Memorial like this statue was to be erected to the memory of a great and valued public servant of the Crown, and at the same time to a highly esteemed and dear friend of myself." His Royal Highness then briefly recounted the chief points in Sir Bartle Frere's long and distinguished career in India and Africa, a career with which all present were doubtless acquainted. Continuing, His Royal Highness remarked :— "For his services in India, whither he first went in the year 1834, in the service of the East India Company, Sir Bartle Frere twice received the thanks of both Houses of Parliament. On his return home he successfully conducted negotiations with the Sultan of Zanzibar for the suppression of the slave trade, and, later, I had the good fortune to have his services during my journey to India in 1876. The last, but no means the least, important of Sir Bartle Frere's duties was as Governor-General of the Cape of Good Hope and Lord High Commissioner to South Africa. There is much more that I might say, but the facts are known to history, and I will, therefore, in conclusion, merely express my thanks for having been asked to perform this ceremony, and remind those present that, on this very day four years ago, when the late Sir Bartle Frere was laid to his rest, the procession passed by the spot where the statue now stands."

NEW GYMNASIUM IN LONG ACRE.

July 6th, 1888.

THE Prince of Wales, accompanied by Prince Albert Victor, opened the new gymnasium connected with the Central Young Men's Christian Association, on the 6th of July, 1888. The gymnasium is in Long Acre, in what was formerly the Queen's Theatre. The King of Sweden and Norway, Lord Aberdeen, President of the Gymnastic Club, Mr. J. Herbert Tritton, President of the Young Men's Christian Association, Lord Charles Beresford, Lord Kinnaird, the Earl of Meath, the Bishop of London, Lord Brassey, Lord Harris, and other distinguished persons were present. The Bishop of London offered a dedicatory prayer. The Earl of Aberdeen read an address, in which it was stated that the Young Men's Christian Association, which had its head-quarters at Exeter Hall, was founded forty-four years ago, and had at the present time nearly 4000 affiliated branches scattered throughout the Colonies and the civilised world (seventy-seven of which are in London), with an aggregate membership of 250,000. It formed a rendezvous for young men, and a centre for the development of a strong, healthy, religious life among them. In recent years the value of athletics had been more fully recognised, and the Committee of the Central Association had availed themselves of that valuable adjunct in the work. The Exeter Hall Gymnasium Team having won (in open competition) the 200-guinea Challenge Shield and Gold Medals offered by the National Physical Recreation Society, it would be deemed a circumstance of the utmost honour by the recipients to have received their medals at the hands of the Prince of Wales. Moreover, the Gymnasium was able to supply voluntary teachers who instructed children and others of the poorer classes in the exercises which they had acquired in that place.

The Prince of Wales said :—

" Your Majesty, Lord Aberdeen, my Lords, Ladies, and Gentlemen,—I am most grateful to you, indeed, Lord Aberdeen, for the address which you have just read to me. I can assure you all that by coming here I receive very great satisfaction, and I am glad to take part in a work in which so many of you are interested. From the account you, Lord Aberdeen, have given us of the Young Men's Christian Association, I have little doubt but that it is an association founded upon excellent and practical principles, and that it is an association likely not only long to continue in existence, but likely to be greatly augmented in its usefulness, as well as in the numbers benefited by it. I am glad that you combine with Christian education healthy recreation, which must, no doubt, tend to be of the greatest benefit to the community at large, and especially to young men who are exposed to so many temptations in a great city like this. It is a great advantage to all young men to have the opportunity of enjoying healthy and useful recreation. Thank you for asking me to take part in the proceedings of the day. And we must all tender our thanks to the King of Sweden and Norway for coming here to-day, knowing, as we all do, how deeply interested his Majesty must be in work of this kind, and of the important part drill has played amongst his people. I have now great pleasure in declaring this gymnasium open."

Mr. Herbert Gladstone, M.P., President of the National Physical Recreation Society, informed the King and Prince that the 200-guinea challenge shield offered by that Society had this year been won by the team of eight sent from Exeter Hall Club to the contest in Dundee, and he asked the Prince of Wales to do them the honour of presenting the shield and gold medals to the winners. Thereupon Mr. E. Sully, the instructor, at the head of the victorious team, advanced up the room, and, after receiving a gold medal each from the Prince, they shouldered the handsome and massive shield, and, at a run, raced away with the trophy.

Then followed an exhibition of drill by thirty members chosen out of 400 members of the Club. These were clad in flannels, and wore red or black stockings. They went through an exposition of musical drill, accompanied by the piano, the exercises consisting of those with dumb-bells, clubs, and bars, Mr. Sully giving the word of command. Occasionally the athletes sang as they drilled, at other moments they whistled as they swung their clubs or poles about.

At the close of the exercises the King rose and said :—" Your Royal Highnesses, I cannot leave this hall without expressing the satisfaction I have had in witnessing the exercises here. I wish also to add my good wishes for the progress and prosperity of this Association. I feel great satisfaction in witnessing the execution of the gymnastic exercises this morning—exercises which are very highly appreciated in my country."

z 2

The Prince of Wales summoned Mr. Sully, shook hands with him, and congratulated him upon the admirable display made by his pupils.   The King of Sweden did the same, very highly praising the manner in which the drill had been executed.

The Prince of Wales, Prince Albert Victor, and the King of Sweden then left the hall amid the cheers of those assembled. The heartiness with which the Prince spoke, and the interest which he showed in the whole proceedings, greatly delighted all who were present.

THE ROYAL MASONIC INSTITUTE FOR GIRLS.

July 6th, 1888.

THE centenary festival of the Royal Masonic Institute for Girls was held on the 6th of July, 1888, in the Royal Albert Hall, the Prince of Wales, Grand Master, presiding.   Between two and three thousand members of the Craft were present, amongst them being the King of Sweden and Norway, Prince Albert Victor, the Earl of Carnarvon, the Earl of Lathom, the Earl of Zetland, Lord Egerton of Tatton, Lord Leigh, and many other eminent Masons.   The galleries were filled by a large number of ladies.

After dinner, the Prince of Wales gave the first toast, which was that of " The Queen and the Craft," and was received with the greatest enthusiasm, the whole of the vast audience rising and joining in singing the National Anthem.

The Prince of Wales then said :—

" Your Majesty and Brethren,—A very high honour and a very high compliment has been conferred upon us this night. At this great and important gathering, probably the largest meeting for a charitable object that has ever taken place anywhere, we have as our guest his Majesty the King of Sweden. I little doubted the manner in which you would receive this toast, because not only are we honouring a distinguished guest, but also a brave ally of ours, and we are further honouring the Grand Master of the Freemasons of Sweden.   We all know the deep interest which his Majesty takes in our Craft, and what excellent Masons the Swedes are.   In proposing this toast it is specially gratifying to me, for I have looked forward to this occasion for many years, because it was through the King and his late brother that, twenty years ago, I was initiated into the mysteries of the Craft, and I am proud to be one of you, and, still more, to be at your head. I am grateful to the King for having made me one of us. Brethren, I know you will drink this toast with cordiality, and at the same time I feel that it will be right to give this toast Masonically, for in doing so we do honour to our guest and to ourselves."

The toast was drunk with Masonic honours.

The King of Sweden, who was loudly cheered on rising, said :—
" Most Worshipful Grand Master and Brethren,—The toast I have the honour of replying to I acknowledge, not only on my own behalf, but on behalf of all the foreign Lodges and Masonic congregations whose principles and constitution are in conformity with yours. On their behalf I would also express the great satisfaction I feel at the honour and distinction to-day conferred upon me by your Grand Master and by you in constituting me a member of your honoured body. I feel much satisfaction in being present at such an enormous gathering as this, and one assembled for purposes of so noble a kind. Patriotic feelings are always noble and honourable, and nowhere have they taken deeper root than in this country, for whose people, ever since my young days, I have felt the most profound esteem. But there is one feeling still more noble than patriotism, and that is the feeling which has its foundation in the Word of God, and unites us in love and charity to mankind. As we sing at Masonic gatherings in my own country, ' There is one God, our Father, so be His sons then, brethren.' This is the bond which exists between us, the rallying cry which unites us, and the lasting tie which binds us. I have the greatest pleasure in giving you ' The Health of our Grand Master, the Prince of Wales.' "

The toast was drunk with full Masonic honours. The Prince of Wales, in reply, said :—

" Your Majesty and Brethren,—You are well aware that during the fourteen years I have held the high office of Grand Master I have striven not to be unmindful of your interests and of those of the Craft, and, though I am prevented by my many duties from meeting you as often as I should like, still I hope that you are convinced that your interests are none the less dear to me. We have heard an address from the King of Sweden this evening which none of us are likely to forget, and I think, if he will allow me to say so, that we Englishmen have reason to envy his facility in speaking our language. It is, I believe, the first time that a foreign Sovereign has honoured a gathering of this kind. I think that we may look upon this as a red-letter day, and we are not likely to forget the King's presence, or the kind and useful words which he has spoken. Our watchword, 'Religion and Charity,' is one which has been inculcated in us ever since we belonged to the Craft, and it is one which we shall do well to remember. If we uphold those principles, and, above all, that idea of patriotism of which the King has spoken, there is little doubt that the Craft will remain as prosperous as it is now, and that our lodges and members will increase. I do not wish to allude to foreign lodges with whom we are not in accord; but I would ask that at any rate we should strive to pick out what is good in them, and remember that we are not only English Freemasons, but Freemasons of the entire universe. I trust that as long as I live, or as long as I may be permitted to hold the high office of your Grand Master, I may continue to do my duty to the Craft and to my country. I wish now to ask his Majesty the King of Sweden to accept the Steward's badge of this festival."

His Majesty was then invested with the badge, amidst loud cheers. The Grand Master then said he had much pleasure in reading a telegram from New York to the following effect:— " Grand Lodge in annual communication congratulates the fraternity in England on the one-hundredth anniversary of the foundation of the Royal Masonic Institute for Girls."

Again rising, the Prince of Wales said :—

" Your Majesty and Brethren,—I have now the honour to give you the last toast, though it may be safely called the most important, as the object with which we have met at this enormous and unprecedented gathering is to celebrate the centenary of the Royal Masonic Institute for Girls. That an institution should have existed a hundred years is one proof that it is a good one, and we have every reason to be grateful to those who, from the commencement up to the present time, have given their energy and their labours to keep going so thoroughly Masonic an Institution.

" As you are aware, the Institution was founded by the Chevalier Ruspini. King George IV. and King William IV. were patrons, besides many members of the Royal Family, and Her Majesty the Queen is patroness now. The school at first contained only fifteen children; it now contains 243, and they are educated up to a high religious standard, combined with education of a general character, including music. Particular attention is paid to needlework and cooking and domestic duties. Only a few days ago I was present here and saw the girls go through their marching exercise, and I never saw anything more satisfactory. There are many commanding officers who would be proud to see their men march and go through their exercise as we saw them performed. I may state the system was established by Miss Davis, who was appointed head governess in 1861, and I am glad to think that at this moment she retains her post. She has been eminently successful, as is manifest by the Cambridge Local, College of Preceptors, and the Science and Art Examinations. It is also satisfactory to notice that, with the exception of Miss Davis, every member of the staff has been educated at the Institution. The Head Governess of the Female Masonic School at Dublin and the Head Governess of the British Orphan Asylum were educated at our school, and during a period of eighty-four years there have been but two matrons, one of whom held the appointment over fifty-two years.

"As you are aware, the object we have in view in meeting here to-night is to make important additions to the present buildings, and provide accommodation for an increased number of children. These additions will cost at least £20,000. In 1838, on the occasion of the jubilee of the Institution, £1000 was subscribed at the annual festival, and in 1871, when I had the honour of presiding, as much as £5200 was collected. But I have now an announcement to make which I think will interest you beyond measure, and that is that I have received the assurance of the Secretary that we have obtained at this centenary festival over £50,000. I may safely challenge anybody to dispute the statement that so large a sum has never been subscribed at a charity dinner. It now affords me great pleasure to propose 'Success to the Institution,' coupled with the name of the Deputy Grand Master, the Earl of Lathom, Chairman of the Executive Committee, and an old and personal friend of my own."

The Earl of Lathom replied, and the proceedings terminated. The grand total of the subscription was £50,472, of which London contributed £22,454, and the Provinces, India, and the Colonies £28,018.

WEST NORFOLK HUNT.

April 9th, 1888.

AMONG the many memorial gifts of the Silver Wedding of the Prince and Princess of Wales was one which would have delighted Sir Roger de Coverley or the Squire of Bracebridge Hall.   The members of the West Norfolk Fox Hunt presented a handsome silver figure of Reynard in full gallop, mounted on a dark mahogany stand.   A beautifully bound morocco album contained the names of the subscribers.   The presentation was made on the 8th of April, the day of the Annual Steeplechase at East Winch, near Lynn.   A marquee had been erected, and a large company assembled.   The Prince and Princess of Wales and all the family were present.

Mr. Hamond, for many years Master of the Hunt, made the presentation, he having been the Chairman of the Committee who had carried on the Hunt during the past two years, in the temporary absence of the Master, Mr. A. C. Fountaine.   He believed that the West Norfolk were the first pack of hounds that the Princess hunted with when she came to England.   The Prince and Princess had entered into the sports and recreations of all classes of Her Majesty's subjects, and the sport which the members of the Hunt had enjoyed with their Royal Highnesses and their sons and daughters would long be remembered.   He asked the acceptance of their gift by the Prince and Princess.

The Prince of Wales said :—

"Mr. Hamond, Ladies, and Gentlemen,—I can assure you that no present which has been offered for our acceptance has been received by us with more pleasure than the one which you have given us to-day—a model of the wily animal that we are all so fond of following.   Norfolk has always been considered to be a shooting county; that may be so to a great extent, but I feel convinced that the hunting is quite as popular, and I sincerely hope that it will long remain so.   There may be difficulties in preserving foxes, but I feel sure that where there's a will there's a way.   For twenty-five years we have enjoyed hunting with the West Norfolk Hunt—both the Princess and myself; and our children have been brought up to follow that Hunt.   I sincerely hope that for many long years we may be able to continue to do so.   We have grateful memories of the mastership of one whose loss we all regretted, the late Mr. Villebois, and also of Mr. Hamond, then Mr. Fountaine, and next of the gentlemen of the Committee who have of late ably carried on the Hunt, whilst Mr. Fountaine was unfortunately away. Most sincerely do I thank you again, in the name of the Princess and myself, for the kind terms in which you have presented us with this handsome and appropriate gift, and most sincerely do I wish prosperity to the West Norfolk Foxhounds, which, I trust, may long continue to exist in this county."

AT BLACKBURN.

May 9th, 1888.

On the return from opening the Exhibition at Glasgow, it was arranged that the Prince and Princess of Wales should visit Blackburn, for laying the foundation-stone of the new Technical and Trades School in that flourishing Lancashire town. The borough was in high festival, the more so as it was the first time on record that it had been honoured with the presence of royalty. At the entrance of the town, the Mayor and Corporation met the Royal party, and conducted them to the marquee which was to be the scene of the ceremony. Here the Prince was presented with the freedom of the borough—being the first honorary freeman—and with an address, to which he replied :—

"Mr. Mayor and Gentlemen,—I can assure you that the Princess of Wales and myself feel very great pleasure in accepting your address, and we thank you warmly for the kind and cordial words of welcome with which you have received us on the occasion of our first visit to the important borough of Blackburn. We thank you most sincerely for your congratulations on our Silver Wedding, and we desire to take this opportunity of publicly stating how infinitely we have been touched by the affectionate tokens of attachment and regard which have universally been shown towards us throughout the whole country on the occasion of that event. We appreciate very highly your allusions to the interest which we take in all things related to the progress and welfare of the kingdom, and more especially to the interest we have taken in the subject of technical education; and I rejoice, therefore, to find that I am able to come here to-day to lay the foundation-stone of an institution which I trust will afford material assistance in maintaining and ad-

vancing the industries and commercial enterprise of your town.
I have very much gratification in complying with your request
that I would accept the honorary freedom of your borough, and
I shall experience a feeling of pride in signing my name as the
first honorary freeman of a town so loyal and prosperous, and
that, I am persuaded, has so great a future before it as Blackburn."

To another address by the Freemasons of Blackburn the Grand
Master expressed his sense of the compliment paid him by their
words of fraternal friendship, and gladly acceded to the wish that the
first stone of so important and useful an institution should be laid
with Masonic honours,—which was done accordingly.

The Mayoress of Blackburn then, on behalf of the ladies of
Blackburn, presented the Princess of Wales with a magnificent
diamond brooch representing Industry. Her Royal Highness said
a few happy words in acknowledgment. The Prince, it should
have been mentioned, received the roll of freedom enclosed in a
very handsome gold casket. The Royal visitors were afterwards
entertained at luncheon in the Town Hall, where numerous guests
were present. In responding to the loyal toasts the Prince said:—

" You may be assured that we are not likely to forget our
visit to Blackburn. The cordial and enthusiastic manner in
which you have received us, the beautiful way in which your
streets and houses have been decorated, and the wonderful order
that was kept throughout will not be forgotten by us. It will
afford me, also, great gratification and pleasure to acquaint the
Queen with the loyalty which has been shown to the Princess
and myself, who are the first members of the Royal families of
England who have visited your borough. The objects we have
had in view in coming here are, we are sure, excellent ones;
and we rejoice that there has been afforded to us the opportunity of laying the foundation-stone of an institution which is
likely to do so much good. As the Mayor has said, I do take a
sincere interest in all that concerns technical instruction, because I feel convinced that, in a vast country like ours, where
so many trades and different manufactures exist, nothing is of
such great importance to the well-being of its manufactures and
trades as a good sound technical education. We cannot erect
too many schools or institutions of the kind in the various parts
of the country. The school the foundation-stone of which we
have laid to-day has been properly started as a remembrance of

the Queen's Jubilee, and, as the special object of it is for the technical education of the operative classes, I sincerely hope that they also will show that they take a great interest in it, and will thoroughly support it. I am glad to hear that there is already existing in this borough a Technical and Art School, which for two years has been in existence. I am told that there are as many as 300 students, and those students who have gone up to London to be examined by the Technical Institute have, I understand, passed the very highest and best examinations. The interest which this town takes in the subject of technical education is a very gratifying one. You must remember that improved talent for the production of more varied and artistic designs in the staple manufacture is essential for the continued prosperity of the town, and the more artisans learn what is necessary to beautify the trade to which they belong, and vary the different specimens which they bring forward, the more likely the town is to flourish. Before sitting down I have a toast to propose to you, ' The Mayor and Corporation of Blackburn, and success to the Blackburn Technical School.' In proposing this toast I am glad to have this opportunity of thanking the Mayor for his kind hospitality and the cordial welcome he has afforded us. He may be assured we shall never forget the kind reception we have received at Blackburn."

The Mayor briefly responded to the toast. The Royal party afterwards proceeded to the Blackburn Railway Station, and left for London.

THE ANGLO-DANISH EXHIBITION.

May 14th, 1888.

THE Anglo-Danish Exhibition at South Kensington had not the official origin of some other similar displays, but the nationality of the scheme, and the promise of its proceeds being applied to a charitable object, secured the patronage of the Prince and Princess of Wales at its opening. This ceremony took place in the Albert Hall, on the 14th of May, 1888.

Their Royal Highnesses were accompanied by the Princesses Louise, Maud, and Victoria of Wales, the Princess Mary of Cambridge and her daughter the Princess Victoria, Prince Karl of

Denmark, Prince George of Greece, the Danish Minister, and many distinguished persons. They were received by Lord Amherst, Chairman of the Committee, who presented an address, to which—after the musical and other ceremonies, and the formal opening of the Exhibition by the Princess of Wales—the Prince replied :—

"Lord Amherst, Ladies, and Gentlemen,—In your address you have expressed the hope that the Exhibition will be a success. We most sincerely hope it will be a success in every sense of the word. The objects, as you are well aware, are, first, to pay a compliment to us in respect of the twenty-fifth anniversary of our wedding-day; and, secondly, to aid an institution which is much in need of funds, and one which is most meritorious and useful. You are anxious that money should be obtained in order to build a new Home for Incurables. Very appropriately this Exhibition has been connected with the institution which was the first with which the Princess became connected when she came to this country. I sincerely hope that the endeavours you have made will be successful, and that the Exhibition will be instructive, agreeable, and useful. It must be gratifying to you to see that the King of Denmark has sent over one of his war ships, manned by all those fine young men who are around us, and it is gratifying to all of us, I am sure, to welcome these ladies whose costumes lend such picturesqueness to the scene. We thank you for your very kind reception of us, and I can only assure you that it has given us the greatest pleasure to take part in this very interesting ceremony, and that we wish the Exhibition the most thorough success."

In the evening, the Duke of Cambridge presided at a special festival, in aid of rebuilding the British Home for Incurables at Clapham, which was held in the Conservatory of the Anglo-Danish Exhibition. There was a numerous attendance, and the donations to the building fund amounted to nearly £5000. This Institution, founded in 1861, provides home with every comfort for hopelessly incurable sufferers (except the idiotic, insane, and the blind, for whom there are other asylums), and also gives pensions to out-patients of £20 per annum.

GREAT NORTHERN HOSPITAL, HOLLOWAY ROAD.

July 17th, 1888.

THE Prince of Wales performed the ceremony of opening the new buildings of the Great Northern Hospital, at Islington, on the 17th of July, 1888. He was accompanied by the Princess of Wales, and by the Princesses Louise, Victoria, and Maude. The event caused much interest in the northern part of London, and vast crowds filled the streets and roads. The Rev. W. H. Barlow, Vicar of Islington, and many of the clergy, Mr. Murdoch, M.P., Chairman of the Hospital, and other official persons, received the Royal visitors in a gaily decorated tent. Their Royal Highnesses, however, were attired in deep mourning, on account of the death of the Emperor Frederick of Germany. An address was read, in which it was stated that Islington is the largest parish in England in population. At the beginning of the reign of the Queen it had 40,000 inhabitants, now it has 320,000. The Great Northern Hospital was established in 1857, but in 1882 it was resolved to erect a building more suitable for the increased population. The wish was to make the new hospital a thanksgiving memorial of the Jubilee year.

The Prince of Wales, in replying to the address, said :—

"Ladies and Gentlemen,—I am most anxious, in my own name, and also in that of the Princess, to acknowledge the most cordial and kind words of the address which we have just heard read by the Vestry Clerk, and also for the kind expressions which have fallen from Mr. Murdoch. We are very glad to be able to take part in so interesting a ceremony as this, and we are glad to think that in so large and ever-increasing a population as this in the North of London is, the project of commemorating the Queen's Jubilee should have been so appropriately celebrated by the building of a hospital. We shall shortly have an opportunity of visiting the wards, and I have little doubt that we shall find everything in the most admirable and efficient state. Amongst the many duties we have to perform, none, I assure you, ladies and gentlemen, gives us greater gratification and pleasure than such a function as this, where we come to give our assistance and support to a philanthropic object, and to a cause the object of which is to alleviate the sufferings of our fellow-creatures. I can only express the pleasure it has given us to have it in our power to open this hospital to-day. You are well aware how much we regretted that it was not in our power to come here and open the hospital on the date originally fixed. You are also aware of the cause, and I well know how much you all sympathise with us and the other members of our family in our sorrow and grief. I am glad to have the opportunity of saying, on this public occasion, that my sister has felt deeply that, although thirty years have elapsed since she left this country, her compatriots have not forgotten her, and that they have sympathised with her, that they have felt for her, in the great and overwhelming sorrow which it has pleased God to inflict upon her. I beg to thank you once more for your kind reception of us to-day, and again to assure you of the sincere gratification it has given us to be present.

The Prince resumed his seat amidst loud cheers, and a number of children and young ladies then presented purses to the Princess, the names of the donors being announced by the Secretary. The total of these subscriptions was £1050. This ceremony being finished, their Royal Highnesses left the pavilion to visit the hospital.

The opening of the new Northern Hospital in London was the last public function performed by the Prince of Wales before his autumn visit to Austria and other regions of Southern Europe. With it our record of his presence at charitable institutions must close. It has been necessary to make only a selection of his speeches on such occasions. The Hospital for Sick Children, the Chelsea Hospital for Women, Queen Charlotte's Lying-in Hospital, Hospital for Diseases of the Chest, the Holloway Sanatorium at Virginia Water, the Cottage Homes at Weybridge, St. Mary's Hospital, University and King's College Hospitals, the Fever Hospital; these, and many other institutions for the help of the poor or the suffering, have had the advantage of the Prince's advocacy.

There have been also many occasions where he has assisted by his presence or his voice other institutions for educational and philanthropic objects, such as the Marine Society's ship " Warspite," and the training-ship " Worcester," the Windsor and Eton Albert Institute, the Church for the Deaf and Dumb, the Dwelling Houses for working people in Soho, the Alexandra Home at Kensington for pupils at the Schools of Art and Music; besides more important educational and charitable establishments, such as the St. Anne's Schools at Redhill, for children of the Clergy, and of others whose means are not equal to their position in life. To have given an account of the proceedings, and reports of the speeches on all these occasions would have required the space of two volumes instead of one.

For the same reason it is with regret that the Editor has to omit descriptions of many important and interesting functions both in the Metropolis and throughout the country. The truth is there are few parts of England, certainly few of the great centres of population and industry, which have not been visited by the Prince, generally accompanied by the Princess of Wales, for some purpose of local and often of national utility. Now it is at Birmingham, to open a new Hospital or an Art Gallery. Now it is at Sheffield to open the Park, which was the munificent gift of its Mayor, Mark Firth. Now it is at York, for opening the New Institute. Now it is at Leeds, for inaugurating the Art Exhibition; and at Leeds the Prince addressed an audience which included the Lord Mayors of London and York, and the Mayors of almost every town in Yorkshire, in the Town Hall, opened many years before by the Queen and the Prince Consort. Another year there was a Royal visit to Lancashire, where a new Infirmary was opened at Wigan, an institution praised by the Prince as due as much to the gifts of the working classes as to the liberality of the employers of labour in that great mining district. At Bolton, for the first time in its history honoured by a Royal visit, the Prince opened the Town Hall, one of the finest edifices of the kind in the provinces. At Hull the new Albert Dock was opened, and new docks at Grimsby. Another time the Prince is among the agricultural people, at Dorchester for a Cattle Show, or at Hunstanton for opening a Convalescent Hospital. Or he is at Newcastle, opening the Coble Dene Dock for the Tyne Commission. Or he is at Southampton laying the foundation-stone of a new church for Canon Wilberforce. Another time he is at Worcester, admiring with the Princess of Wales the splendid Porcelain Works, as well as the Cathedral and antiquities of the loyal city. Many other expeditions have been made during these twenty-five years, and it is noteworthy that in places supposed to be the most democratic and independent, as Birmingham and at Sheffield, the reception of the Royal visitors was the most hearty and enthusiastic. Opening the Victoria Hall at Ealing on December the 15th was the occasion of the latest public appearance in 1888. It adjoins the Parish building, and the Free Library, to which the Prince alluded in his brief speech.

Reference has not been made to occasions of a private kind, such as Regimental and Club Dinners, where the presence of the Prince is always welcomed, and what he says is remembered, though not reported. Perhaps it is right to mention the Savage Club, of which many Press reporters are members, and where the Prince made one of his genial addresses, and drew from the Club very acceptable aid towards founding the Musical Scholarships in which he was then interested.

Any one who could see the engagement book of the Prince of Wales during a season would think there is little exaggeration when it is said he is one of the most busy and hard-working of public men. If it cannot be said *nulla dies sine lineâ*, there are few days on which some important business has not to be attended to, besides his personal or private affairs in town and country. In one of his early addresses, he said that, being excluded by his position from taking active part in political life, he would devote his time to "duties connected with works of charity and of public utility." How far this resolution has been carried out, the readers of this volume have the means of judging.

In many of his speeches the Prince has, in grateful and touching terms, referred to the useful and beneficent services rendered by his revered and lamented father, whose example he desires to follow. That example also influenced the character and the life of the late Emperor of Germany, "Frederick the Noble." In the introduction to the brief biographical memoir of 'Frederick, Crown Prince and Emperor,' recently published by Mr. Rennell Rodd, the widowed Empress—our own Princess Royal—expresses a hope that the book will make his name better known to the English public, and give him a place in their affections beside that of her father, the Prince Consort, "for whom he had so great love, admiration, and veneration." The words of Lord Tennyson are thus recalled with new power:—

> "Dear to thy land and ours; a Prince indeed
> Beyond all titles, and a household name
> Hereafter through all times—ALBERT THE GOOD."

SPEECHES AT ROYAL ACADEMY BANQUETS.

2 A

THE first appearance of the Prince of Wales at the annual dinner of the Royal Academy, with the short speech made on the occasion, has been given under the date, May 4th, 1863. In many subsequent years the Prince has been a welcome and honoured guest, and has been called to address the company. Instead of giving these speeches in the years when they were delivered, it seems better to group them together. The guests at the banquet are in the main the same year by year. After the Royal and official personages, and notable public men always present, and the Academicians and their friends, there remains not much room for variety in the invitations. If any very distinguished stranger is in London at the time, or some hero of the day, he is pretty certain to be invited, and the speech of such a guest is a distinctive feature in the yearly record of the banquets. There is also effort made to secure some eloquent speakers to reply to some of the toasts given from the Chair. But on the whole there is considerable sameness in the reports, the same toasts being always given, and often the same speakers responding. The Prince of Wales has been more than once complimented for his being able to find fresh material for his speeches at these dinners. The simple art in effecting this is that he takes some topic which is before the public at the time, or refers to his own public acts, which interest the audience on account of his personal popularity. We cannot give all the speeches on these occasions, but the following show the general spirit of them, and the variety of subjects touched by him.

1866.

At the banquet of 1866, on the 5th of May, the President, Sir Francis Grant, then recently elected, for the first time occupied the chair. In proposing the health of the Prince of Wales, Sir Francis wished to his Royal guest, "amidst the cares and labours of his exalted station, all the soothing influences of a love of art. He inherits the enlightened appreciation of art, which had distinguished both his illustrious parents. But the title of artist is not confined to the subjects which occupy the Royal Academicians.

2 A 2

In England, especially in the Midland counties, a gentleman who particularly distinguishes himself in riding across country after hounds is popularly called an artist. Gentlemen," continued the President, himself an artist of high repute in both senses of the word, " I am able to assure you from my own personal observation, and I feel sure his Grace the Duke of Rutland will bear me out, that His Royal Highness in his recent visit to Leicestershire, in two very severe runs across the Vale of Belvoir, proved himself a first-rate artist in that particular department of art. Since His Royal Highness has proved himself in one sense an artist, may I, if His Royal Highness will forgive my boldness, claim his sympathy for his brother artists of the brush? Allow me to add, the brush is an important element in both departments of art. I beg to say on the occasion alluded to His Royal Highness was most deservedly presented with the brush. I have the honour to propose ' The health of their Royal Highnesses the Prince and Princess of Wales and the other members of the Royal Family.' "

The Prince, in responding, said :—

" Sir Francis Grant, your Royal Highnesses, my Lords, and Gentlemen,—I thank you most sincerely for the very kind manner in which you have proposed my health, that of the Princess of Wales, and the other members of the Royal Family, and for the cordial manner in which it has been received. I need hardly assure you that it is a source of sincere gratification for me to be present a second time at the annual dinner of the Royal Academy, more especially as I am enabled to have the opportunity of supporting you, Sir Francis, on the first occasion that you take the chair as President of the Royal Academy. Although we are assembled on a festive occasion, I cannot omit referring to the memory of one whose loss we must all deeply deplore. I allude to your late President, Sir Charles Eastlake. You Royal Academicians all knew him so well, and how justly popular he was for his many distinguished qualities, that it would be superfluous for me to pass any eulogy on his name. But I cannot forbear offering my small tribute to his merits, having always considered him as an old friend, and having known him, indeed, since my childhood. I now take the opportunity of thanking you, Sir Francis, for the very kind manner in which you have adverted to me in connection with art. I need not assure you that I shall always be most ready to do my little best in assisting to promote the welfare of art and science, and thus following the bright example of the Queen and my lamented father. I thank you, also, for the allusion you made to me as a brother of the 'brush.' Although, as I observed before, I will do my utmost to support art, still I am afraid I shall never be able to compete with you as a painter, but at the same time I shall always be ready to enter the lists with you in the hunting field as long as you do not attempt to ride over me at the first fence. With respect to the present Exhibition, it may, I think, be said that the pictures in a great measure not only show the progress of art, but record the times in which we live. Taken as a whole, the Exhibition is one of a peaceful character, and indicative of peace. There is only one picture to which I would refer which, at the present moment, bears anything of a warlike character — I mean 'Volunteers at a firing point,' in which there is a picture of a distinguished Highlander (Mr. Ross), a countryman of your own, who is represented as shooting for a prize. That is a very interesting picture, and it reminds us forcibly that the Volunteers who came forward for the protection of their country have not been required in that capacity, and are now employing their time usefully in the art of rifle shooting. Without further trespassing on your time, permit me once more to thank you for the manner in which you have proposed and drunk my health."

The Duke of Cambridge, in responding to the toast of the Army, referred to the distinction in art attained by the President, the brother of one already highly distinguished in arms, his friend Sir Hope Grant. Prince Alfred responded for the Navy.

An interesting fact, not generally known, was mentioned by Sir Francis Grant, who had been called the successor of Sir Charles Eastlake. Sir Edwin Landseer had been elected; and, although he could be only persuaded to retain the office for one week, the Academy had the proud satisfaction of knowing that his name is registered among its Presidents.

The other speeches at this banquet were of unusual interest, from the Archbishop of Canterbury, Earl Russell, and the Earl of Derby. Allusions were made to the loss of Lord Palmerston, and of Mr. Gibson, the sculptor, and also to the approaching marriage of the Princess Mary of Cambridge, for whom the Duke of Teck responded. The Earl of Derby made special reference to the National Exhibition of Portraits at South Kensington, interesting alike to the artist and to the student of history.

1867.

After dinner, the customary loyal toasts were proposed and responded to, the President making special reference to the severe and protracted illness of the Princess of Wales, which they all deplored, with the trust that it would please God soon to restore her to perfect health. The Prince, on rising, was loudly applauded, and spoke with evident emotion, in witnessing the warm sympathy shown by the assembly :—

" Sir Francis Grant, your Royal Highness, my Lords, and Gentlemen,—I beg to tender you my warmest thanks for the very kind manner in which you have proposed and received the health of the Princess of Wales and myself. I feel sure she will be deeply gratified for the kind words you have this evening uttered, and I am glad to say that, although she has now for very nearly two months been kept to her room by a long and tedious illness, she is now progressing towards recovery. I know I can have no more pleasing announcement to make to her Royal Highness than to tell her of the very kind feeling which has always been exhibited to her since her first coming to this country. I beg also, Sir Francis, to thank you for the very kind manner in which you have alluded to the interest I take with regard to science and art. I need not tell you that I do take such an interest. If I may say so, I take the same interest which my parents have always taken, although I may not have the same experience or knowledge; still, I hope I shall always tread in their footsteps in that respect.

" I am flattered, Sir Francis, by your statement that I have shown an appreciation of art in becoming the possessor of a work by so celebrated an artist as Sir Edwin Landseer. I think it would be impossible to find at this table any one who would not feel the same appreciation of so admirable a work of art. I obtained the picture under somewhat peculiar circumstances. It had been painted for a private person who was kind enough to give it up to me. Sir Edwin Landseer, although he has been before the public for many years as a painter, has within the last two months achieved great distinction as a sculptor, and has produced one of the finest monuments of art that exist in this country. He kept us perhaps some time in waiting for his lions, but the result has certainly been a most magnificent one.

" With reference to the Exhibition now before us, I think I may say that for many years we have not seen a finer exhibition. The names of Grant, Watts, Millais, and others I need not particularise. Last year we had to mourn the loss of Sir · C. Eastlake, and now we have to lament the departure from among us of another Royal Academician, Mr. Philip, to the vivid truthfulness of whose pictures from Spanish life I myself, from having been in Spain, can amply testify. I beg, my lords and gentlemen, again to thank you for the kind manner in which you have proposed and received my health, and the still kinder manner in which you have received the health of the Princess of Wales."

1870.

The Royal Academy banquet for 1870 fell on the 30th of April.

Sir Francis Grant, the President, in proposing "The Health of the Queen," stated that Her Majesty had, in May of the previous year, conferred on the Academy the honour of visiting the new galleries in state, and was pleased to express her high approval. At that visit she gave commissions for pictures to several young artists of rising fame ; and she presented to the Academy the beautiful marble bust of herself, executed by her accomplished daughter the Princess Louise.

In next proposing "The Health of the Prince and Princess of Wales and the rest of the Royal Family," the President said that they were all glad to welcome the Prince, for the first time, in the new galleries. "Last year His Royal Highness was well employed elsewhere visiting the historic wonders of ancient Egypt, accompanied by the Princess of Wales, whom we must all rejoice to see returned to this country in perfect health. It must be a gratifying circumstance to all Her Majesty's loyal subjects that the Royal Princes, her sons, are not too delicately reared, as Princes were of old, but are all manly English gentlemen and great travellers, who seek to elevate and enlarge their minds by studying the customs and policy of foreign nations, and to strengthen the cords of sympathy and loyalty which bind our colonies to the mother country. I read with pleasure of His Royal Highness recently presiding at a meeting of the Society of Arts, and the able sentiments he then expressed on the subject of education. I am glad also to learn that the Prince has succeeded the late lamented Lord Derby as President of the Royal Commission of 1851—an institution, if I may so call it, which has done such great things for the progress of art, especially in connection with manufactures, and which owes so much, I might say entirely its great success, to the enlightened genius and active support of the Prince's illustrious father."

His Royal Highness the Prince of Wales, who was received with much cheering, said :—

" Mr. President, your Royal Highness, my Lords, and Gentlemen,—I beg to tender you my warmest thanks for the kind way in which this toast has been proposed and received. It has afforded me great gratification once more to attend the hospitable board of the Royal Academy, and especially as I have this evening for the first time had the pleasure of dining in these new rooms. As the President has remarked, he was kind enough last year to invite me to inaugurate these rooms, but, being abroad, I was unfortunately unable to do so. I regret it, especially as that was the one hundredth anniversary of the Royal Academy. I think I may be allowed to congratulate the President and all the Royal Academicians on the Exhibition of this year. Of course, every artist strives each succeeding year to produce still better pictures and statues, and I think the Academicians have no reason to complain on the present occasion. We must regret, as I am sure all Academicians will, the death of Mr. Maclise, and it is with feelings of sorrow that we shall now for the last time see a picture of his adorn these walls. The President has kindly alluded to me as having recently presided at a meeting of the Society of Arts, and I cannot but thank him for the compliment he has paid me in connection with the observations I made upon that occasion. It afforded me great pleasure to preside at that meeting, and, although my position as President of the Society is to a certain extent an honorary one, I promise that I shall be ready on every occasion to come forward and give as much time as I can in promoting any of its very important objects. I beg also to thank the President for having alluded to me as President of the Commission of 1851. It is with deep regret that I have had to succeed one whose presence we must all miss on occasions like these—one whose name can never be forgotten in the country's history, and who always took the highest interest in the welfare of all our great institutions, and more especially those connected with art—I allude to the late lamented Lord Derby. My lords and gentlemen, I assure you the Princess of Wales will be highly gratified to hear how kindly on this, as on every other public occasion, you have received her name and health, and I beg to thank you for the kind manner in which you have listened to the few remarks I have made."

The usual toasts were afterwards given, and responded to by eminent men, including Mr. Motley, the American Minister, and Charles Dickens.

1871.

At the Royal Academy banquet of 1871, the President, Sir Francis Grant, in proposing "The Health of Her Majesty the Queen," referred to the recent opening of the Albert Hall, a proceeding which, in some degree, tended towards the realisation of the late Prince Consort's constant efforts for the promotion of Science and Art in this kingdom.

In proposing " The Health of the Prince and Princess of Wales and the rest of the Royal family," Sir Francis referred to the zeal of the Prince in the encouragement of Art, and said that he was shortly to preside on two different occasions in connection with Art, at the opening of the International Exhibition, and at the dinner of the Artists' General Benevolent Institution.

The Prince, in responding, said :—

" I feel very much touched by the kind way in which you, Sir Francis, proposed my health, and this company received it, and I beg also to thank you for the very kind terms in which you alluded to the name of the Princess, who, I am confident, will be deeply gratified by the kind way in which you alluded to her name and the company have received this toast. You have referred to the opening of the International Exhibition next Monday, and I sincerely trust that the opening of that series of Exhibitions may be as successful as the others which preceded it, and that the promotion of science and art may be carried forward by the means of these numerous Exhibitions. It is always a great pleasure for me to meet you here at this annual gathering, to see so many distinguished and celebrated persons, and to be surrounded on all sides by the pictures of the most celebrated artists of our own country, and also, by the permission of the Academicians, by the pictures of the most distinguished foreign artists. I feel sure that the artists of this country take it as a great compliment that these pictures should be sent here for exhibition. With respect to the present Exhibition, it must strike all of us on looking around these walls that some pictures are wanting—pictures from an artist whose health, I fear, is failing, although I am sure we all hope most heartily he may yet be spared to us; still we do miss the pictures of Sir Edwin Landseer. Gratifying as it must be for distinguished artists to see their pictures exhibited, and to hear the remarks made on them by critics and others, there are two beautiful drawings in this Exhibition of which, alas! the artists will never hear the praise that may be bestowed upon them, and I feel sure that it will not be considered out of place if on this occasion I offer my condolence to the Royal Academicians for the absence of one of their number, and the cause of it in the terrible bereavement he has sustained (alluding to the death of the son of Mr. Goodall, R.A.). My lords and gentlemen, I thank you for listening to these few remarks, and as many speeches have to be made I will not trespass further upon your attention than by again thanking you for the very kind manner in which my health and that of the Princess have been received by this distinguished assembly."

1874.

The chief interest of the evening was in the speech of Sir Garnet Wolseley, the "hero of Coomassie." His health was proposed by the Prince of Wales, who said he would have preferred that the toast should have been given by some one better qualified, but that he felt it a pleasure and honour to fulfil the duty laid on him by the President.

The Duke of Cambridge, in responding for the Army and Navy, had in very happy terms also referred to the services of Sir Garnet Wolseley, who in his speech gave well-merited praise to the Commander-in-Chief, for his efforts to raise the standard of military education.

Returning to earlier proceedings of the evening, the President of the Academy, Sir Francis Grant, in proposing "The Health of the Prince and the Princess of Wales and the other members of the Royal Family," said :—" It is a subject of infinite satisfaction to the members of the Royal Academy to observe the unmistakable and earnest love of art which His Royal Highness the Prince of Wales manifests on all occasions. Notwithstanding the numerous calls that are made on the time of His Royal Highness, to which he assiduously responds, we learn through the Press of his occasionally visiting the studios of some of our leading artists, thus honouring and encouraging Art in the most gratifying manner. We have also to thank the Prince for the active assistance he gave us in promoting the success of the Landseer Exhibition. It was owing to his personal influence that we are enabled to thank his Majesty the King of the Belgians for two beautiful pictures sent from the royal collection at Brussels, and also his Serene Highness the Duke of Coburg, who sent from Coburg one work of great interest, and besides several other valuable pictures, one of Van Amburgh and the Lions, the property of his Grace the Duke of Wellington, a picture that possesses this special interest, that the subject was suggested and the picture commissioned by the Duke's illustrious father. I am glad to be able to announce that the Prince and Princess of Wales, accompanied by the Duke and Duchess of Edinburgh and the other members of the Royal Family, honoured the Exhibition with their presence on Thursday. I hope the Prince will forgive me for the liberty I take, if I venture to mention that we members of the Academy always witness with pleasure the honest and zealous way in which both the Prince and Princess go over the Exhibition, beginning catalogue with pencil in hand, at No. 1, and working steadily through all the galleries. It cannot but be gratifying, even to the humblest artist who is so fortunate as to obtain a place on these walls, to know that he has good reason to hope that his labours will not escape the observation of the Prince and Princess of Wales."

His Royal Highness the Prince of Wales, who was received with much cheering, said :—

" Mr. President, your Royal Highness, my Lords, and Gentlemen,—I beg to thank you for the very kind manner in which you, Sir Francis, have proposed my health with that of the Princess of Wales and the other members of the Royal Family, and for the cordial way in which you, my lords and gentlemen, have been pleased to receive it. I can assure you, Sir Francis, and the members of the Royal Academy, that it affords me the greatest pleasure and satisfaction to have been able to accept your kind invitation. It is now two years since I had the opportunity of partaking of your hospitality, and you may be sure that whenever I am able to come to the Royal Academy it will always give me the greatest pleasure. Sir Francis Grant has been kind enough to allude to me with reference to the Exhibition at the Royal Academy of pictures by his late distinguished and never-to-be-surpassed colleague, Sir Edwin Landseer. I will only say that any efforts of mine—the efforts were but small, but such as they were, any efforts I could make —were most cheerfully devoted to give the country the opportunity of seeing those magnificent works, some of which, having for many years been in the possession of their proprietors, had

not been placed before the eyes of the public. It gave me very
great pleasure to help in any way such an exhibition. Thanks
to the efforts of the President and the members of the Royal
Academy, that exhibition was a great success, and afforded the
utmost interest and pleasure to all who saw it. I feel assured
that you must all deeply deplore the loss of that great man.
Last year he was still living, though, alas ! his health was such
that it was impossible for him to come among his colleagues as
he used to do. At any rate, he lived to render his name illustrious, and we can never hope to see his fame excelled. Sir
Francis, I hope you will allow me to congratulate you on this
most excellent Exhibition. When we see these walls surrounded with pictures—when we look at the catalogue and see
the names of yourself, of Messrs. Millais, Leighton, Prinsep,
Watts, Ward, Frith, Graves, Calderon, Sant, Alma-Tadema, and
many others I might mention, it is unnecessary to say that we
have here a collection of pictures of the greatest artists which
this country can produce. I am glad to take this opportunity of saying that I hope those gentlemen who have come
to the Royal Academy on this occasion have not forgotten to look
at one picture in the next room, which I think well deserves
attention. It is numbered 142 in the catalogue, and is entitled
' Calling the Roll after an Engagement in the Crimea.' This
picture, painted by a young lady who, I am given to understand,
is not yet twenty-three, is deserving of the highest admiration,
and I am sure she has before her a great future as an artist.
In the next room, the Lecture Room, is a statue of ' A Horse
and his Master,' by Boehm, which I am confident all who take
an interest in sculpture will agree with me is one of the finest
pieces of sculpture of modern times. The name of the artist is
so well known that it is superfluous for me to make any
remarks upon it. I only hope that at no very distant day he
will have the privilege of writing R.A. after his name. My
lords and gentlemen, I beg to thank you for the very kind way
in which this toast has been proposed and accepted by this
distinguished company."

The marked way in which the Prince called attention to the now
celebrated picture of "The Roll Call" was a generous tribute
to rising merit. The young artist thus signalised has more than

fulfilled the anticipations formed of her. The name of Elizabeth Thompson soon became distinguished in Art, and she continues to excel in depicting military scenes, now that her name, Lady Butler, is associated with that of a most gallant and distinguished officer, Sir William Butler, K.C.B. The praise bestowed on " The Roll Call" by the Duke of Cambridge was equally hearty, and was a high compliment as coming from the head of the British Army.

May, 1875.

The President, Sir Francis Grant, in proposing "The Health of the Queen," referred to Her Majesty's constant and cordial encouragement of Art. "In carrying out our Winter Exhibition of the Ancient Masters, Her Majesty has always given us her cordial support; and I hope I may be allowed to remind you that last year, when we held an exhibition exclusively of the works of the late Sir Edwin Landseer, the Queen was so kind as to contribute no fewer than sixty works by that eminent artist. For that and other gracious acts the Academy desire to record their grateful acknowledgments."

On giving the toast of " The Prince and Princess of Wales and the other members of the Royal Family," Sir Francis Grant said :—" I beg to assure His Royal Highness that the members of the Royal Academy are very sensible of the honour he confers on us by his presence on this as on many former occasions. They especially value the compliment as an additional proof of the interest His Royal Highness has at all times manifested in the promotion and encouragement of Art. I am glad to say the Prince and Princess of Wales, accompanied by the Duke and Duchess of Edinburgh and other members of the Royal Family, honoured the Exhibition with their presence on Thursday, and after their usual careful examination of the works of Art were pleased to express their approbation. We cannot but be impressed by the cordial and zealous manner in which both the Princess and the Prince fulfil the many onerous duties which devolve on their exalted position. We can scarcely take up a newspaper without reading of their Royal Highnesses performing some public duty or lending their presence for the support of some charitable institution, combining as they do this honourable desire to do good with the most gracious manner—a graciousness which, I venture to say, does not proceed from mere courtly education, but from the genuine impulses of good and noble natures."

The toast was drunk with all the honours, and His Royal Highness, who was received with much cheering, said:—

" My Lords and Gentlemen,—For the exceedingly kind manner in which my health and that of the Princess of Wales have been proposed by you, Sir Francis, and received by the company here present allow me to return my most sincere thanks. The President of the Royal Academy and the Royal Academicians may be assured that it affords us the greatest pleasure on all occasions to come to the Royal Academy, to attend their annual Exhibition. I am sure, Sir Francis, that you and your brother Academicians have no cause to complain of the Exhibition this year. I am certain that all who have any knowledge of Art will agree with me that this is a very fine Exhibition, in no way inferior to any of its predecessors. For myself, I will only say that it affords me the greatest gratification to be present on an occasion when one meets with the most distinguished men—men of the highest position and talent, surrounded by all that is most beautiful in Art. I beg to return my best acknowledgments for the kind manner in which you have received the health of the Princess of Wales, of myself, and of the other members of the Royal Family, and I sincerely hope that on many future occasions I may have the happiness to be present at the annual gatherings of the Royal Academy."

In responding for the Army, the Duke of Cambridge referred with high praise to the picture of " The Last Muster," and also to that of the young lady who has again distinguished herself by a military picture, " The Square of the 28th Regiment at the Battle of Quatre Bras," and also the picture by a foreign artist in another room delineating an historic "Charge at Waterloo."

In speaking of the Navy, the President said that Mr. Brassey had presented to the nation the fine picture of the *Devastation*. "I believe," said Sir Francis, "this is the first representation of an ironclad that has found a place on these walls—a picture of the *Devastation*—of which the genius of the talented artist has made quite a picturesque object by concealing more than half the vessel in smoke, and adorning what remains with a variety of flags."

1879.

After having missed the anniversary festival at Burlington House for four years, mainly on account of pressing work, partly in connection with Art, the Prince of Wales honoured the President and Council by his presence on the 3rd of May, 1879. There was the customary number of Royal and distinguished guests, but another President now filled the Chair, and other changes were witnessed among the Academicians.

Sir Frederick Leighton, in proposing " The Health of the Queen," said that, " as members of the Royal Academy, we acclaim in this toast the head and immediate patron of this institution—a patron whose patronage has been for forty years not formal merely, but whose interest in its well-being has constantly shown and still shows itself in acts of gracious and enlightened generosity and high examples of support, a generosity and support the fruits of which were but a few weeks ago again magnificently evident on our walls. Deep gratitude, therefore, mingles with loyalty in the toast which I have now the honour to propose—'The Health of Her Majesty the Queen.'"

The President said of the Prince of Wales, that " his absence for a time had not been caused by any diminution of the interest which he has ever evinced in this Academy and in the arts which are its care, but, on the two last occasions at least, by the performance of self-imposed and onerous duties in which the furtherance of English Art had no small share. Those who had the honour to co-operate with His Royal Highness in the work to which I allude—and not a few are seated at this table—know by experience with what steadfast zeal and devotion and with what inexhaustible kindness in his dealings with all he carried it out; but no one, perhaps, so well as myself knows how desirous the Prince of Wales has been throughout that English Art should receive at the International Exhibition that recognition and honour which in his view it deserved, and which in the event was measured out to it by the opinion of Europe." The Princess of Wales, as all knew, co-operated with never-failing grace with the Prince in fulfilling the duties of their high station. As to the other members of the Royal Family, " all had grown up in the love of arts, and several of them practise one or other of those arts with enthusiasm and with marked success. I give ' The Prince and Princess of Wales, and the rest of the Royal Family.'"

The Prince, in responding, said :—

" Sir Frederick Leighton, your Royal Highnesses, my Lords, and Gentlemen,—I am very grateful for the excessively kind manner in which this toast has been proposed and received by this large and distinguished company. As the President, Sir Frederick Leighton, has said, it is four years since I last had the advantage of being present at your annual celebration. It was a matter of great regret to me that so long a time should elapse, but it has given me great pleasure to come here to-night and take part in your proceedings. During those four years events have occurred in the history of the Royal Academy which have awakened deep regret. The members of the Royal Academy— I may say all who sit at these tables—feel that they lost a friend in the death of Sir Francis Grant, who so long presided with so much geniality and kindness at these anniversaries.

But of the Academy, as of Royalty, it may be said, '*Le Roi est mort ! Vive le Roi !*' The President is dead ; another President is elected. Sir Frederick Leighton is an old friend of mine—a friend of upwards of twenty years' standing. I congratulate him most cordially and sincerely on the high office he now holds. I may also congratulate the Royal Academy on having such a man to preside over their meetings.

"I have to return my thanks, and those of my colleagues, to Sir F. Leighton for the able assistance he has rendered during the recent International Exhibition in Paris. Your President was unanimously elected chairman of the Section of Fine Arts, and he presided over a jury of at least forty members, and I think we have every reason to congratulate ourselves on the results.

"Let me now congratulate you, Sir Frederick, and the Royal Academy generally, on the magnificent Exhibition which we see before us this evening. I have not yet had sufficient time to enable me to speak to its merits, but I hope on some future occasion to have the opportunity of going over it more carefully. I thank you again for the kind way in which my health and that of the Princess of Wales have been proposed and for the very warm reception you have given me."

The Duke of Cambridge, in responding for the Army, referred to wars now being carried on in different parts of the world. He also spoke with praise of two pictures in this year's Exhibition by Miss Thompson. Mr. W. H. Smith spoke for the Navy. Lord Beaconsfield responded for Her Majesty's Ministers, Mr. Froude for Literature, the Lord Chief Justice for the Guests, and the Lord Mayor for the Corporation of London. The Lord Chief Justice (Sir Alexander Cockburn) gave an eloquent description of the chief works of Sir Frederick Leighton, beginning with the "Procession of Cimabuc," nearly a quarter of a century ago, from which men felt that "a new genius had arisen who was to add to the lustre and renown of British Art." Sir Frederick Leighton, in his concluding speech, paid a generous tribute to the memory of Sir Francis Grant, and also of Mr. E. M. Ward, in whom the Academy had lost "one of the few artists who made the history of our country a constant subject for study."

1880.

At the annual banquet in 1880, the President, Sir Frederick Leighton, paid to the Prince of Wales a handsome compliment when he said : "Sir, of the graces by which your Royal Highness has won and firmly retains the affectionate attachment of Englishmen, none has operated more strongly than the width of your sympathies; for there is no honourable sphere in which Englishmen move, no path of life in which they tread, wherein your Royal Highness has not, at some time, by graceful word or deed, evinced an enlightened interest." Coming from Sir Frederick Leighton, this was not the mere language of flattery.

In replying, the Prince, after expressing his sincerest thanks, said :—

"Year by year the members of my family and myself receive invitations to take part in the proceedings at this anniversary banquet. You can therefore well understand that I find some difficulty in replying to the toast. At the same time I can assure the President and the members of the Academy that, though year by year we visit these exhibitions and take part at these banquets, the interest we take in them does not in any way diminish. I may be allowed to congratulate him and his colleagues on the very great success of this Exhibition. I had the opportunity two or three days ago of going through these rooms, and, though I do not profess to be in any way an art critic, I am quite sure they have no reason to fear any criticism upon the works of art which adorn these walls.

"I have been charged by my brothers, who generally take part in this day's proceedings, to express their great regret that they have not been able to be present. My brother, the Duke of Edinburgh, has been for the last five or six weeks absent on duty in Ireland, where he is employed on an important and, I trust, useful mission, not only as Admiral Superintendent of the Naval Reserve, but in doing what he can to relieve the distress which exists in Ireland. He has lately had the opportunity of taking the supplies for distribution on the West Coast from that gallant ship the *Constitution*, sent over by our American cousins, so nobly and generously, to afford relief to their distressed brethren in Ireland. In a letter I received from him two days ago he says the distress still exists, and both food and clothing are much wanted; in many instances the corn is not yet sown. I will not touch more upon this topic, and I should not have mentioned it had I not been particularly requested to do so."

2 B

1881.

At the banquet of 1881, the most notable incident was the special toast in honour of Sir Frederick Roberts. The President, Sir Frederick Leighton, said that " it was unusual at that table to single out a guest, however distinguished, when the profession to which he belongs has already been made the subject of a toast. But the brilliant achievements of Sir Frederick Roberts, especially the now famous march from Cabul to Candahar, had stirred all hearts." Sir Frederick, while grateful for the hearty welcome, spoke of the services of Sir Donald Stewart, and said that officers and men were all animated by one spirit—to do their duty, and to uphold the honour of their Queen and country.

Other events, that had occurred since their last assembly, were touched upon by the Prince of Wales, in responding to the toast with which his name is usually associated at these banquets. He said:—

"It is always a great gratification to myself and any other members of our family who may be present to come to this annual gathering of the Royal Academy, and we greatly regret when any cause arises to prevent us being present. It is a matter of great interest not only to be surrounded by all that is finest in modern art, but also to meet so distinguished an assembly, although we who come year by year find that gaps are made which we must all deeply regret. One of the most recent of these has been occasioned by the death of the great statesman just taken from us, who but two years ago made in this room one of his most eloquent speeches, which must be in the memory of all who were then present, many of whom are here to-night. I will not allude to the late Earl of Beaconsfield further than to say how gratifying it is to see that fine portrait of him in the next room, executed by one of our first artists, Mr. Millais. I might also allude to the removal from among us of the late Lord Chief Justice of England, opposite to whom I had often the pleasure of sitting at this table. The Academy, I am sure, also deplores the loss of Mr. Elmore, and Mr. Knight, who was many years Secretary, and we must all sympathise with the Academy for the loss they have thus sustained.

"It is not for me on this occasion to offer any criticism on the pictures which adorn these walls. I have only had the opportunity of taking a very cursory glance at them, and even if I were able I should not indulge in any critical remarks. But I will say this—neither the President nor the members of the Academy have any reason to deprecate fair and just criticism. One of the greatest pictures in the Exhibition is the portrait of the President, painted by himself. In this he has only followed the example of some of the great masters, who painted their own portraits. As there are so many more speeches to be made—some of the greatest possible interest—I will not weary you with more words. I will only again thank you, in my own name, in the name of the Princess, and of my brothers who are present, for your very kind reception."

The Duke of Cambridge said the Artists' Corps was one of the smartest and most efficient in the Volunteer Army, and he was glad of the opportunity of paying this tribute to them.

1885.

At the banquet of 1885, the Prince of Wales was accompanied for the first time by Prince Albert Victor. In the speech in reply to the usual toast from the Chair, the Prince referred to his being accompanied by his son in a very different place from the Academy of Art.

"You, sir" (addressing the President), "have kindly alluded to our late visit to Ireland. I can only assure you that, if that visit was a labour at all, it was a labour of love. We had for a long time past looked forward to a fitting opportunity for once more visiting Ireland, and we were glad to avail ourselves of the opportunity recently afforded us. I was sure that on going there we should meet with a kind and hearty reception, and such was the case with very few exceptions. We received as kind and loyal a reception as it could be the good fortune of any one to meet with. You, sir, have touched upon a subject of interest to us. My son and I had the opportunity of visiting, although the time allowed us was too short to do all that we could have wished to do, those districts of the town of Dublin in which the houses, although they might have picturesqueness, were certainly not calculated to promote the happiness and welfare of their inhabitants. This reminds me that I have had the honour of serving for upwards of a year on the Commission

which has for its object the improvement of the dwellings of
the poorer classes of this country. I will not anticipate our
first report, which will be shortly issued. I will only say before
sitting down that not only has it been to me a sincere pleasure
and satisfaction to have aided so important and valuable a
work, but I have had the advantage of working with some of
the most distinguished of my countrymen, some of whom are
here to-night."

The Duke of Cambridge made touching reference to the death
of General Gordon. "I feel that the remarks of the President
call for a sympathetic sentiment on my part and that of the
Army. The allusion to General Gordon is one that touches the
heart of every English soldier, from myself down to the youngest
soldier of us all. I can only deplore the fact that he is no longer
among us, and that his brilliant career is now over."

1888.

At the banquet of 1888, the President, Sir Frederick Leighton,
after the toast of "The Queen," in proposing "The Prince and
Princess of Wales and the rest of the Royal Family," referred to
this year being the "Silver Wedding," and also alluded to the
anxiety then darkening the home of "the Princess Royal of
England," the Empress of Germany.

The Prince, in reply, said :—

"Mr. President, my Lords, and Gentlemen,—This toast has
been proposed in far too flattering terms, but the words which
have fallen from Sir Frederick Leighton have not failed to touch
me deeply, as they also will touch the Princess. I thank you,
therefore, Mr. President, for the kind manner in which you have
given the toast, and you, gentlemen, for the way in which you
have received it. My coming here this evening marks, as it
were, a double anniversary. This is not only the year of my
silver wedding, which your President has kindly referred to,
but it is now just a quarter of a century ago since I first had
the pleasure and gratification of accepting the kind hospitality
of this great Academy. There have, no doubt, been many
changes during that interval in this body. Many illustrious
and distinguished members of the Academy have passed away ;
but, while we cannot but regret them, we know that there has
been no lack of others to fill their places. When one thinks of

the old buildings in which we used to assemble, which are now devoted to the purposes of the National Gallery, and when one sees this new edifice, which has existed now for nineteen years, and the beautiful objects that adorn its walls, one can form some idea of the great progress that has been made in art in this country. It is a remarkable fact that, although many new galleries are constantly springing up, there appears to be no difficulty in adorning their walls and filling them with pictures and sculpture. In 1869, 3000 works of art were offered for acceptance by this Academy; but this year, I am told, no less than 9300 were sent in. Unfortunately, of that number upwards of 7000 had to be returned, because you have only room for 2000 odd. The responsibility which rests upon the President, and especially upon that most hard-working and perhaps I may say also best-abused body, the hanging committee, is very great, and their labours increase as years go on. They, of course, cannot give satisfaction to everybody; but those distinguished artists who must be disappointed at not seeing their works upon these walls may perhaps find some consolation in observing how very high is the general standard of excellence attained by their more fortunate brethren whose works have been accepted.

"Before sitting down I wish to acknowledge on behalf of my sister and her husband the kind sympathy which you, sir, have expressed to-night in such feeling words. I wish it were possible for me to give on this occasion greater hopes of the life of one so near and dear to me, of one of such value, not only to his own country, but, I maintain, to the world at large. The recent news which we have received has been rather more favourable, and God grant that such news may continue. At any rate, as long as there is life there is hope. I thank you once more, Mr. President, for the cordial terms in which you have proposed my health and the kind way in which you have alluded to the members of my family."

The Duke of Cambridge, who has the pleasurable duty every year of responding to the toast of the Army, must naturally feel increasing difficulty in varying the subject of his discourses. He was, however, never more happy in his remarks than at the banquet of 1888. "Every year that I come here," said the Duke, "I feel more at home among you, and for this reason, because I believe that there is great sympathy between artists and military men. It has been said that the services seem to some extent out of place in a company composed of artists, because artists are concerned with art and science and peaceful pursuits; but I believe, on the other hand, that artists derive a great advantage from observing our profession, because it supplies them with many subjects which they love to portray. And the military sentiment among artists is by no means to be considered as effaced. When I see what a splendid corps of Volunteers the artists supply, I think I may claim them as one of the elements of strength which we should use should any emergency arise. God forbid that it should ever arise; but, if it should, may the services be in a condition to prevent danger from approaching this country." These last words form the burden of most of the wise and patriotic speeches which the Duke of Cambridge delivers at the Academy and elsewhere.

ROYAL BANQUETS AT TRINITY HOUSE.

ROYAL BANQUETS AT THE TRINITY HOUSE.

July 2nd, 1866

THE Corporation of the Trinity House received its first charter in
1514, from King Henry VIII. It was then a guild or brotherhood
for the encouragement of the science and art of navigation, and
was first empowered to build lighthouses and erect beacons by an
Act passed in the reign of Queen Elizabeth. This has gradually
come to be the chief duty of the Corporation, and a very important
one it is to a nation with such vast commerce. The Scottish coasts
are under a separate Board, but all others are under the charge of
the Trinity House. The Mastership of the Company has in recent
times been an honourable post, held by Princes and Statesmen.
Lord Liverpool was Master in 1816, and was followed by the
Marquis Camden, the Duke of Clarence, afterwards William IV.,
the Duke of Wellington, the Prince Consort, and Lord Palmerston,
since whose death the office has been held by the Duke of Edinburgh.
The post was offered to the Prince of Wales, but was declined by
him, in behalf of his sailor brother, "with graceful delicacy and
characteristic manliness," as Sir Frederick Arrow, the Deputy-
Master said, in proposing his health at the first banquet where he
was a guest.

This first festival meeting after the election of the Duke of
Edinburgh as Master took place on the 2nd of July, 1866.
Among the guests were the King of the Belgians, the Prince of
Wales, the Premier and several members of the Cabinet, the Lord
Chief Justice, the Lord Mayor, and other distinguished persons.
The guests were received by the Elder Brethren in the Court Room
of the Corporation, a stately apartment, adorned with portraits of
Royal personages and of former Masters.

His Royal Highness the Master proposed the health of "Her
Majesty the Queen," and then that of the "King of the Belgians,"
who in his reply warmly thanked a Corporation which rendered important services to all maritime and commercial nations. In giving
the toast of "The Prince of Wales, the Princess of Wales, and the
other members of the Royal Family," the Master said: "It has
never before been my pleasing duty to propose the health of my
brother in his presence, and I should feel very shy if I were to
make any remarks further than that, as Master of your Corporation,
and as his brother, I beg you to give him a most hearty welcome."

His Royal Highness the Prince of Wales said :—

" May it please your Majesty, your Royal Highness, my Lords,
and Gentlemen,—Under any circumstances it would have been
a source of gratification to me to be present on such an occasion
as this, but more especially when I have been invited by my
own brother and have the pleasure of supporting him on the
first occasion of his taking the chair as Master of this Company.
Perhaps you will allow me on this occasion merely to mention
that, after the death of that distinguished and lamented statesman whose loss we must always deplore, the office of Master
was most kindly offered to me by the Brethren of this Company.
I begged to decline—at least, I begged to offer the suggestion
that the office should be offered to my brother, who was far
more fit to undertake its duties. Among the distinguished
personages who are present on this occasion it is, you will allow
me to say, very gratifying to have the honour of the presence of
his Majesty the King of the Belgians. After the very kind
manner in which he has spoken of his attachment to this
country, which I know is a real attachment, and not merely a
form of words, because I have often heard the same sentiment
expressed by him in private—after such expressions from his
Majesty I think I may say that we as Englishmen feel a strong
attachment to his country—a country distinguished in its own
position among the nations of the Continent, and a country
for which his ever lamented father did so much. I beg to
thank you for the honour you have done me in drinking my
own health in connection with the health of her Royal Highness
the Princess of Wales and the other members of the Royal
Family."

July 20th, 1868.

At the banquet of 1868, on the 20th of July, the Prince was
formally installed as one of the " Younger Brethren " of the
Trinity House, the oaths having been administered by the Duke
of Edinburgh, as Master. In proposing the usual loyal toasts, the
Master said it gave him much satisfaction to be supported by his
brother, who, however, on this occasion was present as a member
of the Corporation. The Prince, on speaking to the toast, said :—

" Your Royal Highnesses, my Lords, and Gentlemen,—I return
my best thanks to my illustrious relative for the kind way in

which he has proposed this toast, and for coupling with it the health of the Princess of Wales and that of the other members of the Royal Family. I am very grateful for the reception which has been accorded him in this room, and I have great pleasure in being here this evening. This is not the first time I have been present at the hospitable board of the Trinity House. It is the second time I have supported my brother, and I come here now in a double capacity, for I have the honour of being present to-day as a member of this Corporation and as his 'younger brother.' I am sure I may say even in his presence that it is a source of the greatest satisfaction to me to be present at the first dinner at which he has presided since his return from Australia. I know I am only speaking his wishes when I say that, although the season is now far advanced, he thought, consistently with the duties he had to perform on board the *Galatea,* now off Osborne, he could not refrain from taking the chair at the anniversary dinner of this ancient Corporation, of which he has the honour of being the Master. I thank you for the kind way in which this toast has been received."

The Duke of Richmond, as President of the Board of Trade, acknowledged the great services to the Mercantile Marine rendered by the Trinity House. Lord Napier of Magdala, in response to the toast of " The Visitors," spoke of the efficient manner in which the Transport Service had been carried out during the Abyssinian Expedition.

July 4th, 1869.

In 1869 the Duke of Edinburgh was absent, and the Prince of Wales undertook the office of presiding at the dinner on the 4th of July. Sir Frederick Arrow, Deputy Master, and the Elder Brethren, among whom were Mr. Disraeli and Mr. Gladstone, honorary Brethren, received the invited guests, among whom were Prince Arthur, Prince Christian, Prince Teck, Prince Edward of Saxe Weimar, and numerous men of high distinction in public life.

The Prince having proposed " The Health of The Queen, the protectress of this ancient Corporation," Sir Frederick Arrow gave " The Health of the Prince and Princess of Wales and the rest of the Royal Family." The Deputy Master referred to the sympathy of the Prince with naval service in all departments, and especially his love of yachting. He also referred to his tour in the East, since they last assembled at their annual festival. The Prince replied :—

" Your Royal Highnesses, my Lords, and Gentlemen,—I am gratified by the honour you have done me in drinking my health and that of the Princess of Wales and the other members of the Royal Family. I can assure you it has given me great pleasure to be present on this occasion, but I feel I have hardly any right to occupy this chair. The last time I was here I was elected a younger member of your Corporation. To-day I have become an elder member, and Sir Frederick Arrow asked me to take the chair in place of my brother, the Master, who is now in a far distant land. You may be sure that I shall always be ready to assist in every way I can to promote the good of this excellent institution. Sir Frederick Arrow has been pleased to allude to my yachting. It is true I am fond of yachting, but I cannot claim to be either a nautical or a naval man. You may, however, always reckon upon any services I can render in any way in which you may think I can be useful to your Corporation."

Other customary toasts were then given, and responded to. To the toast of " The Master of the Corporation," his Royal Highness the Duke of Edinburgh, " wishing him a happy, prosperous, and safe voyage from the Southern hemisphere, and a quick return home," the Prince of Wales replied : —

" Your Royal Highnesses, my Lords, and Gentlemen,—I feel I am in rather a difficult position in having to return thanks for one who is absent. At the same time, I feel assured my brother would be gratified by my thanking you for the manner in which his health has been proposed and welcomed. According to the French proverb, ' *Les absens ont toujours tort.*' But I hope you will think differently, seeing that my brother is a post captain in Her Majesty's Navy, and is visiting one of Her Majesty's far distant colonies. I am sure if he knew you were drinking his health at this time his heart would be with you. Before I sit down I have the honour of proposing to you a toast—the principal toast of the evening. I call upon you to drink, ' Prosperity to the Corporation of Trinity House.' It would be almost superfluous in me to make any remarks on the Corporation or its present or future development. It has existed since the time of Henry VIII., and ever since that time to the present the community has taken the deepest interest in its prosperity.

It has also been connected through its honorary Brethren 'with some of the most distinguished men, and many of those honorary Brethren are present here this evening. Its object is to protect our ships and our sailors, and that object is never forgotten. As the First Lord of the Admiralty has just said, while the Navy is called upon to protect our commerce, the Corporation of Trinity House is called upon to protect our sailors and our ships. The first electric light put up in this country was that at Dungeness, and the great Wolf Rock, which has long been the terror of our sailors, will before long cease to be so. This will show you that the Trinity House authorities are anxious to do their duty and to maintain their great name, which I am sure is honoured here and in other countries. Before I resume my seat I give you ‘ The Health of Sir Frederick Arrow, the Deputy Master,’ and I am sure you will drink it with enthusiasm, knowing as you do how justly he merits your applause. He has done his duty in every way to maintain the interests of the Corporation, and I think the honour was eminently due which his Sovereign conferred in making him Sir Frederick Arrow. I call upon you to drink ‘ Prosperity to the ancient Corporation of Trinity House,’ coupling with the toast the name of Sir Frederick Arrow.”

Sir Frederick Arrow, having briefly responded, gave the toast of “ Her Majesty's Ministers,” saying that, although politics are unknown at the Trinity House, it was their duty to mark their respect for the Government of the day. Mr. Gladstone responded. The toast of “ The Maritime and Commercial Interests of the Country,” was coupled with the name of Mr. Bright, as President of the Board of Trade. Mr. Bright made an eloquent reply, discoursing on the benefits to this nation, and to all nations, of the works of the Trinity House Corporation. He said that he believed that “at this time the merchant ships of England are equal, or nearly equal—I have heard it said they surpass—in number and tonnage the seagoing merchant ships of all other countries in the world. This is an extraordinary thing, if it be true. But, whether it be exactly true or not, there can be no doubt with regard to foreign commerce—with regard to ships on the ocean—this country has a position at this moment which I believe it never held before, and one I think we may fairly be proud of. I delight, therefore, to dilate on the grandeur of our merchant navy, and I agree with Mr. Cardwell in hoping that the time is coming when the resources of this country may not be expended to an extravagant extent in maintaining our military establishments.”

In dilating on the magnitude of British commerce and the

number of British merchant ships, it probably never occurred to
Mr. Bright that in case of war, a few swift armed cruisers would
make these ships fly, like doves before hawks, and the seas be cleared
of our now countless merchant steamers.   The *Alabama* and a few
swift rovers speedily swept all the commerce of the United States
from the sea; and the same would be the fate of the vaster commerce of Great Britain, if there are not armed vessels, swift,
powerful, and numerous, to protect our mercantile navy in every
region of the globe.   There is no political question in this, but the
common prudential principle of insurance against possible peril
and disaster.   Our coasts may be adequately defended, but there
is need of a naval volunteer service as well as of volunteer riflemen
and gunners on land.   It may be one of the future national
services rendered by the Prince of Wales to get the yachting men
of the day to form themselves into naval volunteers, in case of the
protection of swift armed cruisers being needed for protecting the
fleets of merchantmen on which the people of England depend for
supplies.

After Mr. Bright's speech, the toast of " The Honorary Brethren "
was responded to by Mr. Disraeli, who was followed by Sir Stafford
Northcote, Sir R. Phillimore, and Sir John Burgoyne.   Seldom has
the banqueting hall of the Trinity House been honoured by the
presence of so many illustrious and eloquent guests.

June 24th, 1871.

In 1871, the Duke of Edinburgh, Master of the Trinity House, had
returned to England, and on the 24th of June took his place as
President at the annual banquet.   The Prince of Wales was
present, and a distinguished company.

In proposing the health of the Prince of Wales, the Master
thanked him for having performed the duties of the Mastership
during his absence.   Three years before he had jocularly called the
Prince his younger Brother.   He had since become an Elder
Brother, but, in respect of the Trinity House, he, as Master, was
still the eldest brother.   The Prince, in reply, said :—

" It is a great pleasure to me to have my health proposed by
my brother in the kind manner in which he has proposed it.
He has been pleased to allude to what I call the small duties
which I have had to perform at the Trinity House in his absence.
I think all the Brethren are well aware that it gave me great
satisfaction to be able to do anything during my brother's
absence; and I only regret that I had not more to do; but the
real duties were, in fact, performed by a gentleman who now
sits on my right (the Deputy Master), and I have to thank him

and all the Brethren for the assistance they rendered during the interregnum. My brother is now on half-pay, but the time may come when he will again have an important command. In that event I shall be glad again to be of any service during his absence, and the Trinity House may always count upon my placing myself at their disposal."

The usual toasts were given, and responded to. His Royal Highness the Prince of Wales gave Her Majesty's Ministers, saying:—

" To whatever party they belonged, so long as they performed their duty to the Crown and upheld the dignity and honour of the country, they were entitled to the compliment he now asked the company to pay to them, and he had great pleasure in coupling the toast with the name of his noble and learned friend the Lord Chancellor."

The Lord Chancellor responded, saying that there was not among the methods of preserving peace any greater or more effective means than that of maintaining in its full force and activity the great Navy of England, which must be looked upon by every Government with unmixed admiration; and he trusted, whatever differences might exist on other subjects, Her Majesty's Government would show that they had one common object, the maintenance of the maritime reputation, honour, and dignity of the country.

Mr. Milner Gibson, by command of the Master, proposed a toast always given at the Trinity House anniversaries: " The maritime and commercial interests of the country, and the President of the Board of Trade." Having himself long held the office of President of the Board of Trade, Mr. Milner Gibson bore testimony to the efficient administration by the Trinity House of the funds placed at their disposal. As the funds came from a tax on the shipping and trade of the country, it is a right and constitutional thing that the expenditure should be controlled by the Minister of Commerce, responsible to Parliament. He could say that the lights on the coast of the United Kingdom were equal, if not superior, to the lights which existed in any other country in the world. Under the control of the Board of Trade we had made great improvement in the system of lighting our coasts, coupled with a reduced charge upon the trade of the country.

It might have been added that it was when the Prince Consort was Master that more constitutional relations between the Trinity House and the Government came into operation, the funds being supplied by the Board of Trade, and administered by the Corporation, who then had what they called " new Sailing Orders " for their guidance.

June 27th, 1874.

The banquet at the Corporation Hall on June 27, 1874, was presided over by His Royal Highness the Prince of Wales, in the absence of the Master, the Duke of Edinburgh. The Deputy Master Sir Frederick Arrow, after the usual loyal and patriotic toasts, gave " The Health of the Prince of Wales," who responded in brief and appropriate terms, and afterwards proposed the toast of " Prosperity to the Corporation of the Trinity House." He said :—

" Your Royal Highnesses, my Lords, and Gentlemen,—I have now the honour of proposing to you a toast which I only wish had been placed in better hands than mine. Although I have the honour of being connected with this ancient Guild, I do not feel that I possess that nautical knowledge which a person ought to have who proposes a toast like ' Prosperity to the Corporation of Trinity House '; but I am sure it is a toast which will meet with your approval this evening. I will begin by stating that the few remarks with which I shall preface the toast are not of my own knowledge, the facts having been supplied to me by the kindness of the Deputy Master, and if I get out of my depth or among the quicksands I must trust you will excuse me. I speak with sincerity when I say that since we met here last year the duties of the Trinity House have been carried on as successfully as on any previous occasion, and that the whole of its proceedings have been of a highly satisfactory character. There have been several new lighthouses built—one, I believe, has been completed to-day, and is to be opened on the 1st of July. It is on Hartland Point, and, with reference to our commercial interests, is considered to be of great importance. It will do much to facilitate our trade with the Welsh coal ports. The Goodwin Sands is a name which fills every sailor with alarm ; and, although everything has been done to prevent the fearful wrecks with which the name is associated, we have only to read the daily newspapers to be aware of the fearful disasters that often occur at sea outside those terrible sands. The Trinity House has lately put a second lighthouse eastward of Beachy Head.

" There is another subject in connection with which the Trinity House has taken a very active part, and it is one of great importance, especially to nautical men. I mean the subject of sound-signals in foggy weather. The Trinity House has every reason to feel deeply indebted to Professor Tyndall, who, I regret to say, could not be with us upon this occasion owing to his absence from England. Some most interesting experiments in connection with sound-signals have been carried out by him, and a most able report has been written by him on the subject. I am sure you will all agree with me in thinking this a most important matter, and one in which it is natural that the Trinity House should take a prominent interest. At a great many stations it has been determined to place these fog-signals where lights can be of no avail.

" There is another matter in connection with which the Trinity House has every reason for congratulation. I mean the reduction of dues to the amount of £80,000, in addition to the reduction of £60,000 in 1872. There are many other important facts connected with the Trinity House which the Deputy Master has been kind enough to place at my disposal, but which I need not now detain you by mentioning. In proposing the toast of ' Prosperity to the Corporation of the Trinity House,' it is my pleasing duty to connect it with the health of one who not only does everything to make our annual gatherings here most agreeable, but who performs the arduous and responsible duties which he has to discharge in a most praiseworthy and effective manner. I am sure that you will drink most cordially the health of the Deputy Master. My Lords and gentlemen, I give you ' Prosperity to the Corporation of the Trinity House, coupled with the name of Sir Frederick Arrow, the Deputy Master.' "

At a later period of the evening His Royal Highness proposed the toasts of " Her Majesty's Ministers," to which the Lord Chancellor responded, and the " Distinguished Visitors," coupling with it the name of the Lord Chief Justice of England (Sir Alexander Cockburn).

June 2nd, 1875.

In 1875 the Duke of Edinburgh was not abroad, and presided at the annual dinner on the 2nd of June. The seamen of the *Galatea* lined the way to the Hall, on Tower Hill, in honour of the occasion, and of the presence of their captain. In the room where

2 c

the guests were received was a portrait of the Master, painted as a companion picture to those already on the walls, by a Russian artist, G. Koberwein. Count Shouvaloff, the Russian Ambassador, was among the guests. In responding to the customary toast of " The Royal Family," the Prince of Wales expressed his gratification at his brother Prince Leopold having become a member of the Corporation. The Duke of Cambridge responded for the Army.

1877.

The banquet of 1877 was again presided over by the Prince of Wales, in the absence of the Master, the Duke of Edinburgh. There was the usual select company, including Royal and other distinguished guests, especially General Grant, who, in his travels throughout the old world, was received with as great honour as any king could be.

In proposing the health of the Prince of Wales, the Earl of Derby said :—" No one particularly likes to listen to his own panegyric, even at a public dinner, and therefore I will say nothing with regard to the illustrious subject of my toast beyond that which you all know to be the simple and literal truth. His Royal Highness has not only now, but for many years past, done all that is in the power of man to do, by genial courtesies towards men of every class, and by his indefatigable assiduity in the performance of every social duty, to secure at once that public respect which is due to his exalted position and that social sympathy and personal popularity which no position, however exalted, can of itself be sufficient to secure. We regret the absence of the illustrious Master of the Corporation, the Duke of Edinburgh, but we regret it the less because he is doing what each of us in our humble spheres desires and endeavours to do—he is serving his country. I give you " The Health of His Royal Highness the Prince of Wales and the rest of the Royal Family."

The toast was drunk with all the accustomed honours, and the Prince in reply said :—

" My Lords and Gentlemen,—I return you my sincere thanks for the kind way in which the toast of my health has been proposed and the manner in which it has been received. I can assure the whole company that I feel it a great honour to be present on this occasion, especially connected as I have the honour to be with your Master. I regret that my brother is not here this evening. It is now two years since I was present at this annual gathering, and I regret to say I miss the kind and genial face of the late Deputy Master, Sir Frederick Arrow ; but in Admiral Collinson we have an excellent substi-

tute. On the present occasion it is a matter of peculiar gratification to us as Englishmen to receive as our guest General
Grant. I can assure him, for myself and for all the loyal
subjects of the Queen, that it has given us the greatest pleasure
to see him as a guest in this country. My lords and gentlemen,
before resuming my seat, it is my privilege to propose to you
another toast—one which always recommends itself most
heartily to the public, and that is ' The Army, Navy, and Reserve
Forces,' connecting with it on this occasion the name of a distinguished officer, Lord Strathnairn, and that of the Hon. Sir
Henry Keppel."

The toast was received with three times three. Lord Strathnairn
and Sir H. Keppel replied to the compliment, and the Chancellor
of the Exchequer responded to the toast of "Her Majesty's
Ministers," proposed by His Royal Highness the Chairman. Other
toasts having been given and acknowledged, the Earl of Carnarvon
proposed " The Health of the Guests," coupled with the name of
General Grant; saying that "there never has been one to
whom we willingly accord a freer, a fuller, a heartier welcome
than we do to General Grant on this occasion. We accord it to
him, not merely because we believe he has performed the part of
a distinguished General in many a 'well-foughten field,' nor
because he has twice filled the highest office which the citizens of
his great country can fill, but because we look upon him here
present to-night as representing, so to speak, that good-will and
that affection which ought to subsist between us and the United
States of America. It is not a century since there befell this
country what we believe to have been the greatest misfortune
that her pages record. Not a hundred years ago the States of
America separated from us ; and, great as the loss was, I do not
think that the separation was the greatest part of the calamity.
The disaster lay in this, that the separation on each side was
effected amid the storms of passion, resentment, and animosity.
Yet not a century has rolled by, and I believe, and thank God for
believing, that in a great measure that animosity and resentment
have passed away, and we are entering on a new stage of mutual
trust, of mutual sympathy, and of mutual support and strength.
I have had, perhaps, special opportunities of observing this in the
office I have the honour to hold. It has been my duty to be
connected with the great dominion of Canada, stretching, as it
does, several thousand miles along the frontier of the United
States, and during the last three or four years I can truthfully
say that nothing impressed me more or gave me livelier satisfaction than the interchange of friendly and good offices between the
two countries under the auspices of President Grant.

General Grant was loudly cheered on rising to respond. He spoke in such a low voice as not to be heard distinctly, but he was understood to say that he felt more impressed than possibly he had ever felt before on any occasion. He came there under the impression that this was the Trinity House, and that the trinity consisted of the Army, the Navy, and Peace. He therefore thought it was a place of quietude, where there would be no talk or toasts. He had been therefore naturally surprised at hearing both one and the other. He had heard some remarks from His Royal Highness the President of the evening which compelled him to say one word in response to them. The remarks he referred to were complimentary to him. He begged to thank His Royal Highness for those remarks. There had been other things said during the evening highly gratifying to him. Not the least gratifying among them was to hear that there were occasionally in this country party fights as well as in America. He had seen before now as much as a war between the three departments of the State—the executive, the judicial, and the legislative departments. He had not seen the political parties of England go so far as that since he had come to this country. He would imitate their Chairman, who had set the good example of oratory—that was brevity—and say no more than simply to thank His Royal Highness and the company for the visitors.

This is one of the longest speeches ever made by General Grant, whose allusion to party fights was suggested by what had been said by the Chancellor of the Exchequer: " There have been reports and rumours of dissensions in the Cabinet, and of them I do not mean to say anything but this—there is one subject on which there is no dissension. Among all the ministers who have ever dined at the Trinity House there is no dissension as to the manner in which they have been received in this hospitable hall."

THE ROYAL COLLEGE OF MUSIC.

THE ROYAL COLLEGE OF MUSIC.

THE Royal College of Music has occupied so much of the time and labour of the Prince of Wales, and promises to be an institution of so great national importance, that it seems well to present in order the various movements that led up to the foundation of the College, and to group together the successive speeches of the Prince on this subject.

NATIONAL TRAINING SCHOOL FOR MUSIC.

June 15th, 1875.

THE need for extending musical education, and for improving musical taste in England, has long been felt. That there is no lack of musical genius or skill in our country is sufficiently attested by the great array of eminent composers and distinguished performers, whether in vocal or instrumental music, both in former and in recent times. Nor has the love of the art, and delight in its exercise, ever been wanting. There was a time when what we now call "old English" rounds and catches, glees and madrigals, and all kinds of choral compositions, were popular, in the widest sense of the word. The love of orchestral harmony has also been great in England, where Handel found his home, and the best field for his wonderful powers. In those days Ireland was truly one with England, in appreciation of high classical music. It was in Dublin that the *Messiah* was first heard, and best appreciated. Even in the depressed period of music, in the early decades of this century, there were always competitions of well-trained choirs and bands, which showed the love and practice of musical art to be still widely diffused and ardently cultivated.

Notwithstanding all this, it had come to be necessary to take some measures for advancing musical art throughout the country, where great towns and busy centres of industry had multiplied, without the civilising influence of music being to a corresponding degree diffused. No one felt this more strongly than the Prince. Consort, but the opportunity of carrying out his ideas did not arise in his lifetime. The Royal Academy of Music, founded in 1822, and incorporated in 1830, did good service in its limited

way, for training its pupils and awarding a few scholarships; but
some institution was needed, with larger expansiveness, and
capable of diffusing the love and the practice of music more
widely among the people.

It was in furtherance of this national purpose that the Prince
of Wales, who put himself at the head of the movement, held
a conference at Marlborough House, on the 15th of June, 1875.

The immediate object was to promote the establishment of free
scholarships, to be held in the National Training Schools for
Music, then being erected, close to the Royal Albert Hall, at
Kensington Gore. The Duke of Edinburgh, Prince Christian,
and the Duke of Teck were present; and representatives of many
public bodies in Church and State, including the Archbishops and
several Bishops, the Lord Mayor of London and the Mayors of
many provincial towns, the Masters or Prime Wardens of the
City Companies, the head masters of public schools, the Chairman
and members of the London School Board, the Parliamentary
representatives of the Metropolitan boroughs, and a very numerous
company, of the most distinguished name and position.

The Prince of Wales, in opening the proceedings, expressed his
gratification at the large attendance, which augured well for the
object they all had in view. He then called on the Duke of Edinburgh to move the first resolution, in introducing which he gave a
lucid and interesting statement of the history of the movement.

In 1854, the Royal Academy of Music made an application to the
Commissioners of the Exhibition of 1851 to grant a site upon their
estate for a building in which they could carry on their labours.
The negotiations were not successful, and matters remained in
abeyance until 1865, when the Society of Arts appointed a Committee to consider and report on the whole subject of musical
education in this country. Of this committee the Prince of Wales
consented to act as chairman. Inquiries were made as to the
methods employed in the management of musical academies in
Paris, Berlin, Munich, Milan, and other Continental schools.
Reports were drawn up, one of the main points in which dealt
with the necessity for instituting scholarships to be competed for
openly, so as to draw out the best musical talent throughout the
country. Assistance should be given in cases where the scholars
were unable to provide education for themselves.

In 1872 negotiations were reopened with the Royal Academy,
with the idea of removing the head-quarters of the Academy from
Tenderden Street to South Kensington. It became more evident
that the purposes contemplated by the Committee of the Society
of Arts could be better accomplished by the establishment of a
new and independent institution as a National Training School
for Music. The foundation-stone of the new institution had been
laid in 1873, at which time a member of the Council, Mr. Freake,
had liberally offered to undertake the whole cost of the building.
At first Mr. Freake intended to give the use only of the building

for some years, but he now requested the acceptance of it as a free gift. It was further stated by the Duke of Edinburgh that there was ample accommodation for above 300 students. It only remained to obtain the foundation of Scholarships in sufficient numbers for the appointment of a permanent Staff of Professors, and other arrangements for efficiently carrying on the new training school.

The Duke of Edinburgh then moved a resolution for the appointment of a Committee for taking steps to found Free Scholarships for the City of London and the Metropolitan districts. This resolution was seconded by the Archbishop of Canterbury, and supported by the Lord Mayor and the Archbishop of York.

The Prince of Wales, in responding to a vote of thanks for having convened and presiding over the meeting, said, " he thought the initiative in this matter was really due to his brother, the Duke of Edinburgh, who had taken great interest in music since his childhood. The same was the case with their father, the late Prince Consort, whose name would always be remembered with gratitude for the powerful influence he had exercised on the intellectual advancement of the country, and to whose efforts might be traced in great measure the important place which music now held in the estimation of all classes.

" On the whole, they had reason to congratulate themselves on the success of the meeting, and he was glad to have the opportunity of returning his thanks to the Lord Mayor and to all the gentlemen representing the great City Companies for their cooperation on this occasion, feeling that that meeting would be the commencement of a movement which he trusted would be a success. In conclusion, he wished to move a resolution conveying a vote of thanks to Mr. Freake for the handsome and liberal manner in which he had so kindly behaved in giving the building for the National Training School of Music. It was already a great exercise of liberality to offer the use of it rent free for five years, and certainly he was sure none present could have expected that he would have made them a present of it. He was therefore anxious that they should on that occasion record a unanimous vote of thanks to him for his great liberality, and for the interest he had taken in the welfare of that which they had so much at heart."

The Duke of Edinburgh seconded the resolution, which was carried unanimously.

FOUNDING THE ROYAL COLLEGE OF MUSIC.

February 28th, 1882.

As far back as June, 1875, the Prince of Wales, we have seen, had taken steps to secure improvement of musical education throughout the kingdom. With this purpose he had invited many influential persons to a Conference at Marlborough House, which was held on the 15th of June of that year, and which resulted in the establishment of the National Training School of Music, with Sir Arthur Sullivan as its Principal. Ten years earlier, in 1865, the Prince had induced the Society of Arts to appoint a Committee to consider and report on the whole subject of musical education in this country, and of this Committee he gladly consented to act as President.

In 1878 the Prince summoned a number of gentlemen to a meeting at Marlborough House, where the proposal to found a National College of Music, uniting the Academy and the Training School, was first mooted. A committee was appointed, and the assent both of the Academy and the School had been obtained, when the Academy withdrew, and declined to accept the proposals of union. It was not till after the lapse of several years that the way was clear for the establishment of a new and truly national institution.

On the 28th of February, 1882, the Prince of Wales presided at a meeting held in the Banqueting Hall, St. James's Palace, for the purpose of soliciting public support for founding a "Royal College of Music." This meeting is destined to be a memorable event, not only in musical annals, but in the history of the nation. What was the character and influence of that meeting was stated in eloquent terms by Sir George Grove, in his speech at the inauguration of the Royal College in the following year. This statement will be given in full on a subsequent page, the following words being sufficient to quote here : "A meeting so truly national in its aspect gave, if I may use a not inappropriate figure, the key-note of the movement; and the key-note thus struck at St. James's Palace resounded through the country, and met with a ready and harmonious response."

Larger meetings the Prince has frequently addressed, but never one more broadly representative of all the most distinguished and influential classes in the kingdom. The Ambassadors and Ministers of most of the Continental Powers were also among the audience.

The Prince of Wales, who on rising was most cordially greeted, opened the proceedings by reading letters from the Duke of Connaught and Prince Christian, expressing regret that circumstances prevented them from being present, and their hearty sympathy with the objects of the meeting. Prince Christian in his letter briefly recounted the history of the fruitless attempt which had been made to induce Professor Macfarren and the directors of the Royal Academy of Music to consent to a union of their institution with the National Training School of Music, with a view to form a Royal College of Music on a more extended basis. The Prince of Wales then said :—

"My Lords and Gentlemen,—I have called you together to-day, the representatives of the counties and towns in England, the dignitaries of the Church and other religious and educational bodies, distinguished colonists now resident in England, and the representatives of foreign Powers, to aid me in the promotion of a national object by obtaining contributions for the establishment of a Royal College of Music. Were the object less than of national importance, I should not have troubled you—the heads of social life—to meet me here to-day, and I should not myself have undertaken the responsibility of acting as the leader and organiser of the movement. I have invited to meet you the leading musicians and publishers of music, the most eminent musical instrument makers, the most influential amateurs and patrons of music, and I trust that by the co-operation and union of some of the most powerful elements of society, we may succeed in establishing a Royal College of Music on a more extended basis than any existing institution in United Kingdom ; worthy alike of this meeting and of this country, for whose benefit you are asked to give your time, your money, and your influence.

" I do not propose to trouble you with any proofs of the advantages that would be derived from the establishment of a National College of Music. That subject has been fully discussed by the Duke of Albany at Manchester, and his address is before the world. He showed that relatively to foreign countries England occupied three centuries ago a higher place in the musical world than she does at the present time, and he proved that the almost universal establishment of central and national musical institutions abroad, and the want of such an institution in England, had been one cause why musical progress has not in this country kept pace with the increase of wealth and population and the corresponding development of science and art.

" Again, the necessity of public aid formed the groundwork of the appeal made at Manchester by the Duke of Edinburgh and Prince Christian. Music, as they showed, is far more expensive to teach than other arts, and the natural capacity for instruction in music is more rare than in almost any other art. You are compelled, then, if you would have good musicians, to provide means by which those to whom nature has been bountiful in giving good ears and good voices, but niggardly in giving worldly wealth, may be sought out in their obscurity and brought up to distinction by a proper course of instruction.

"What I have said naturally leads me to deal with free education in music, coupled in certain cases with free main-tenance of the pupil as the first branch of the subject on which I desire to engage your sympathies and ask your aid. This system of gratuitous education is one of the principal features which will distinguish the new college from the Royal Academy and other excellent existing schools of music. I do not mean to say that we intend to exclude paying pupils. To adopt such a course would be to deprive musical ability in the upper classes of any means of access to the college, and would stamp it with a narrow and contracted character, which is above all to be avoided in a national institution intended to include in its corporate character all classes throughout the United Kingdom. What I seek to create is an institution bearing the same relation to the art of music as that which our great public schools—Eton and Winchester, for example—bear to general education. On the one side you have scholars who are on the foundation and educated by means of endowments; on the other side, pupils who derive no direct benefit from the foundation. Both classes of pupils follow the same course of study ; their teachers are the same, their rewards are the same. They differ only in the fact that the collegers derive aid from the college, while those who are not on the foundation pay for the whole of their education. I lay great stress on this combination of the two systems of education—that by endowment and that by payment. Finan-cially, it enables us to have salaried teachers of the greatest eminence, who will give so much of their time as they devote to teaching exclusively to the instruction of pupils at the college. But, more than all, a union of different classes in a common and elevating pursuit is the best mode of binding in one tie of common enthusiasm the different grades of society, varying alike in wealth and social influence. Each has much to learn from the other, and this learning is best acquired in an institution where all meet on common ground, and on a footing of artistic equality. A further object, and one most material, is sought to be attained by including in our college persons who do not intend to make music their profession. To advance music as an art in its highest aspects, resort must be had to those who possess the best opportunities for general mental culture. The most highly educated classes are those who have the greatest power of disseminating the influence of art throughout the country. They are the sources from which the civilising stream proceeds downwards, and penetrates through every channel of our complex social life.

" I will now proceed to explain the details of the scheme for which I ask your support, beginning with the foundation, as being that branch of the college for which public money will be required. The least number of scholars which would be worthy to constitute a foundation for the college would be 100. Of these, 50 should have their education free and 50 should be maintained as well as educated. These scholars will be selected by open competition throughout the United Kingdom. A system of examination will be organised by which every town— nay, every village—in the kingdom may be afforded a chance of participating in the public benefaction. Only let eminent ability be found in the village choir, the pupil will be brought to London and may, if he do but possess the requisite ability, become a Beethoven or a Mendelssohn, and any school of music may put forward its best pupil as a candidate for collegiate honours. The expense of maintenance and education of pupils I estimate at about £80 a year; that of education alone at about £40 a year. I should hope also that your liberality will grant me means to found at least two fellowships, in order that rising musicians, who have acquired distinction at the college, may not be tempted on commencing their professional career to sacrifice the higher aspirations of their art to the necessity of providing immediate means of subsistence.

" Having settled the number of our foundationers, where are we to place them ? In London, I need not say, land is sold by the yard, and not by the acre, and a square yard in a good locality is often equal in value to a square acre in a remote district. Yet, for the health of a young communi'y, we must have open space and pure air, and space is particularly necessary in a music school, for, as the Duke of Edinburgh showed in his address at Manchester, pupils in an ordinary school may be grouped and classified, but musical pupils require space for the performance either of vocal or instrumental music, and the individual attention of their masters to an extent quite unknown in the education of pupils in other branches of knowledge. Again, the locality in which a school is placed must be easy of access in order to accommodate the staff of teachers, for, though I hope to have a resident staff to a greater extent than has yet been tried in any other musical school, yet undoubtedly extraneous teaching must form a considerable portion of our instruction. Now, on the point of site, I am happy to say I can give the meeting the most satisfactory assurances without making any calls on their liberality. It is due to the foresight of my father, the Prince Consort, that at a time when South Kensington was comparatively remote from London, the large estate held by the Exhibition Commissioners was purchased with a view to furnish sites for future public buildings. In the few years that have elapsed since that purchase a suburb has been converted into a city. The estate lies between two stations of the Metropolitan District Railway, and is skirted on the north by one of the most frequented roads in the Metropolis. Here already we have a nucleus for the college in the building constructed by the great liberality of Mr. Freake, and I am enabled to state, as Chairman of the Commission of 1851, that, in proportion as the public contributions enable us to construct our buildings, in the same proportion will the Commissioners be prepared to grant a sufficiency of site on which to erect them. The Commissioners have also a considerable portion of the Albert Hall under their control, and, by connecting that hall with the new college by a tunnel or a bridge, practising rooms, sitting-rooms, dining-rooms, and two small theatres will be immediately at the disposal of the college. The Commissioners will also be prepared to assist the college with an annual grant of money. To maintain the college with 100 pupils on the foundation apart from the expense of buildings an income of not less than from £10,000 to £12,000 a year will be required. The plan will admit of any degree of development in proportion as the munificence of the public or the Government supplies the requisite funds. A charter for incorporating the college has already been prepared and laid before the Privy Council. I have myself undertaken to be President. The governing body consist of a council, intrusted with the function of making by-laws for the regulation of the college, and of an executive committee charged with the details of the administration. The names of the gentlemen who form the council and the executive committee will be published, and will, I am satisfied, command the confidence alike of the public and of the musical world.

"I have now laid my plan before you. I commend it to your favourable consideration. A few words I would fain add to prevent any misunderstanding of my intentions. I have not brought you here to ask your aid for the support only of a school calculated to advance music by giving the best instruction continued over a course of years. This might be done by strengthening existing schools. I have not brought you here for the sole purpose of asking for assistance whereby to educate young and deserving musicians. Such an institution is but a branch of what I desire to found. My object is above and beyond all this. I wish to establish an institution having a wider basis and a more extended influence than any existing school or college of music in this country. It will teach music of the highest class; it will have a foundation for the education, and in some cases for the free maintenance, of scholars who have obtained by merit the right to such privileges. But it will do more than this. It will be to England what the Berlin Conservatoire is to Germany, what the Paris Conservatoire is to France, or the Vienna Conservatoire to Austria—the recognised centre and head of the musical world. Why is it that Germany, France, Italy have national styles of music? Why is it that England has no music recognised as national? It has able composers, but nothing indicative of the national life or national feeling. The reason is not far to seek. There is no centre of music to which English musicians may resort with confidence and thence derive instruction, counsel, and inspiration. I hope by the breadth of my plan to interest all present in its success. You who are musicians must desire to improve your art, and such will be the object of the Royal College.   You who are only lovers of music must wish well to a plan which provides for all classes of Her Majesty's subjects a pleasure which you yourselves enjoy so keenly.   To those who are deaf to music, as practical men I would say thus much—to raise the people, you must purify their emotions and cultivate their imaginations.   To satisfy the natural craving for excitement, you must substitute an innocent and healthy mode of acting on the passions for the fierce thirst for drink and eager pursuit of other unworthy objects.   Music acts directly on the emotions, and it cannot be abused, for no excess in music is injurious.

"In laying this great national question before you, I have followed the example of my father, by offering to place myself at the head of a great social movement.   I have asked you for assistance, I await your answer with confidence.   I am sure that it will be worthy of the nation of which you are representatives.   To you, my Lords-Lieutenant, I would address myself with an intimation that I trust you will assemble meetings throughout your counties, for it is desirable that contributions should be received from all parts of the country as showing the interest taken by the people in music.   My Lord Mayor of London and other Mayors who are here,—I am sure I may hope that you will assist me by presiding at assemblies of your fellow-townsmen, and will urge them to contribute to so national an institution.   I may, I doubt not, look with confidence to the representatives of the Church and of other religious and educational denominations who have been good enough to attend here, to remind their choirs and their flocks that any contributions will be a grateful testimony that the population of England are interested in improving an art which, more than others, excites devotional feelings, and inspires with enthusiasm public and private worship.   From those who are directly interested in music, either professionally or as amateurs, I trust I have a right to expect the greatest measure of assistance which they can afford; for on their behalf, and with a view to extend the influence of the science to which they are devoted, we are met here to-day for the purpose of establishing a national central musical institution. I know the loyalty of our Colonial brethren; they will not be behindhand in aiding the mother country. From foreign countries I have ever received so many tokens of regard and sympathy, that I may look with confidence to them to give their support to an institution the doors of which will be thrown open to all nations. One practical observation in conclusion. I trust that those present here to-day will each and every one of them from time to time communicate to me the steps they are taking to procure contributions, and will forward to the honorary secretaries the amount of contributions they may receive. For my part, I will take care, as soon as I am enabled to form some judgment of the extent to which the nation will support this demand, to communicate to the contributories and to the public the details of the foundation and establishment of the College, of which I have only set forth in my address the general outline."

The first resolution was proposed to the meeting by the Duke of Edinburgh, and seconded by the Archbishop of Canterbury. The speech of the Duke of Edinburgh was so clear and practical, supplementing and confirming that of the Prince of Wales, who has always generously attributed to his brother the initiation in this great national movement, which, however, could not have been carried out without the personal aid and influence of the Prince. He thus concluded:—

"I wish to express my own personal hope that the Royal College will not be a mere teaching institution, but will become a centre for groups of affiliated colleges, the members of which will, with the Council of the Royal College, form a musical senate, to which all questions of importance relating to music and musicians may be referred for determination. This may perhaps be deemed somewhat Utopian, but I do not despair of a time when the musical colleges throughout the country will ally themselves with the Royal College, and form a body united by a common tie and a general system. I will go one step further, though I do not conceal from myself that I am treading on somewhat delicate ground, and possibly trenching on the honoured privileges of the Universities; yet I will express my personal hope that, as London is the chief City of the United Kingdom, so the Royal College should be the chief musical college, invested with the power of conferring musical degrees, and the source from which all musical honours should legitimately flow.

"In proposing the first resolution, it only remains, my lords and gentlemen, for me to express my hope that the Prince of Wales will be supported on the present occasion earnestly and faithfully.

2 D

A large sum of money is required for our enterprise. England is rich, and ready at all times to forward a worthy national undertaking. Why should I say England only, when we are assured of the generous support of our Colonial brethren, and when we trust that our American cousins will not be behind in furthering the foundation of an establishment which may act as a home to their musical students on this side of the Atlantic? The representatives of many foreign countries are here also. We look to them in many cases as examples in our new enterprise, and I feel sure that their kind advice and co-operation will not be wanting when we have occasion to seek them. I will now read the resolution intrusted to me:—

"'That this meeting approves of the proposal to establish a Royal College of Music as a national institution, and undertakes that meetings shall be called throughout the country, and the utmost exertions used, individually and collectively, to forward the movement by obtaining the necessary funds for founding and endowing a College of Music for the British Empire.'"

The speeches of the Archbishop of Canterbury, of the Earl of Rosebery, the Lord Mayor, and of Mr. Gladstone all touched upon points illustrating the importance of the movement, and the national benefits to be expected from it.

It is a wonder that no reference in this matter has been made to the great German reformer and patriot, Martin Luther, who was a strenuous advocate of State education, including music. He placed music as next to religion in the training of the young. He would have every schoolmaster a lover of music, and capable of teaching it. This training of teachers is one of the most important functions of the College, and should be steadily kept in mind.

When the thanks of the meeting had been moved, by Sir Stafford Northcote, to the Royal Chairman, and carried with acclamation,—

The Prince of Wales mentioned, in his reply, that "he had received a touching letter from some one who had anonymously sent £50 for the Royal College of Music—one whose earliest recollection was the singing of the National Anthem on the Coronation of the Queen, when as a poor lad he joined in the procession of Sunday-school children."

Many munificent donations and subscriptions were announced, but none more touching and interesting than this.

THE COLONIES AND THE COLLEGE OF MUSIC.

March 23rd, 1882.

THE meeting at St. James's Palace on the 28th of February, 1882, was followed up by other important, though subsidiary meetings, at the instance of the Prince of Wales, who was now fully set on the success of his grand scheme. As, formerly, he had been ably supported by the speeches of the Duke of Edinburgh, the lamented Prince Leopold, Duke of Albany, and Prince Christian, at influential meetings in Manchester, so now he enlisted the Duke of Connaught in the cause, who addressed, with great ability and tact, a meeting of Merchants, Bankers, and leading men in the City, at the Mansion House, on the 20th of March, the Lord Mayor in the Chair.

Not satisfied with this, the Prince of Wales invited a large number of influential gentlemen connected with the Colonial Empire to meet him at Marlborough House, on Thursday, the 23rd of March, 1882, to consider what steps could be taken to secure the benefits of the Royal College of Music for all parts of the Empire. The record of the origin of this great institution would not be complete without giving the speech of His Royal Highness on that occasion. The following is the address delivered at that meeting :—

" You are, doubtless, aware of the efforts at present being made to establish a Royal College of Music—a work which, I venture to think, is one of national importance.

" It is intended to place the institution on a broad and liberal basis ; that its advantages shall not be confined to residents of the United Kingdom, but be open to our fellow-subjects in all parts of the Empire ; and the gratuitous education of scholars, selected by competition on the claim of merit only, will be one of its principal features.

" The scheme has been received with marked favour throughout the United Kingdom, but I should consider it wanting in one of its main objects if I did not succeed in enlisting the sympathy and co-operation of our fellow-subjects residing in the Colonial portions of the Empire.

" I have on so many occasions experienced the advantages of their ready and earnest concert in promoting schemes of public utility in relation to material progress, that I have some confidence they will exhibit the like friendly rivalry in furthering

2 D 2

our efforts in favour of an elevating pursuit, which in all ages and among all communities has exercised no slight influence on national character, and the promotion of which may constitute a bond tending to unite us as strongly in sentiment and feeling as we now are in loyalty and material interest.

" For these reasons I was anxious to meet as many of the leading gentlemen connected with the Colonies as might now be temporarily in London, as well as those who permanently reside here ; and I am gratified at the readiness with which so many of you have acceded to my invitation.

" My object is partly to make it understood how much importance I attach to the element of Colonial co-operation and sympathy, not only as affecting the immediate success of the work, but bearing on the higher objects of national unity, by inspiring among our fellow-subjects in every part of the Empire those emotions of patriotism which national music is calculated so powerfully to evoke.

" I further desired to apprise you of the steps which had been and were being taken to carry out this purpose.

" Immediately after the Meeting at St. James's Palace I directed that full reports of the proceedings should be prepared, with the view of transmitting them to Lord Kimberley, the Secretary of State for the Colonies, to be forwarded by him for the information of the Governments of the various Colonies, in the hope that the good-will of these Governments might be attracted in our favour, and such public encouragement afforded as they might feel it becoming to extend.

" It seemed doubtful, however, whether an official communication of this character was calculated to accomplish the full object we had in view, viz. to stimulate popular feeling and sympathy among our Colonial fellow-subjects. It was thought that such an end might be better attained by a direct appeal to themselves and by a more general distribution of the reports of our proceedings among the various institutions, religious bodies, heads of municipalities, and leading persons in the Colonies.

" I accordingly propose to supplement this communication by a further letter, and to send a sufficient number of copies of our proceedings to meet the necessary requirements, for transmission to the Colonies.

" I am not insensible to the engrossing nature of the pursuits of Colonial life, nor to the claims which material interests have on young communities. We must all recognise with pride and admiration how much the enlightened enterprise and perseverance of our Colonial fellow-subjects have already contributed to the greatness and wealth of the Empire; and I am far from suggesting any relaxation of these efforts.

" My purpose is to provide for the leisure hours which must come to the busiest among us—no matter where we live or what sphere of life we occupy—an elevating source of enjoyment, which is at the same time calculated to strengthen those emotions that have so much influence in perpetuating a common love of country.

" I have endeavoured in my further letter to Lord Kimberley to convey fully the object I have at heart; and, although its terms are in some measure a repetition of what I have now stated to you, I think it well you should be apprised of its contents :—

" ' My Lord,—I am anxious that no possible steps should be omitted which may be calculated to bring the proposal to found a Royal College of Music under the favourable notice of Her Majesty's subjects in the Colonies.

" ' It appears to me that the communication which I request you in the accompanying letter to be good enough to transmit for the information of the Governments of the various Colonies might advantageously be supplemented by a somewhat more general distribution within these Colonies of the proceedings which have taken place here in connection with the movement.

" ' The objects of such distribution would be to awaken public interest among all classes of Her Majesty's subjects more thoroughly than even proposals on the part of any of the Colonial Governments to extend their practical aid are calculated to do.

" ' I have therefore directed further copies of these proceedings to be transmitted to you, and would again request that you will be good enough to forward these further copies, for distribution among such religious or educational institutions, Municipal or other Public Bodies, or private persons in the various Colonies, as may be thought most likely to help the project.

" ' I trust that the efforts now being made here may meet

with general support on the part of the Clergy of all denominations in the Colonies, and that they, as well as the Heads of Colleges and Municipal Bodies, may interest themselves in their several localities to make known the advantages offered by the establishment of the Royal College of Music, and especially that all these advantages (including free instruction) will be open as unreservedly to Her Majesty's Colonial subjects as to those residing in the United Kingdom.

"'Her Majesty's Colonial subjects have indeed already shown that the possession of musical talent exists among them in as great a degree as in any other nation, for they may claim with pride that they have produced one of the most accomplished vocalists of the present age.

"'I have in past years had occasion in many ways—especially through the medium of the various International Exhibitions over which I have presided—to notice the manifold benefits which have resulted from the combined action of the Colonies and the Mother Country in the development of commerce and the advancement of industrial and other material interests, and I cannot but think that the friendly rivalry of all portions of the Empire will not now be wanting in the effort to cultivate a refined and elevating pursuit which in all ages and among all nations has exercised so important an influence on national character, and done so much to strengthen the common love of country.

"'I have the more confidence in making this appeal, from the readiness and public spirit which the Colonies have always evinced to promote every object tending to strengthen the ties that now so happily unite us.

"'Your Lordship will, I am sure, be glad to learn that I have had the advantage of communicating with a number of gentlemen resident in several of the Colonies, who are temporarily in England, as well as with former Colonists permanently residing here, and they have kindly undertaken by their individual exertions to further the present more extended movement, which I trust will also meet with your Lordship's encouragement and approval.

"'I have the honour, &c.,

"'ALBERT EDWARD, P.'

"I have no doubt but that the different Colonial Governments will exercise a judicious discretion in the use of these papers, and that we may rely on their hearty co-operation and support in applying them to the best advantage.

"If there are any gentlemen present who may think themselves warranted by their connections with the Colonies in aiding to insure a friendly reception of my communication there, it will be a source of gratification both to me and my colleagues to view such efforts, so entirely in unison with our own, and to welcome them as fellow-workers in the same cause.

"I have thus endeavoured to place before you the object we have in view, and the means by which we hope to accomplish it, and I trust you will find both worthy of your support.

"I do not, therefore, presume to indicate the precise course which it might be expedient to adopt in any of the Colonies, believing that this had better be left to the practical sagacity and zeal of our friends there, who must be considered to have the best knowledge of what plans are most calculated to insure local success. I have, however, thought that a brief reference to some of the steps which are contributing to our success here, as well as an enumeration, in a comprehensive form, of some of the advantages which the College offers to Colonists, might be attended with advantage, and, at all events, serve as a ground-work for their operations.

"I have, accordingly, directed a memorandum in that sense to be prepared, which will be forwarded, with the other papers, to the proper quarter.

"In conclusion, I cannot but again express my cordial thanks to the many gentlemen connected with the Colonies who have favoured me with their attendance to-day, and repeat the expression of my hope, not unmixed with a large measure of confidence, that your encouragement and help may not be withheld from an undertaking which may, I trust, in the fulness of time prove to be one more of the many fibres in the silken cord that binds the Mother Country to her Colonial offspring.

"I would finally say that we shall be most happy to receive any practical suggestion from our Colonial friends either here or resident in the Colonies."

Lord Kimberley said that, as Colonial Minister, he would give

every assistance in his power, by forwarding papers and information. Private individuals in the Colonies might be willing to
found scholarships, and have the nomination of students; but any
response on the part of the Colonial Governments must be from
their free and spontaneous action.

The Prince of Wales said, at the opening of his speech, that he
deemed this work as "one of national importance." It is because
of the high "imperial" tone and spirit of the address, a spirit
which it is pleasant to witness in all the Prince's public actions,
that there is especial interest attached to this meeting at Marlborough House in 1882.

INAUGURATION OF THE ROYAL COLLEGE
OF MUSIC.

May 7th, 1883.

THE ceremony of inaugurating the Royal College of Music took
place on the 7th of May, 1883, in the presence of a small but
select company. The building, hitherto used by the National
Training School of Music, has rooms amply sufficient for teaching
purposes, but not large enough for a large assembly. By permission of Her Majesty's Commissioners for the Exhibition of
1851, the use of rooms in the Albert Hall for choral and instrumental practice was granted to the College.

The Prince, accompanied by the Princess of Wales, the Duke
and Duchess of Edinburgh, and the Princess Christian, was
received by the Trustees, the Duke of Westminster, Lord Charles
Bruce, Sir Richard Wallace, M.P., Sir John Rose, Sir George
Grove, and the honorary secretary, Mr. Charles Morley. Among
the company were many distinguished persons and eminent
musicians. The Archbishop of Canterbury offered the following
special prayer: "O God, who art the only author of order and
beauty, Bless, we beseech Thee, this College to the perfecting of
science and skill in Thy pure gift of Music; and grant that the
good intent of its Founders may be so answered in the diligence
and virtue of its students, that both the restful delight of man,
and the glory of the Divine worship may be enhanced ever more
and more; through Jesus Christ Our Lord. Amen."

The collect, "Prevent us, O Lord," and the Lord's Prayer, closed
the religious service. Sir George Grove, Director, then said: "It
is now almost exactly fourteen months since your Royal Highness
held the remarkable meeting which assembled at St. James's
Palace on the 28th of February, 1882, and in which your proposi-
tion of the Royal College of Music was launched on the country.

It may well be called remarkable—first, because of the place in which it was held ; secondly, because of the lucid and exhaustive statement which your Royal Highness vouchsafed to address to it ; thirdly, because for the first time in English history music was taken out of the domain of personal and professional questions to which it is too often relegated, and placed upon that national basis which its social and civilising powers entitle it to demand. Your Royal Highness's hearers embraced many of the most distinguished English musicians of the day, but these were not the main constituents of the meeting. The bulk of your audience consisted of the representatives of the counties, cities, and towns of England, the lords lieutenant, mayors, and town clerks of the United Kingdom, while surrounding your Royal Highness on the platform were His Royal Highness the Duke of Edinburgh, the leader of the Government, the leader of the Opposition, the head of the Established Church, an eminent Scotch peer, and the Lord Mayor of London. A meeting so truly national in its aspect gave, if I may use a not inappropriate figure, the key-note of the movement.

" The hope so long entertained by your Royal Highness, and your advisers, that the chief existing musical institution of the country would join your movement, was unfortunately dissipated. But the absence of the Royal Academy of Music from your Royal Highness's project was counterbalanced by the active adherence of the towns and cities of the country which through their municipal officers, with hardly an exception, rallied as if by instinct round a movement so boldly conceived and so happily inaugurated. The key-note thus struck at St. James's Palace resounded through the country, and met with a ready and harmonious response. Meetings were speedily organised by the lords lieutenant and mayors in the provinces. In the short period of fourteen months forty-four meetings have been held—from Exeter, Plymouth, and Hastings, in the South, to Newcastle-on-Tyne in the North; from Swansea and Shrewsbury, on the one hand, to Lincoln and Norwich on the other; while the great manufacturing and commercial centres of Nottingham, Leicester, Leeds, Bradford, Liverpool, and Blackburn, have all testified their interest in your Royal Highness's new institution. In the City of London several meetings were held at the Mansion House, and a remarkable gathering of provincial mayors, under the sympathetic presidency of Sir. J. Whittaker Ellis, the then Lord Mayor, gave your Royal Highness an opportunity of again enforcing your views upon your audience. By these meetings, and by the personal exertions of your Royal Highness and your illustrious brothers, a sum of money, amounting to over £110,000, has been raised, of which nearly £5000 was due to the gracious action of Her Royal Highness the Princess of Wales."

Sir George Grove announced " the foundation already of many scholarships for tuition, fifteen of which include maintenance.

Four of the scholarships were founded by private liberality, and two by Australian benefactors." He then announced "the names of the professors selected by the Prince of Wales for the teaching of the College, who were such as to give assurance as to the quality and range of the instruction. The piano is in the hands of Mr. Pauer, Madame Arabella Goddard, Mr. Franklin Taylor, and Mr. John Francis Barnett. To forward our interests, Madame Lind-Goldschmidt has emerged from her retirement, and singing will be taught by her, Mr. Deacon, and Signor Visetti. The violin is in the charge of Mr. Henry Holmes and Mr. Gompertz; the organ of Mr. Walter Parratt. Counterpoint and composition are taught by Dr. Bridge, Mr. Villiers Stanford, and Dr. Hubert Parry; while among the professors of other instruments are the honoured names of Harper, Lazarus, Thomas, and other ornaments of the English school. Declamation will be specially cared for, and for this the names of Mrs. Kendal and Mrs. Arthur Stirling are sufficient guarantee.

"The competition," continued Sir George Grove, "which has taken place throughout the country for the fifty scholarships is in itself an ample proof, if proof were needed, of the justness of your Royal Highness's idea. Following the method adopted in launching the institution, your Royal Highness appealed to the mayors, corporations, and Local Boards throughout the country, and in the Metropolitan districts to the Vestries, to make known the fact of the competition, and to organise the preliminary examinations, selecting the examiners from the most eminent local musicians. The result was as successful as might have been anticipated. The municipal buildings were put at the disposal of the College, and the best musicians were prompt to give their services as honorary local examiners to a task which in many cases involved great labour and severe sacrifice. Throughout the United Kingdom and Ireland 1588 candidates sent in their names as competitors. Of these 480 were sent up to the final examination, which was conducted personally in this building by the various professors in sections; and, lastly, before the entire Board of Professors and myself as Director. The result was the unanimous election of seventeen scholars for the pianoforte, thirteen for singing, eight for the violin, six for composition, two for the violoncello, one for the organ, one for the clarionet, one for the flute, and one for the harp. In addition to the fifty scholars, forty-two persons have entered their names as paying students in the College.. Time will not allow me more than an allusion to various acts of private generosity by which the College has benefited. Prominent among them is the gift of the library of the late Sacred Harmonic Society, through Sir Philip Cunliffe Owen, and various other gifts of pianos, furniture, &c., by Sir Charles Freake, Messrs. Broadwood, Messrs. Erard, Messrs. Chappell, Messrs. Holland, Feetham, and others. The professors, scholars, and students are awaiting your Royal Highness's notice at the close of these proceedings, and I trust your Royal Highness will believe that we are all alike animated by a sincere and enthusiastic desire to carry out to the full those wise and gracious designs which have brought us to this first step in our career. That your Royal Highness may long live to preside over us and guide us in the right path is, Sir, our humble and earnest hope and prayer."

The Prince of Wales, in reply, said :—

"I have heard your address with pleasure, and I feel great gratification in opening to-day the Royal College of Music, in the promotion of which I have taken so deep an interest. I avail myself of this, the first public opportunity that has offered itself, of expressing the deep personal gratification I feel at the manner in which the country has replied to my appeal for aid in establishing the College. There is no class of Her Majesty's subjects capable of affording assistance to which I have addressed myself in vain. The Corporation of London and the London companies have led the way in giving pecuniary assistance; and I owe a debt of gratitude to the Mayors throughout the kingdom for the valuable aid they have afforded by granting facilities for holding local examinations essential to the proper selection of scholars. I thank these great bodies for their services, and I trust that I may yet expect from them further help in completing the task so auspiciously begun. I thank the donors of scholarships for their liberality. I thank the general public for the sums they have subscribed at a time when agriculture has been depressed and the prospects of trade have not been encouraging; and, above all, I thank the many kind friends who have responded so cordially and liberally to my appeal for assistance. I have noticed also with the greatest pleasure the contributions for Colonial scholarships that have been given by two eminent colonists, the one on behalf of the colony of Victoria, and the other on behalf of the colony of South Australia. The object I have in view is essentially Imperial as well as national, and I trust that ere long there will be no colony of any importance which is not represented by a scholar at the Royal College.

"Much, indeed, has been done, but I am aware that much remains to be done. I am conscious that I may be thought to have taken a bold step in beginning so great an enterprise with only the resources at present at my command. But I am unwilling that any delay should take place in giving effect to the generous intentions of those who have already contributed so liberally.   I am sanguine enough to think that the example set during the last year by corporate bodies, representatives of the colonies, private donors, and the general public will be followed in ensuing years.   Ours is an institution which admits of almost indefinite extension, for, wherever a scholarship is founded, we know now that we shall find a deserving candidate to hold it.

"Let me now pass to an account of what has been actually accomplished.   Fifty scholarships have been established, of which thirty-five confer a free education in music, and fifteen provide not only a free education, but also maintenance for the scholars.   Of these scholarships half are held by boys and half by girls.   I observe with pleasure that the various districts from which the scholars are drawn indicate the widespread distribution of a taste for music, and an adequate cultivation of music throughout the United Kingdom.   London, with its vast population, sends only twelve out of the fifty.   The remaining thirty-eight come as follows :—twenty-eight from fourteen different counties in England, two from Scotland, six from Ireland, one from Wales, and one from Jersey.   The occupations of the scholars are as various as the places from which they come.   I find that a mill-girl, the daughter of a brickmaker, and the son of a blacksmith take high places in singing, and the son of a labourer in violin playing.

"The capacity of these candidates has been tested by an examination of unusual severity.   Each of these scholars who returns to his native place furnished with the highest instruction in music will form a centre from which good musical education will spread around; while those who obtain musical engagements elsewhere will stimulate and encourage by their success the cultivation of music in the places whence they have come.   Surely, then, it is not too much to expect that many years will not pass away before our College has so popularised music as to place England on a par with those countries on the Continent which have acquired the distinction of being called musical people.

"I feel, then, that one great object of a College of Music has been secured—namely, the discovery of latent musical ability and the extension to those who, with great natural gifts, have been blessed with little of this world's goods, of the opportunity of obtaining instruction in music, to say the least, not inferior to any which this kingdom can afford. That these words are not the language of exaggeration will be apparent to those who read the names of the eminent staff who have placed their services at the disposal of the College. Side by side with these scholars will be educated a group of paying pupils, who think that music is an art which, if worth studying at all, is worth studying well. They are, then, prepared to enter on a systematic course of instruction, of less severity and continuance than that of the scholars, but still far removed from the musical dilettantism of those who, induced by fashion, not by taste, to study music, make progress enough to torment themselves and distract their friends.

"I lay great store by the meeting of the various classes of society in pursuit of a common yet elevating study. Such a union softens asperities, inspires kindly feeling between various classes, and proves that all mankind are akin when engaged in an art which gives the highest expression to some of the best and purest feelings af the human heart.

"The observations I have hitherto made relate only to the Royal College of Music in its character of a teaching body. It is not proposed, however, that the functions of the College should be restricted to teaching. The charter under which we are incorporated provides that the council are to cause examinations to be held of pupils of the College, and of other persons who may present themselves for examination, and after examination to confer on those who deserve such distinctions the degrees of Bachelor of Music, Master of Music, and Doctor of Music, certificates of proficiency, and other rewards. I propose that this power should be exercised by an independent board of examiners chosen by the Royal College in conjunction with the Universities, and after consultation with the great musical authorities of the United Kingdom. I trust thus to secure an examining body whose impartiality will be above suspicion and capacity beyond all question. I hope thus, through the instrumentality of the Royal College, to raise the standard of music throughout the United Kingdom and to create a central influence which may be beneficially exercised over all music-teaching bodies who recognise the advantage of a common system of examination.

"Beyond and above all this I trust, as I stated on a previous occasion, that the College will become the recognised centre and head of the musical world in this country.   It has been a reproach to England that, with her vast resources, her large benevolence, her eagerness to instruct all classes of society in other branches of knowledge, one thing has hitherto been wanting—a national institution for music.   Yet music is in the best sense the most popular of all arts.   If that government be the best which provides for the happiness of the greatest number, that art must be the best which at the least expense pleases the greatest number.   I trust that to-day we have removed the reproach.   England, by a national subscription, has acquired an institution worthy to be called national, and with the establishment of such an institution we may look forward with confidence to the creation of a national school of music. England has the composers already ; all she wants is a general centre, such as a Royal College of Music, to which they may resort for mutual aid and common inspiration.

"Such are the aims, not mean nor ignoble aims, proposed for the College which we open to-day. It remains for you, gentlemen of the council, to be careful that the aims are fully realised.   A young institution requires fostering care and constant super-vision.   You must not relax your efforts, no pains must be spared to gain fresh support and obtain the establishment of new scholarships.   We want much ; we are, I trust, entitled to ask for much of the public.   In addition to scholarships we want more extended premises, a music-hall, lodgings for our scholars, houses for masters, and all the appurtenances of a great College.   I am sure I may trust to the generosity of the public to supply these wants ; but you, gentlemen, must by your careful supervision make our institution worthy of support, and no efforts of mine shall be wanting to secure the objects we have in view.

"I will say only one word in conclusion.   The establishment of an institution such as I open to-day is not the mere creation of a new musical society.   The time has come when class can no longer stand aloof from class, and that man does his duty best who works most earnestly in bridging over the gulf between different classes which it is the tendency of increased wealth and increased civilisation to widen. I claim for music the merit that it has a voice which speaks, in different tones, perhaps, but with equal force, to the cultivated and the ignorant, to the peer and the peasant. I claim for music a variety of expression which belongs to no other àrt, and therefore adapts it more than any other art to produce that union of feeling which I much desire to promote. Lastly, I claim for music the distinction which is awarded to it by Addison—that it is the only sensuous pleasure in which excess cannot be injurious. What, more, gentlemen, can I say on behalf of the art for the promotion of which we are to-day opening this institution—an institution which I trust will give to music a new impulse, a glorious future, and a national life? Before I quit this room a further duty devolves on me—a most gratifying one, I admit. I am called upon to announce a most gracious act by which the Queen has been pleased to mark her interest in the opening of the Royal College. Her Majesty authorises me to say that she proposes to confer the honour of knighthood on Professor Macfarren and Dr. Sullivan. If anything could add to my satisfaction in making this statement it is this, that these honours are bestowed by the advice of the Prime Minister, who has taken so kind an interest in the promotion of the Royal College, and who could have devised no better mode of celebrating its opening than by recommending that honour should be done on this occasion to music by conferring knighthood on men so celebrated in their art as Professor Macfarren and Dr. Sullivan, and that honour should be done to our college by awarding a like distinction to its director, Dr. Grove, who, eminent in general literature, has specially devoted himself to the preparation and publication of a dictionary of music, and has earned our gratitude by the skill and success with which he has worked in the difficult task of organising the Royal College. I have only to add that the Prime Minister (Mr. Gladstone) by his presence to-day proves that neither the cares of State, nor the overwhelming press of business by which he is surrounded, prevents him from giving personal countenance to a national undertaking which, if I am right in what I have said, is calculated to advance the happiness and elevate the character of the English people."

The Royal College of Music, incorporated by Royal Charter in 1883, is now one of the established institutions of the Empire. There lies before us the Report of the Fifth Annual Meeting of the Corporation, with Report of the Council and other official documents and statements.   This meeting was held at the Concert Hall of the Alexandra House, adjoining the College, on Tuesday, July 24th, 1888, Prince Christian, K.G., one of the Vice-Presidents, in the chair.   There was a very large attendance of the Council, members of the Corporation, teachers and pupils of the College. The Report of the Council was of the most satisfactory nature. The progress of the pupils has been very encouraging, and the discipline and efficiency of the College thoroughly well maintained. The number of foundation scholars at the end of April, 1888, was fifty-nine.   Its number of paying students on the books at the same date, was 170, an increase of 24, during the preceding twelve months.   These students were in various years of their training. The total number of pupils was 229.

The Examiners, Mr. W. G. Cusins, Sir Charles Hallé, Mr. C. H. Lloyd, Mr. A. Randegger, Mr. Carl Rosa, and Mr. Prosper Sainton, gave a most favourable report of steady progress, especially by the students of stringed instruments, piano, and organ.   As an educational institution, the Royal College has already proved itself able to exert a powerful influence on the condition of musical art in this country.

The results of examinations and competitions were then given in detail, and various incidents of the year were recorded, including visits of Dr. Joachim and Dr. Hans Richter, who delighted the pupils by their presence and their performing.   Various changes in the teaching staff were announced.   The finances of the College are in good state, the available balance at the close of the year being nearly £2484, a clear increase during the past year of nearly £470.   Various donations and benefactions were reported, but the great event of the meeting—which H.R.H. Prince Christian announced with a cheerful emphasis, in keeping with the warm interest he has always taken in the College—this was the generous gift of £30,000 by Mr. Samson Fox, for a building worthy of the institution; met by Her Majesty's Commissioners of 1851 by the grant of a site on their estate at South Kensington.

We must not give more space to this subject of the Royal College of Music.   Those who wish further information must apply to the Secretary or Director of the College.   In connection with the present volume it only remains to congratulate His Royal Highness the Prince of Wales on the successful accomplishment of a work, which is an honour to the reign of Queen Victoria, and will be of perennial benefit to the British Empire.

GENERAL INDEX.

2 E